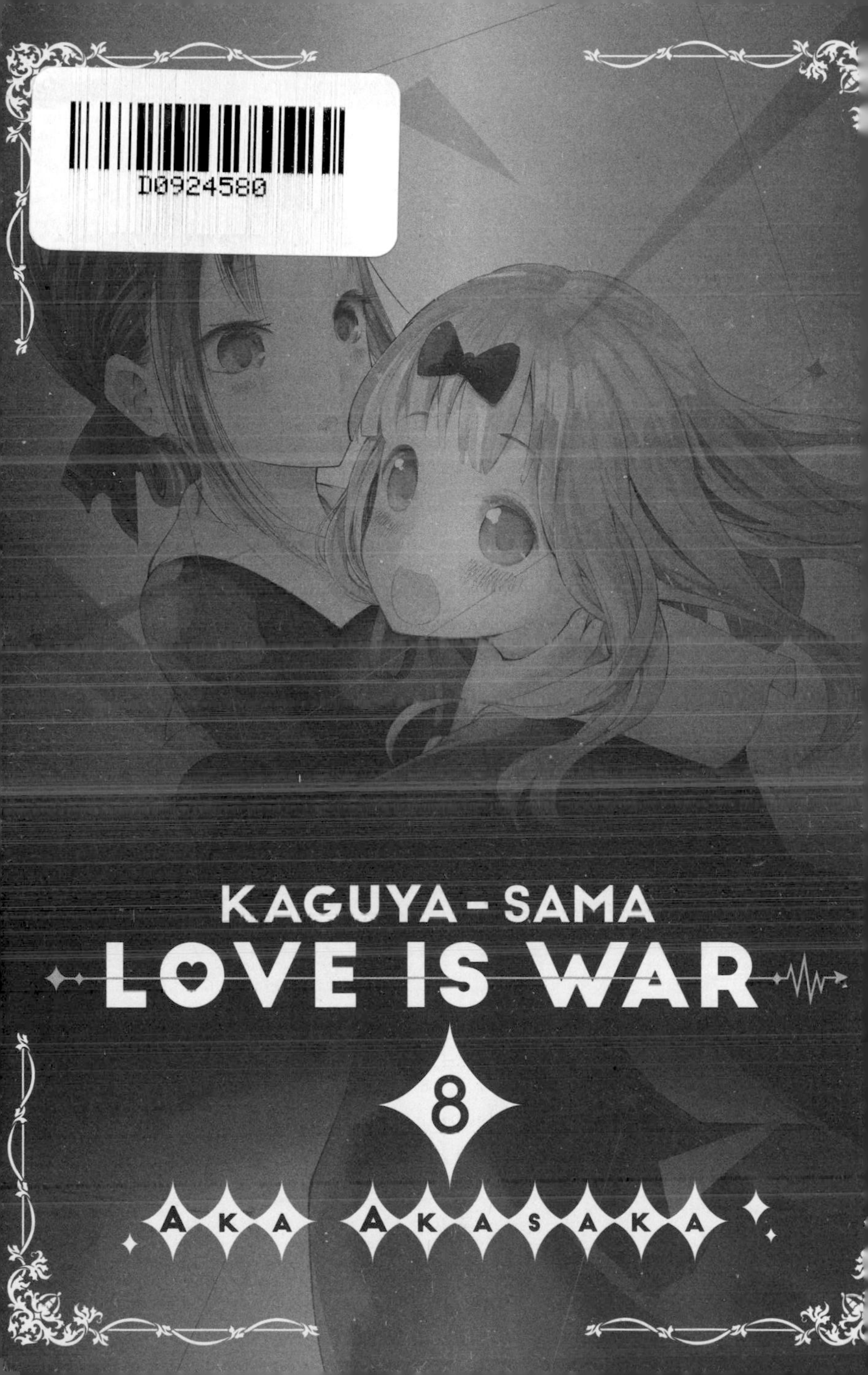

KAGUYA-SAMA
LOVE IS WAR

8

AKA AKASAKA

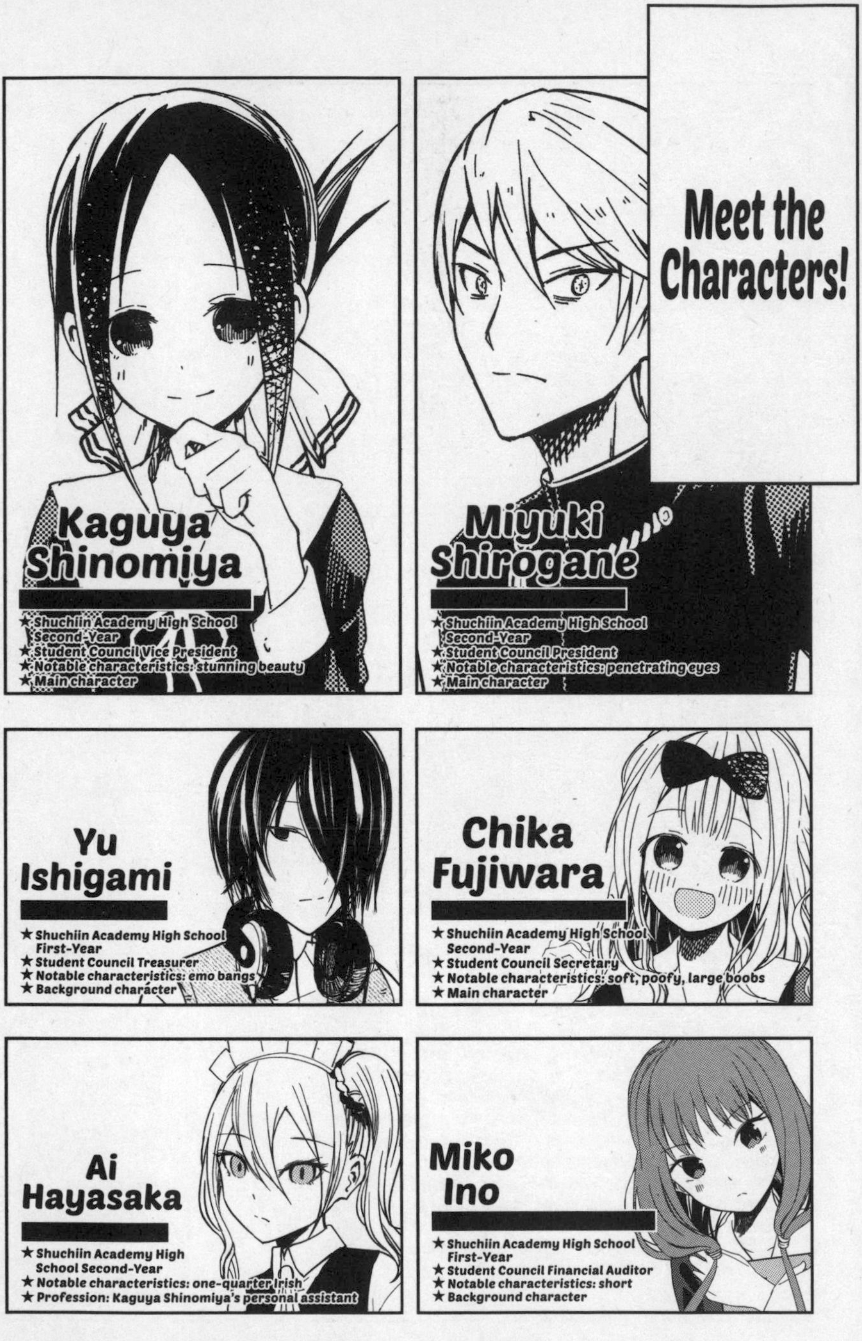
Meet the Characters!
Miyuki Shirogane
★Shuchiin Academy High School Second-Year
★Student Council President
★Notable characteristics: penetrating eyes
★Main character
Kaguya Shinomiya
★Shuchiin Academy High School Second-Year
★Student Council Vice President
★Notable characteristics: stunning beauty
★Main character
Chika Fujiwara
★Shuchiin Academy High School Second-Year
★Student Council Secretary
★Notable characteristics: soft, poofy, large boobs
★Main character
Yu Ishigami
★Shuchiin Academy High School First-Year
★Student Council Treasurer
★Notable characteristics: emo bangs
★Background character
Miko Ino
★Shuchiin Academy High School First-Year
★Student Council Financial Auditor
★Notable characteristics: short
★Background character
Ai Hayasaka
★Shuchiin Academy High School Second-Year
★Notable characteristics: one-quarter Irish
★Profession: Kaguya Shinomiya's personal assistant

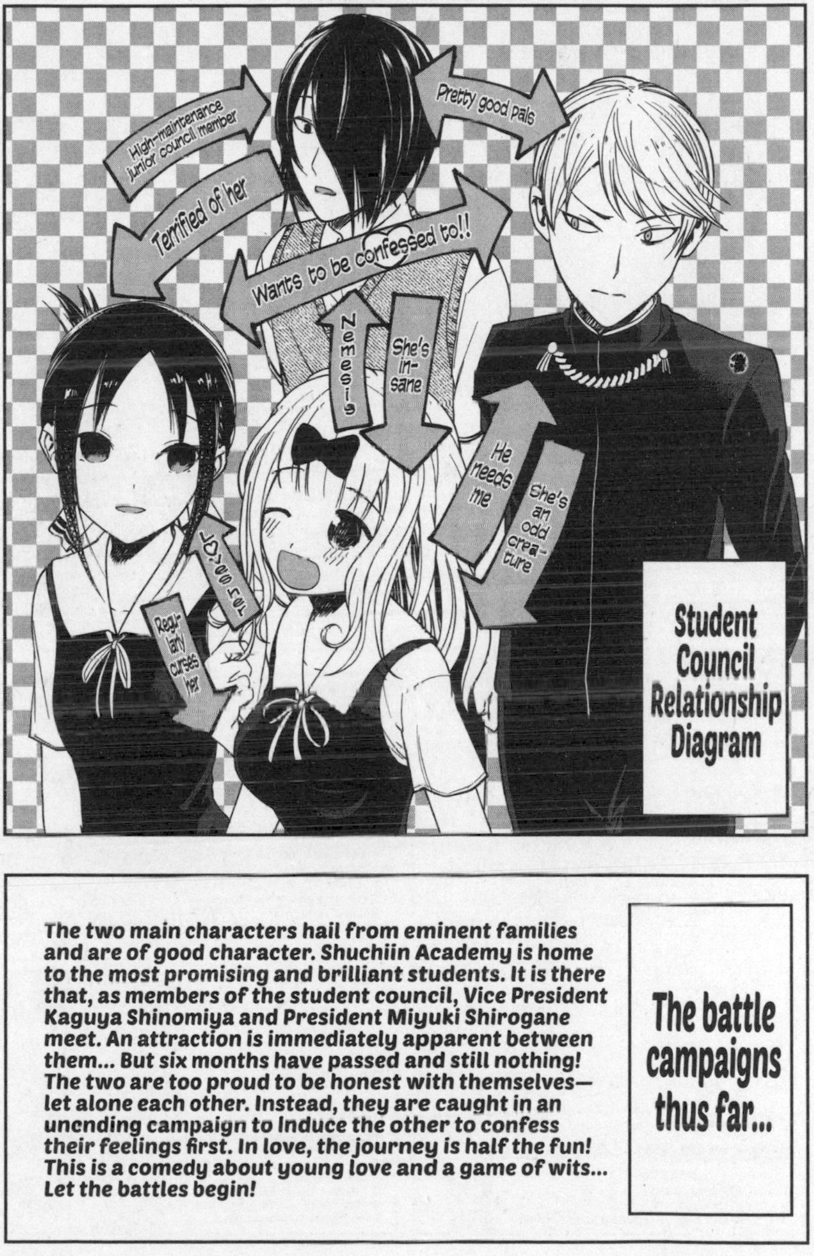
Student Council Relationship Diagram
Pretty good pals
High-maintenance junior council member
Terrified of her
Wants to be confessed to!!
She's in-sane
Nemesis
He needs me
She's an odd crea-ture
Loves her
Regu-larly curses her

The battle campaigns thus far...

The two main characters hail from eminent families and are of good character. Shuchiin Academy is home to the most promising and brilliant students. It is there that, as members of the student council, Vice President Kaguya Shinomiya and President Miyuki Shirogane meet. An attraction is immediately apparent between them... But six months have passed and still nothing! The two are too proud to be honest with themselves—let alone each other. Instead, they are caught in an unending campaign to induce the other to confess their feelings first. In love, the journey is half the fun! This is a comedy about young love and a game of wits... Let the battles begin!

KAGUYA-SAMA ♡ LOVE IS WAR

BATTLE CAMPAIGNS 8

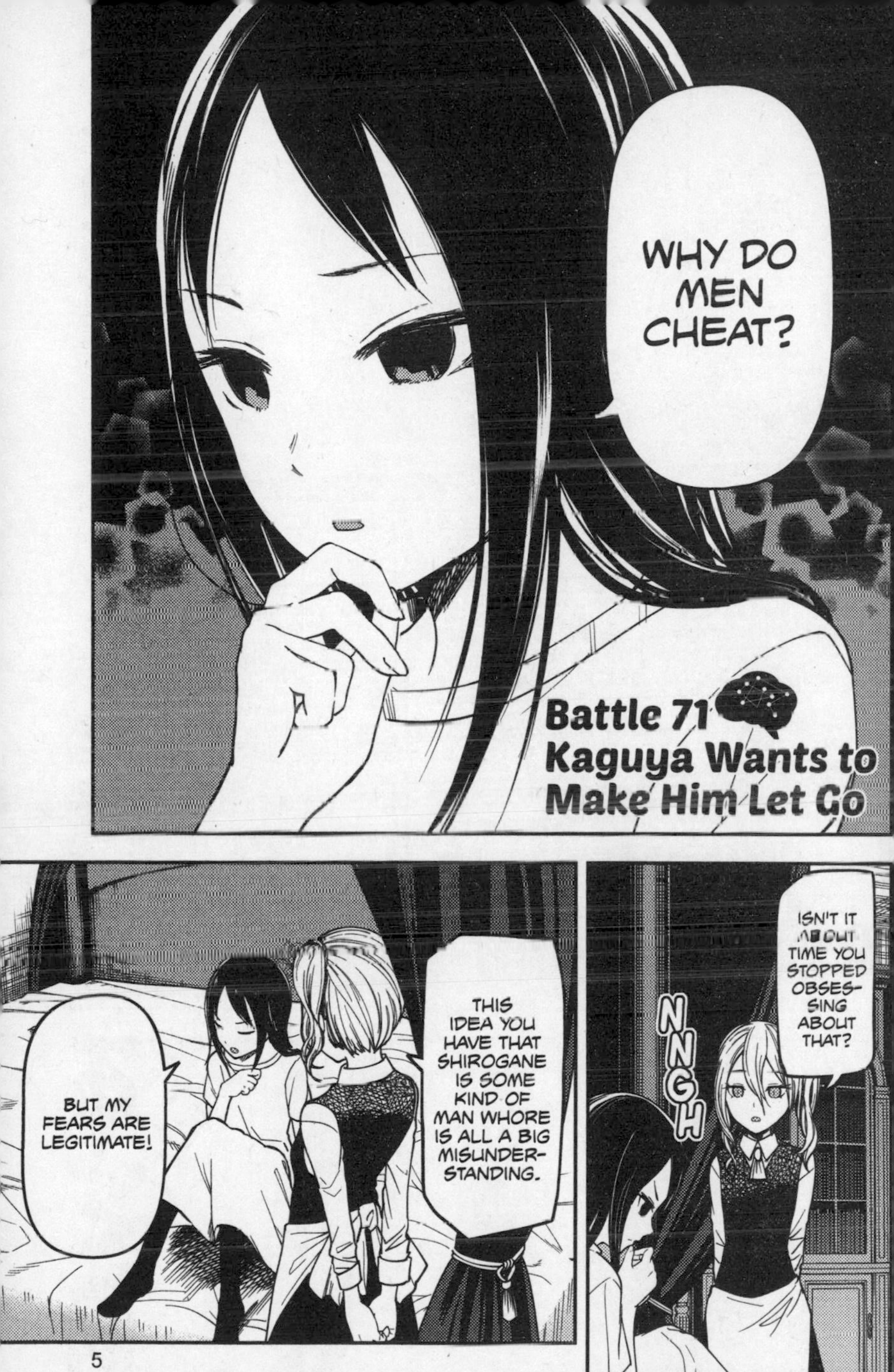
WHY DO MEN CHEAT?
Battle 71
Kaguya Wants to Make Him Let Go
ISN'T IT ABOUT TIME YOU STOPPED OBSES-SING ABOUT THAT?
NNGH
THIS IDEA YOU HAVE THAT SHIROGANE IS SOME KIND OF MAN WHORE IS ALL A BIG MISUNDER-STANDING.
BUT MY FEARS ARE LEGITIMATE!

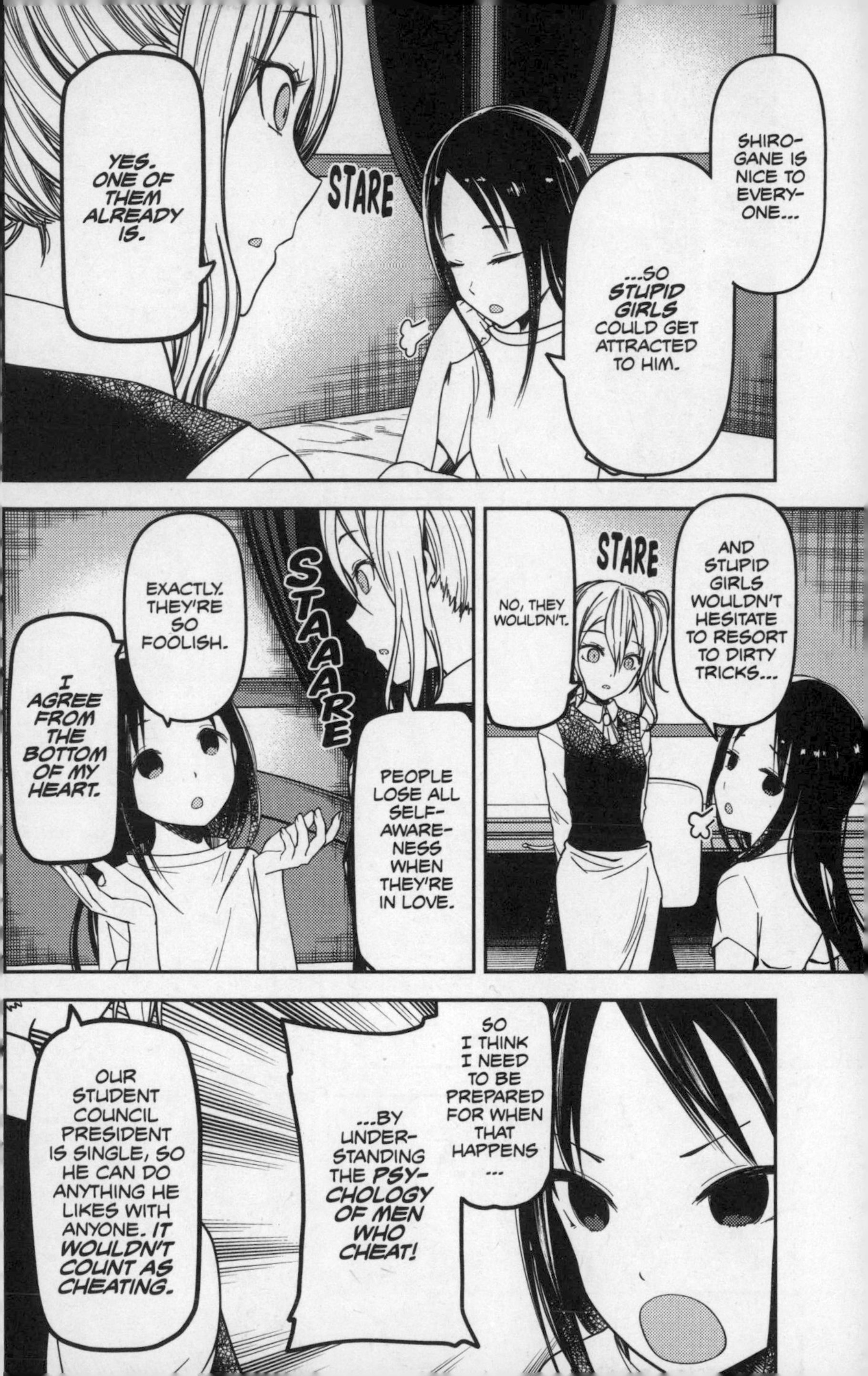
SHIRO-GANE IS NICE TO EVERY-ONE...
...SO STUPID GIRLS COULD GET ATTRACTED TO HIM.
STARE
YES. ONE OF THEM ALREADY IS.
AND STUPID GIRLS WOULDN'T HESITATE TO RESORT TO DIRTY TRICKS...
STARE
NO, THEY WOULDN'T.
PEOPLE LOSE ALL SELF-AWARENESS WHEN THEY'RE IN LOVE.
STAAAARE
EXACTLY. THEY'RE SO FOOLISH.
I AGREE FROM THE BOTTOM OF MY HEART.
SO I THINK I NEED TO BE PREPARED FOR WHEN THAT HAPPENS...
...BY UNDERSTANDING THE PSYCHOLOGY OF MEN WHO CHEAT!
OUR STUDENT COUNCIL PRESIDENT IS SINGLE, SO HE CAN DO ANYTHING HE LIKES WITH ANYONE. IT WOULDN'T COUNT AS CHEATING.

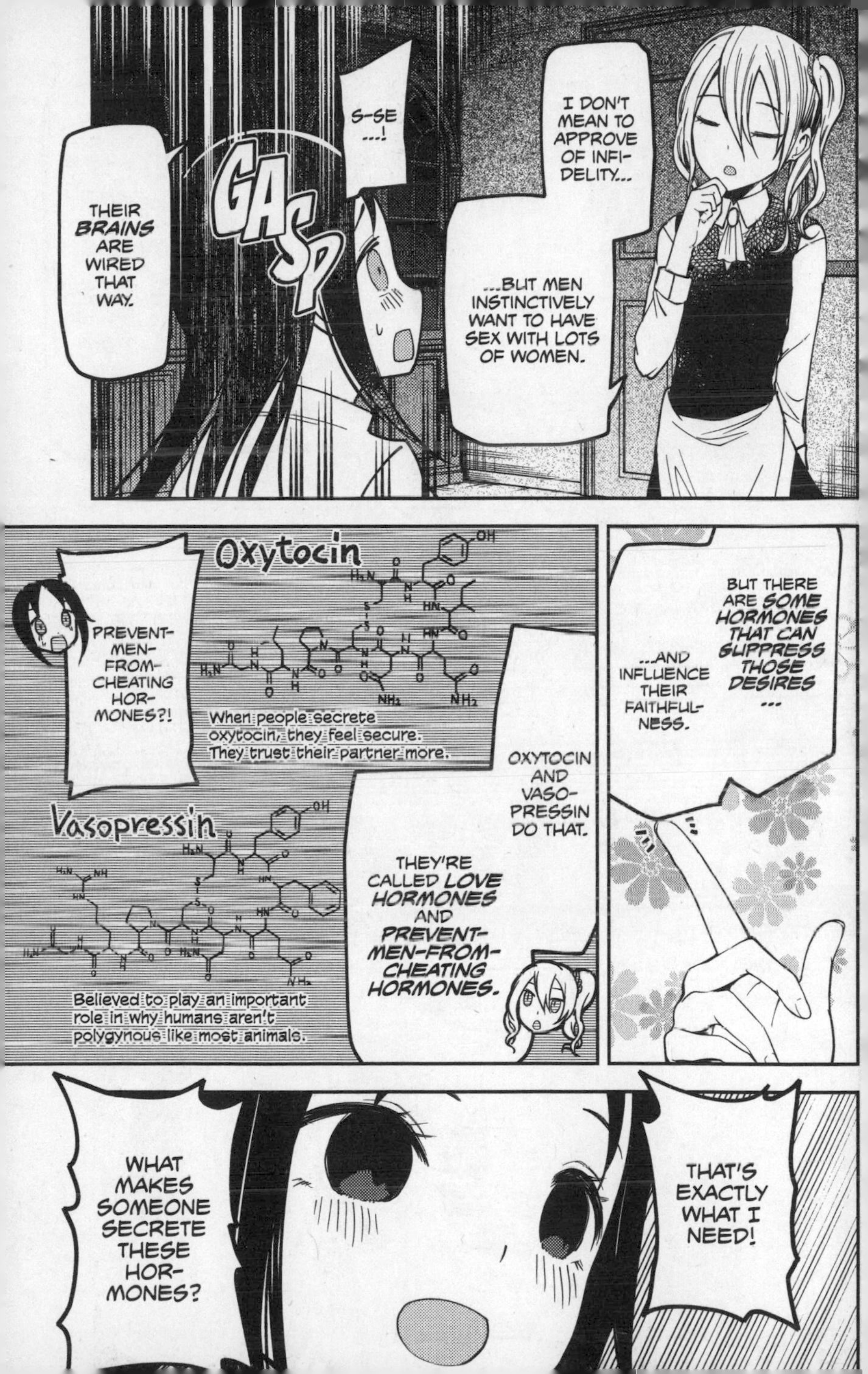
I DON'T MEAN TO APPROVE OF INFIDELITY...
...BUT MEN INSTINCTIVELY WANT TO HAVE SEX WITH LOTS OF WOMEN.
S-SE...!
GASP
THEIR BRAINS ARE WIRED THAT WAY.
BUT THERE ARE SOME HORMONES THAT CAN SUPPRESS THOSE DESIRES...
...AND INFLUENCE THEIR FAITHFULNESS.
OXYTOCIN AND VASOPRESSIN DO THAT.
THEY'RE CALLED LOVE HORMONES AND PREVENT-MEN-FROM-CHEATING HORMONES.
Oxytocin
When people secrete oxytocin, they feel secure. They trust their partner more.
PREVENT-MEN-FROM-CHEATING HORMONES?!
Vasopressin
Believed to play an important role in why humans aren't polygynous like most animals.
THAT'S EXACTLY WHAT I NEED!
WHAT MAKES SOMEONE SECRETE THESE HORMONES?

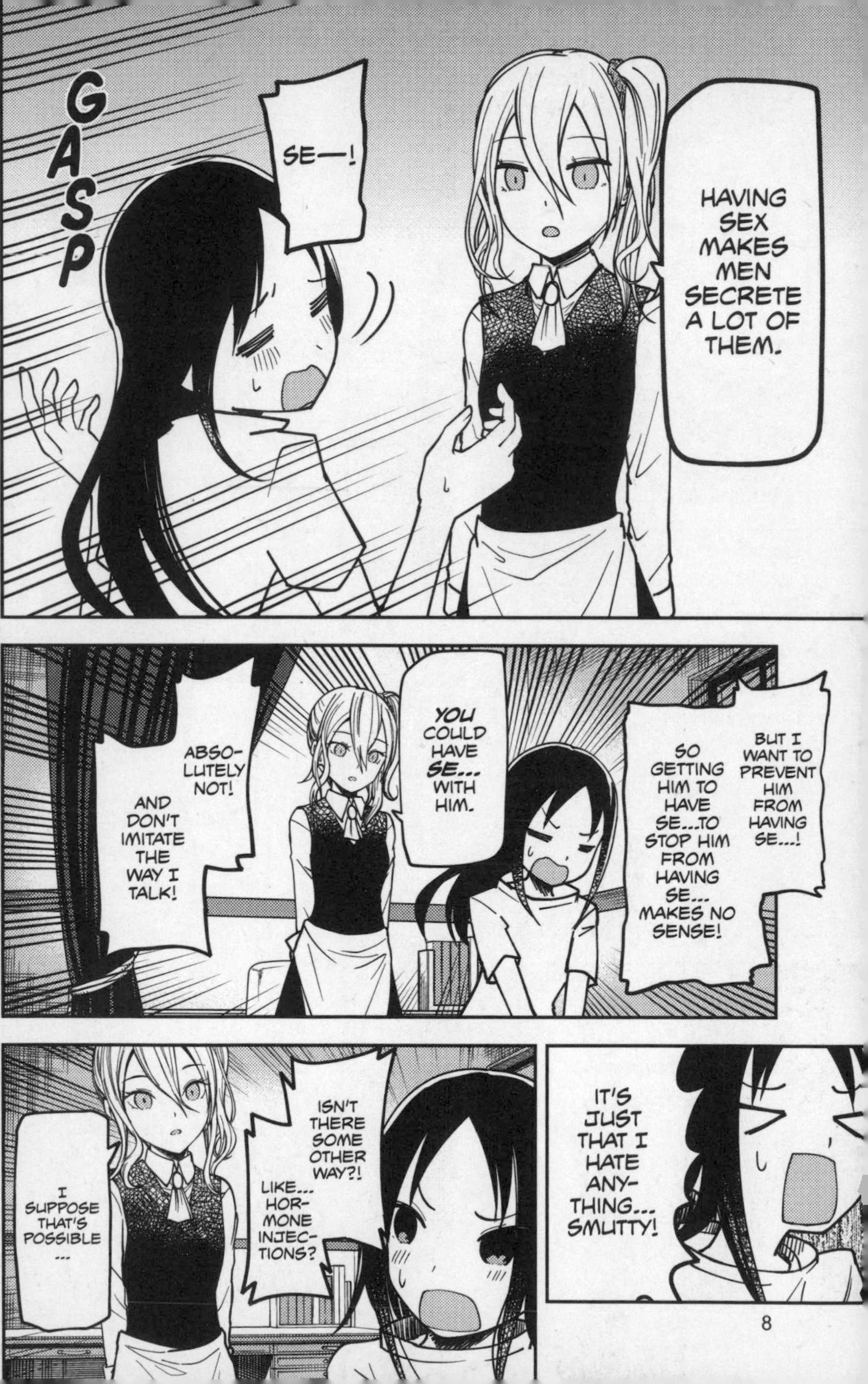
HAVING SEX MAKES MEN SECRETE A LOT OF THEM.
SE—!
GASP
BUT I WANT TO PREVENT HIM FROM HAVING SE...!
SO GETTING HIM TO HAVE SE...TO STOP HIM FROM HAVING SE... MAKES NO SENSE!
YOU COULD HAVE SE... WITH HIM.
ABSO-LUTELY NOT!
AND DON'T IMITATE THE WAY I TALK!
IT'S JUST THAT I HATE ANY-THING... SMUTTY!
ISN'T THERE SOME OTHER WAY?!
LIKE... HOR-MONE INJEC-TIONS?
I SUPPOSE THAT'S POSSIBLE ...

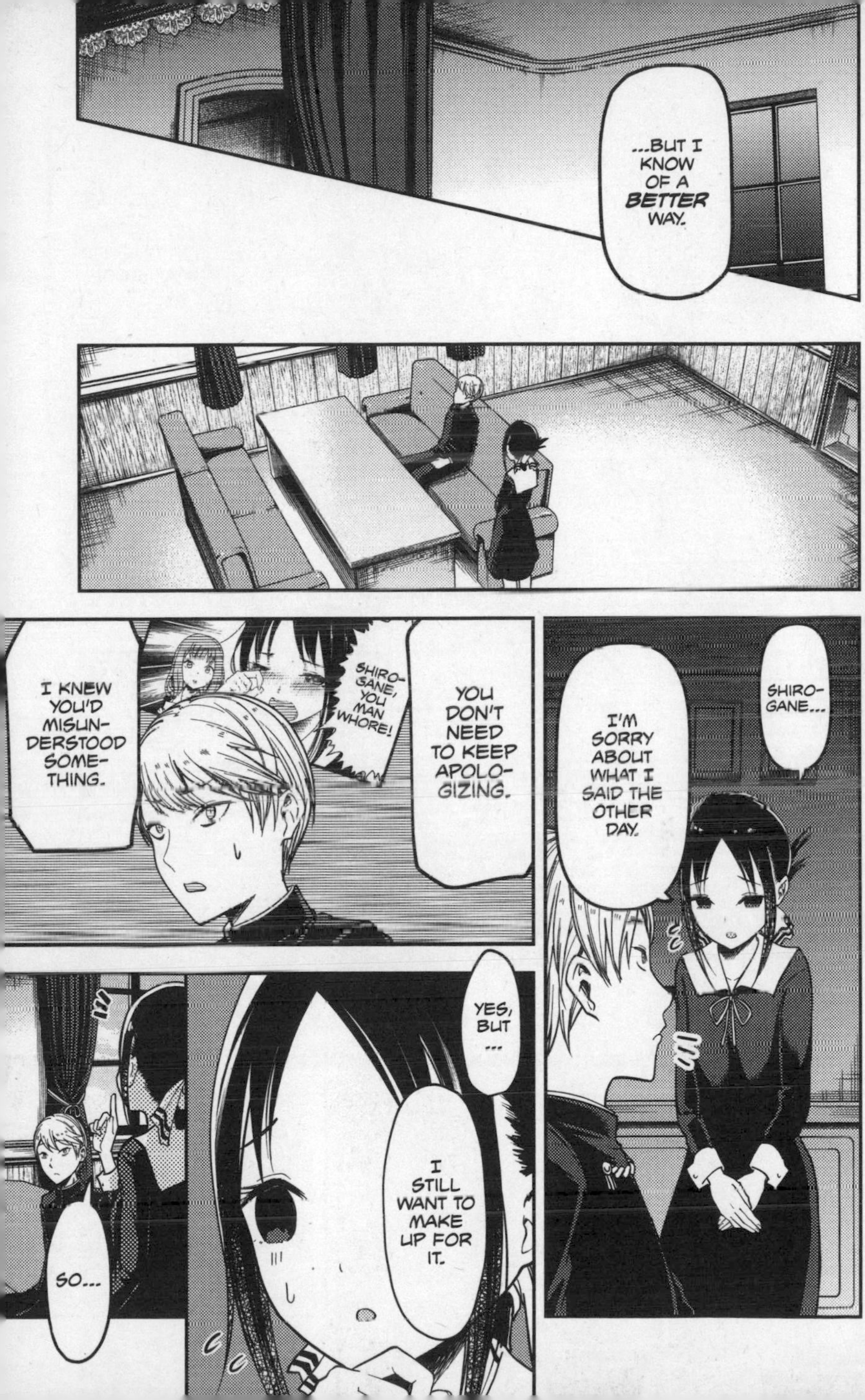
...BUT I KNOW OF A BETTER WAY.
SHIRO-GANE...
I'M SORRY ABOUT WHAT I SAID THE OTHER DAY.
YOU DON'T NEED TO KEEP APOLOGIZING.
SHIRO-GANE, YOU MAN WHORE!
I KNEW YOU'D MISUN-DERSTOOD SOME-THING.
YES, BUT...
I STILL WANT TO MAKE UP FOR IT.
SO...

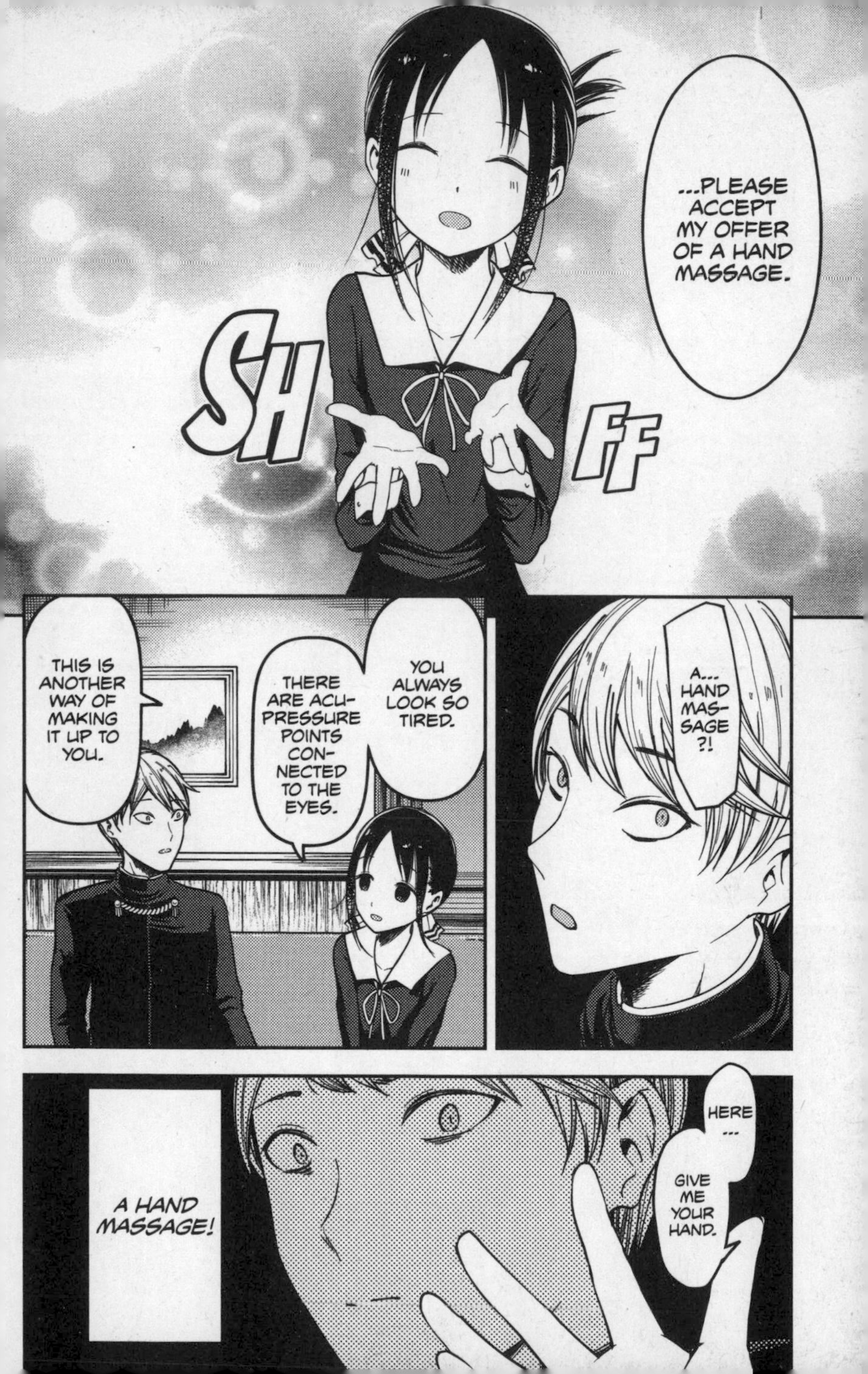
...PLEASE ACCEPT MY OFFER OF A HAND MASSAGE.
SH
FF
A... HAND MAS-SAGE?!
YOU ALWAYS LOOK SO TIRED.
THERE ARE ACU-PRESSURE POINTS CON-NECTED TO THE EYES.
THIS IS ANOTHER WAY OF MAKING IT UP TO YOU.
HERE...
GIVE ME YOUR HAND.
A HAND MASSAGE!

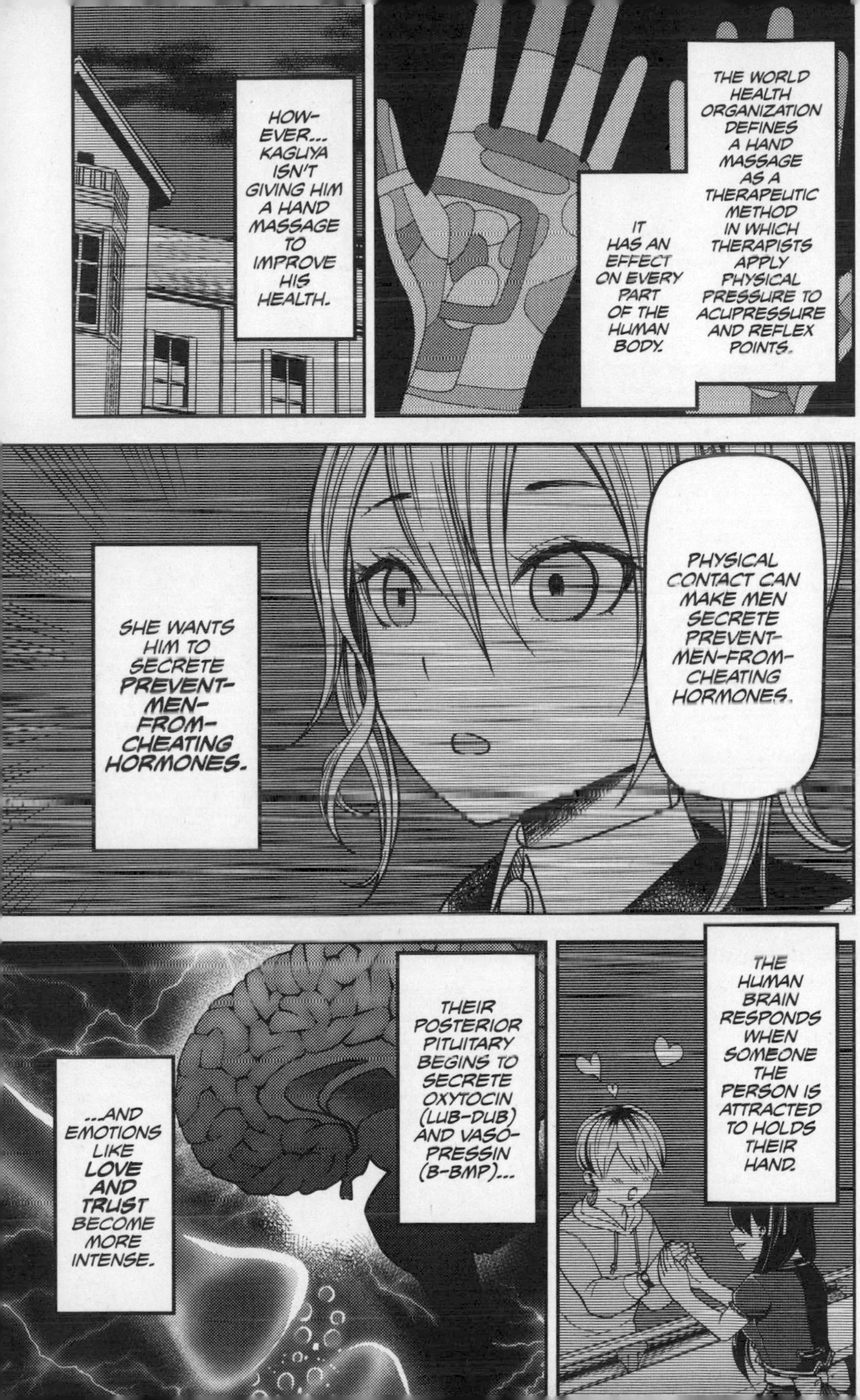
THE WORLD HEALTH ORGANIZATION DEFINES A HAND MASSAGE AS A THERAPEUTIC METHOD IN WHICH THERAPISTS APPLY PHYSICAL PRESSURE TO ACUPRESSURE AND REFLEX POINTS.
IT HAS AN EFFECT ON EVERY PART OF THE HUMAN BODY.
HOW-EVER... KAGUYA ISN'T GIVING HIM A HAND MASSAGE TO IMPROVE HIS HEALTH.
PHYSICAL CONTACT CAN MAKE MEN SECRETE PREVENT-MEN-FROM-CHEATING HORMONES.
SHE WANTS HIM TO SECRETE **PREVENT-MEN-FROM-CHEATING HORMONES.**
THE HUMAN BRAIN RESPONDS WHEN SOMEONE THE PERSON IS ATTRACTED TO HOLDS THEIR HAND.
THEIR POSTERIOR PITUITARY BEGINS TO SECRETE OXYTOCIN (LUB-DUB) AND VASO-PRESSIN (B-BMP)...
...AND EMOTIONS LIKE **LOVE AND TRUST** BECOME MORE INTENSE.

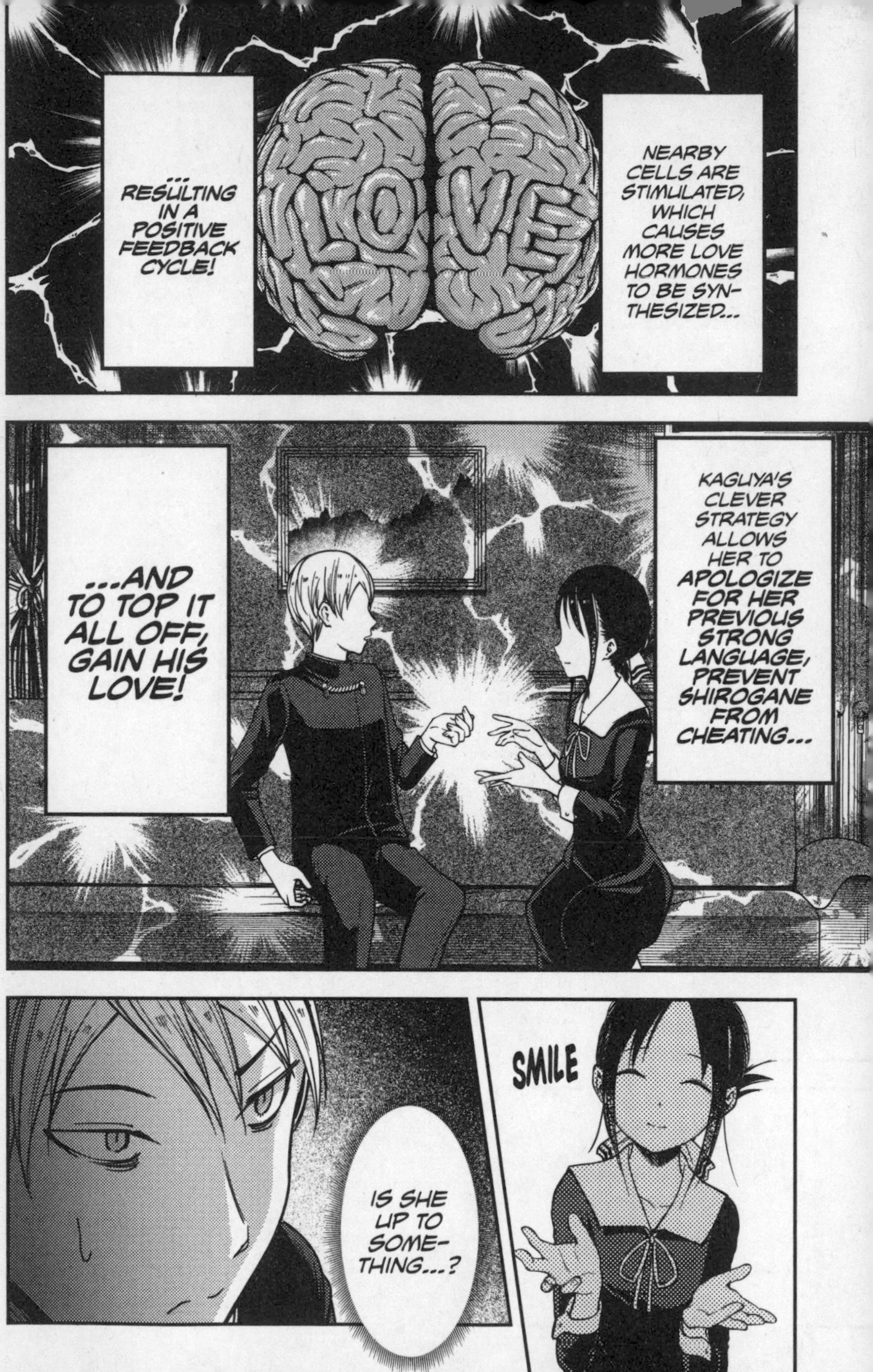
NEARBY CELLS ARE STIMULATED, WHICH CAUSES MORE LOVE HORMONES TO BE SYN-THESIZED...
...RESULTING IN A POSITIVE FEEDBACK CYCLE!
LOVE
KAGUYA'S CLEVER STRATEGY ALLOWS HER TO APOLOGIZE FOR HER PREVIOUS STRONG LANGUAGE, PREVENT SHIROGANE FROM CHEATING...
...AND TO TOP IT ALL OFF, GAIN HIS LOVE!
SMILE
IS SHE UP TO SOME-THING...?

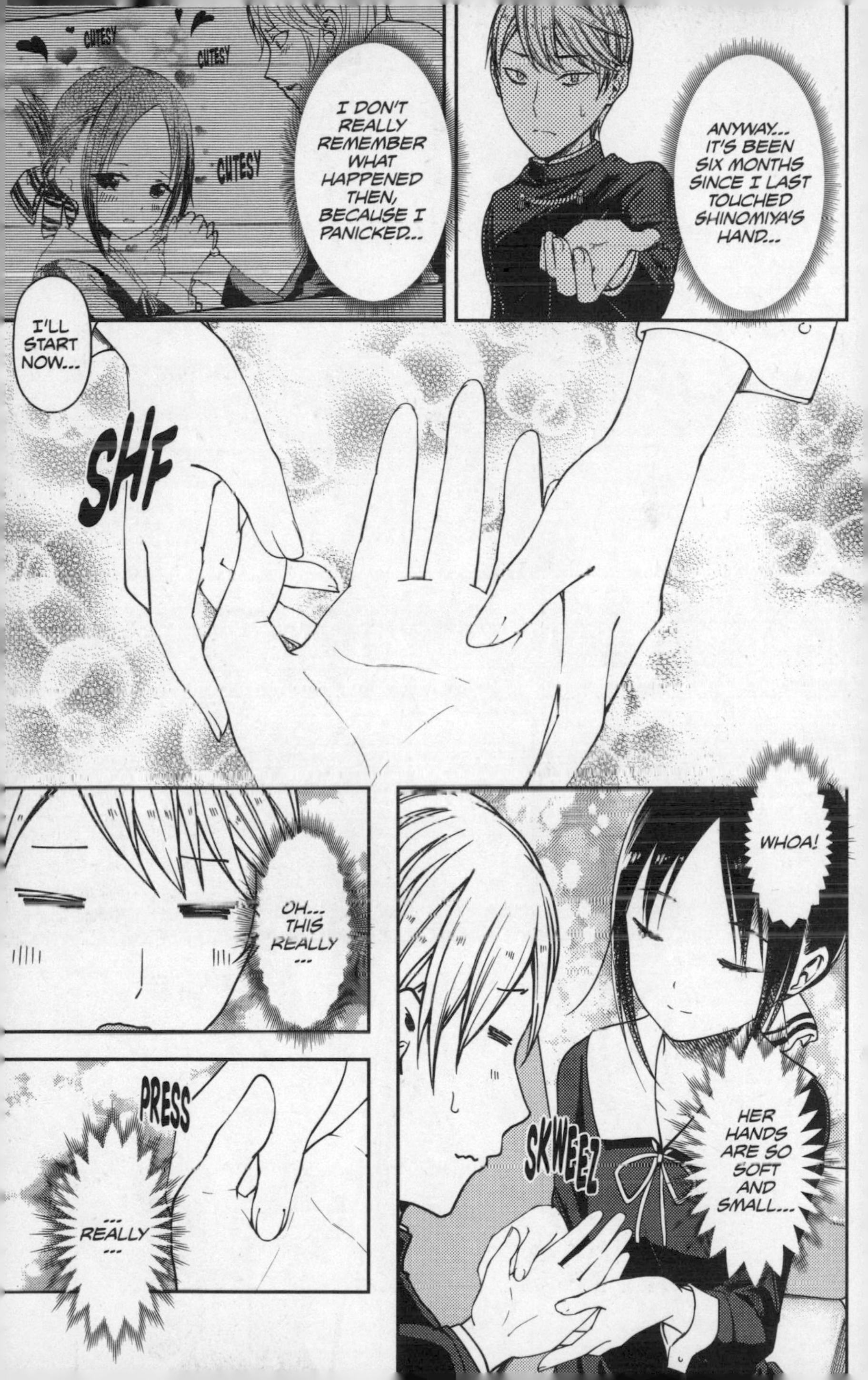
ANYWAY... IT'S BEEN SIX MONTHS SINCE I LAST TOUCHED SHINOMIYA'S HAND...
I DON'T REALLY REMEMBER WHAT HAPPENED THEN, BECAUSE I PANICKED...
CUTESY
CUTESY
CUTESY
I'LL START NOW...
SHF
WHOA!
SKWEEZ
HER HANDS ARE SO SOFT AND SMALL...
OH... THIS REALLY ...
PRESS
... REALLY ...

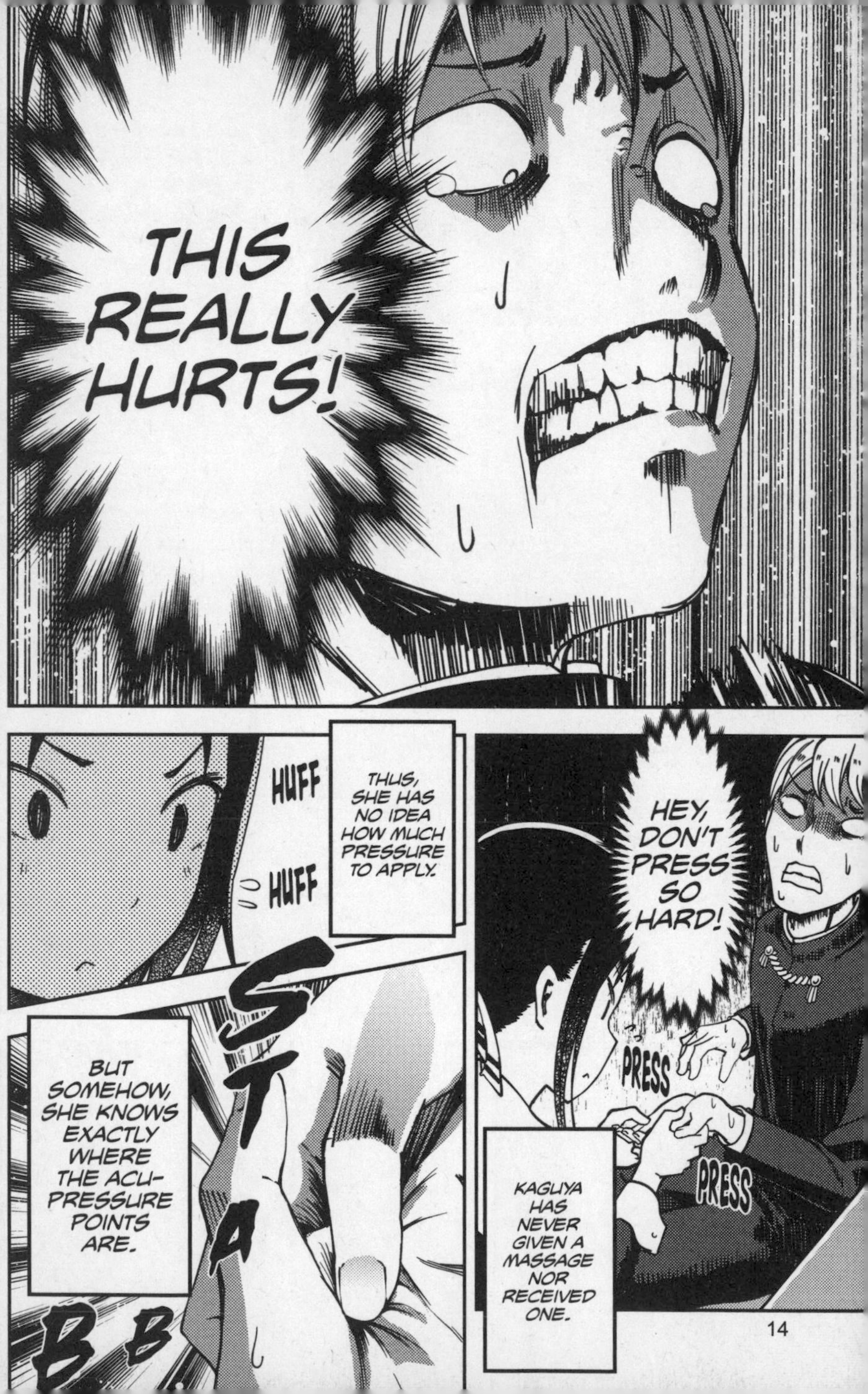
THIS REALLY HURTS!
HEY, DON'T PRESS SO HARD!
PRESS
PRESS
KAGUYA HAS NEVER GIVEN A MASSAGE NOR RECEIVED ONE.
THUS, SHE HAS NO IDEA HOW MUCH PRESSURE TO APPLY.
HUFF
HUFF
STABB
BUT SOMEHOW, SHE KNOWS EXACTLY WHERE THE ACU-PRESSURE POINTS ARE.

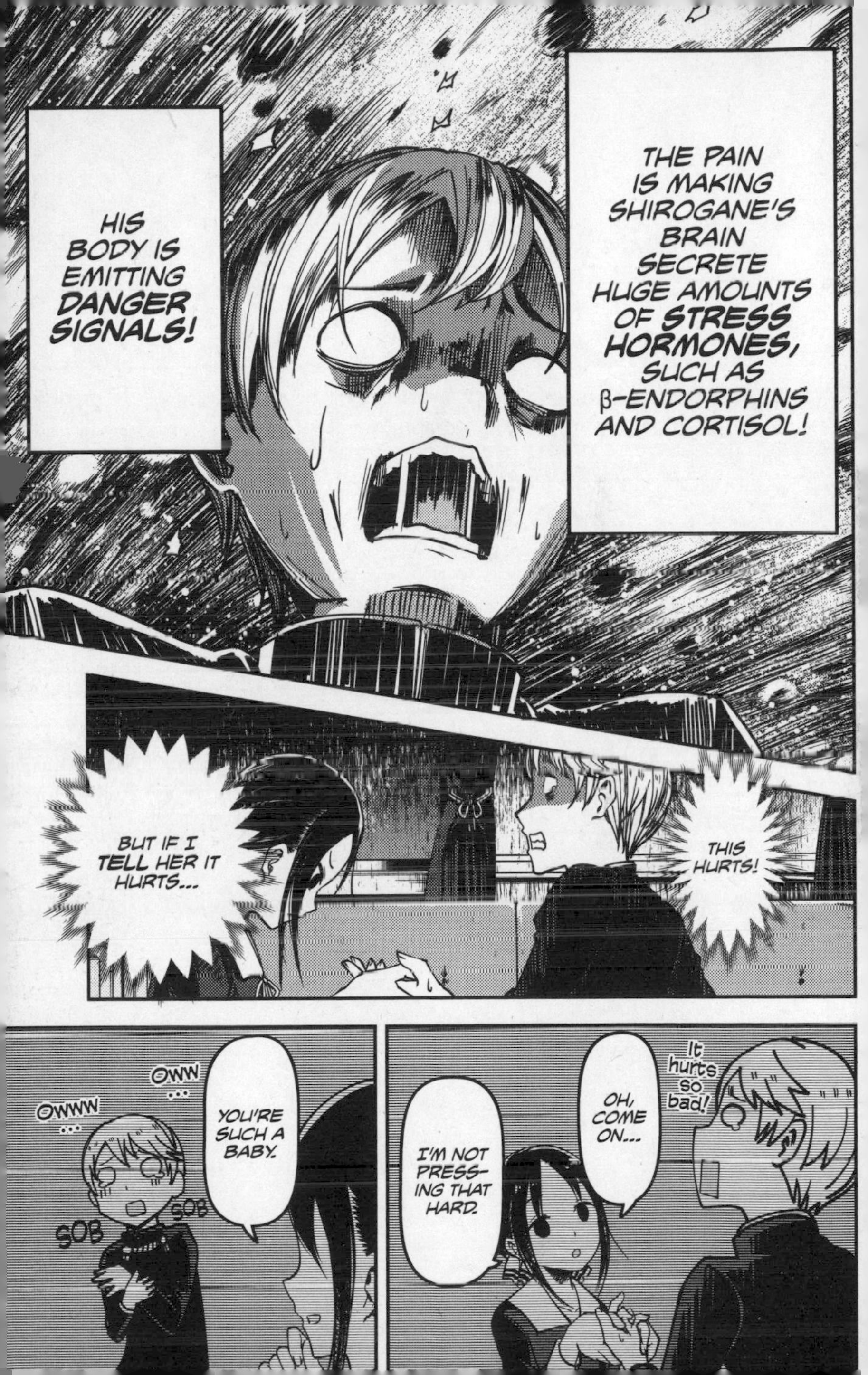
THE PAIN IS MAKING SHIROGANE'S BRAIN SECRETE HUGE AMOUNTS OF STRESS HORMONES, SUCH AS β-ENDORPHINS AND CORTISOL!
HIS BODY IS EMITTING DANGER SIGNALS!
THIS HURTS!
BUT IF I TELL HER IT HURTS...
It hurts so bad!
OH, COME ON...
I'M NOT PRESS-ING THAT HARD.
YOU'RE SUCH A BABY.
OWW...
OWWW...
SOB
SOB

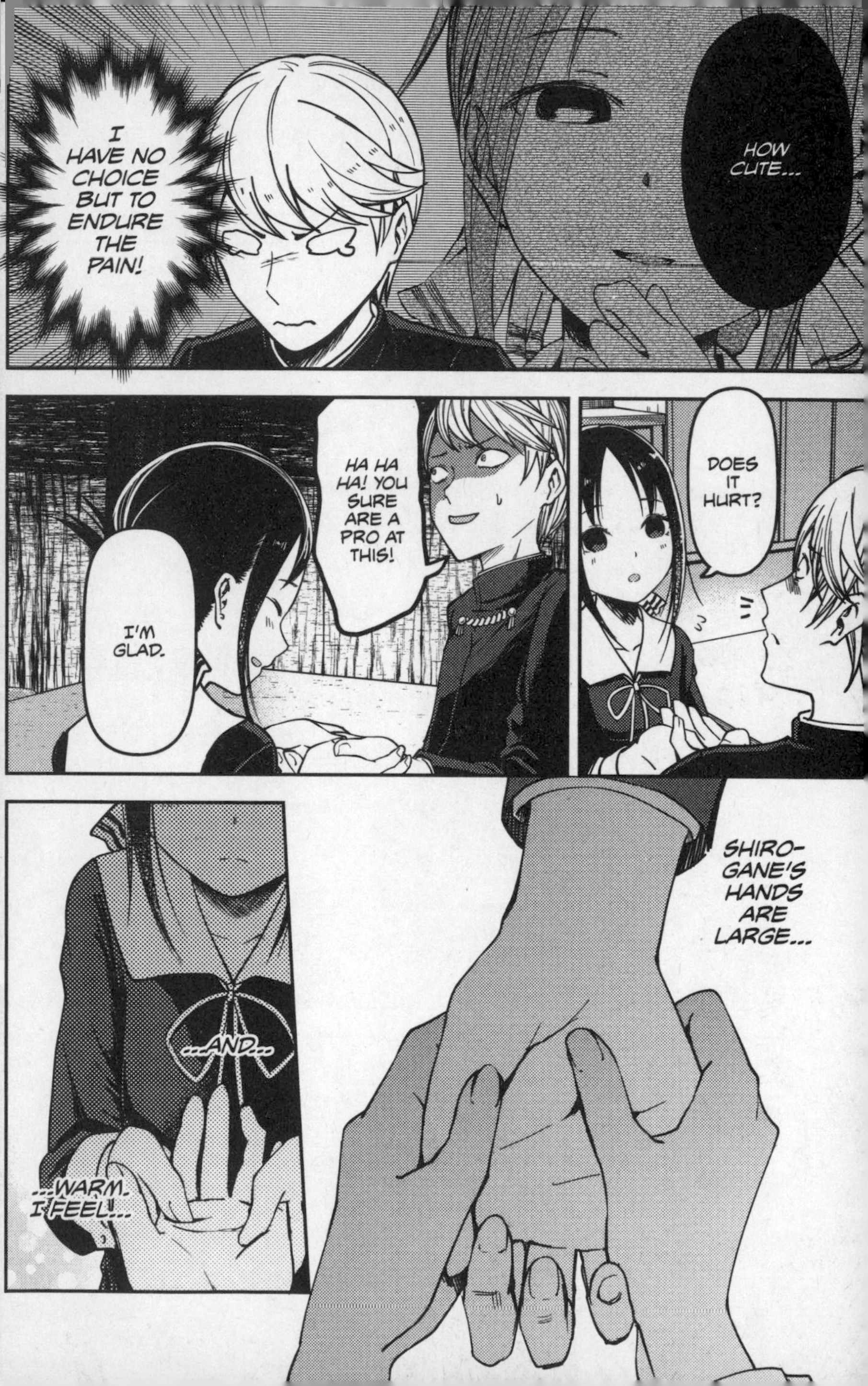
HOW CUTE...
I HAVE NO CHOICE BUT TO ENDURE THE PAIN!
DOES IT HURT?
HA HA HA! YOU SURE ARE A PRO AT THIS!
I'M GLAD.
SHIRO-GANE'S HANDS ARE LARGE...
...AND...
...WARM. I FEEL...

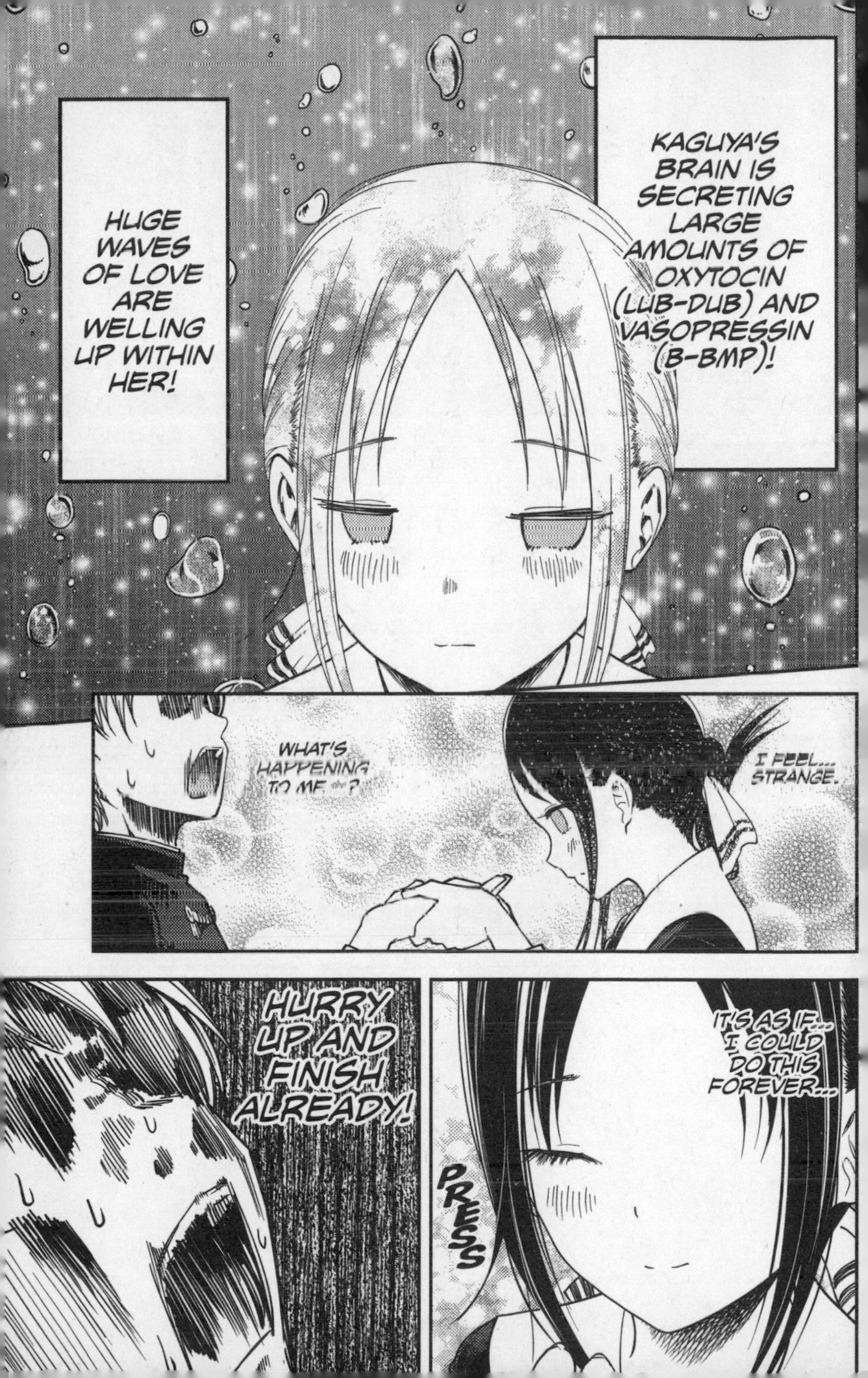
KAGUYA'S BRAIN IS SECRETING LARGE AMOUNTS OF OXYTOCIN (LUB-DUB) AND VASOPRESSIN (B-BMP)!
HUGE WAVES OF LOVE ARE WELLING UP WITHIN HER!
I FEEL... STRANGE.
WHAT'S HAPPENING TO ME...?
IT'S AS IF... I COULD DO THIS FOREVER...
PRESS
HURRY UP AND FINISH ALREADY!

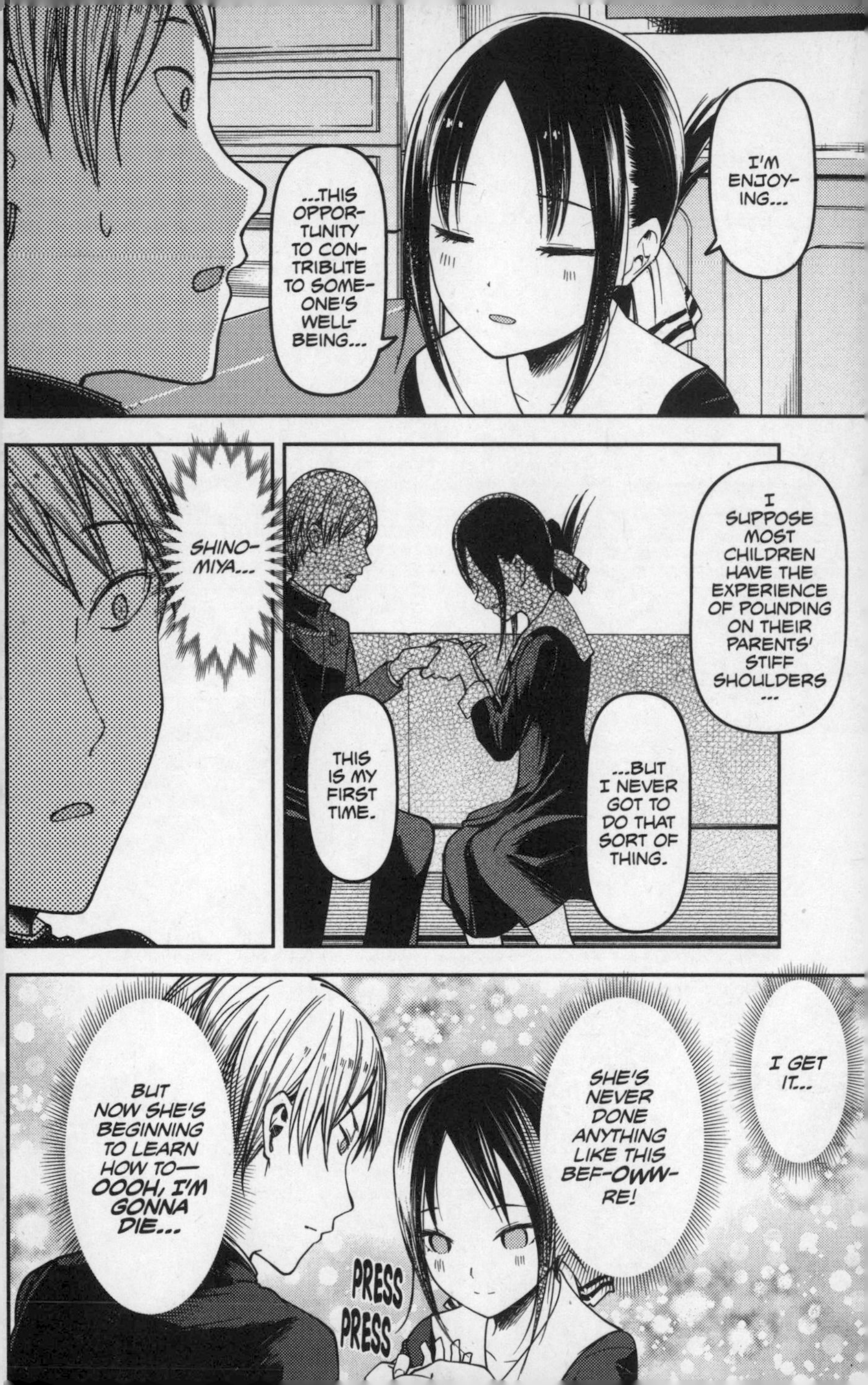
I'M ENJOYING...
...THIS OPPORTUNITY TO CONTRIBUTE TO SOMEONE'S WELL-BEING...
I SUPPOSE MOST CHILDREN HAVE THE EXPERIENCE OF POUNDING ON THEIR PARENTS' STIFF SHOULDERS...
...BUT I NEVER GOT TO DO THAT SORT OF THING.
THIS IS MY FIRST TIME.
SHINOMIYA...
I GET IT...
SHE'S NEVER DONE ANYTHING LIKE THIS BEF-OWW-RE!
PRESS PRESS
BUT NOW SHE'S BEGINNING TO LEARN HOW TO—OOOH, I'M GONNA DIE...

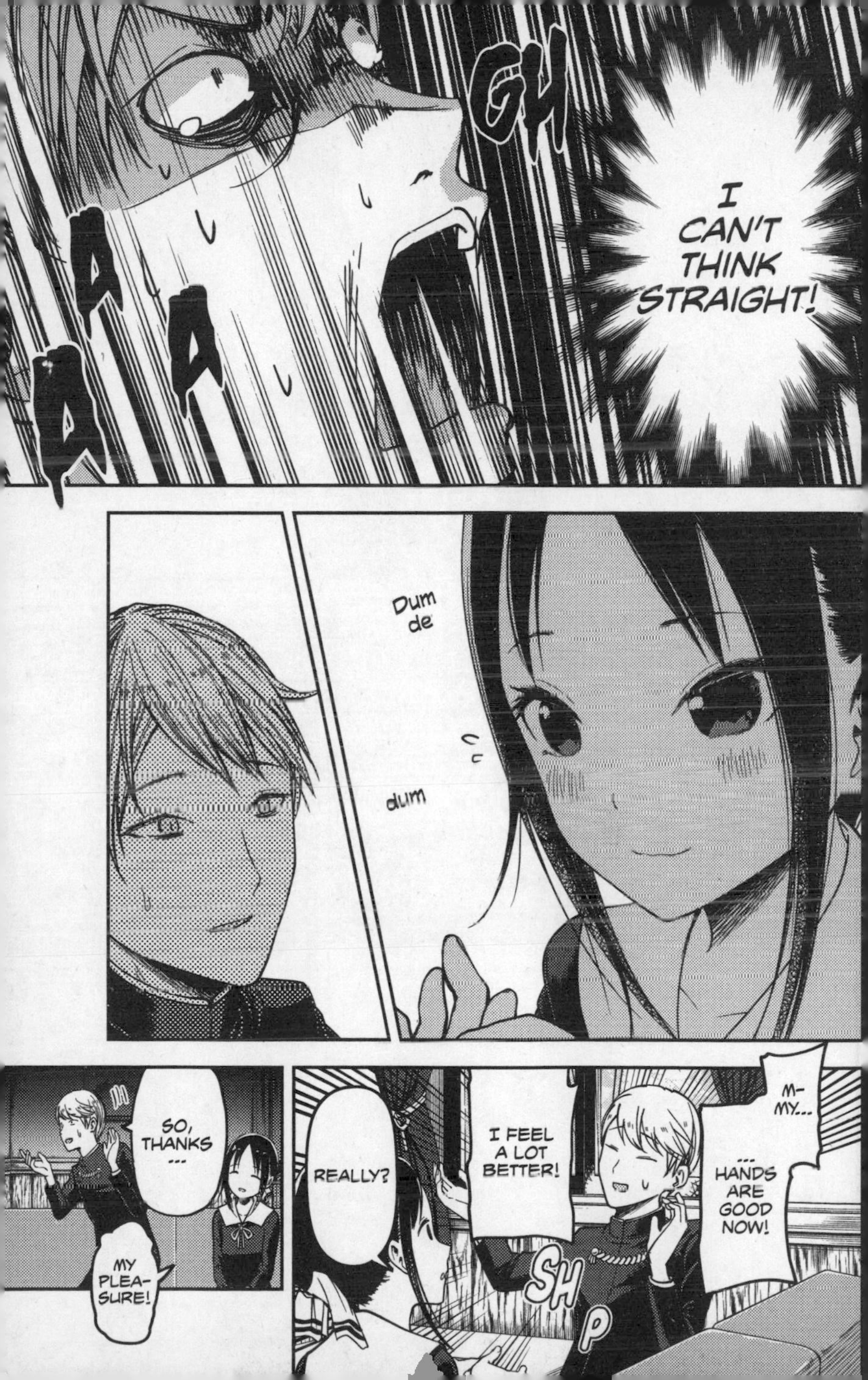
GH
I CAN'T THINK STRAIGHT!
Dum de dum
M-MY...
...HANDS ARE GOOD NOW!
I FEEL A LOT BETTER!
REALLY?
SHP
SO, THANKS...
MY PLEASURE!

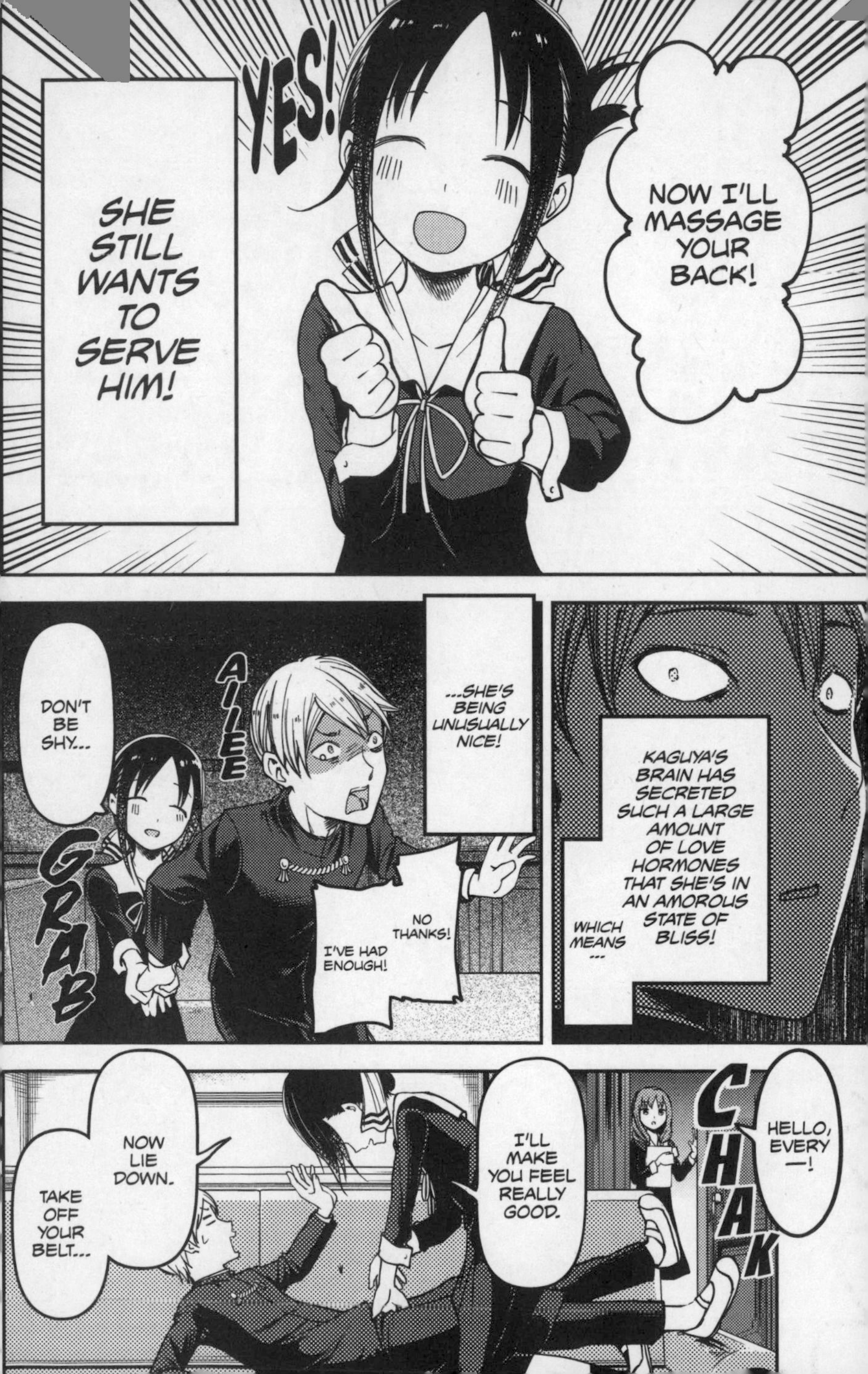
NOW I'LL MASSAGE YOUR BACK!
YES!
SHE STILL WANTS TO SERVE HIM!
KAGUYA'S BRAIN HAS SECRETED SUCH A LARGE AMOUNT OF LOVE HORMONES THAT SHE'S IN AN AMOROUS STATE OF BLISS!
WHICH MEANS ...
...SHE'S BEING UNUSUALLY NICE!
AIIEE
NO THANKS!
I'VE HAD ENOUGH!
DON'T BE SHY...
GRAB
HELLO, EVERY—!
CHAK
I'LL MAKE YOU FEEL REALLY GOOD.
NOW LIE DOWN.
TAKE OFF YOUR BELT...

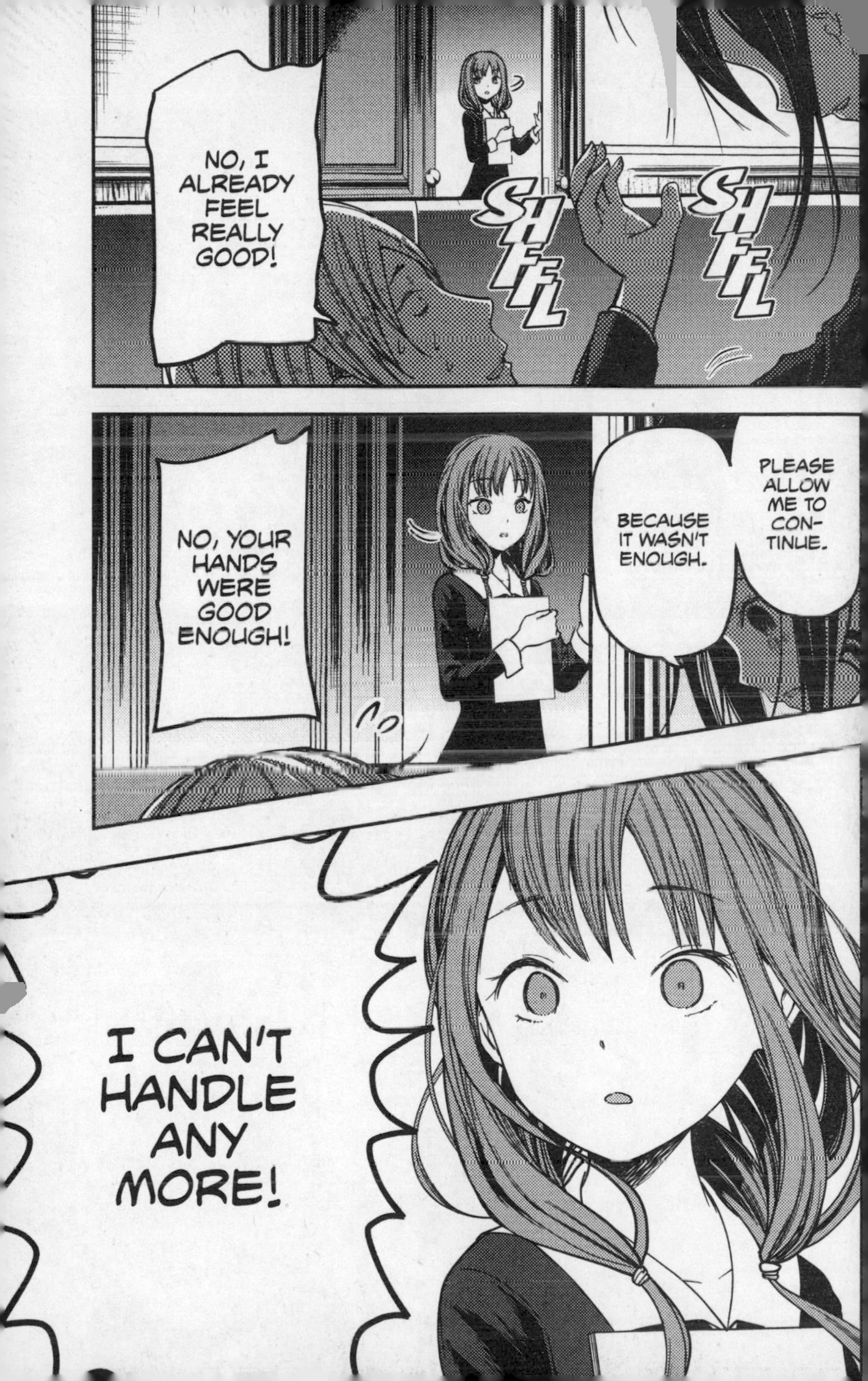
SHFFL
SHFFL
NO, I ALREADY FEEL REALLY GOOD!
PLEASE ALLOW ME TO CONTINUE.
BECAUSE IT WASN'T ENOUGH.
NO, YOUR HANDS WERE GOOD ENOUGH!
I CAN'T HANDLE ANY MORE!

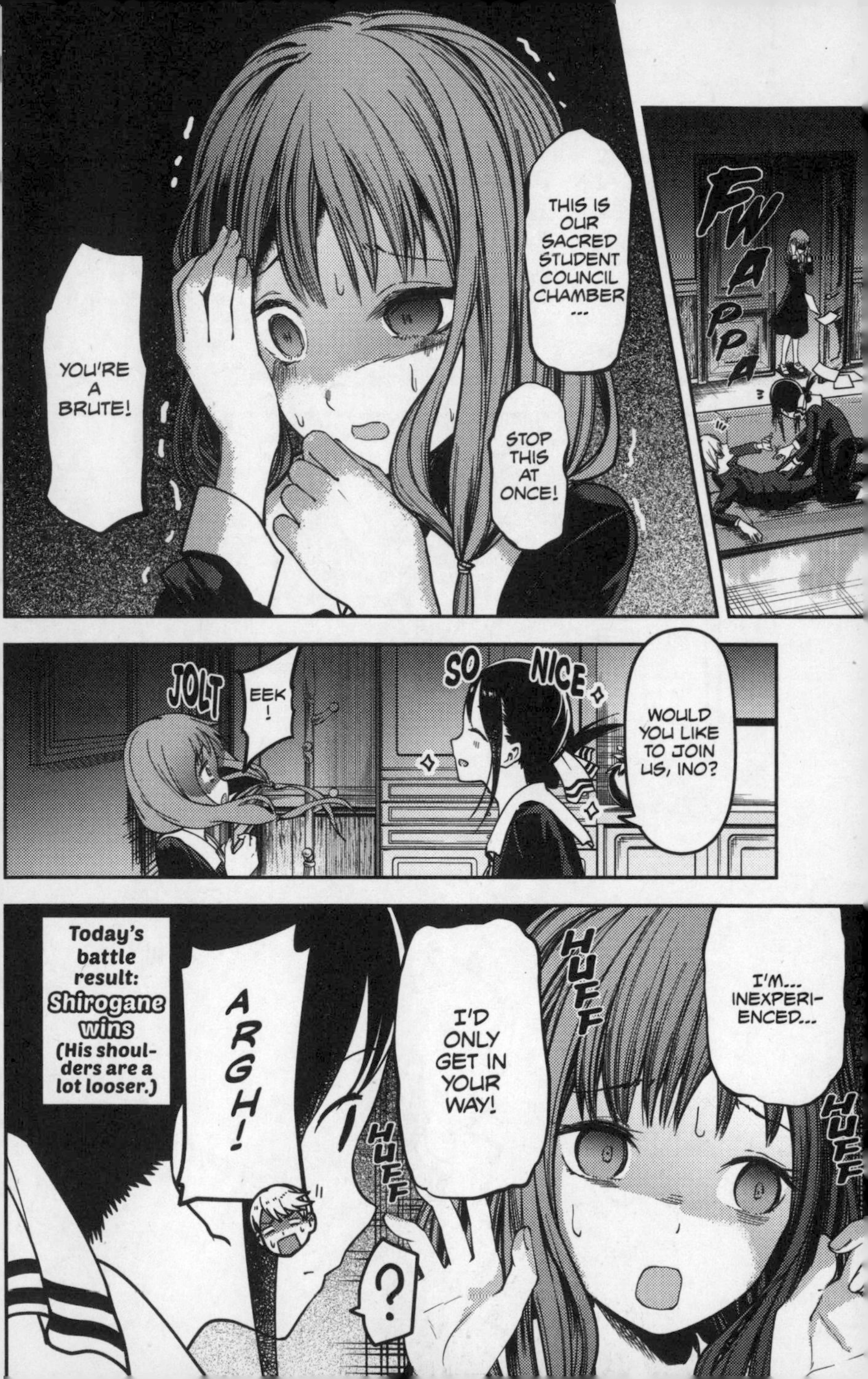
FWAPPA
THIS IS OUR SACRED STUDENT COUNCIL CHAMBER...
STOP THIS AT ONCE!
YOU'RE A BRUTE!
WOULD YOU LIKE TO JOIN US, INO?
SO NICE
EEK!
JOLT
I'M... INEXPERI-ENCED...
HUFF
HUFF
I'D ONLY GET IN YOUR WAY!
HUFF
?
ARGH!
Today's battle result: Shirogane wins (His shoulders are a lot looser.)

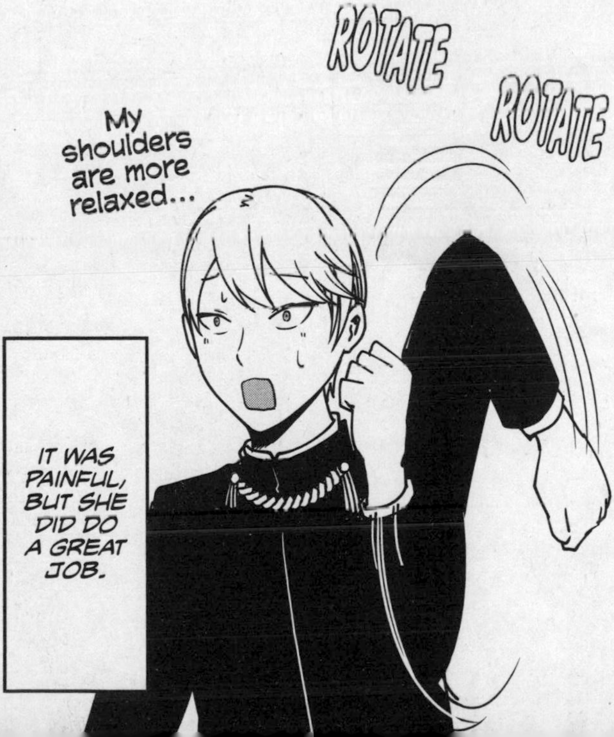
ROTATE
ROTATE
My shoulders are more relaxed...
IT WAS PAINFUL, BUT SHE DID DO A GREAT JOB.

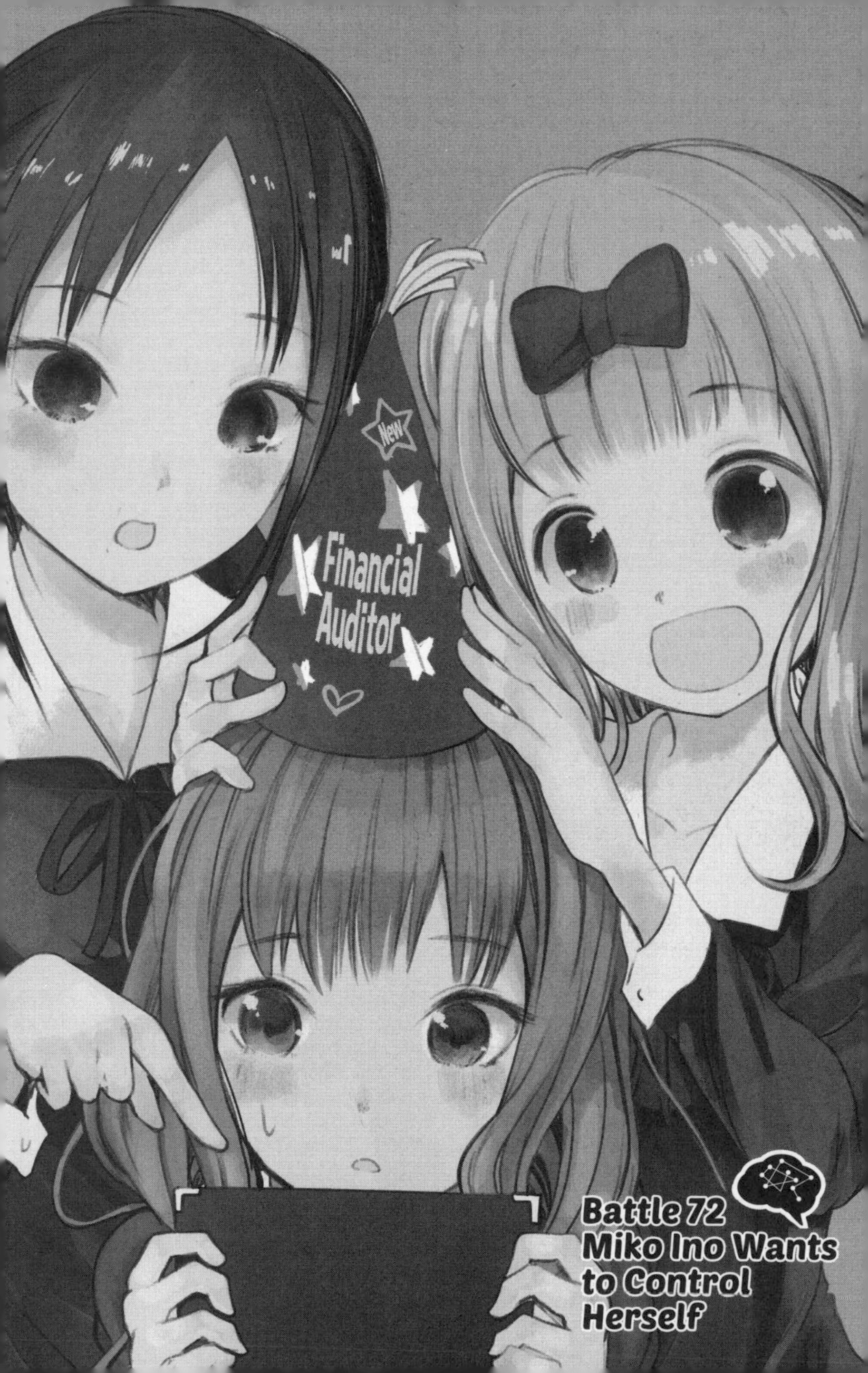
New
Financial Auditor
Battle 72
Miko Ino Wants to Control Herself

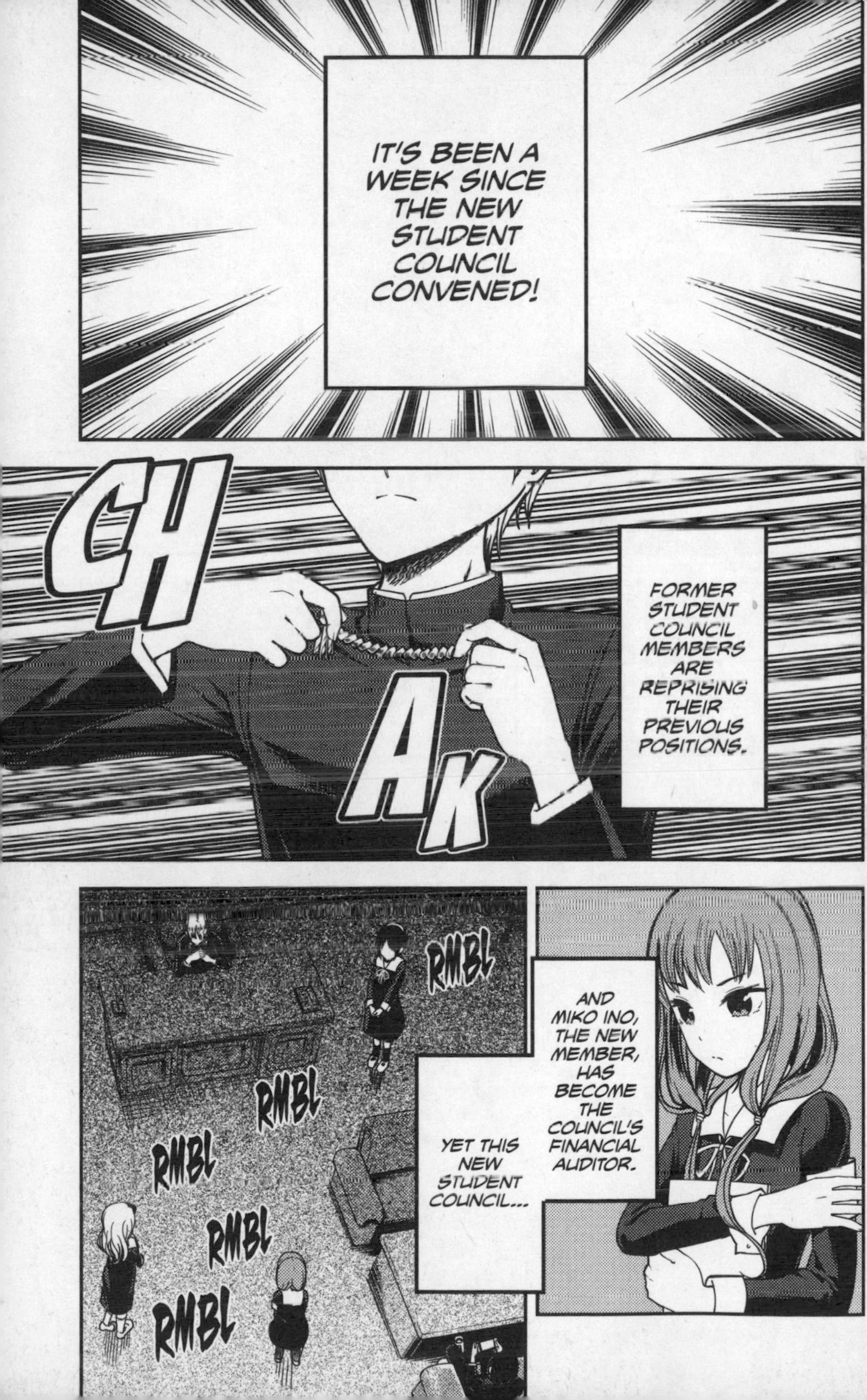
IT'S BEEN A WEEK SINCE THE NEW STUDENT COUNCIL CONVENED!
FORMER STUDENT COUNCIL MEMBERS ARE REPRISING THEIR PREVIOUS POSITIONS.
CH
AK
AND MIKO INO, THE NEW MEMBER, HAS BECOME THE COUNCIL'S FINANCIAL AUDITOR.
YET THIS NEW STUDENT COUNCIL...
RMBL
RMBL
RMBL
RMBL
RMBL

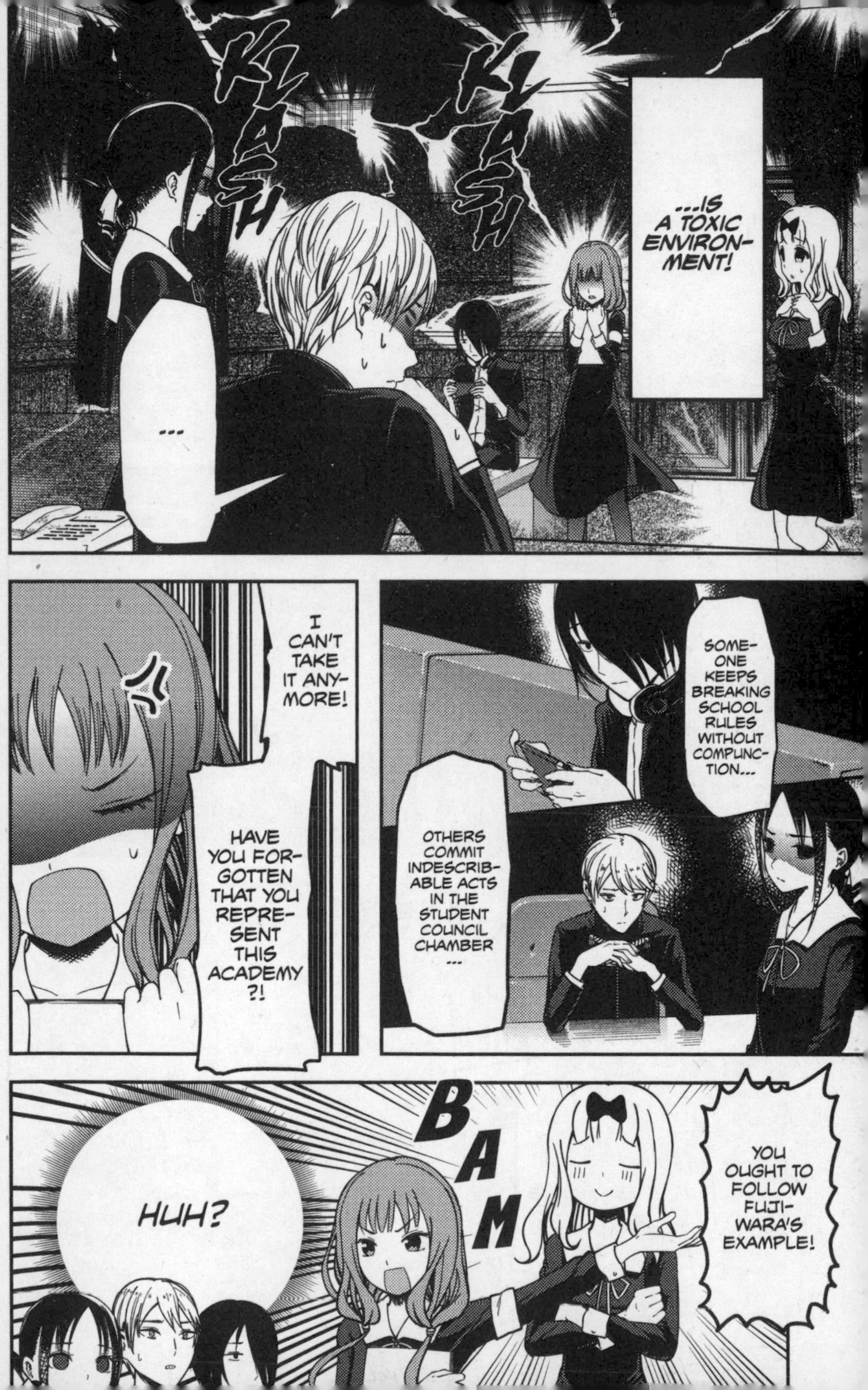
KLASH
...IS A TOXIC ENVIRONMENT!
KLASH
...
SOMEONE KEEPS BREAKING SCHOOL RULES WITHOUT COMPUNCTION...
OTHERS COMMIT INDESCRIBABLE ACTS IN THE STUDENT COUNCIL CHAMBER...
I CAN'T TAKE IT ANYMORE!
HAVE YOU FORGOTTEN THAT YOU REPRESENT THIS ACADEMY?!
YOU OUGHT TO FOLLOW FUJIWARA'S EXAMPLE!
BAM
HUH?

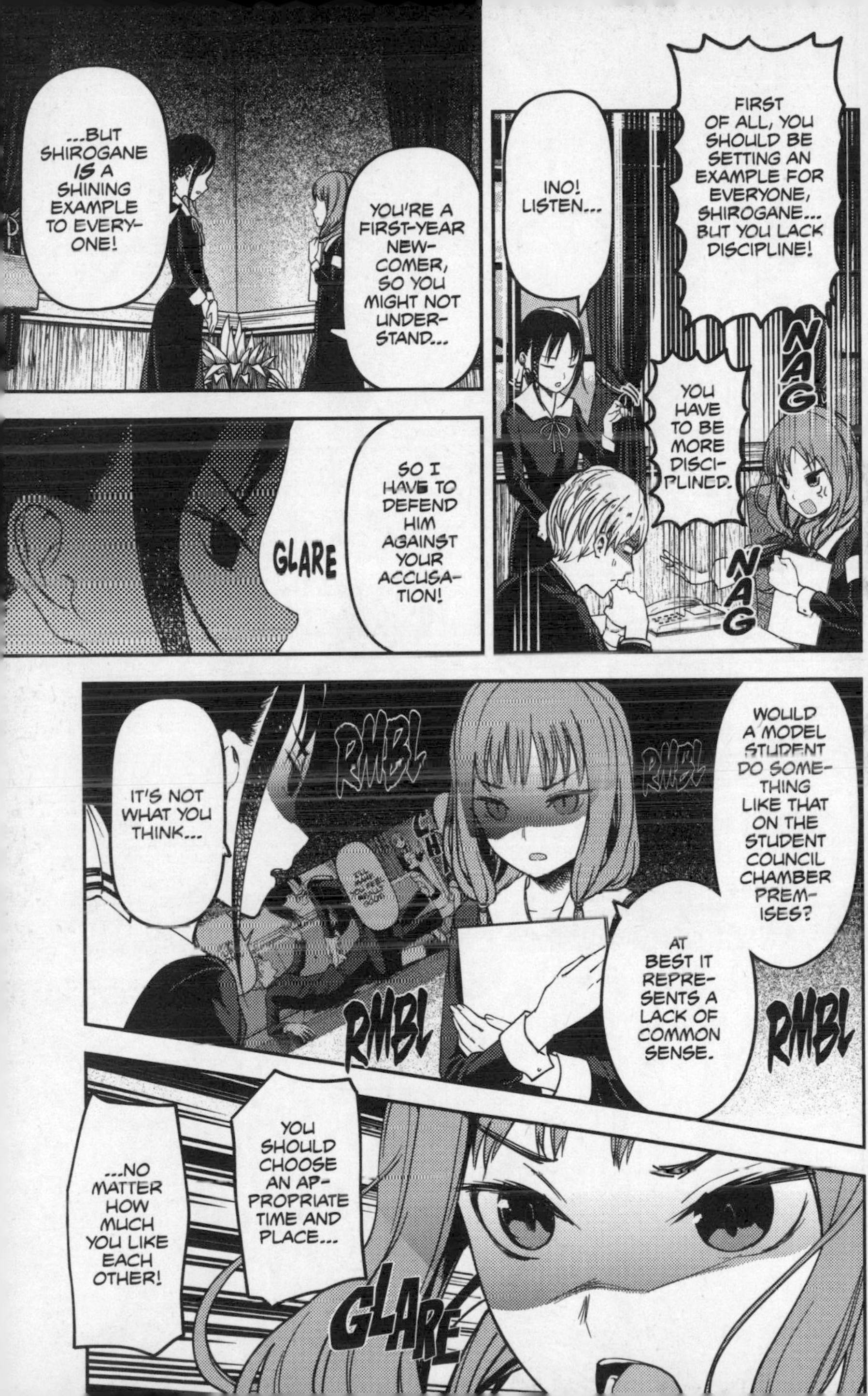
FIRST OF ALL, YOU SHOULD BE SETTING AN EXAMPLE FOR EVERYONE, SHIROGANE... BUT YOU LACK DISCIPLINE!
INO! LISTEN...
NAG
YOU HAVE TO BE MORE DISCIPLINED.
NAG
YOU'RE A FIRST-YEAR NEWCOMER, SO YOU MIGHT NOT UNDERSTAND...
...BUT SHIROGANE IS A SHINING EXAMPLE TO EVERYONE!
SO I HAVE TO DEFEND HIM AGAINST YOUR ACCUSATION!
GLARE
WOULD A MODEL STUDENT DO SOMETHING LIKE THAT ON THE STUDENT COUNCIL CHAMBER PREMISES?
RMBL
RMBL
AT BEST IT REPRESENTS A LACK OF COMMON SENSE.
RMBL
IT'S NOT WHAT YOU THINK...
RMBL
YOU SHOULD CHOOSE AN APPROPRIATE TIME AND PLACE...
...NO MATTER HOW MUCH YOU LIKE EACH OTHER!
GLARE

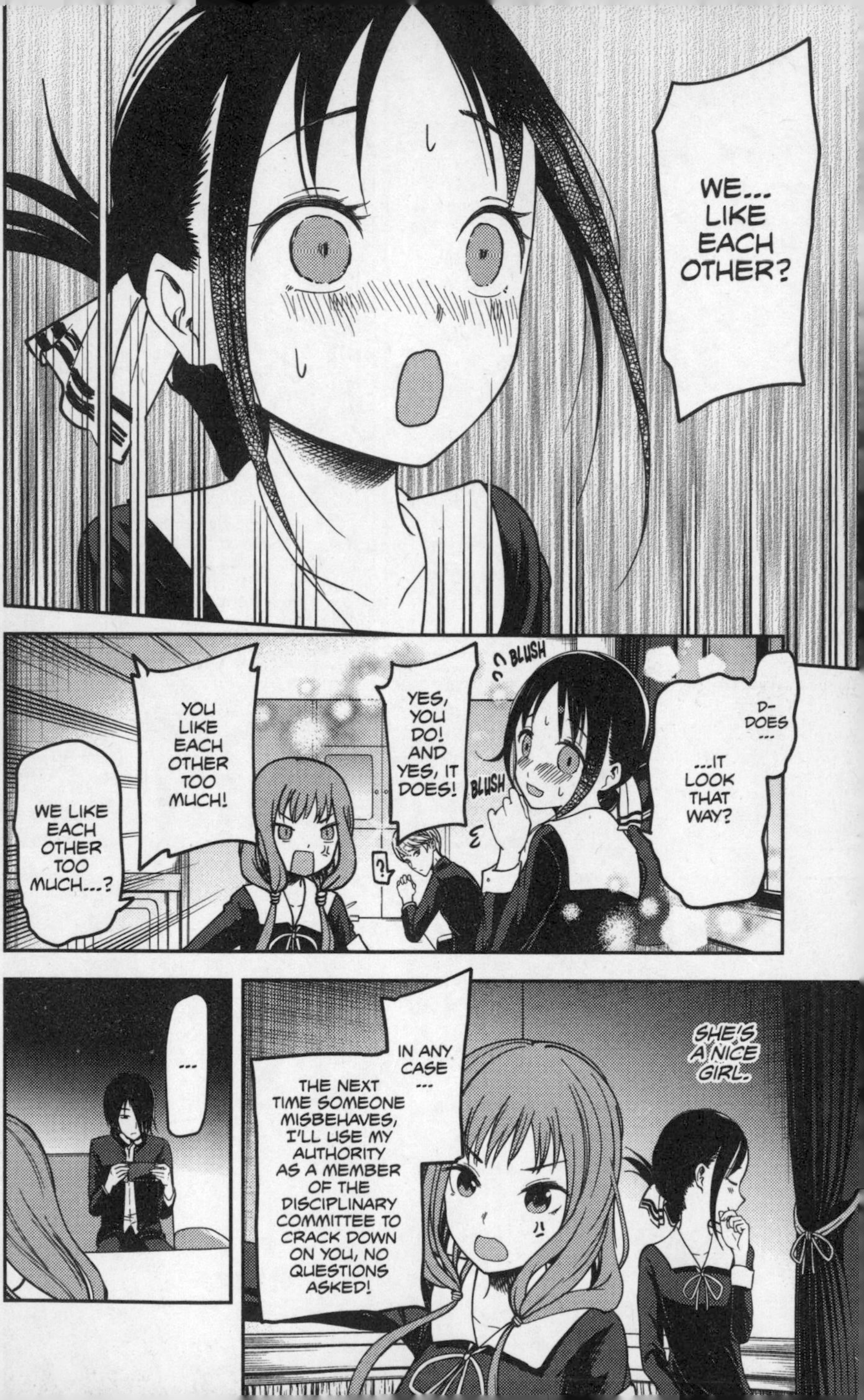
WE... LIKE EACH OTHER?
D-DOES...
...IT LOOK THAT WAY?
BLUSH
BLUSH
YES, YOU DO! AND YES, IT DOES!
YOU LIKE EACH OTHER TOO MUCH!
WE LIKE EACH OTHER TOO MUCH...?
?
SHE'S A NICE GIRL.
IN ANY CASE...
THE NEXT TIME SOMEONE MISBEHAVES, I'LL USE MY AUTHORITY AS A MEMBER OF THE DISCIPLINARY COMMITTEE TO CRACK DOWN ON YOU, NO QUESTIONS ASKED!
...

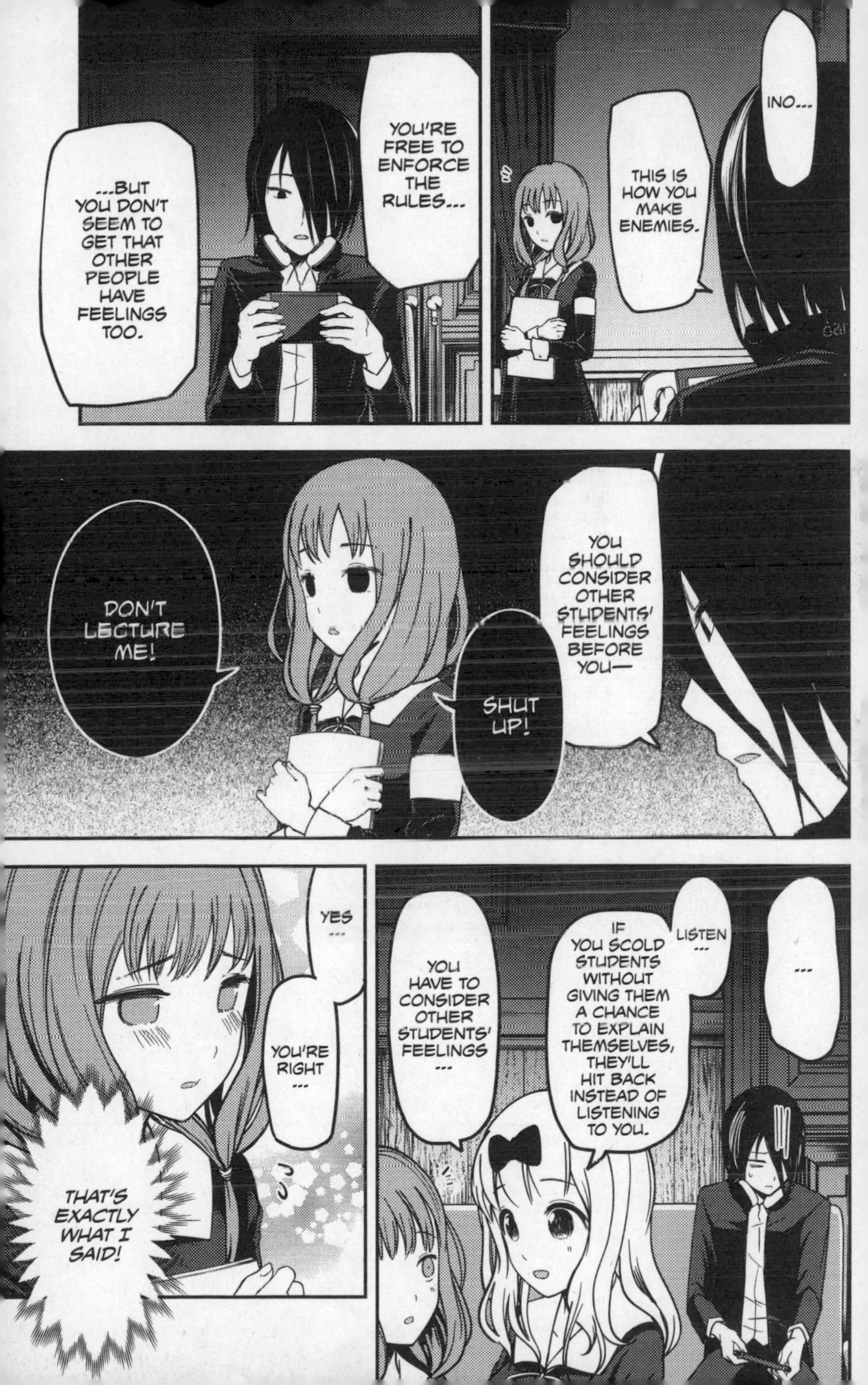
INO...
THIS IS HOW YOU MAKE ENEMIES.
YOU'RE FREE TO ENFORCE THE RULES...
...BUT YOU DON'T SEEM TO GET THAT OTHER PEOPLE HAVE FEELINGS TOO.
YOU SHOULD CONSIDER OTHER STUDENTS' FEELINGS BEFORE YOU—
SHUT UP!
DON'T LECTURE ME!
...
LISTEN...
IF YOU SCOLD STUDENTS WITHOUT GIVING THEM A CHANCE TO EXPLAIN THEMSELVES, THEY'LL HIT BACK INSTEAD OF LISTENING TO YOU.
YOU HAVE TO CONSIDER OTHER STUDENTS' FEELINGS...
YES...
YOU'RE RIGHT...
THAT'S EXACTLY WHAT I SAID!

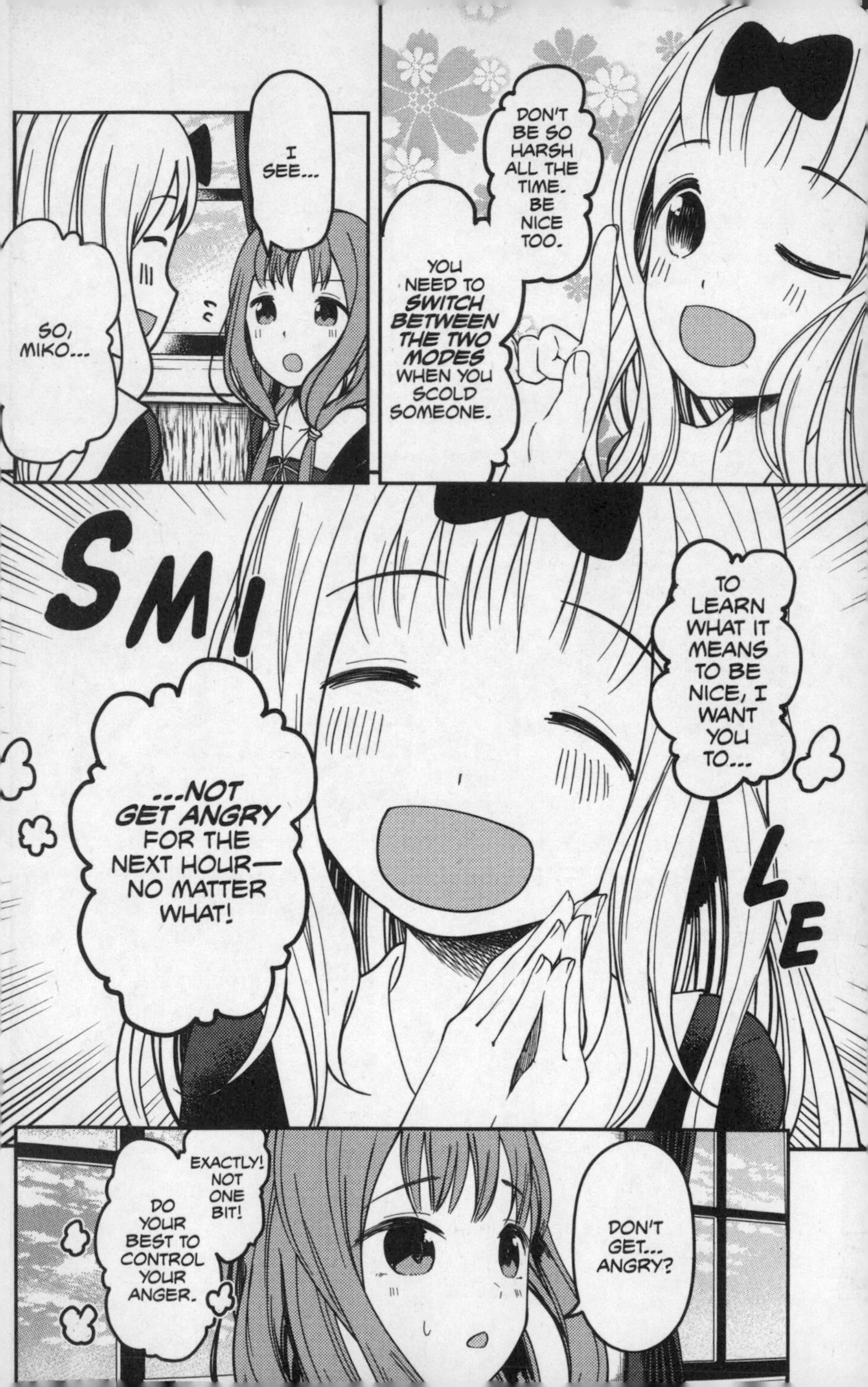
DON'T BE SO HARSH ALL THE TIME. BE NICE TOO.
YOU NEED TO SWITCH BETWEEN THE TWO MODES WHEN YOU SCOLD SOMEONE.
I SEE...
SO, MIKO...
SMILE
TO LEARN WHAT IT MEANS TO BE NICE, I WANT YOU TO...
...NOT GET ANGRY FOR THE NEXT HOUR— NO MATTER WHAT!
DON'T GET... ANGRY?
EXACTLY! NOT ONE BIT!
DO YOUR BEST TO CONTROL YOUR ANGER.

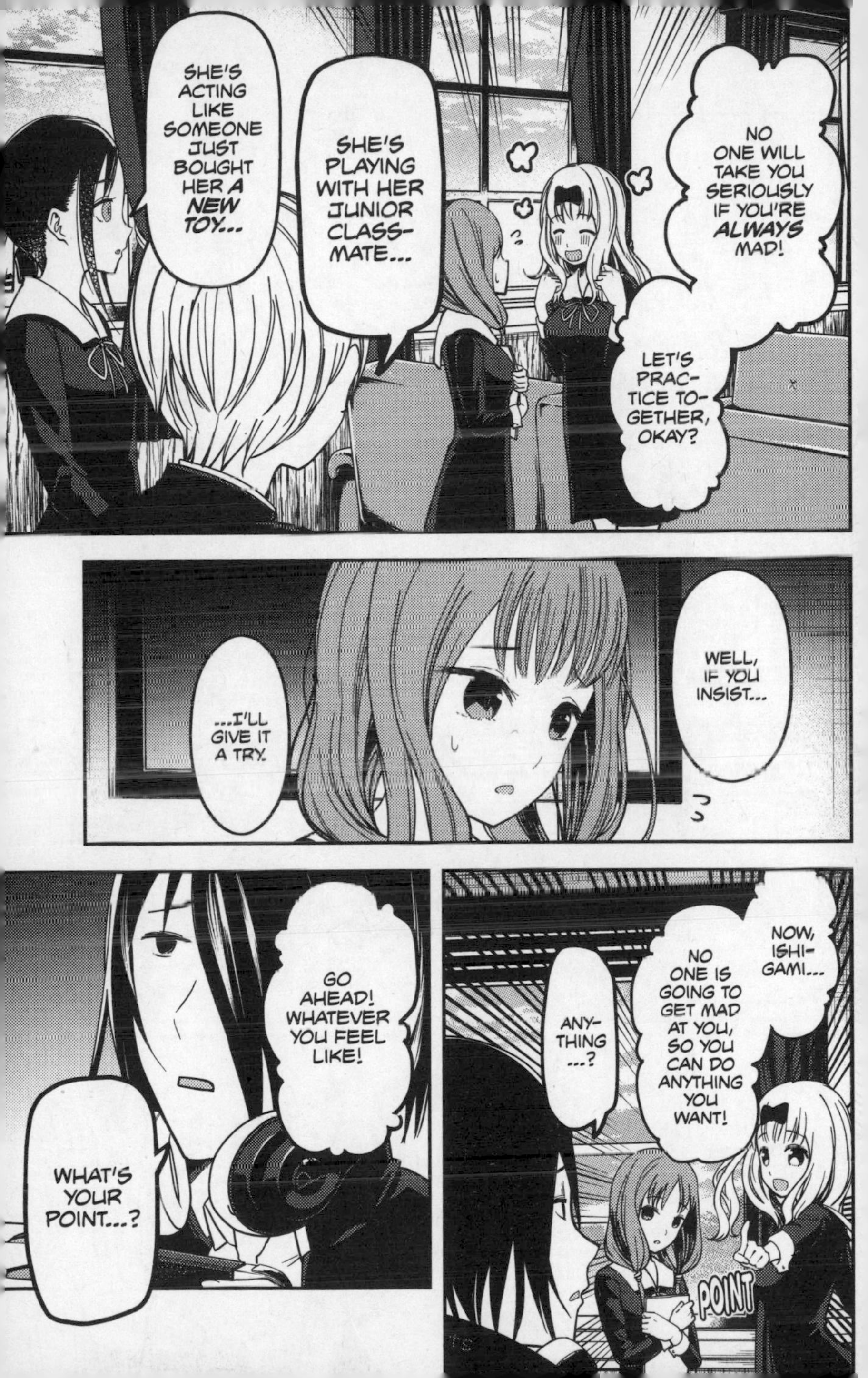
NO ONE WILL TAKE YOU SERIOUSLY IF YOU'RE ALWAYS MAD!
LET'S PRACTICE TOGETHER, OKAY?
SHE'S PLAYING WITH HER JUNIOR CLASSMATE...
SHE'S ACTING LIKE SOMEONE JUST BOUGHT HER A NEW TOY...
WELL, IF YOU INSIST...
...I'LL GIVE IT A TRY.
NOW, ISHIGAMI...
NO ONE IS GOING TO GET MAD AT YOU, SO YOU CAN DO ANYTHING YOU WANT!
ANYTHING...?
POINT
GO AHEAD! WHATEVER YOU FEEL LIKE!
WHAT'S YOUR POINT...?

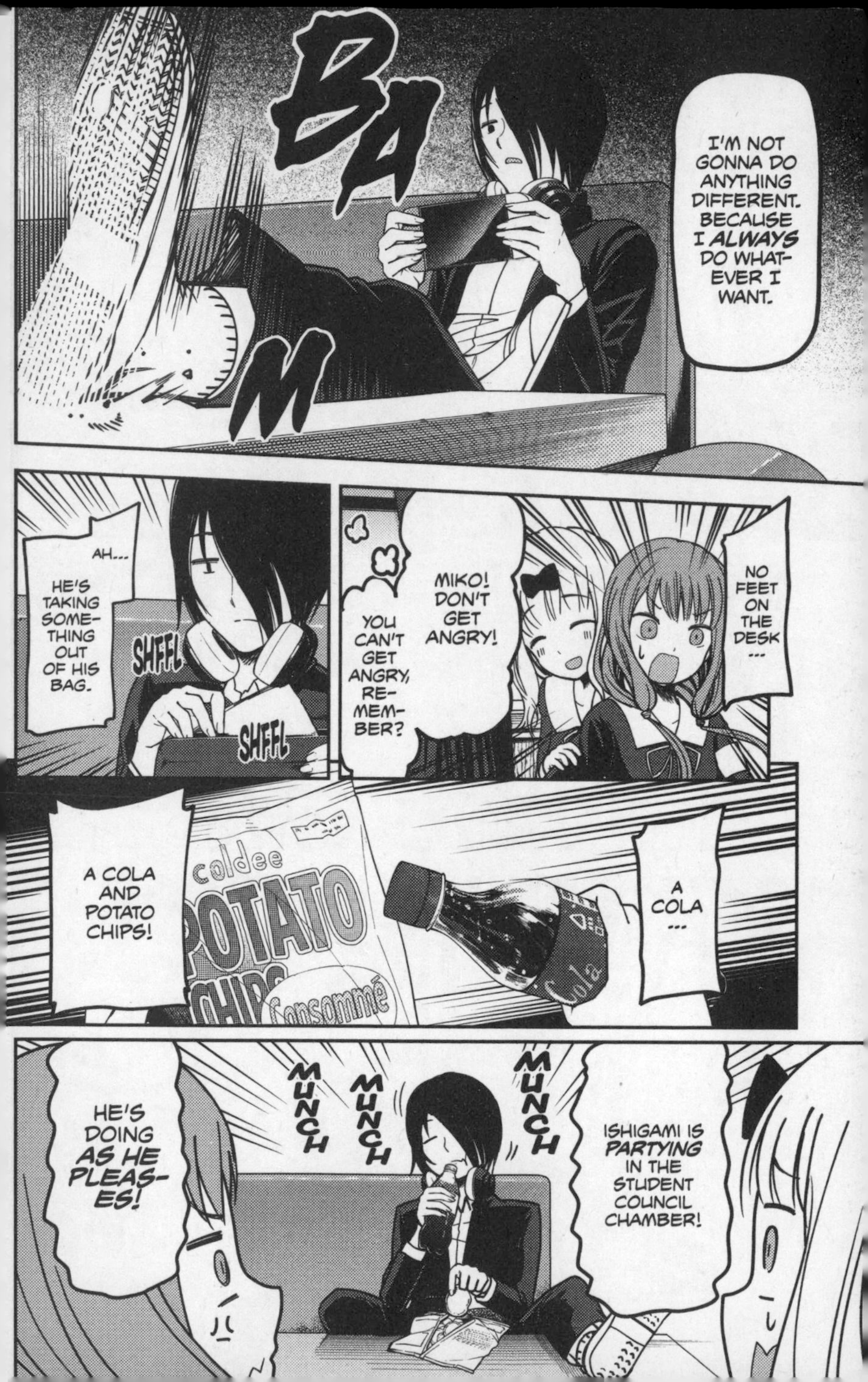
BAM
I'M NOT GONNA DO ANYTHING DIFFERENT. BECAUSE I ALWAYS DO WHATEVER I WANT.
NO FEET ON THE DESK...
MIKO! DON'T GET ANGRY!
YOU CAN'T GET ANGRY, REMEMBER?
AH... HE'S TAKING SOMETHING OUT OF HIS BAG.
SHFFL
SHFFL
A COLA...
coldee POTATO CHIPS Consommé
Cola
A COLA AND POTATO CHIPS!
ISHIGAMI IS PARTYING IN THE STUDENT COUNCIL CHAMBER!
MUNCH
MUNCH
MUNCH
HE'S DOING AS HE PLEASES!

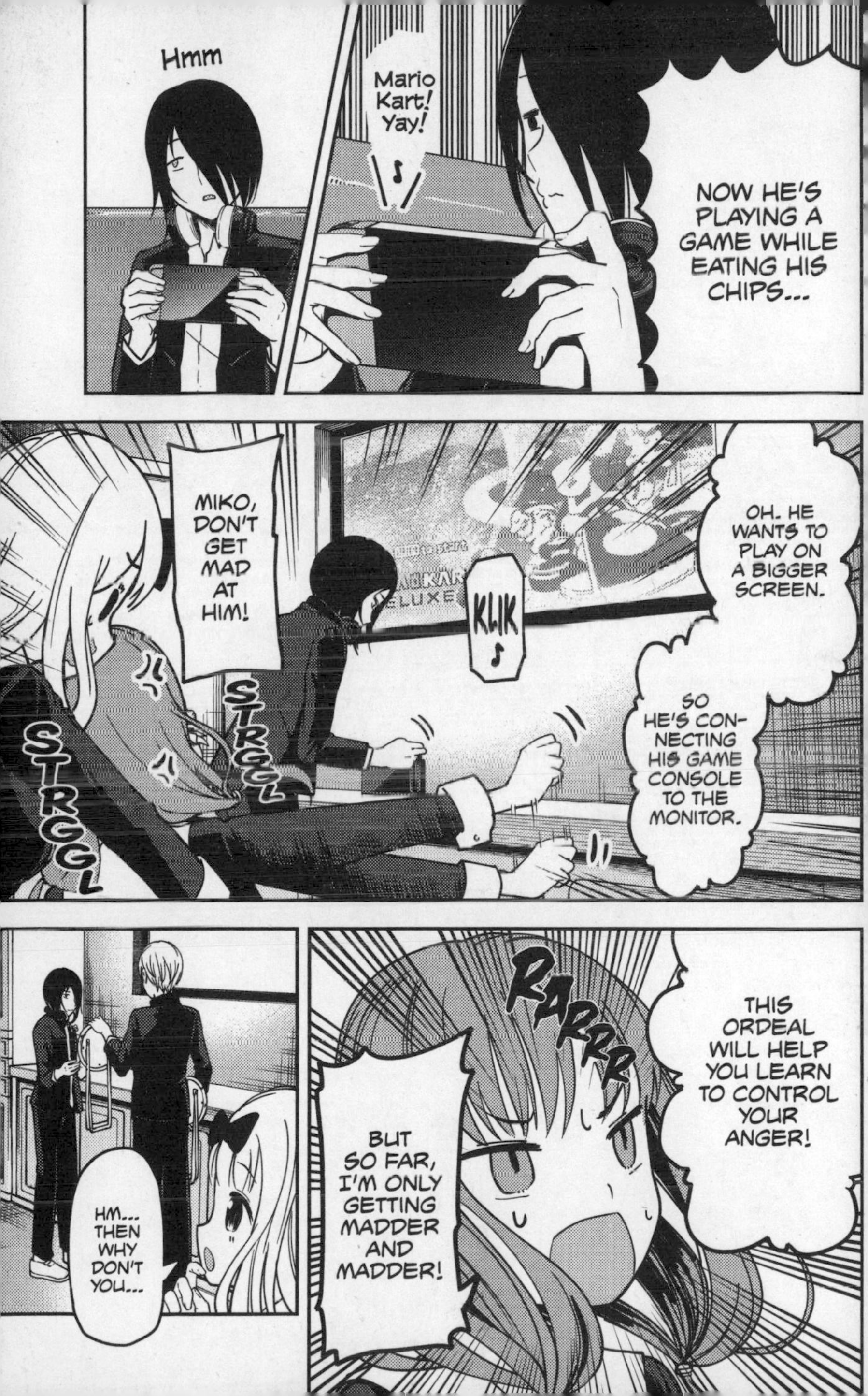
NOW HE'S PLAYING A GAME WHILE EATING HIS CHIPS...
Mario Kart! Yay!
Hmm
OH. HE WANTS TO PLAY ON A BIGGER SCREEN.
SO HE'S CONNECTING HIS GAME CONSOLE TO THE MONITOR.
KLIK
MIKO, DON'T GET MAD AT HIM!
STRGGL
STRGGL
THIS ORDEAL WILL HELP YOU LEARN TO CONTROL YOUR ANGER!
RARRR
BUT SO FAR, I'M ONLY GETTING MADDER AND MADDER!
HM... THEN WHY DON'T YOU...

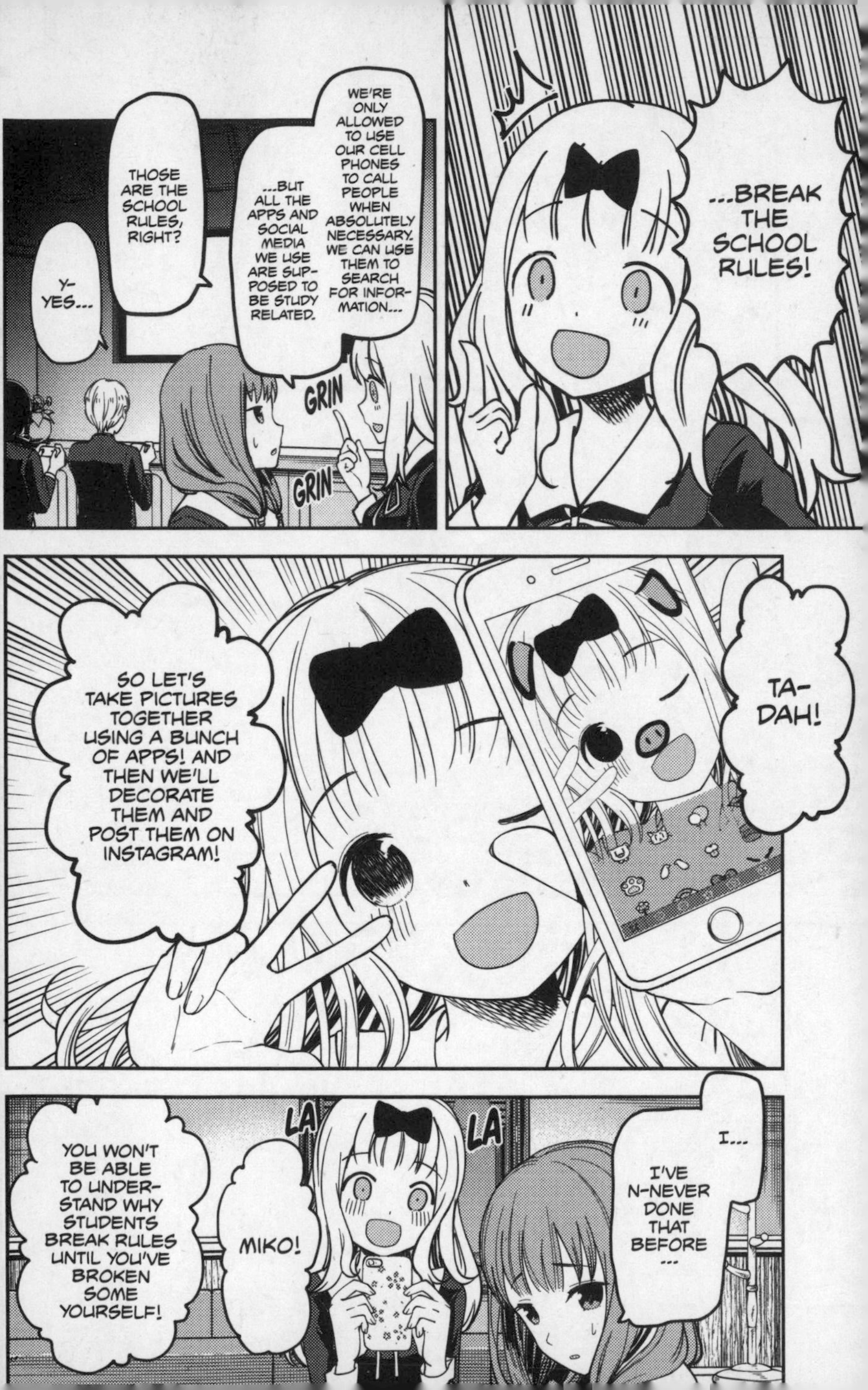
...BREAK THE SCHOOL RULES!
WE'RE ONLY ALLOWED TO USE OUR CELL PHONES TO CALL PEOPLE WHEN ABSOLUTELY NECESSARY. WE CAN USE THEM TO SEARCH FOR INFORMATION...
...BUT ALL THE APPS AND SOCIAL MEDIA WE USE ARE SUPPOSED TO BE STUDY RELATED.
THOSE ARE THE SCHOOL RULES, RIGHT?
GRIN
GRIN
Y-YES...
TA-DAH!
SO LET'S TAKE PICTURES TOGETHER USING A BUNCH OF APPS! AND THEN WE'LL DECORATE THEM AND POST THEM ON INSTAGRAM!
I...
I'VE N-NEVER DONE THAT BEFORE...
LA
LA
MIKO!
YOU WON'T BE ABLE TO UNDERSTAND WHY STUDENTS BREAK RULES UNTIL YOU'VE BROKEN SOME YOURSELF!

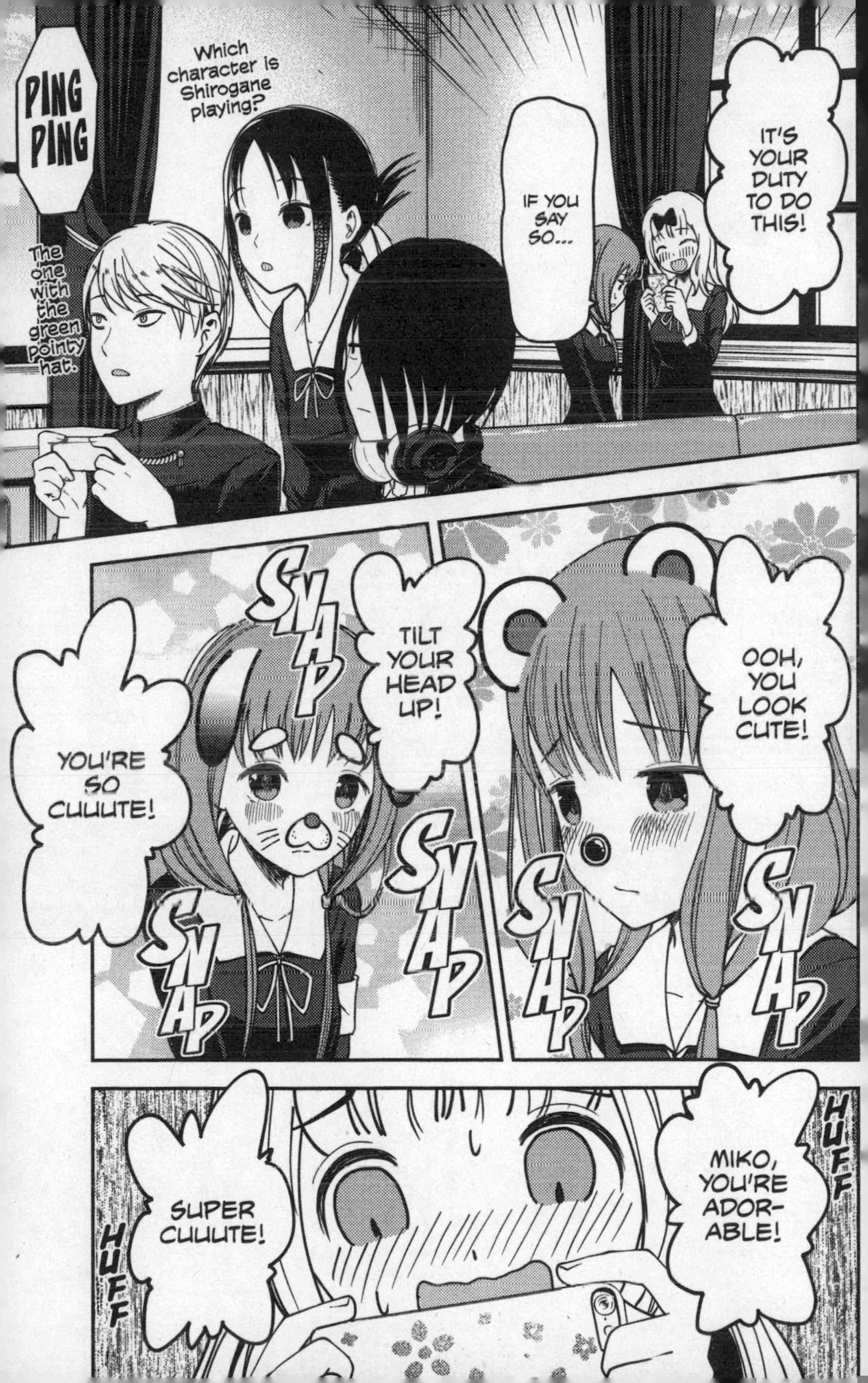
IT'S YOUR DUTY TO DO THIS!
IF YOU SAY SO...
Which character is Shirogane playing?
PING PING
The one with the green pointy hat.
OOH, YOU LOOK CUTE!
SNAP
SNAP
TILT YOUR HEAD UP!
SNAP
SNAP
YOU'RE SO CUUUTE!
SNAP
HUFF
MIKO, YOU'RE ADORABLE!
SUPER CUUUTE!
HUFF

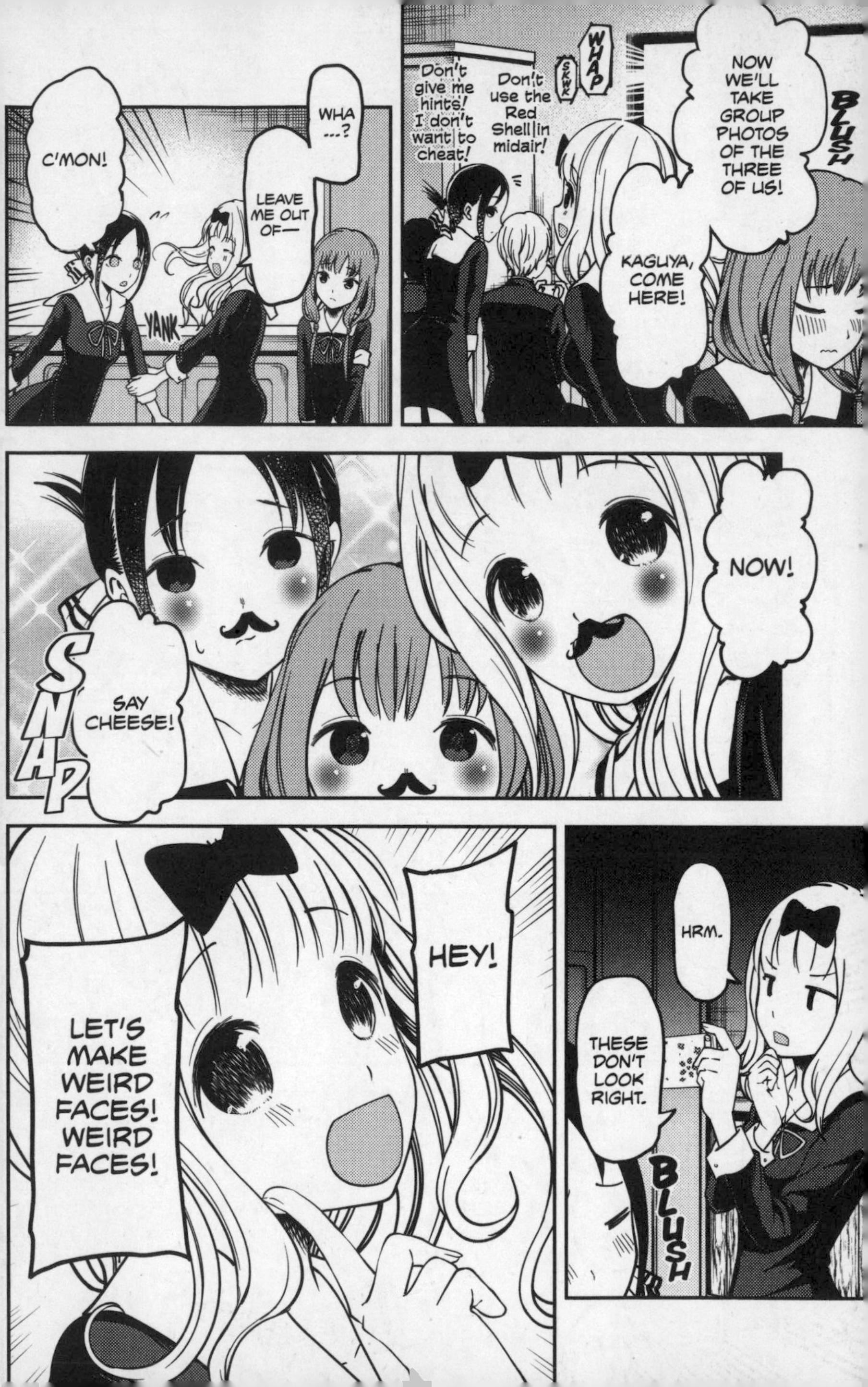

NOW WE'LL TAKE GROUP PHOTOS OF THE THREE OF US!
BLUSH
WHAP
SKWK
Don't use the Red Shell in midair!
Don't give me hints! I don't want to cheat!
KAGUYA, COME HERE!
WHA ...?
C'MON!
LEAVE ME OUT OF—
YANK
NOW!
SAY CHEESE!
SNAP
HRM.
THESE DON'T LOOK RIGHT.
BLUSH
HEY!
LET'S MAKE WEIRD FACES! WEIRD FACES!

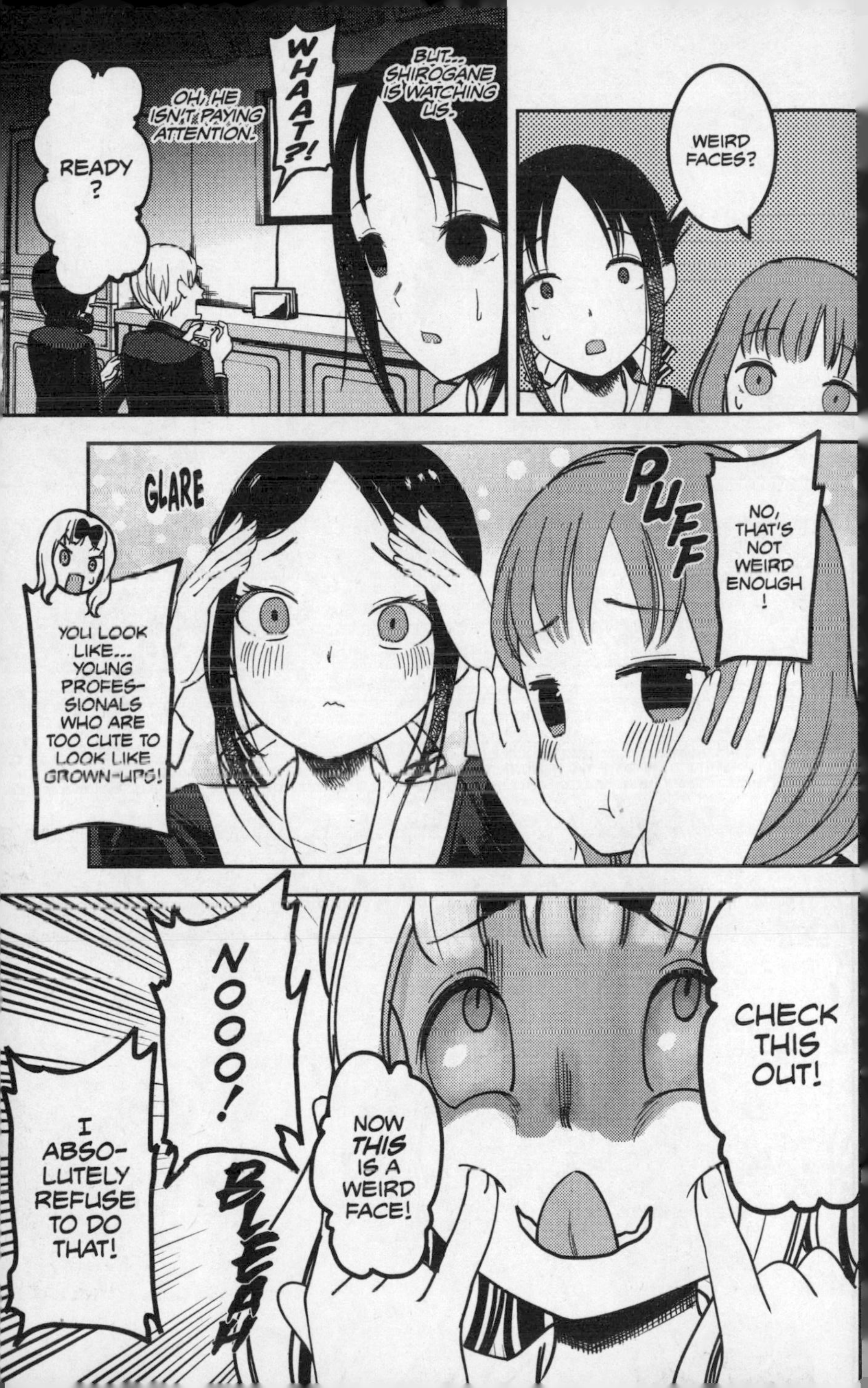
WEIRD FACES?
BUT... SHIROGANE IS WATCHING US.
WHAAAT?!
OH, HE ISN'T PAYING ATTENTION.
READY?
NO, THAT'S NOT WEIRD ENOUGH!
PUFF
GLARE
YOU LOOK LIKE... YOUNG PROFES-SIONALS WHO ARE TOO CUTE TO LOOK LIKE GROWN-UPS!
CHECK THIS OUT!
NOW THIS IS A WEIRD FACE!
BLEAH
NOOOO!
I ABSO-LUTELY REFUSE TO DO THAT!

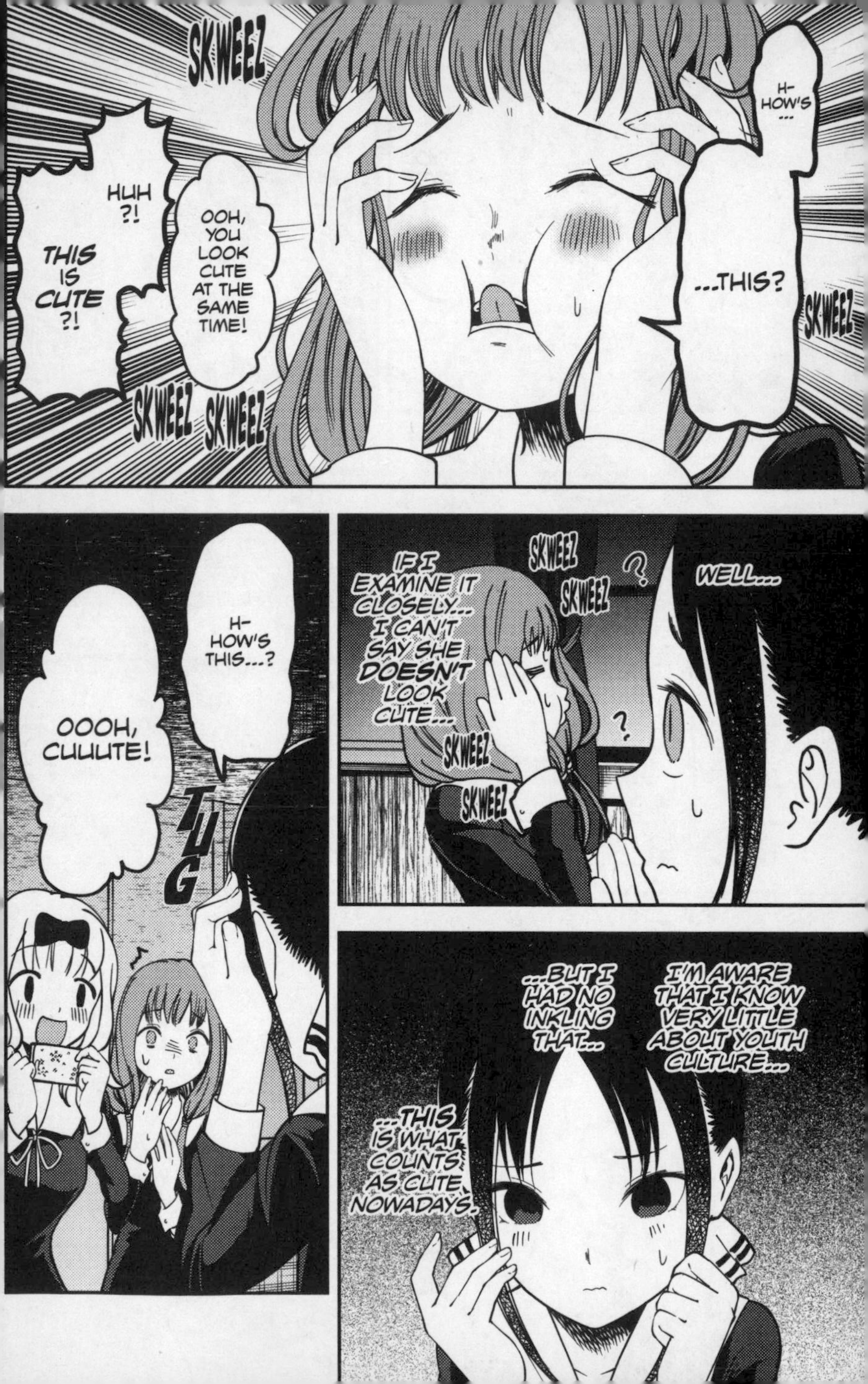
SKWEEZ
H- HOW'S ...
...THIS?
SKWEEZ
OOH, YOU LOOK CUTE AT THE SAME TIME!
HUH?!
THIS IS CUTE?!
SKWEEZ
SKWEEZ
WELL...
SKWEEZ
SKWEEZ
IF I EXAMINE IT CLOSELY... I CAN'T SAY SHE DOESN'T LOOK CUTE...
SKWEEZ
SKWEEZ
I'M AWARE THAT I KNOW VERY LITTLE ABOUT YOUTH CULTURE...
...BUT I HAD NO INKLING THAT...
...THIS IS WHAT COUNTS AS CUTE NOWADAYS.
H- HOW'S THIS...?
OOOH, CUUUTE!
TUG

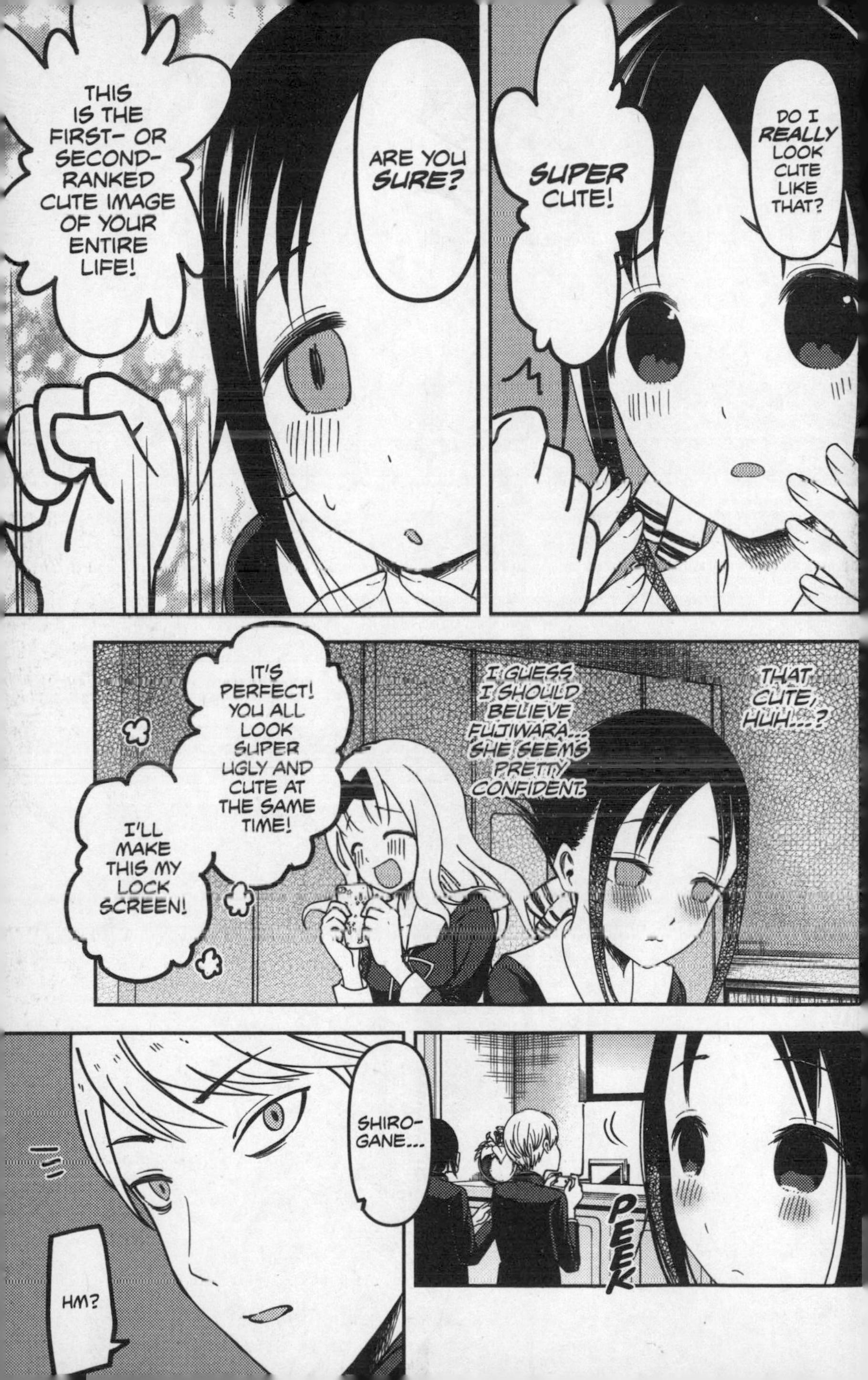
DO I REALLY LOOK CUTE LIKE THAT?
SUPER CUTE!
ARE YOU SURE?
THIS IS THE FIRST- OR SECOND-RANKED CUTE IMAGE OF YOUR ENTIRE LIFE!
THAT CUTE, HUH...?
I GUESS I SHOULD BELIEVE FUJIWARA... SHE SEEMS PRETTY CONFIDENT.
IT'S PERFECT! YOU ALL LOOK SUPER UGLY AND CUTE AT THE SAME TIME!
I'LL MAKE THIS MY LOCK SCREEN!
PEEK
SHIRO-GANE...
HM?

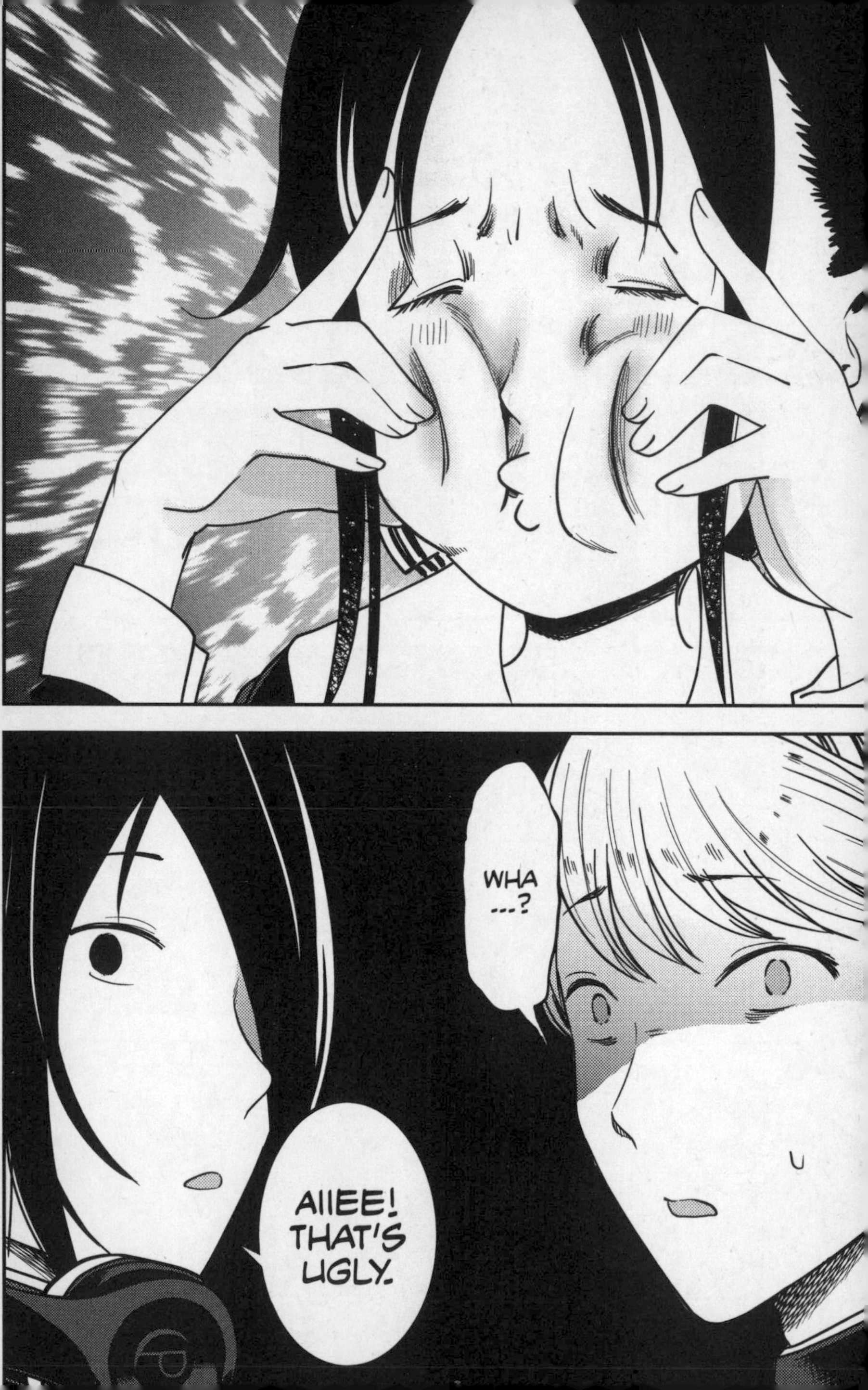
WHA---?
AIIEE! THAT'S UGLY.

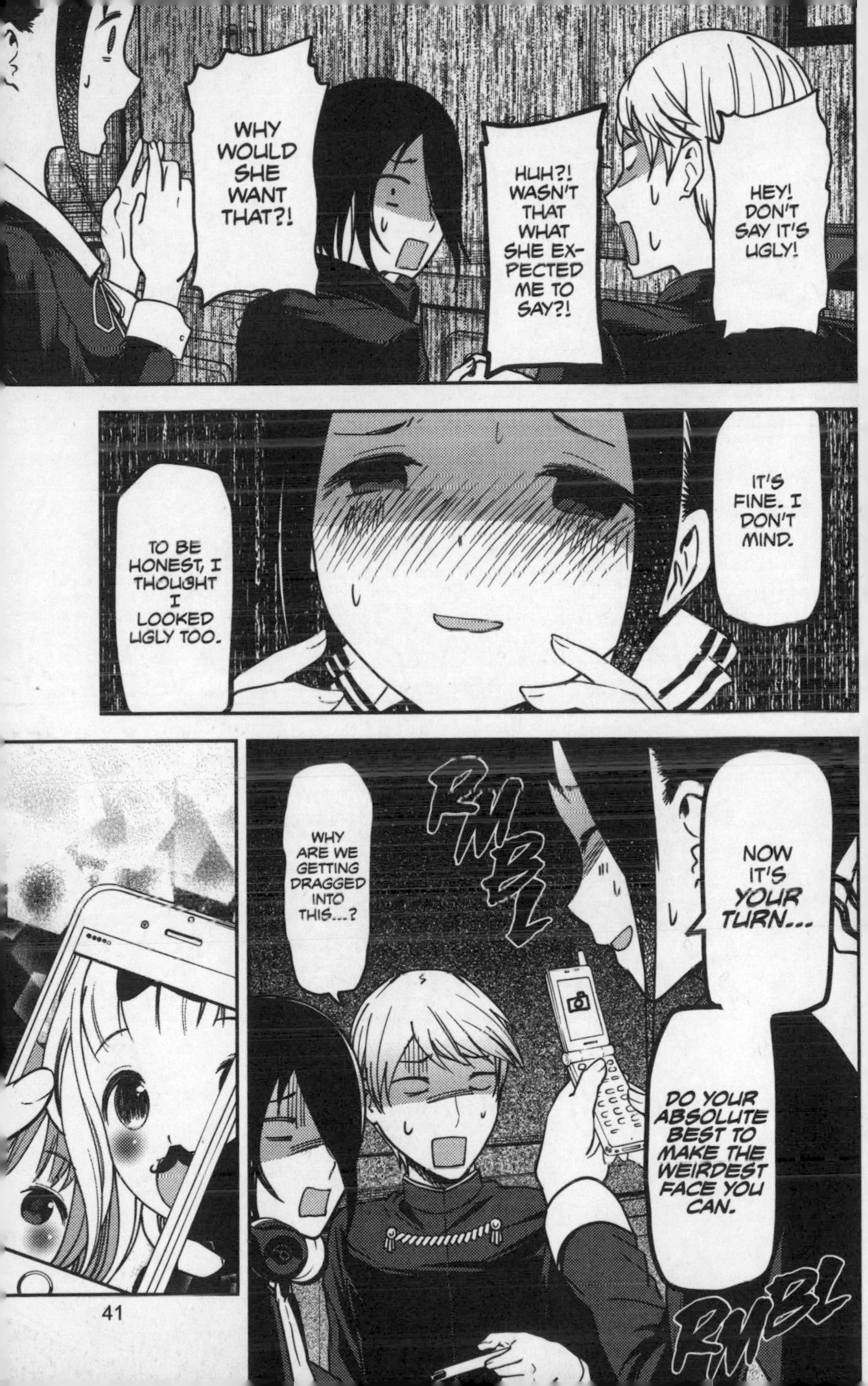
HEY! DON'T SAY IT'S UGLY!
HUH?! WASN'T THAT WHAT SHE EX-PECTED ME TO SAY?!
WHY WOULD SHE WANT THAT?!
IT'S FINE. I DON'T MIND.
TO BE HONEST, I THOUGHT I LOOKED UGLY TOO.
NOW IT'S *YOUR* TURN...
DO YOUR ABSOLUTE BEST TO MAKE THE WEIRDEST FACE YOU CAN.
RMBL
WHY ARE WE GETTING DRAGGED INTO THIS...?
RMBL

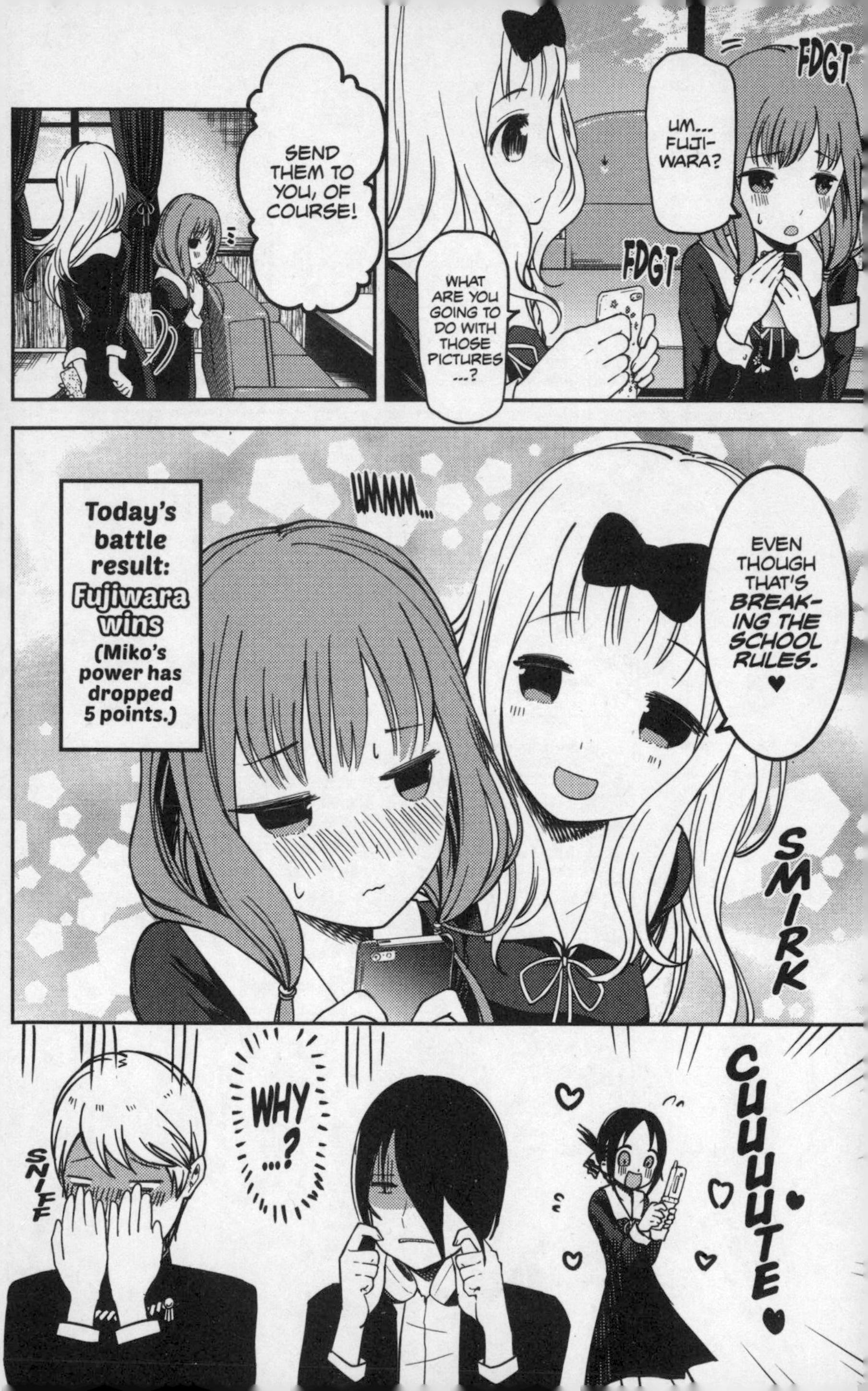
FDGT
UM... FUJI-WARA?
FDGT
WHAT ARE YOU GOING TO DO WITH THOSE PICTURES ...?
SEND THEM TO YOU, OF COURSE!
EVEN THOUGH THAT'S BREAKING THE SCHOOL RULES. ♥
SMIRK
UMMM...
Today's battle result: Fujiwara wins (Miko's power has dropped 5 points.)
CUUUUTE
WHY ...?
SNIFF

KAGUYA-SAMA

LOVE IS WAR

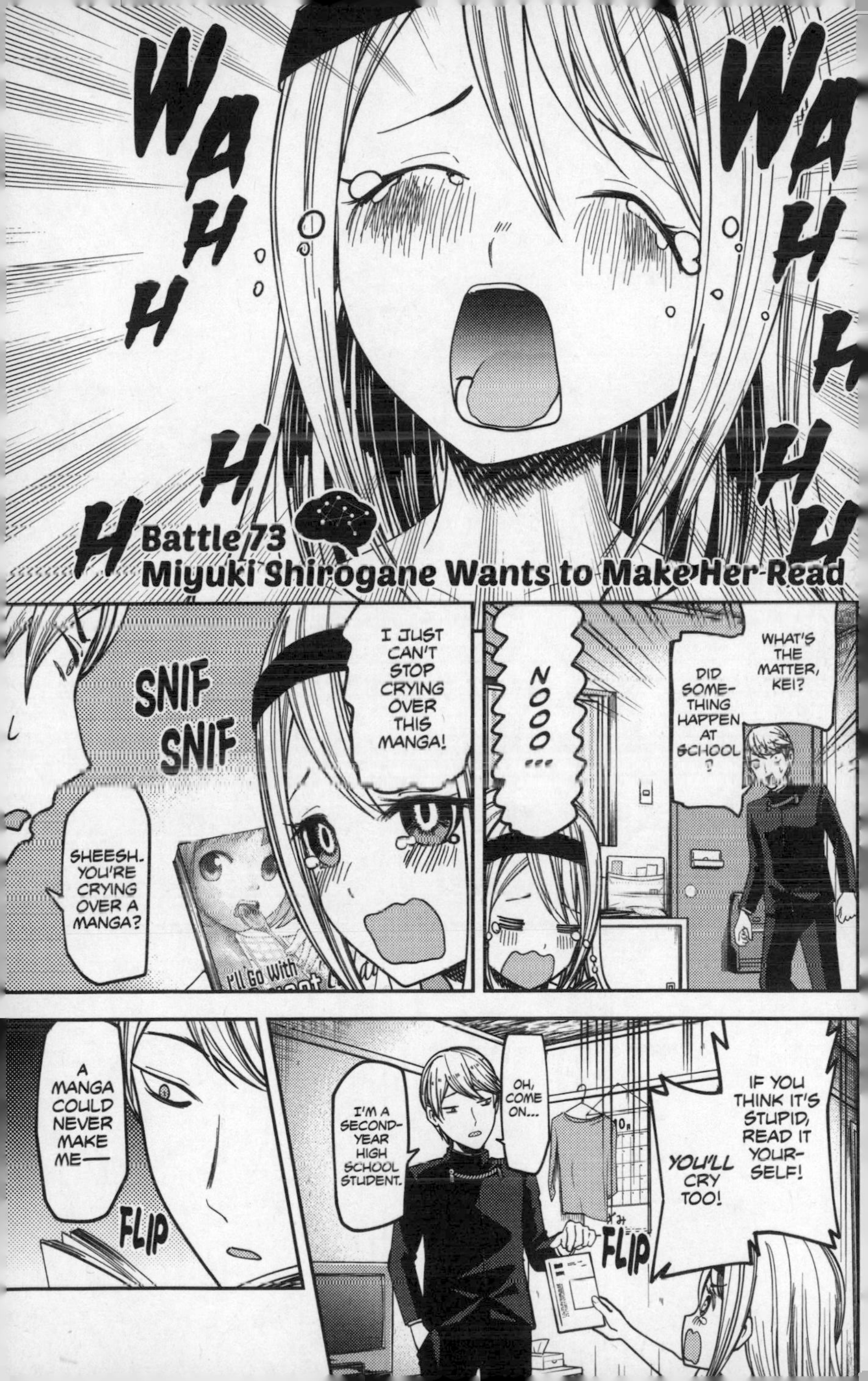
WAHHHHHH
WAHHHHH
Battle 73
Miyuki Shirogane Wants to Make Her Read
WHAT'S THE MATTER, KEI?
DID SOMETHING HAPPEN AT SCHOOL?
NOOO...
I JUST CAN'T STOP CRYING OVER THIS MANGA!
SNIF SNIF
SHEESH. YOU'RE CRYING OVER A MANGA?
I'll Go With
OH, COME ON...
I'M A SECOND-YEAR HIGH SCHOOL STUDENT.
IF YOU THINK IT'S STUPID, READ IT YOURSELF!
YOU'LL CRY TOO!
FLIP
A MANGA COULD NEVER MAKE ME—
FLIP

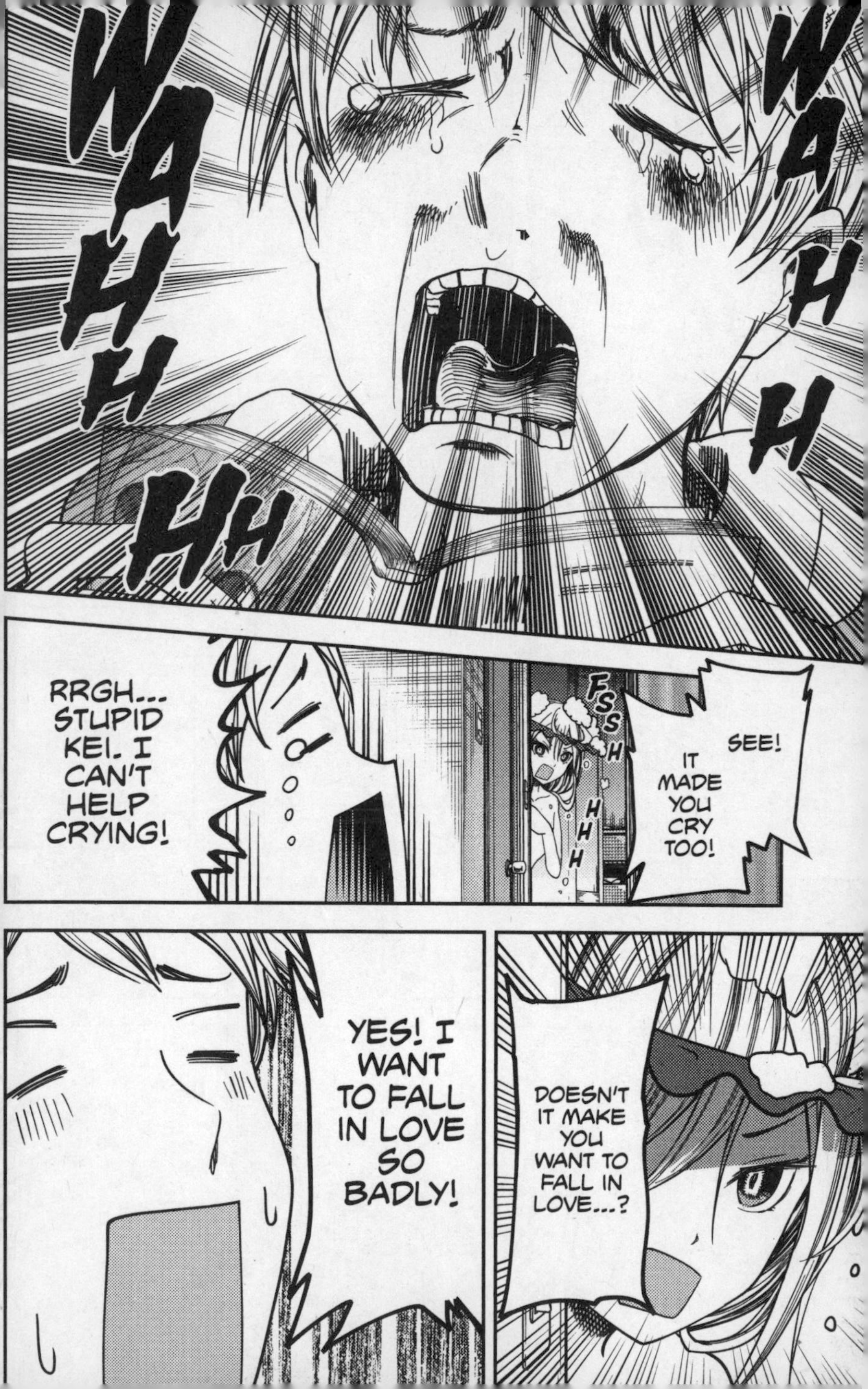
WAHHH
WAHHH
HHH
SEE! IT MADE YOU CRY TOO!
FSSHHHH
RRGH... STUPID KEI. I CAN'T HELP CRYING!
DOESN'T IT MAKE YOU WANT TO FALL IN LOVE...?
YES! I WANT TO FALL IN LOVE SO BADLY!

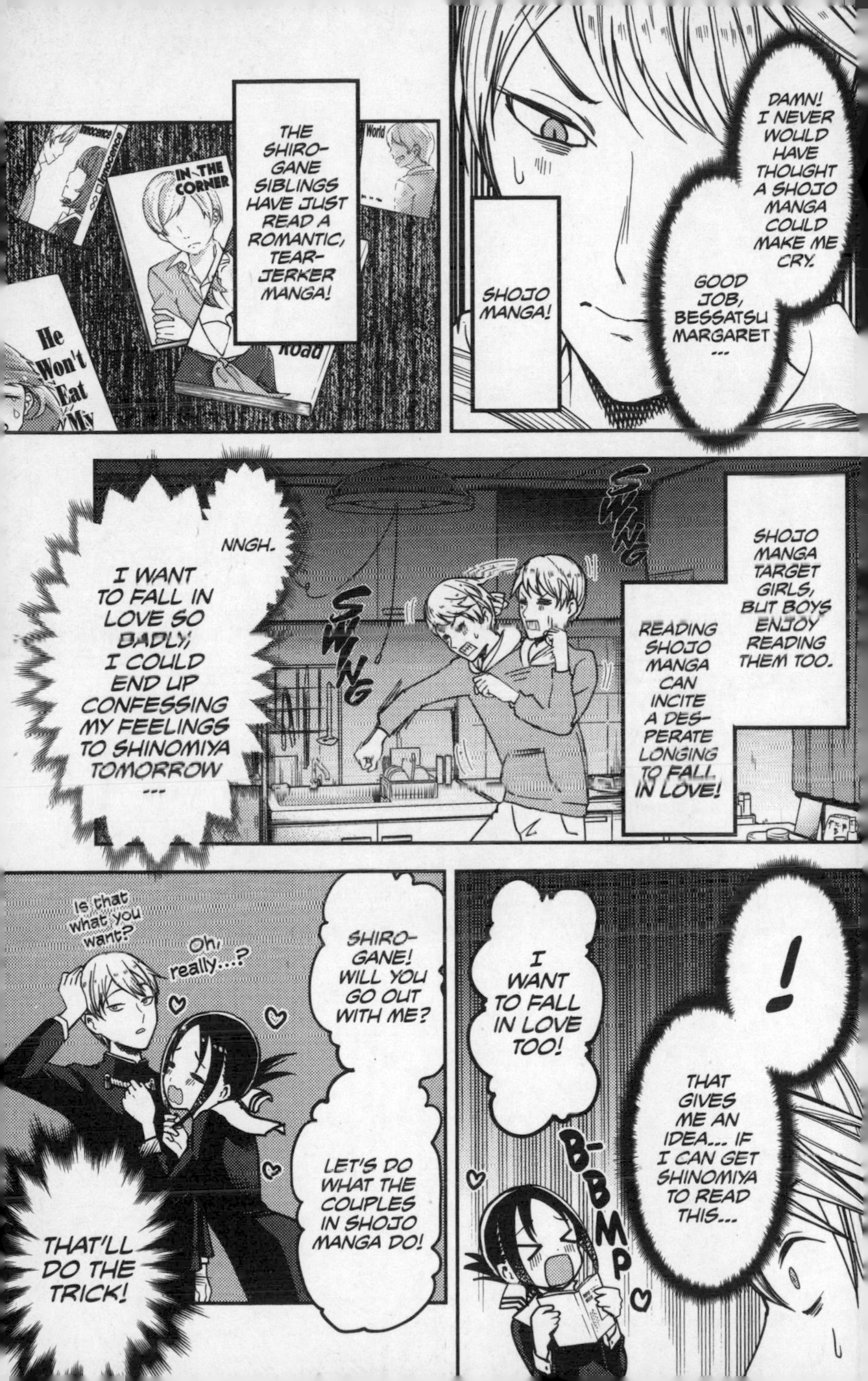
DAMN! I NEVER WOULD HAVE THOUGHT A SHOJO MANGA COULD MAKE ME CRY.
GOOD JOB, BESSATSU MARGARET...
SHOJO MANGA!
THE SHIRO-GANE SIBLINGS HAVE JUST READ A ROMANTIC, TEAR-JERKER MANGA!
World
Innocence
IN THE CORNER
Road
He Won't Eat My
SHOJO MANGA TARGET GIRLS, BUT BOYS ENJOY READING THEM TOO.
READING SHOJO MANGA CAN INCITE A DES-PERATE LONGING TO FALL IN LOVE!
SWING
SWING
NNGH.
I WANT TO FALL IN LOVE SO BADLY, I COULD END UP CONFESSING MY FEELINGS TO SHINOMIYA TOMORROW...
!
THAT GIVES ME AN IDEA... IF I CAN GET SHINOMIYA TO READ THIS...
I WANT TO FALL IN LOVE TOO!
B-BBMP
SHIRO-GANE! WILL YOU GO OUT WITH ME?
LET'S DO WHAT THE COUPLES IN SHOJO MANGA DO!
Oh, really...?
Is that what you want?
THAT'LL DO THE TRICK!

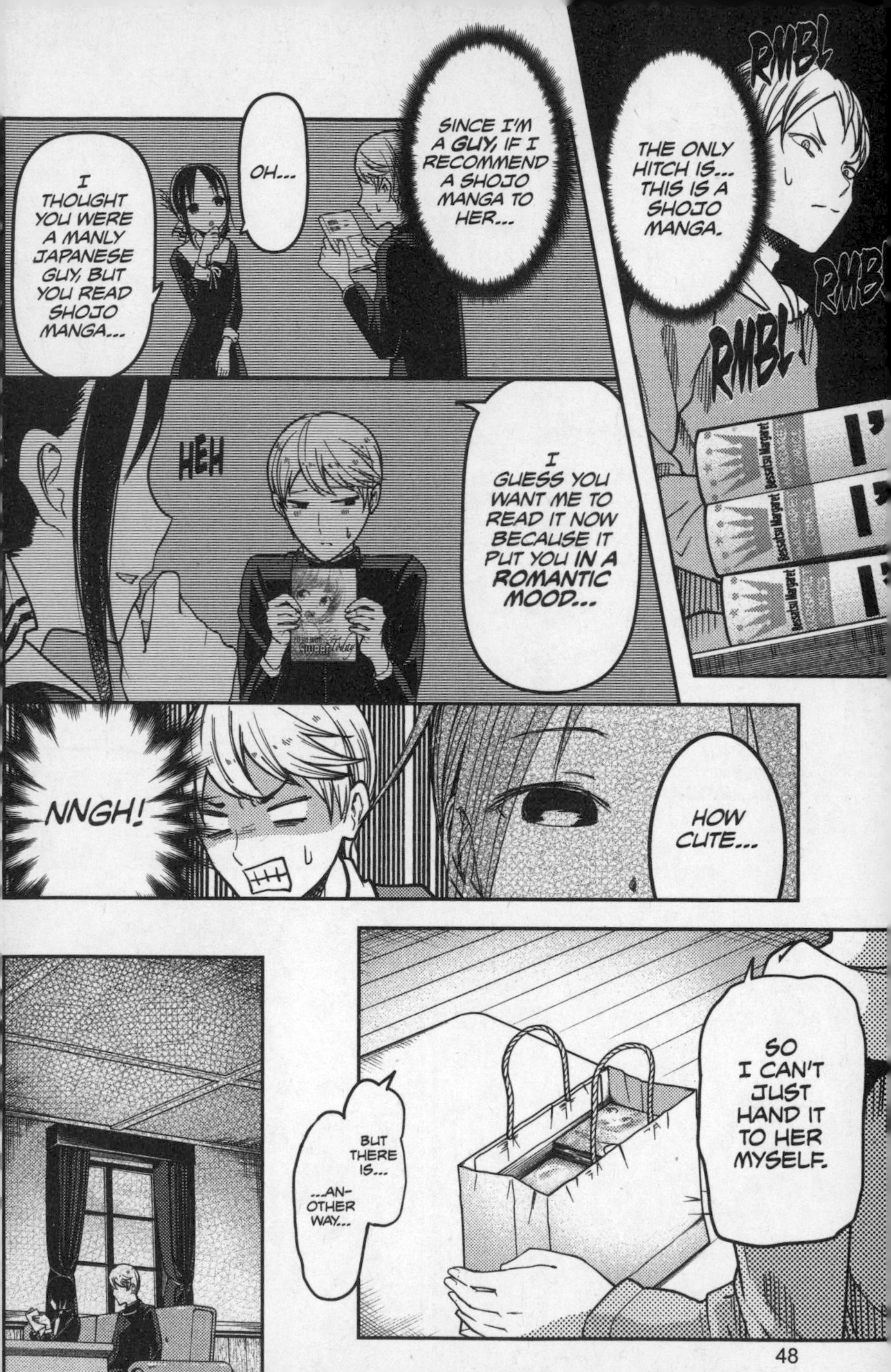
RMBL
THE ONLY HITCH IS... THIS IS A SHOJO MANGA.
RMBL
RMBL
Bessatsu Margaret
Bessatsu Margaret
Bessatsu Margaret
SINCE I'M A GUY, IF I RECOMMEND A SHOJO MANGA TO HER...
OH...
I THOUGHT YOU WERE A MANLY JAPANESE GUY, BUT YOU READ SHOJO MANGA...
I GUESS YOU WANT ME TO READ IT NOW BECAUSE IT PUT YOU IN A ROMANTIC MOOD...
HEH
HOW CUTE...
NNGH!
SO I CAN'T JUST HAND IT TO HER MYSELF.
BUT THERE IS...
...AN-OTHER WAY...

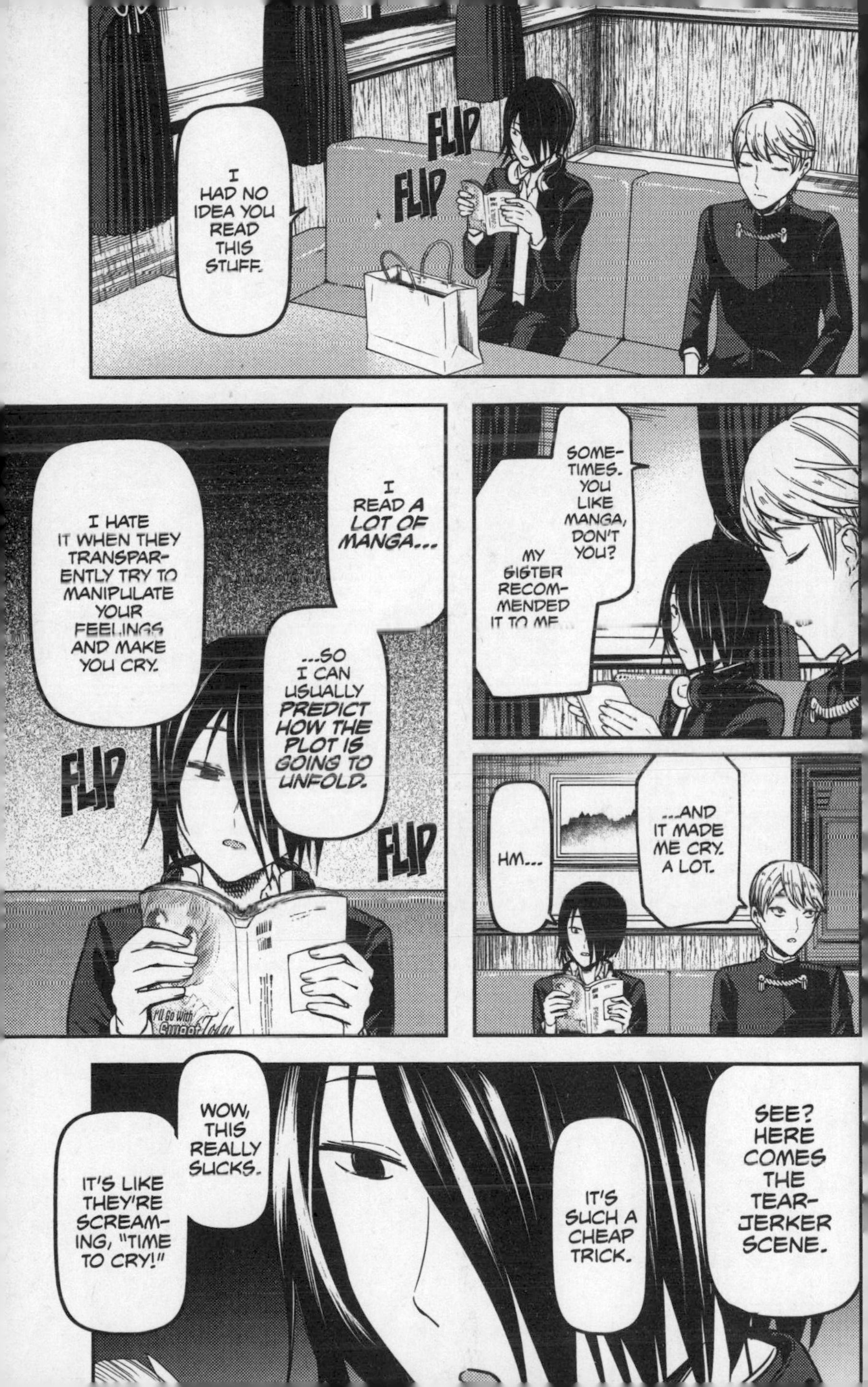
I HAD NO IDEA YOU READ THIS STUFF.
FLIP
FLIP
SOMETIMES. YOU LIKE MANGA, DON'T YOU?
MY SISTER RECOMMENDED IT TO ME...
...AND IT MADE ME CRY. A LOT.
HM...
I READ A LOT OF MANGA...
...SO I CAN USUALLY PREDICT HOW THE PLOT IS GOING TO UNFOLD.
I HATE IT WHEN THEY TRANSPARENTLY TRY TO MANIPULATE YOUR FEELINGS AND MAKE YOU CRY.
FLIP
FLIP
SEE? HERE COMES THE TEARJERKER SCENE.
IT'S SUCH A CHEAP TRICK.
WOW, THIS REALLY SUCKS.
IT'S LIKE THEY'RE SCREAMING, "TIME TO CRY!"

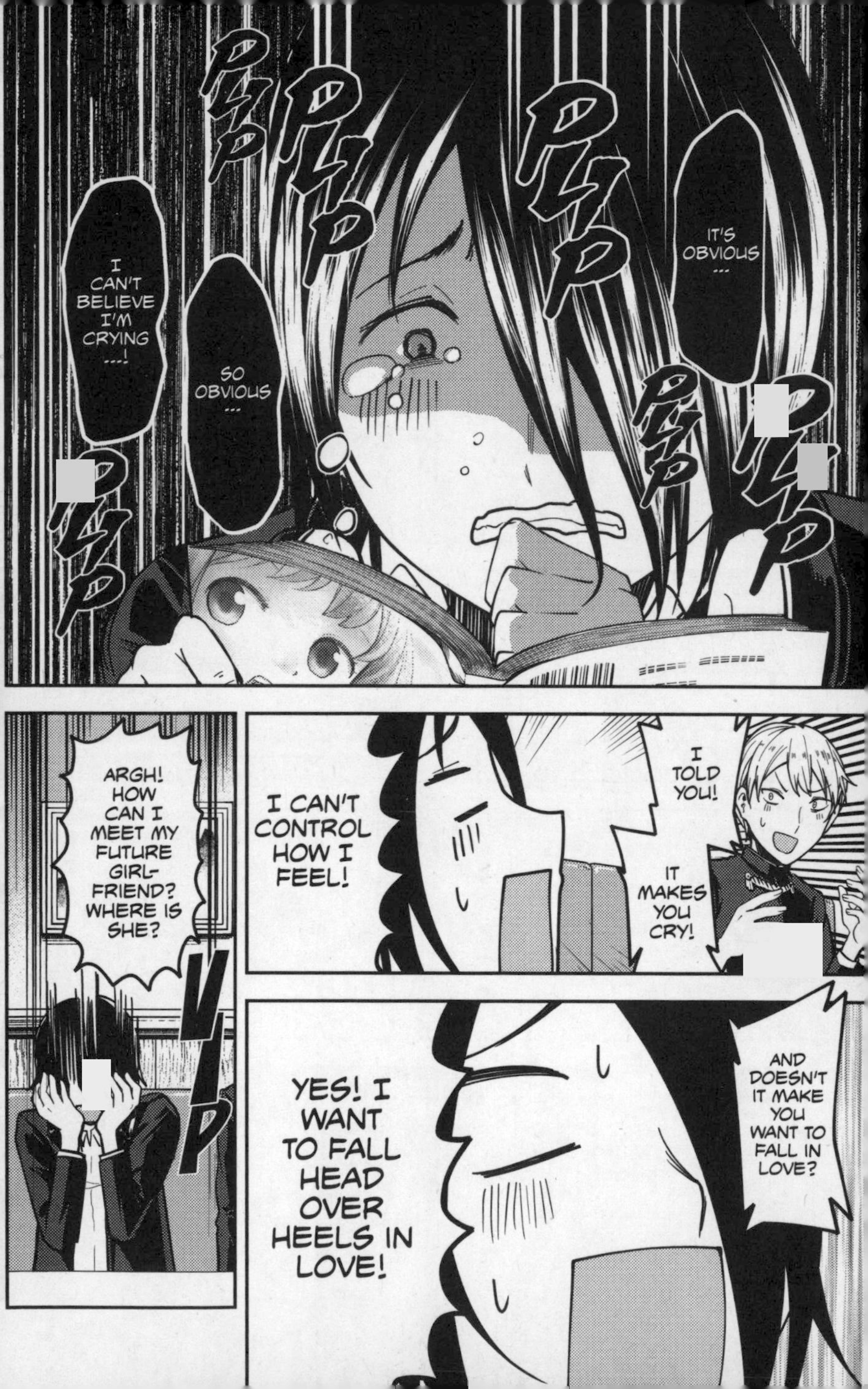
PLIP
IT'S OBVIOUS...
PLIP
SO OBVIOUS...
PLIP
I CAN'T BELIEVE I'M CRYING...!
PLIP
I TOLD YOU!
IT MAKES YOU CRY!
I CAN'T CONTROL HOW I FEEL!
AND DOESN'T IT MAKE YOU WANT TO FALL IN LOVE?
YES! I WANT TO FALL HEAD OVER HEELS IN LOVE!
ARGH! HOW CAN I MEET MY FUTURE GIRL-FRIEND? WHERE IS SHE?

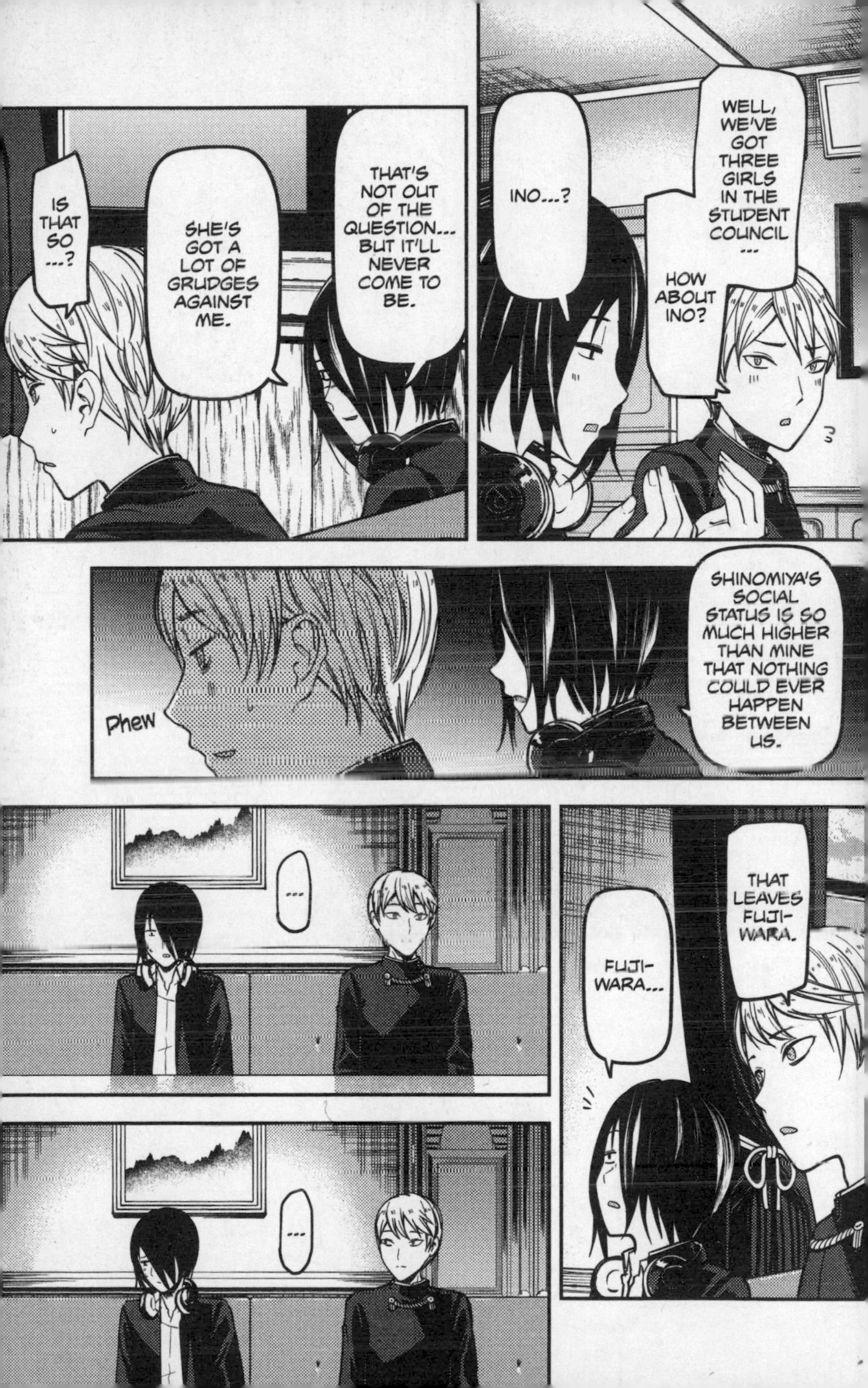
WELL, WE'VE GOT THREE GIRLS IN THE STUDENT COUNCIL ...
HOW ABOUT INO?
INO...?
THAT'S NOT OUT OF THE QUESTION... BUT IT'LL NEVER COME TO BE.
SHE'S GOT A LOT OF GRUDGES AGAINST ME.
IS THAT SO ...?
SHINOMIYA'S SOCIAL STATUS IS SO MUCH HIGHER THAN MINE THAT NOTHING COULD EVER HAPPEN BETWEEN US.
Phew
THAT LEAVES FUJI-WARA.
FUJI-WARA...
...
...

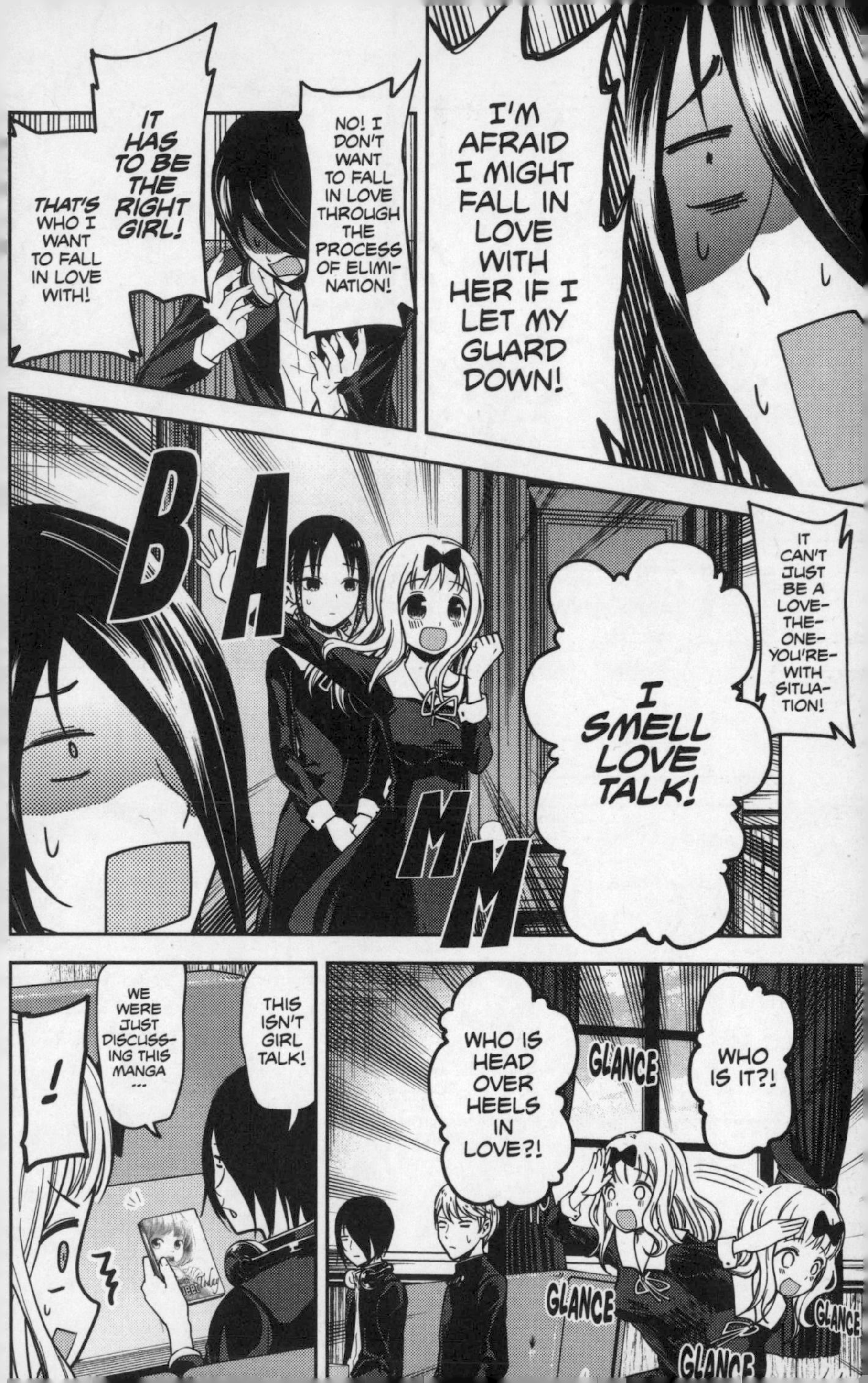
I'M AFRAID I MIGHT FALL IN LOVE WITH HER IF I LET MY GUARD DOWN!
NO! I DON'T WANT TO FALL IN LOVE THROUGH THE PROCESS OF ELIMINATION!
IT HAS TO BE THE RIGHT GIRL!
THAT'S WHO I WANT TO FALL IN LOVE WITH!
IT CAN'T JUST BE A LOVE-THE-ONE-YOU'RE-WITH SITUATION!
I SMELL LOVE TALK!
BAMM
WHO IS IT?!
GLANCE
WHO IS HEAD OVER HEELS IN LOVE?!
GLANCE
GLANCE
GLANCE
THIS ISN'T GIRL TALK!
WE WERE JUST DISCUSSING THIS MANGA ...
!

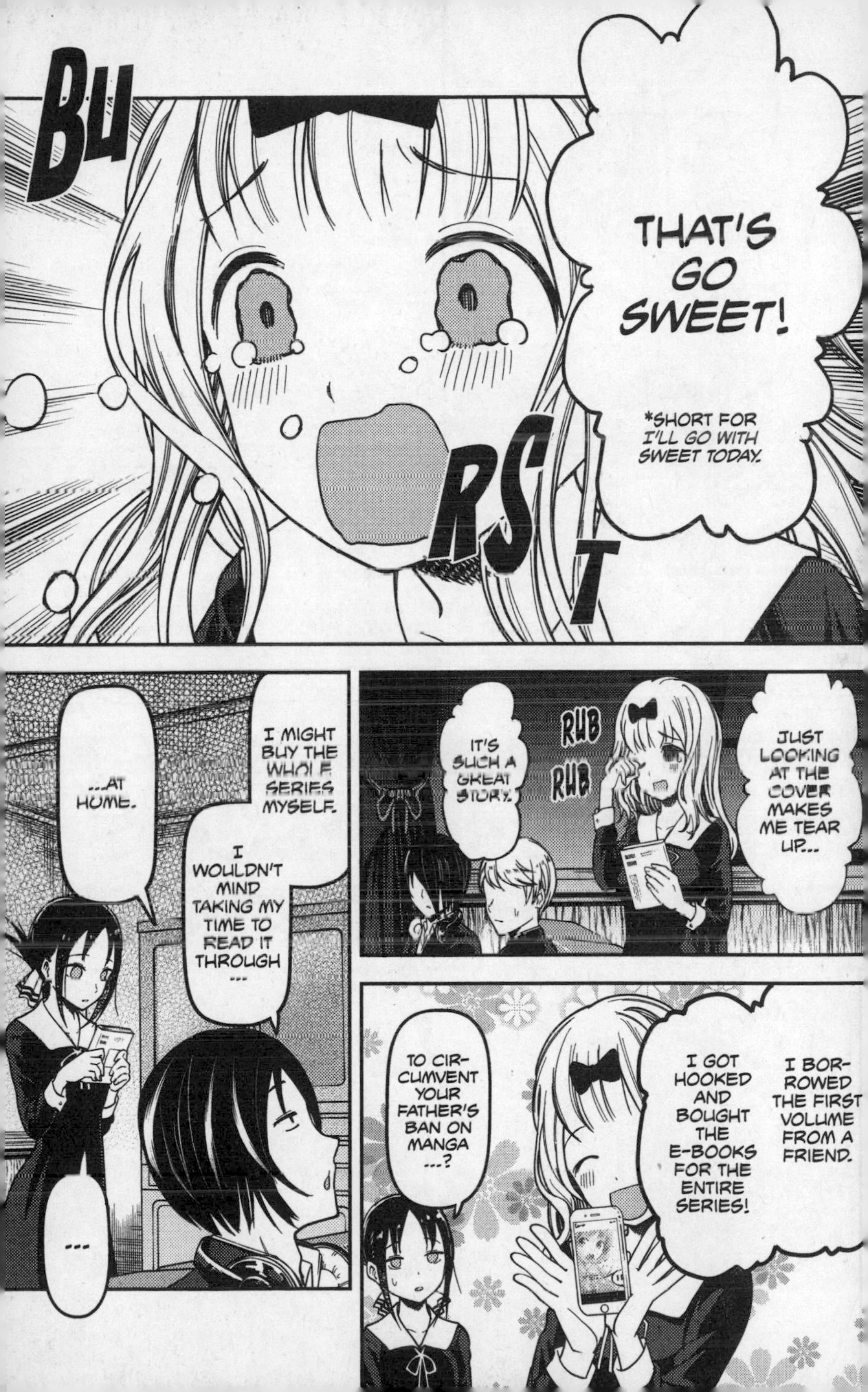
BURST
THAT'S GO SWEET!
*SHORT FOR I'LL GO WITH SWEET TODAY.
JUST LOOKING AT THE COVER MAKES ME TEAR UP...
RUB RUB
IT'S SUCH A GREAT STORY.
I BORROWED THE FIRST VOLUME FROM A FRIEND.
I GOT HOOKED AND BOUGHT THE E-BOOKS FOR THE ENTIRE SERIES!
TO CIRCUMVENT YOUR FATHER'S BAN ON MANGA...?
I MIGHT BUY THE WHOLE SERIES MYSELF.
...AT HOME.
I WOULDN'T MIND TAKING MY TIME TO READ IT THROUGH...
...

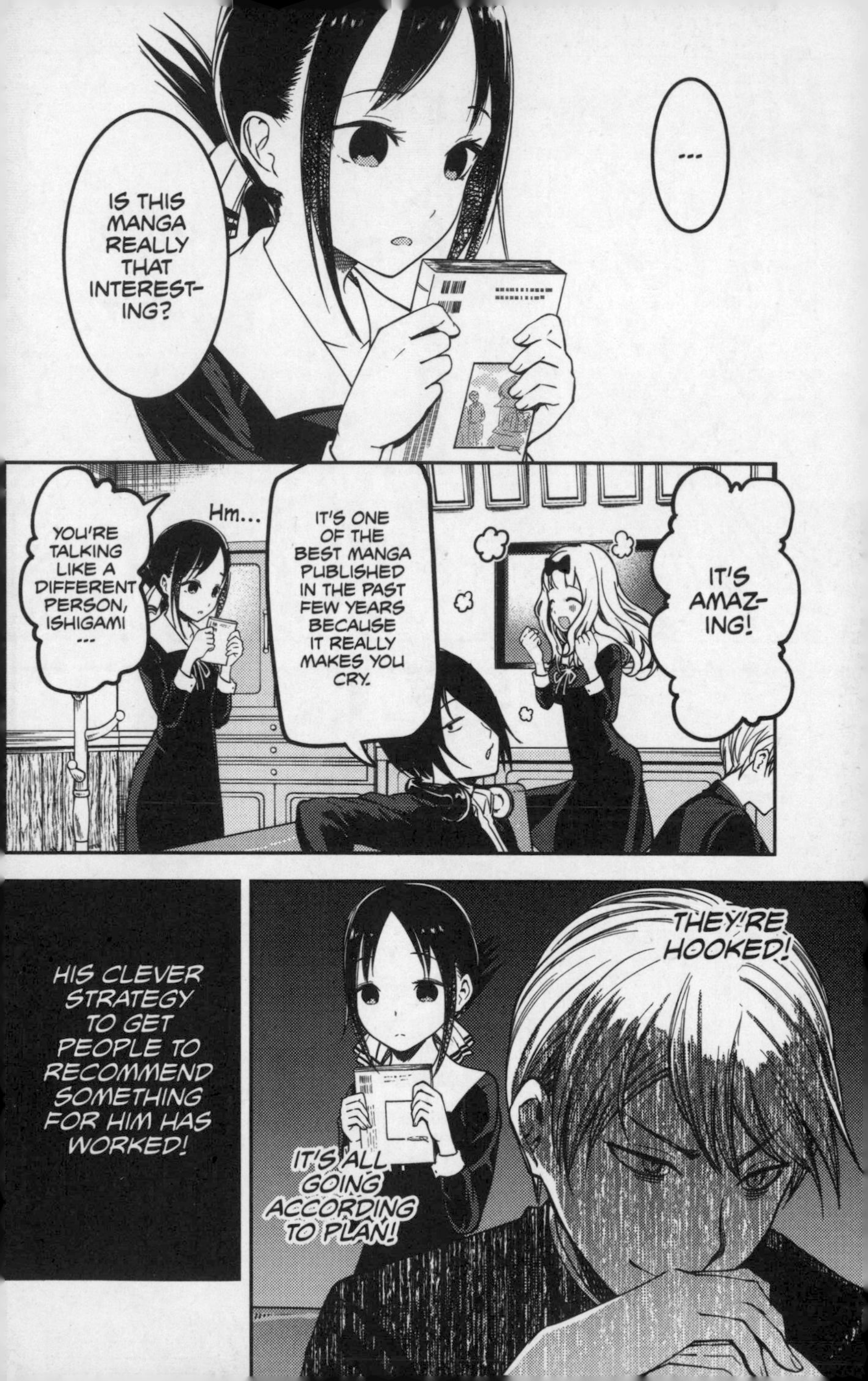
...
IS THIS MANGA REALLY THAT INTEREST-ING?
IT'S AMAZ-ING!
IT'S ONE OF THE BEST MANGA PUBLISHED IN THE PAST FEW YEARS BECAUSE IT REALLY MAKES YOU CRY.
Hm...
YOU'RE TALKING LIKE A DIFFERENT PERSON, ISHIGAMI ...
THEY'RE HOOKED!
IT'S ALL GOING ACCORDING TO PLAN!
HIS CLEVER STRATEGY TO GET PEOPLE TO RECOMMEND SOMETHING FOR HIM HAS WORKED!

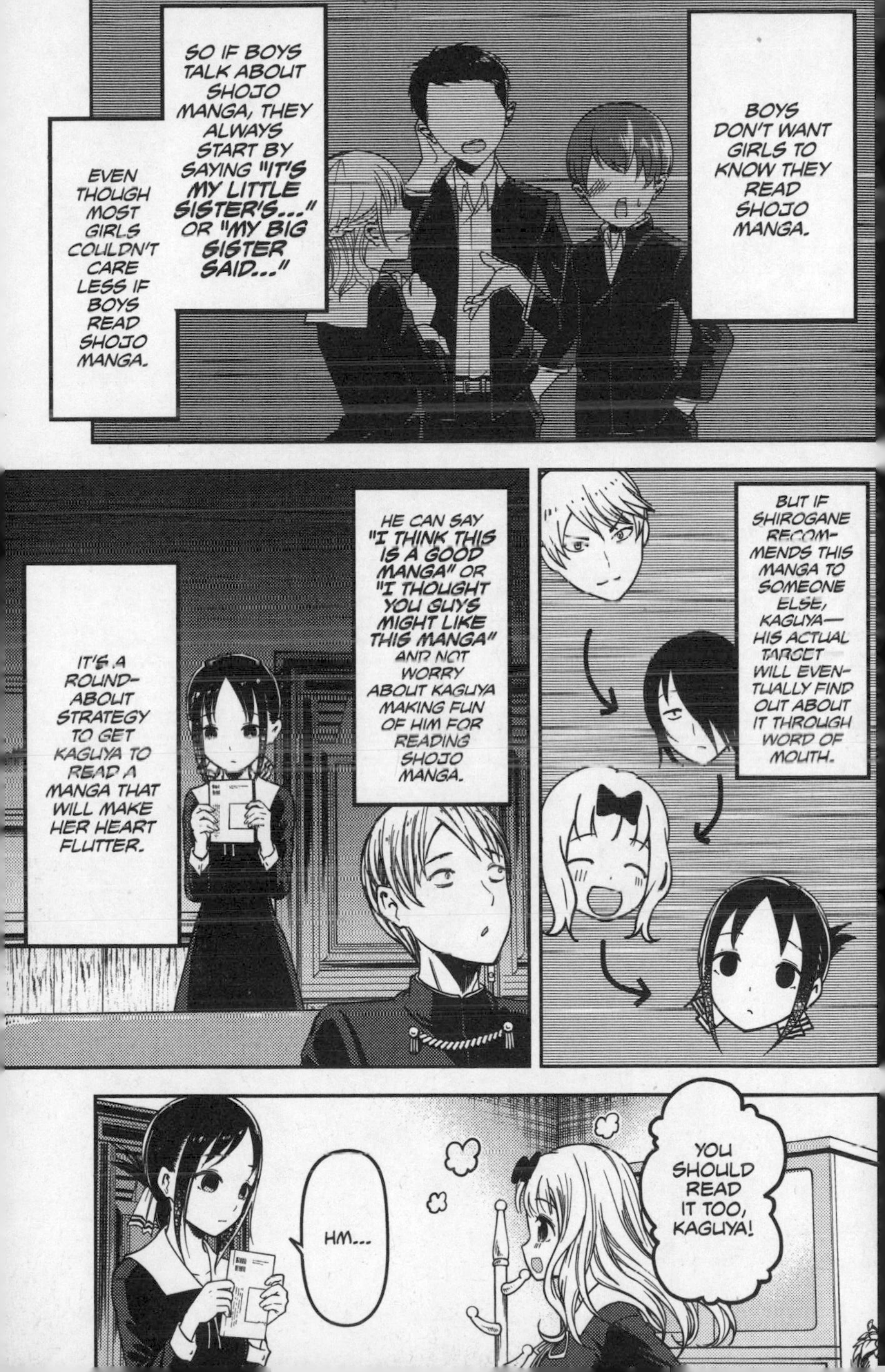
BOYS DON'T WANT GIRLS TO KNOW THEY READ SHOJO MANGA.
SO IF BOYS TALK ABOUT SHOJO MANGA, THEY ALWAYS START BY SAYING "IT'S MY LITTLE SISTER'S..." OR "MY BIG SISTER SAID..."
EVEN THOUGH MOST GIRLS COULDN'T CARE LESS IF BOYS READ SHOJO MANGA.
BUT IF SHIROGANE RECOMMENDS THIS MANGA TO SOMEONE ELSE, KAGUYA—HIS ACTUAL TARGET—WILL EVENTUALLY FIND OUT ABOUT IT THROUGH WORD OF MOUTH.
HE CAN SAY "I THINK THIS IS A GOOD MANGA" OR "I THOUGHT YOU GUYS MIGHT LIKE THIS MANGA" AND NOT WORRY ABOUT KAGUYA MAKING FUN OF HIM FOR READING SHOJO MANGA.
IT'S A ROUNDABOUT STRATEGY TO GET KAGUYA TO READ A MANGA THAT WILL MAKE HER HEART FLUTTER.
YOU SHOULD READ IT TOO, KAGUYA!
HM...

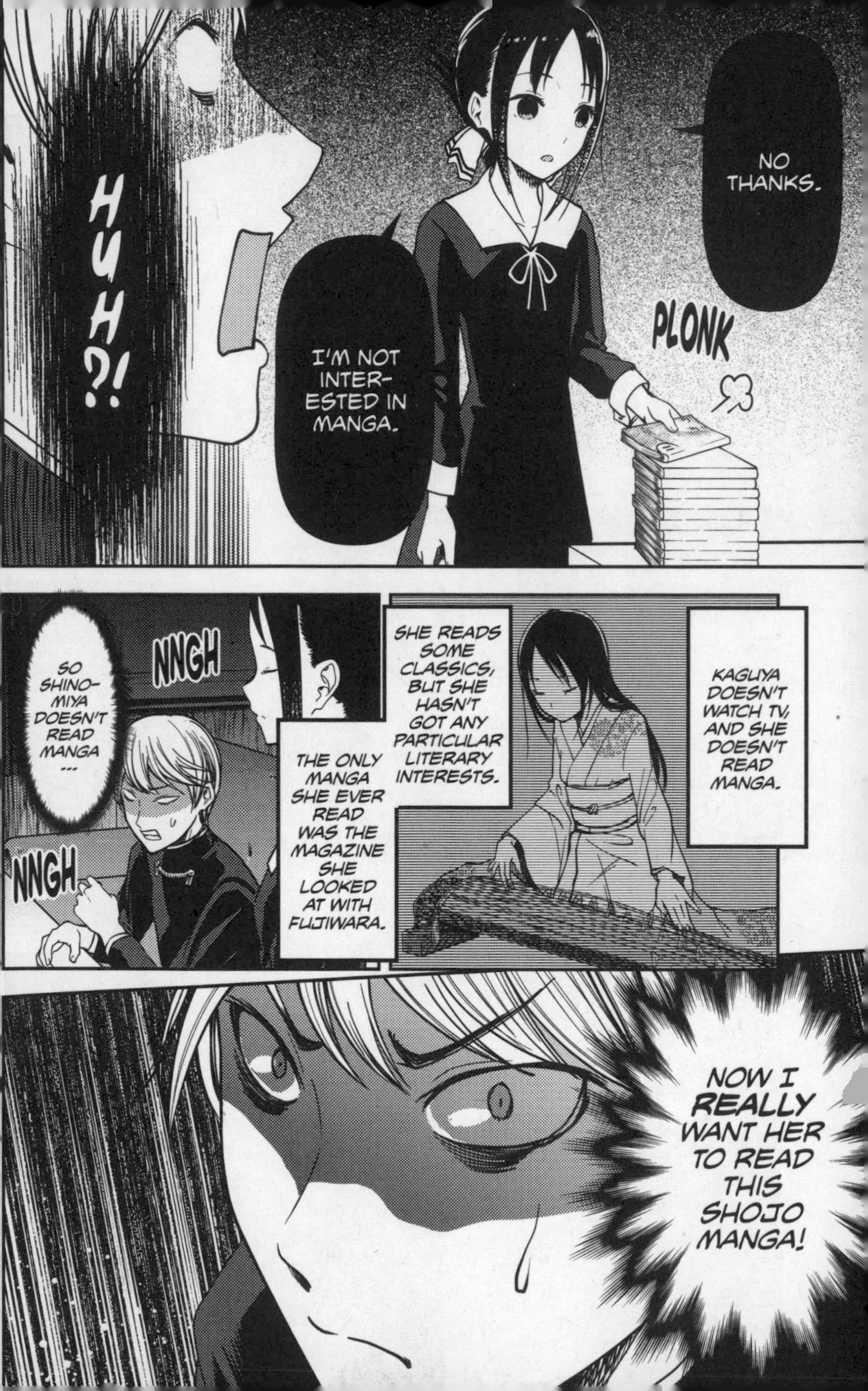
NO THANKS.
PLONK
I'M NOT INTER-ESTED IN MANGA.
HUH?!
KAGUYA DOESN'T WATCH TV, AND SHE DOESN'T READ MANGA.
SHE READS SOME CLASSICS, BUT SHE HASN'T GOT ANY PARTICULAR LITERARY INTERESTS.
THE ONLY MANGA SHE EVER READ WAS THE MAGAZINE SHE LOOKED AT WITH FUJIWARA.
NNGH
SO SHINO-MIYA DOESN'T READ MANGA...
NNGH
NOW I **REALLY** WANT HER TO READ THIS SHOJO MANGA!

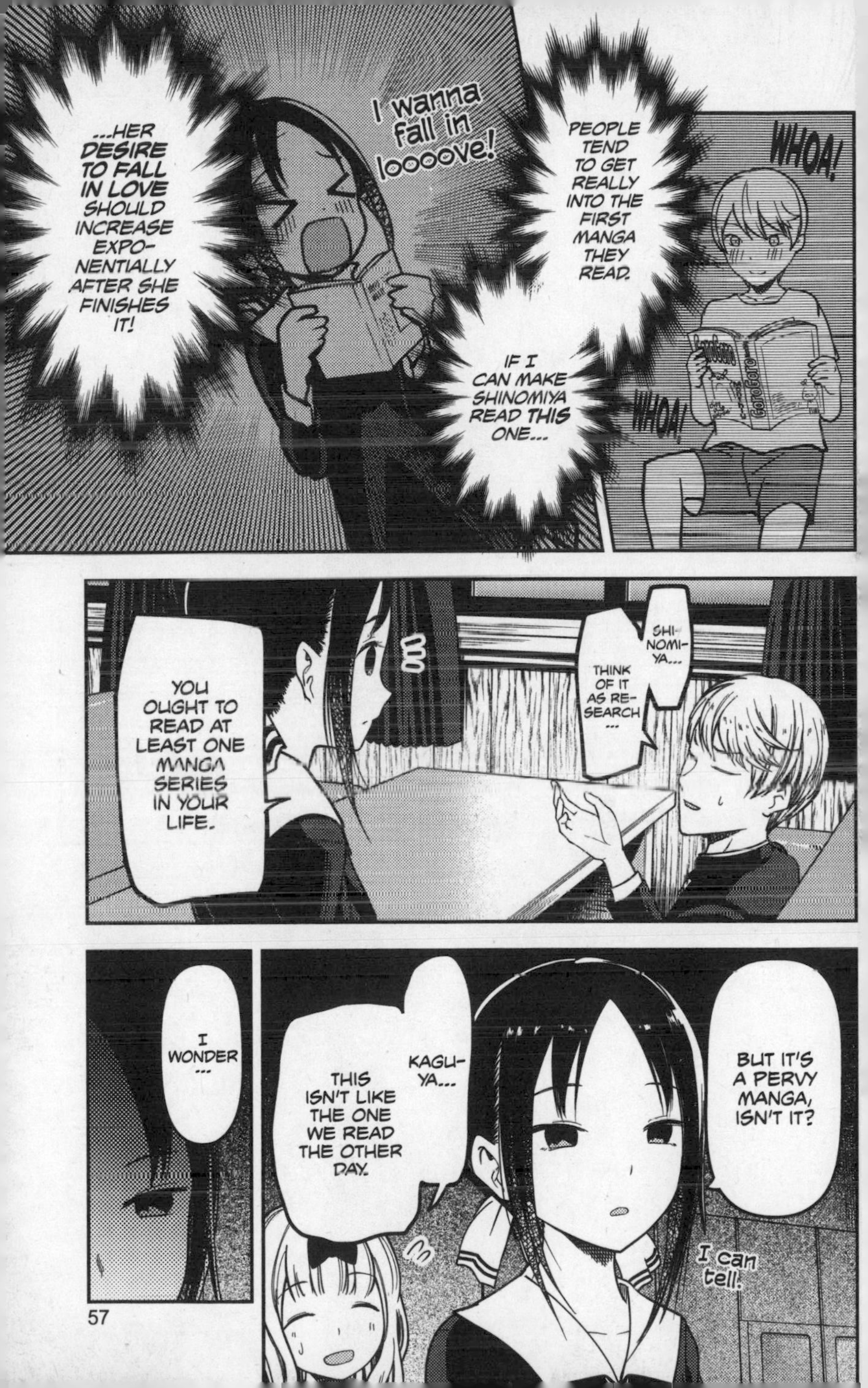
WHOA!
PEOPLE TEND TO GET REALLY INTO THE FIRST MANGA THEY READ.
WHOA!
IF I CAN MAKE SHINOMIYA READ THIS ONE...
I wanna fall in loooove!
...HER DESIRE TO FALL IN LOVE SHOULD INCREASE EXPONENTIALLY AFTER SHE FINISHES IT!
SHINOMIYA...
THINK OF IT AS RESEARCH...
YOU OUGHT TO READ AT LEAST ONE MANGA SERIES IN YOUR LIFE.
BUT IT'S A PERVY MANGA, ISN'T IT?
I can tell.
KAGUYA...
THIS ISN'T LIKE THE ONE WE READ THE OTHER DAY.
I WONDER...

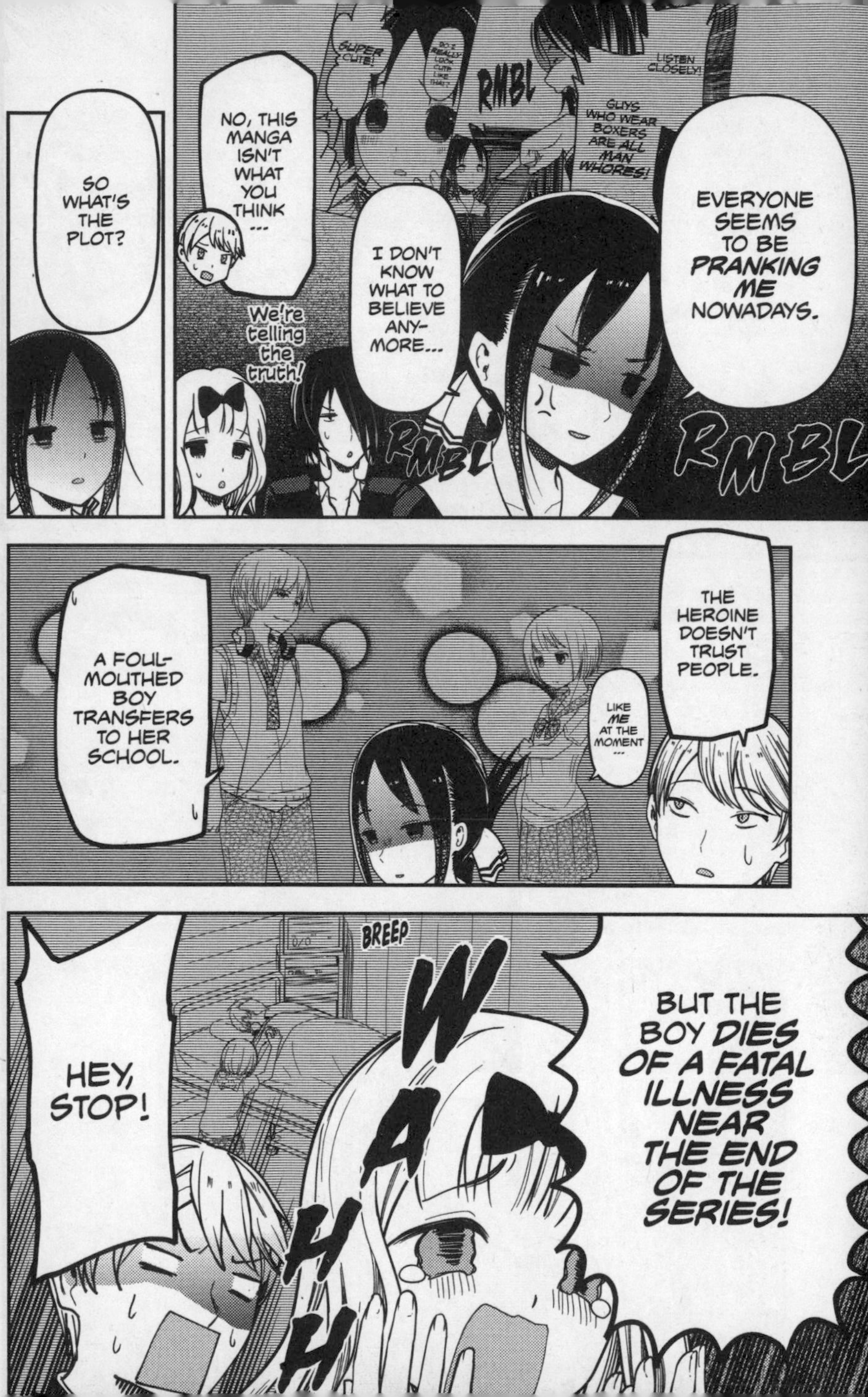
LISTEN CLOSELY!
GUYS WHO WEAR BOXERS ARE ALL MAN WHORES!
RMBL
DO I REALLY LOOK CUTE LIKE THAT?
SUPER CUTE!
EVERYONE SEEMS TO BE PRANKING ME NOWADAYS.
RMBL
I DON'T KNOW WHAT TO BELIEVE ANYMORE...
NO, THIS MANGA ISN'T WHAT YOU THINK...
We're telling the truth!
RMBL
SO WHAT'S THE PLOT?
THE HEROINE DOESN'T TRUST PEOPLE.
LIKE ME AT THE MOMENT...
A FOUL-MOUTHED BOY TRANSFERS TO HER SCHOOL.
BUT THE BOY DIES OF A FATAL ILLNESS NEAR THE END OF THE SERIES!
BREEP
WAHH
HEY, STOP!

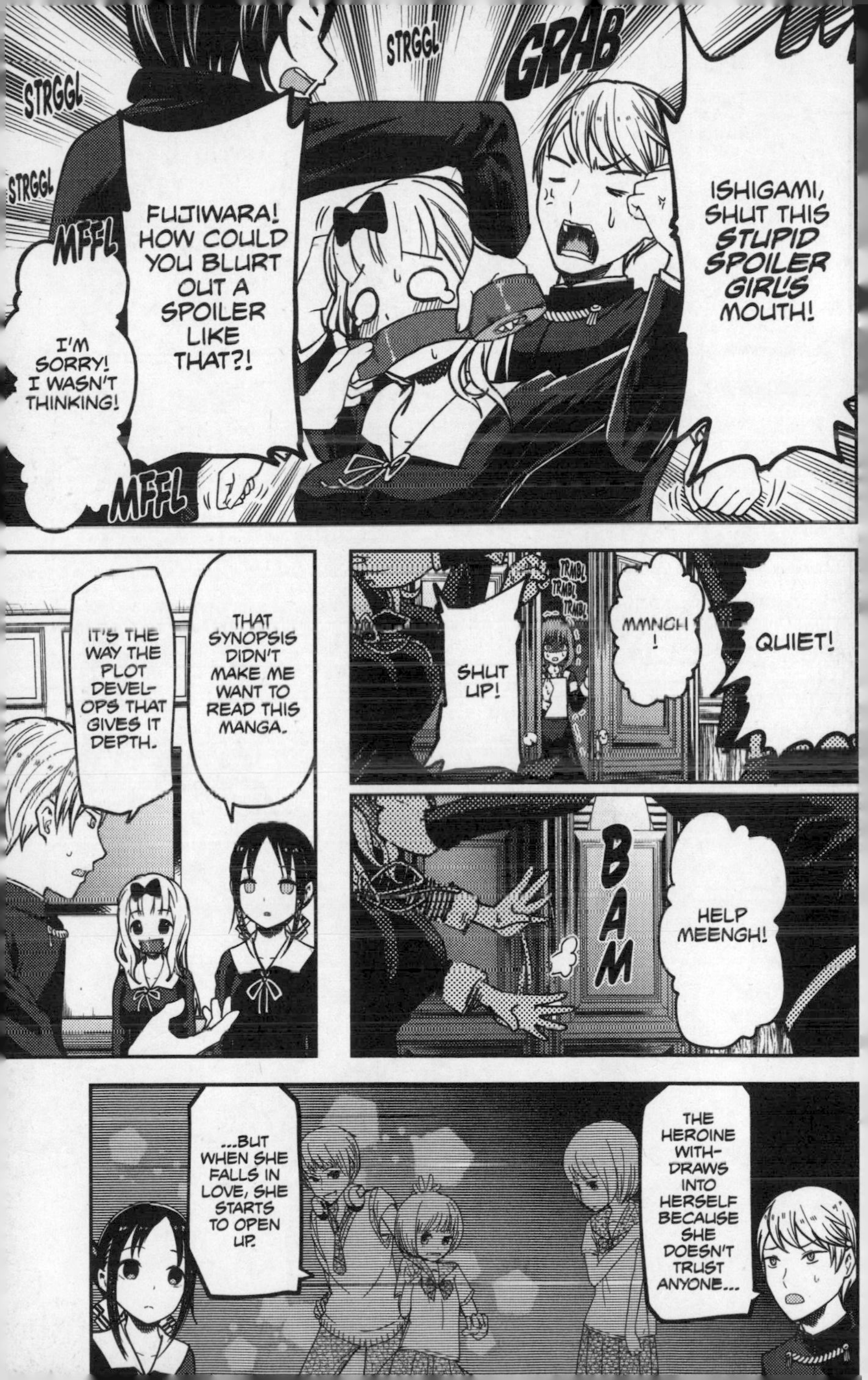
GRAB
ISHIGAMI, SHUT THIS STUPID SPOILER GIRL'S MOUTH!
STRGGL
FUJIWARA! HOW COULD YOU BLURT OUT A SPOILER LIKE THAT?!
STRGGL
STRGGL
MFFL
I'M SORRY! I WASN'T THINKING!
MFFL
QUIET!
MMNCH!
TRMBL TRMBL TRMBL
SHUT UP!
HELP MEENGH!
BAM
THAT SYNOPSIS DIDN'T MAKE ME WANT TO READ THIS MANGA.
IT'S THE WAY THE PLOT DEVEL-OPS THAT GIVES IT DEPTH.
THE HEROINE WITH-DRAWS INTO HERSELF BECAUSE SHE DOESN'T TRUST ANYONE...
...BUT WHEN SHE FALLS IN LOVE, SHE STARTS TO OPEN UP.

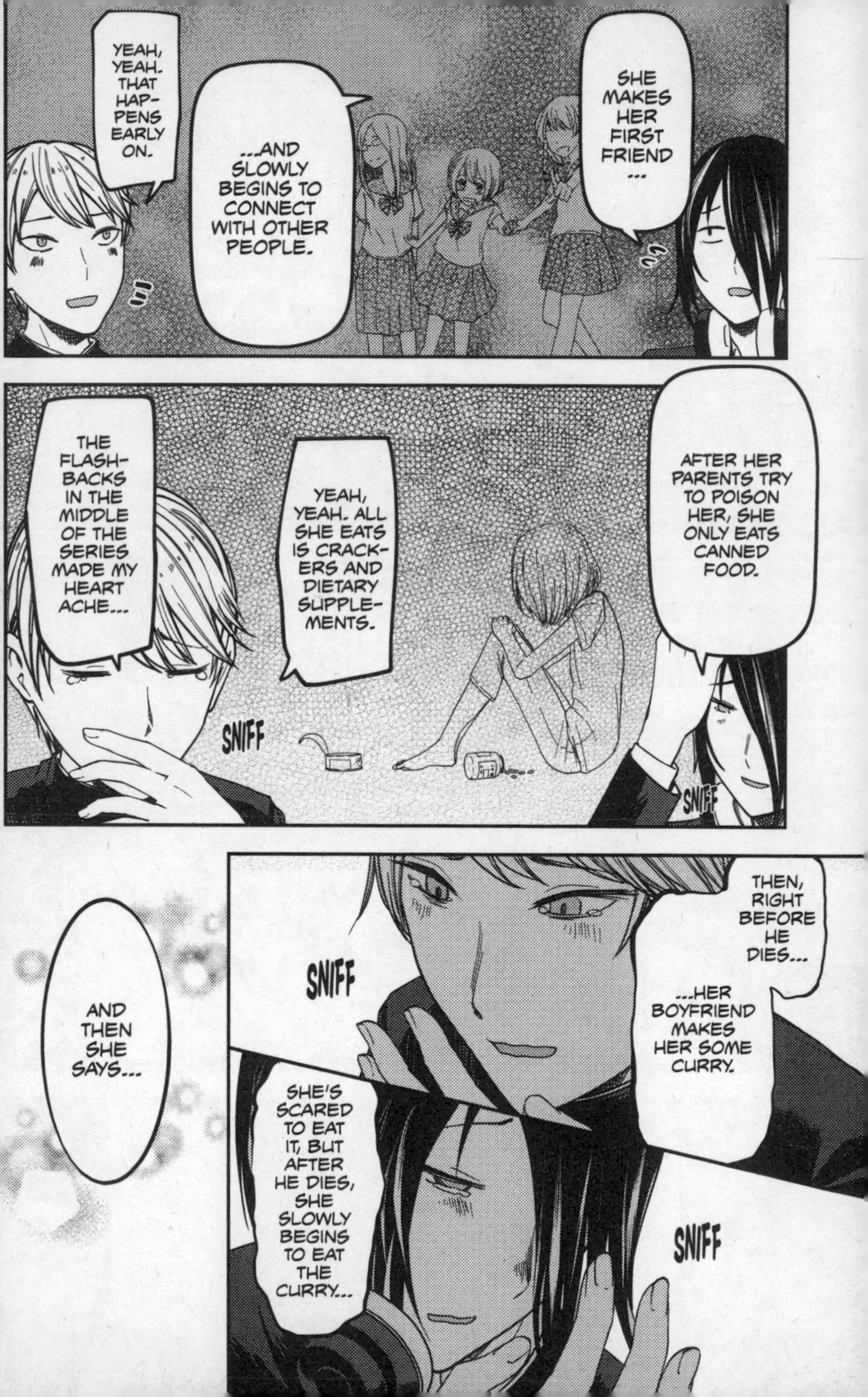
SHE MAKES HER FIRST FRIEND ...
...AND SLOWLY BEGINS TO CONNECT WITH OTHER PEOPLE.
YEAH, YEAH. THAT HAPPENS EARLY ON.
AFTER HER PARENTS TRY TO POISON HER, SHE ONLY EATS CANNED FOOD.
SNIFF
YEAH, YEAH. ALL SHE EATS IS CRACKERS AND DIETARY SUPPLEMENTS.
THE FLASHBACKS IN THE MIDDLE OF THE SERIES MADE MY HEART ACHE...
SNIFF
THEN, RIGHT BEFORE HE DIES...
...HER BOYFRIEND MAKES HER SOME CURRY.
SNIFF
SNIFF
SHE'S SCARED TO EAT IT, BUT AFTER HE DIES, SHE SLOWLY BEGINS TO EAT THE CURRY...
AND THEN SHE SAYS...

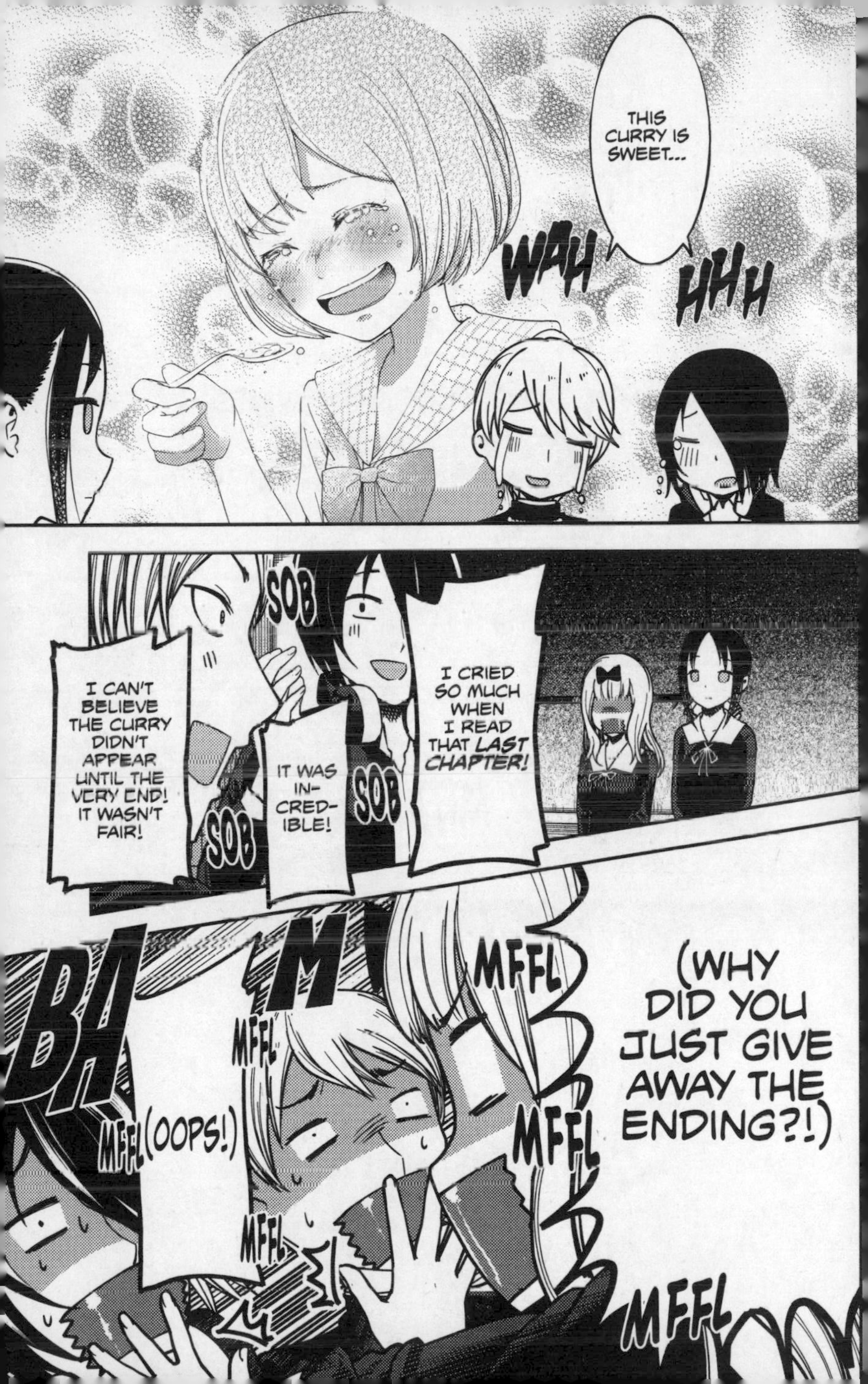
THIS CURRY IS SWEET...
WAH HHH
I CRIED SO MUCH WHEN I READ THAT *LAST CHAPTER!*
SOB
IT WAS IN-CRED-IBLE!
SOB
I CAN'T BELIEVE THE CURRY DIDN'T APPEAR UNTIL THE VERY END! IT WASN'T FAIR!
SOB
SOB
(WHY DID YOU JUST GIVE AWAY THE ENDING?!)
MFFL
MFFL
BA M
MFFL
(OOPS!)
MFFL
MFFL
MFFL

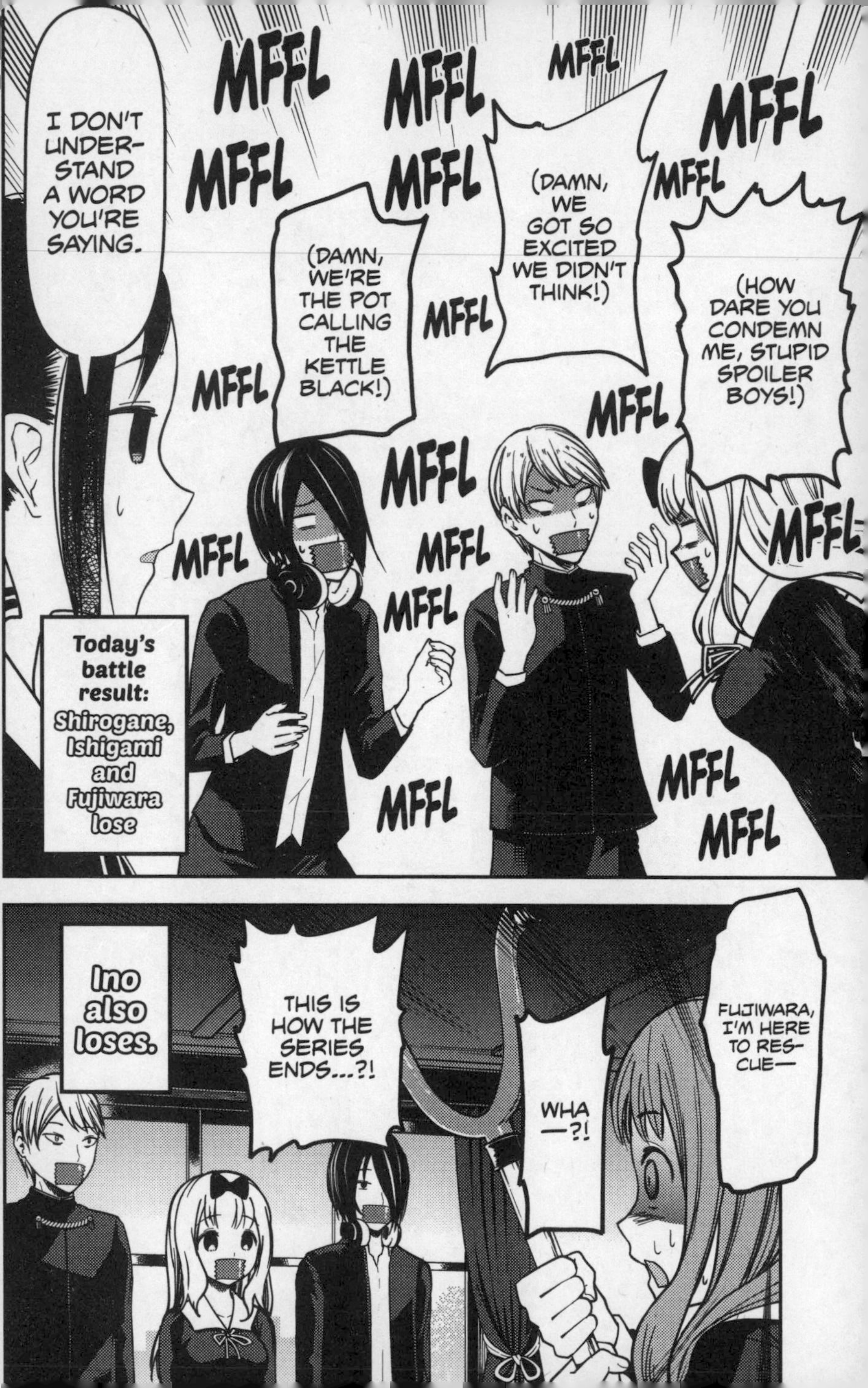
MFFL
MFFL
(HOW DARE YOU CONDEMN ME, STUPID SPOILER BOYS!)
(DAMN, WE GOT SO EXCITED WE DIDN'T THINK!)
(DAMN, WE'RE THE POT CALLING THE KETTLE BLACK!)
I DON'T UNDER-STAND A WORD YOU'RE SAYING.
Today's battle result: Shirogane, Ishigami and Fujiwara lose
FUJIWARA, I'M HERE TO RES-CUE—
WHA —?!
THIS IS HOW THE SERIES ENDS...?!
Ino also loses.

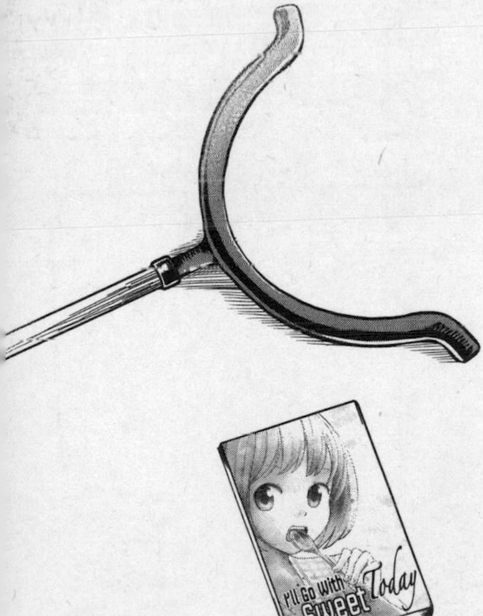
I'll Go With
Sweet
Today

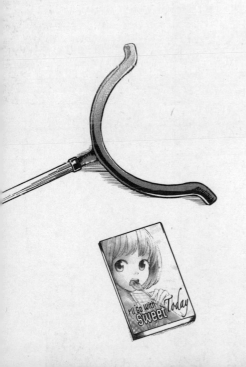

KAGUYA-SAMA
LOVE IS WAR

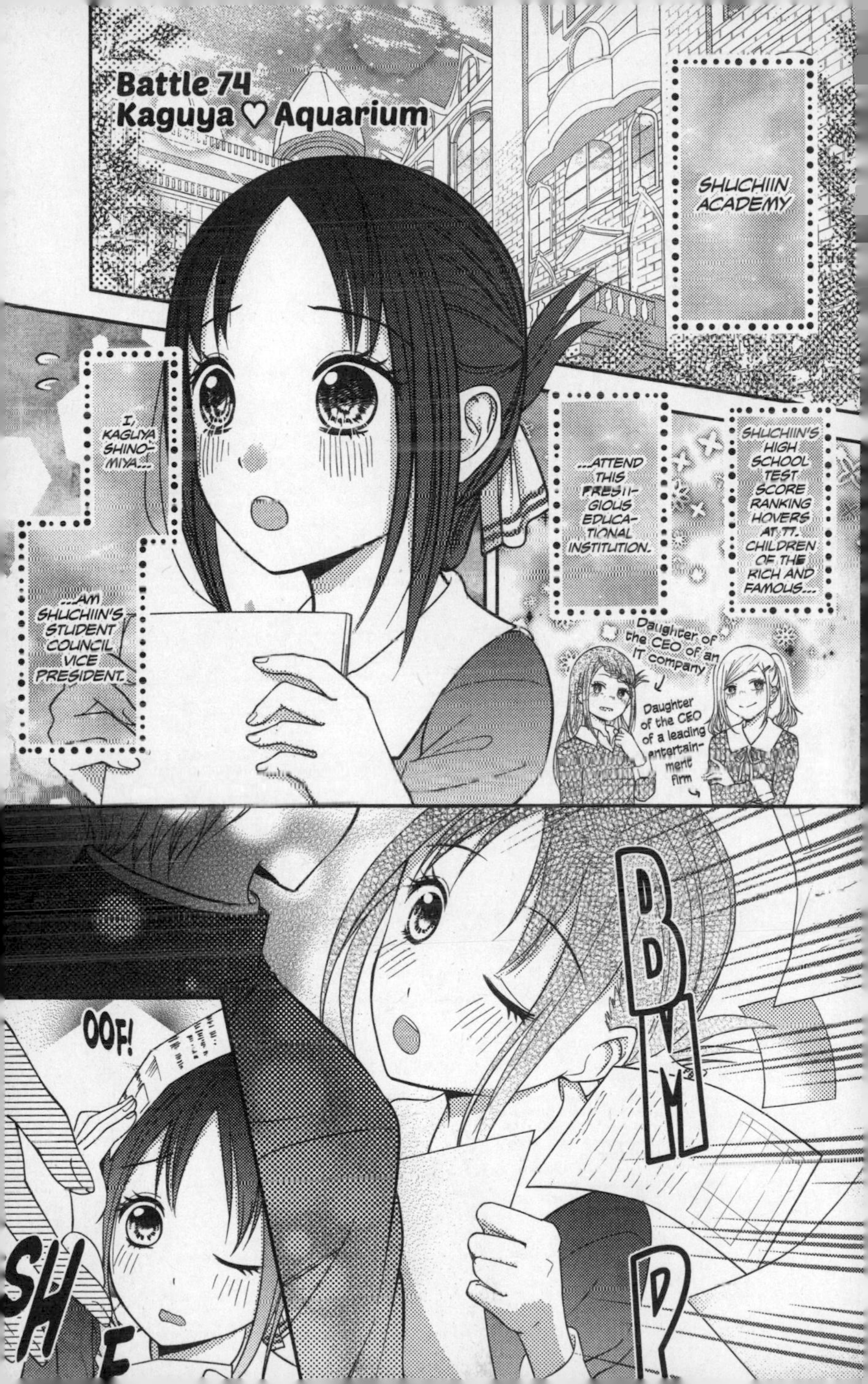
Battle 74
Kaguya ♡ Aquarium
SHUCHIIN ACADEMY
SHUCHIIN'S HIGH SCHOOL TEST SCORE RANKING HOVERS AT 77. CHILDREN OF THE RICH AND FAMOUS...
...ATTEND THIS PRESTI-GIOUS EDUCA-TIONAL INSTITUTION.
Daughter of the CEO of an IT company
Daughter of the CEO of a leading entertain-ment firm
I, KAGUYA SHINO-MIYA...
...AM SHUCHIIN'S STUDENT COUNCIL VICE PRESIDENT.
BUMP
OOF!

Battle 74 Kaguya ♡ Aquarium

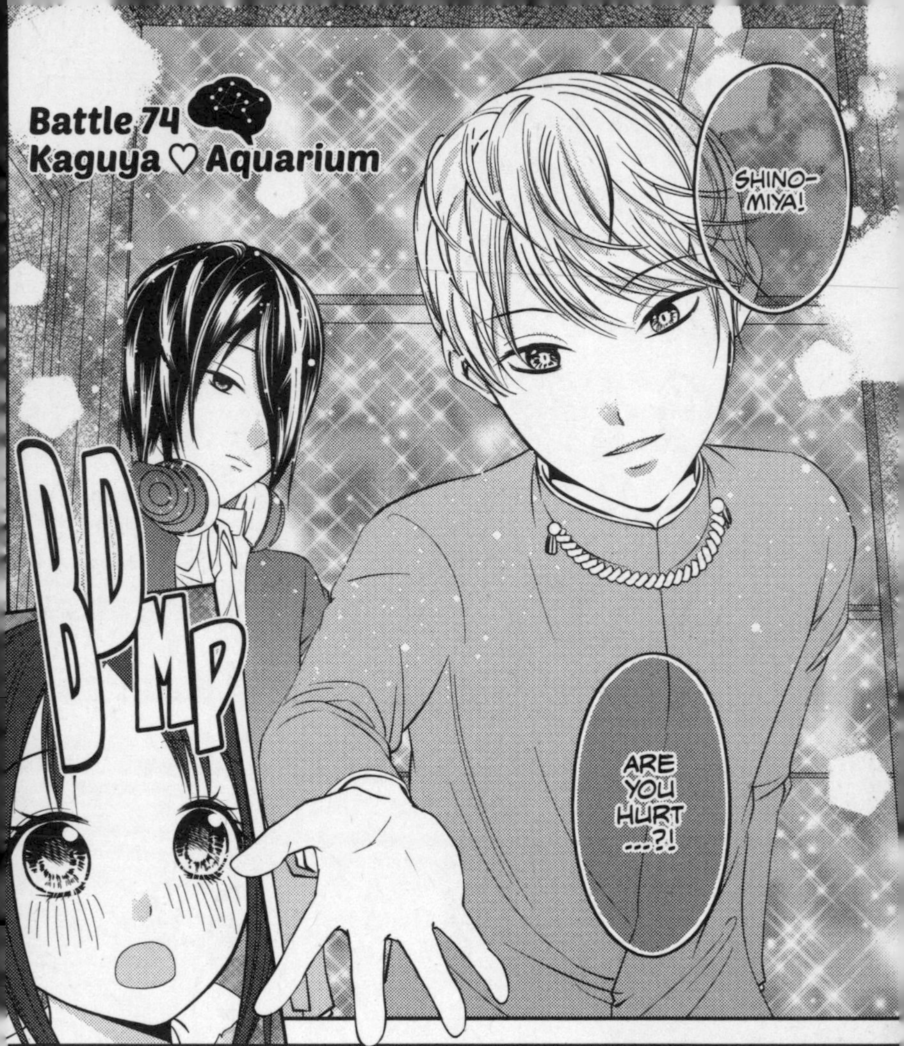
SHINO-MIYA!
BDMP
ARE YOU HURT...?!

The story thus far...

For some reason, Kaguya Shinomiya was forced to join the student council, whose members are all geniuses. Miyuki Shirogane—a super-genius at the top of his grade and the handsome student council president—has grown fond of her...

The two are initially hostile to each other, but over time an inexorable attraction develops between them...♡

It's obvious that Shirogane likes Kaguya, but he is too proud to confess his love and shows no signs of softening. So Kaguya goes on the offensive, concocting plots to induce him to ask her to go out with him...

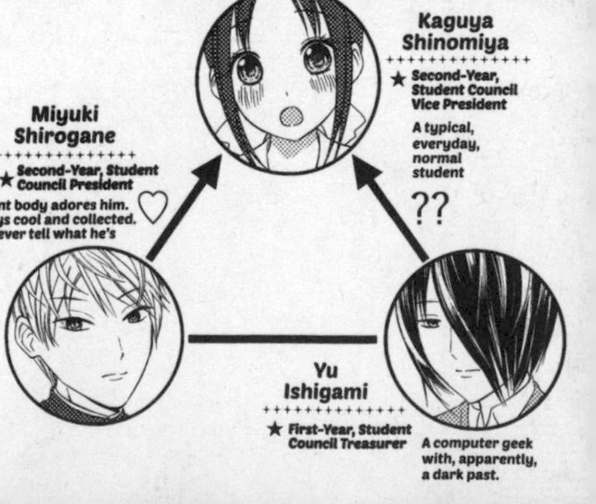
Kaguya Shinomiya
★ Second-Year, Student Council Vice President
A typical, everyday, normal student
??
Miyuki Shirogane
★ Second-Year, Student Council President
The student body adores him. He's always cool and collected. You can never tell what he's thinking.
♡
Yu Ishigami
★ First-Year, Student Council Treasurer
A computer geek with, apparently, a dark past.

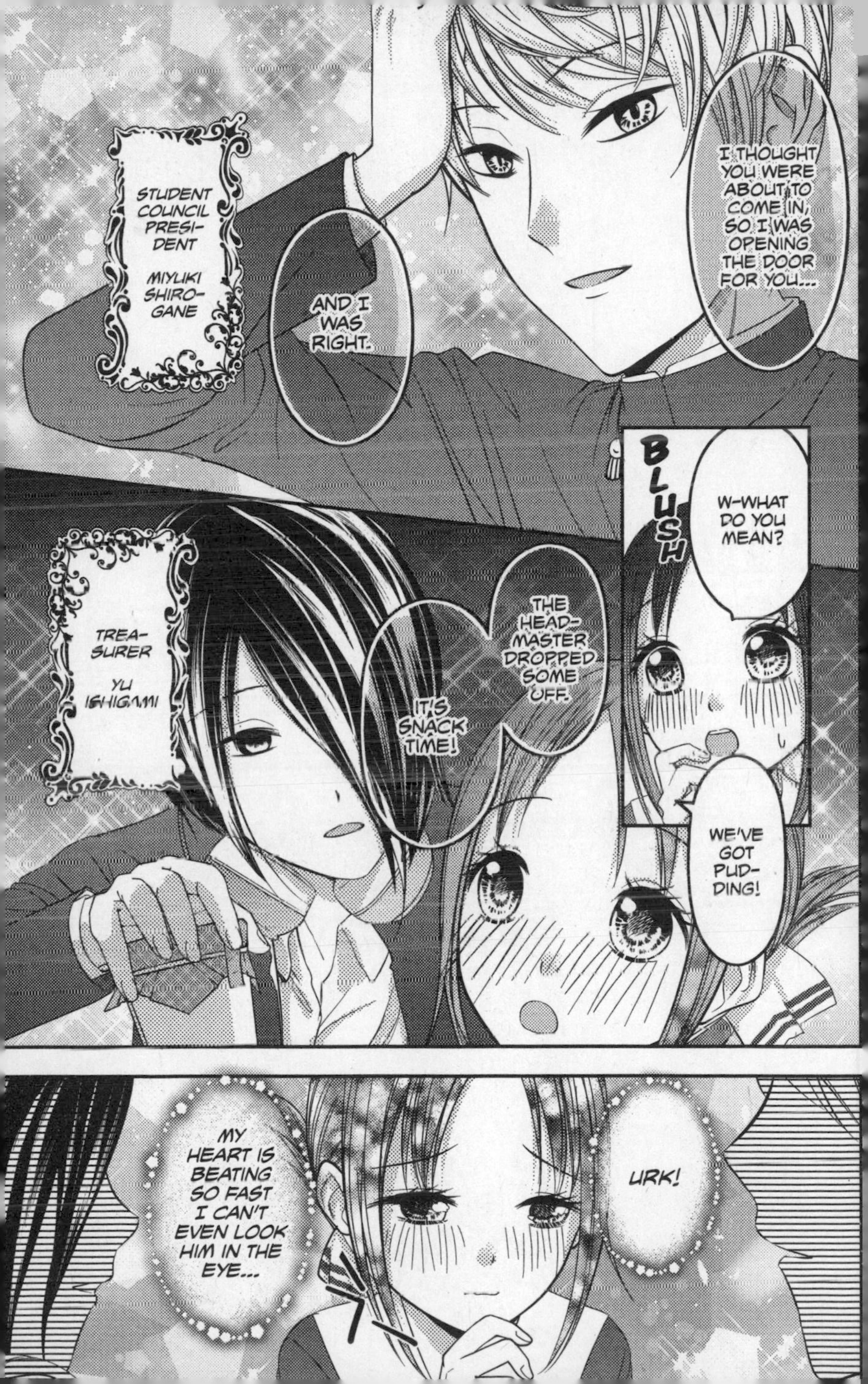
I THOUGHT YOU WERE ABOUT TO COME IN, SO I WAS OPENING THE DOOR FOR YOU...
AND I WAS RIGHT.
STUDENT COUNCIL PRESIDENT
MIYUKI SHIROGANE
BLUSH
W-WHAT DO YOU MEAN?
WE'VE GOT PUDDING!
THE HEADMASTER DROPPED SOME OFF.
IT'S SNACK TIME!
TREASURER
YU ISHIGAMI
URK!
MY HEART IS BEATING SO FAST I CAN'T EVEN LOOK HIM IN THE EYE...

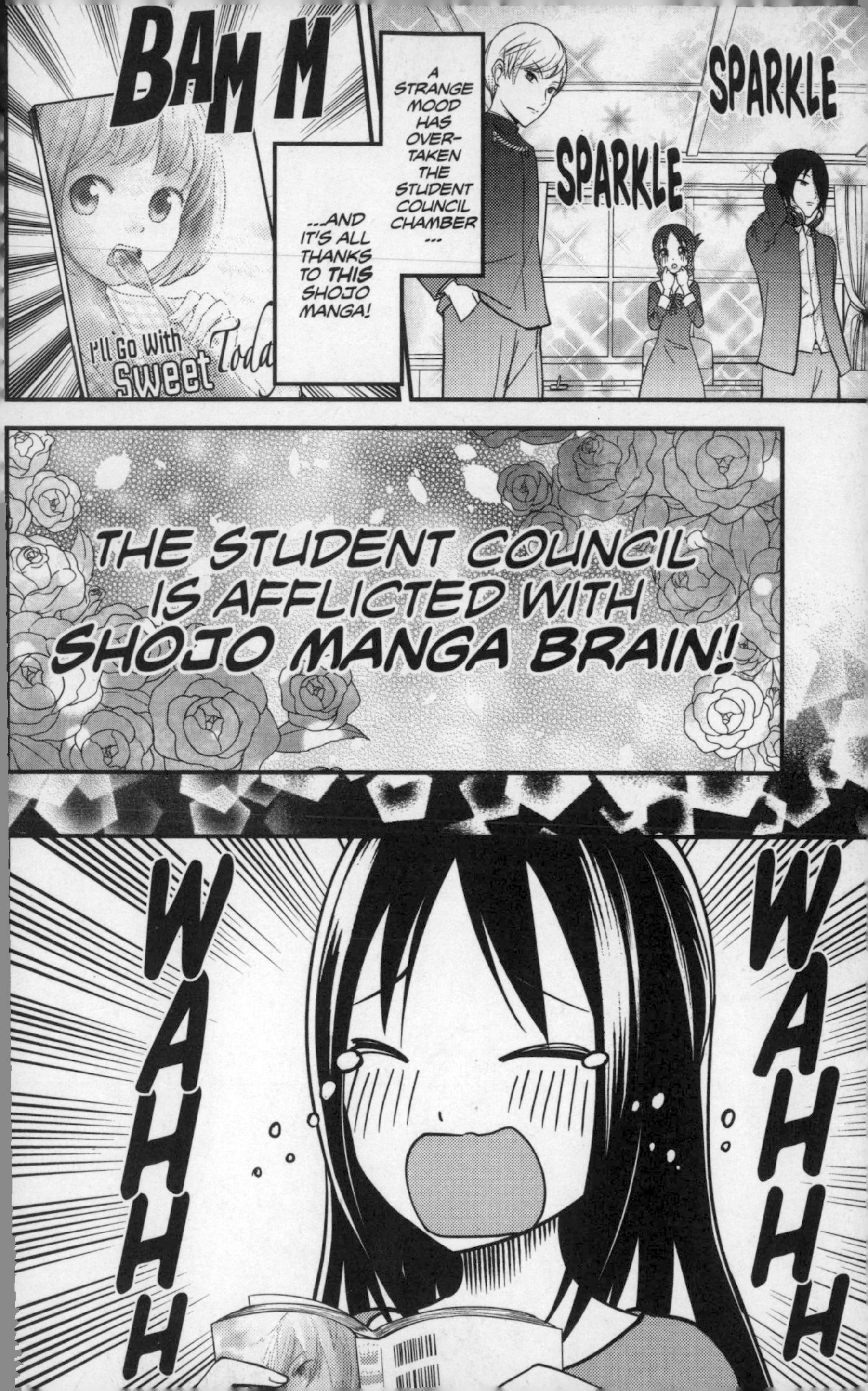
SPARKLE
SPARKLE
A STRANGE MOOD HAS OVER-TAKEN THE STUDENT COUNCIL CHAMBER ...
...AND IT'S ALL THANKS TO THIS SHOJO MANGA!
BAM M
I'll Go With Sweet Toda
THE STUDENT COUNCIL IS AFFLICTED WITH SHOJO MANGA BRAIN!
WAHHH
WAHHH

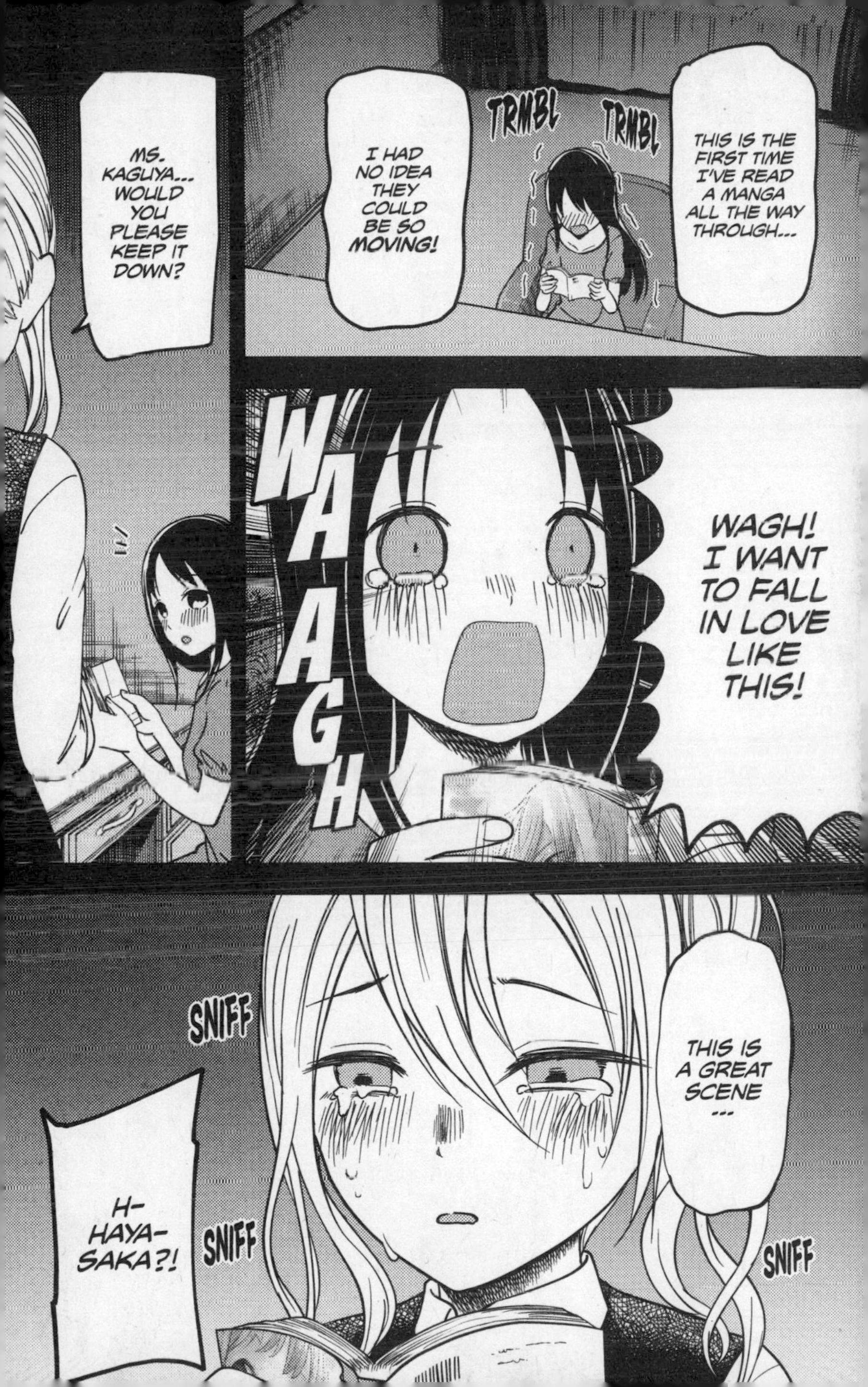
TRMBL
TRMBL
THIS IS THE FIRST TIME I'VE READ A MANGA ALL THE WAY THROUGH...
I HAD NO IDEA THEY COULD BE SO MOVING!
WAGH! I WANT TO FALL IN LOVE LIKE THIS!
WAAAGH
MS. KAGUYA... WOULD YOU PLEASE KEEP IT DOWN?
THIS IS A GREAT SCENE ...
SNIFF
SNIFF
SNIFF
H-HAYA-SAKA?!

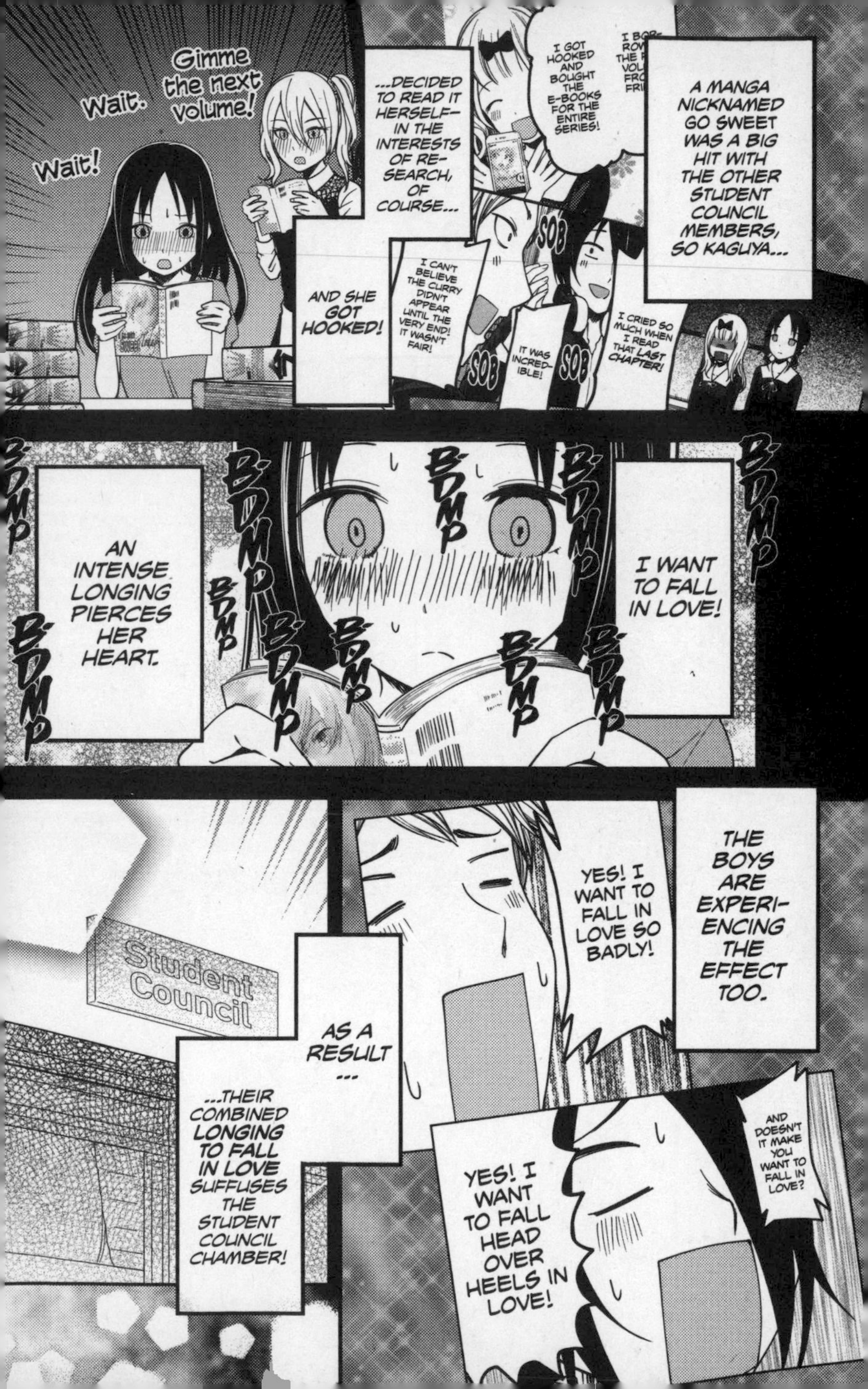

A MANGA NICKNAMED GO SWEET WAS A BIG HIT WITH THE OTHER STUDENT COUNCIL MEMBERS, SO KAGUYA...
I GOT HOOKED AND BOUGHT THE E-BOOKS FOR THE ENTIRE SERIES!
I CRIED SO MUCH WHEN I READ THAT LAST CHAPTER!
SOB
SOB
IT WAS INCREDIBLE!
SOB
SOB
I CAN'T BELIEVE THE CURRY DIDN'T APPEAR UNTIL THE VERY END! IT WASN'T FAIR!
...DECIDED TO READ IT HERSELF—IN THE INTERESTS OF RE-SEARCH, OF COURSE...
AND SHE GOT HOOKED!
Gimme the next volume!
Wait.
Wait!
I WANT TO FALL IN LOVE!
B-DMP
B-DMP
B-DMP
AN INTENSE LONGING PIERCES HER HEART.
B-DMP
B-DMP
THE BOYS ARE EXPERI-ENCING THE EFFECT TOO.
YES! I WANT TO FALL IN LOVE SO BADLY!
AND DOESN'T IT MAKE YOU WANT TO FALL IN LOVE?
YES! I WANT TO FALL HEAD OVER HEELS IN LOVE!
Student Council
AS A RESULT...
...THEIR COMBINED LONGING TO FALL IN LOVE SUFFUSES THE STUDENT COUNCIL CHAMBER!

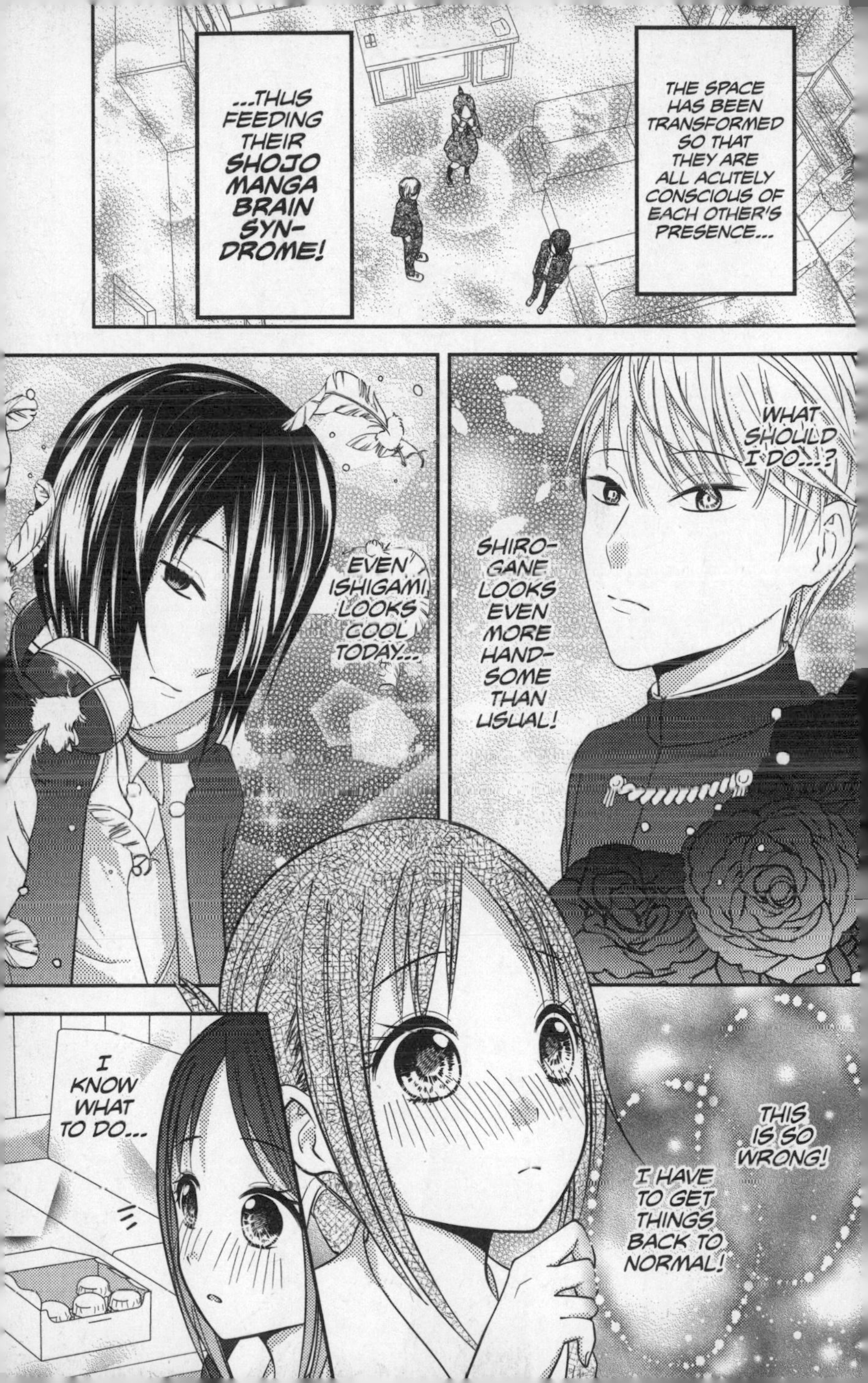
THE SPACE HAS BEEN TRANSFORMED SO THAT THEY ARE ALL ACUTELY CONSCIOUS OF EACH OTHER'S PRESENCE...
...THUS FEEDING THEIR SHOJO MANGA BRAIN SYN-DROME!
WHAT SHOULD I DO...?
SHIRO-GANE LOOKS EVEN MORE HAND-SOME THAN USUAL!
EVEN ISHIGAMI LOOKS COOL TODAY...
THIS IS SO WRONG!
I HAVE TO GET THINGS BACK TO NORMAL!
I KNOW WHAT TO DO...

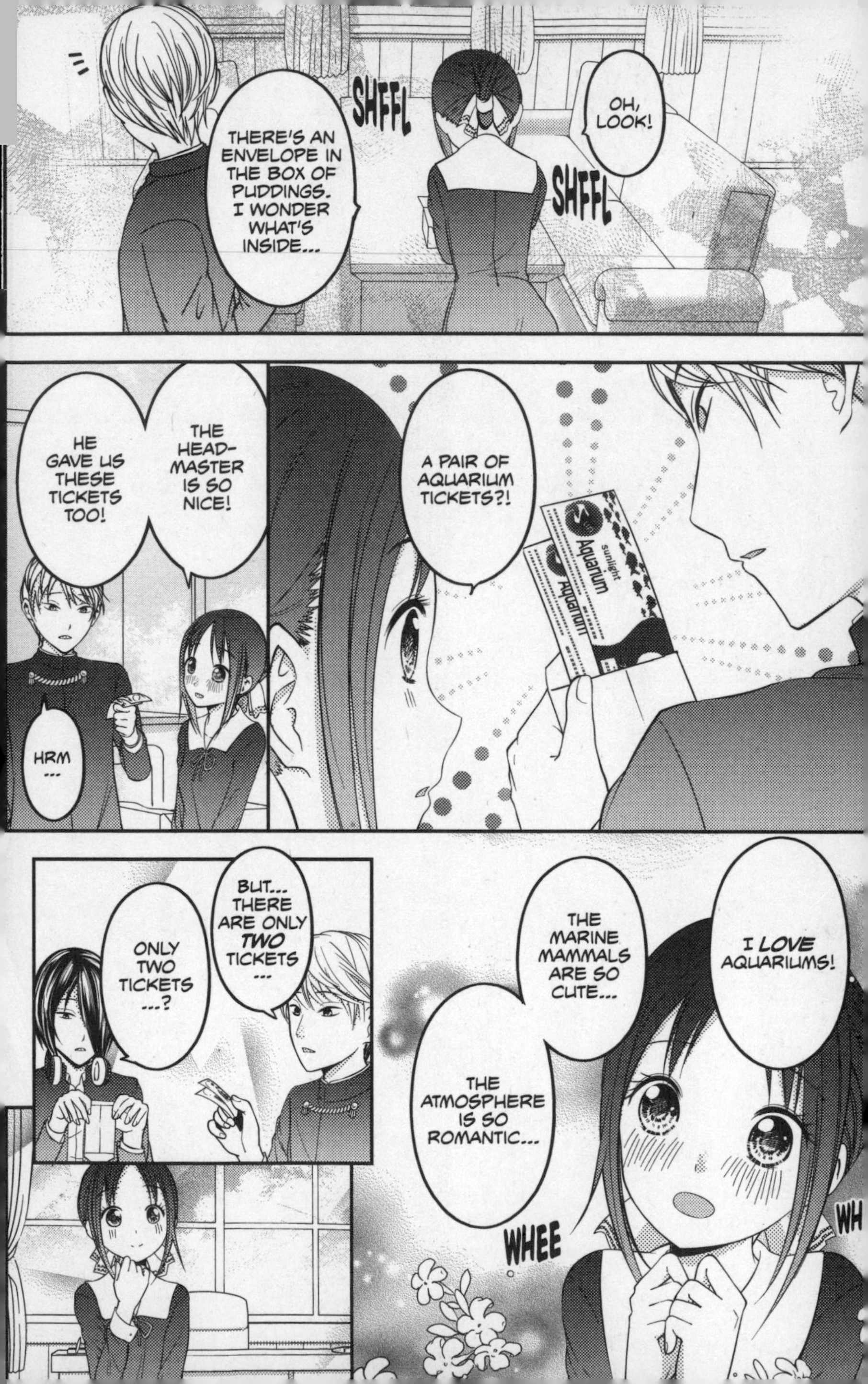
OH, LOOK!
SHFFL
SHFFL
THERE'S AN ENVELOPE IN THE BOX OF PUDDINGS. I WONDER WHAT'S INSIDE...
A PAIR OF AQUARIUM TICKETS?!
sunlight Aquarium
Aquarium
THE HEAD-MASTER IS SO NICE!
HE GAVE US THESE TICKETS TOO!
HRM...
I *LOVE* AQUARIUMS!
THE MARINE MAMMALS ARE SO CUTE...
THE ATMOSPHERE IS SO ROMANTIC...
WH
WHEE
BUT... THERE ARE ONLY ***TWO*** TICKETS...
ONLY TWO TICKETS...?

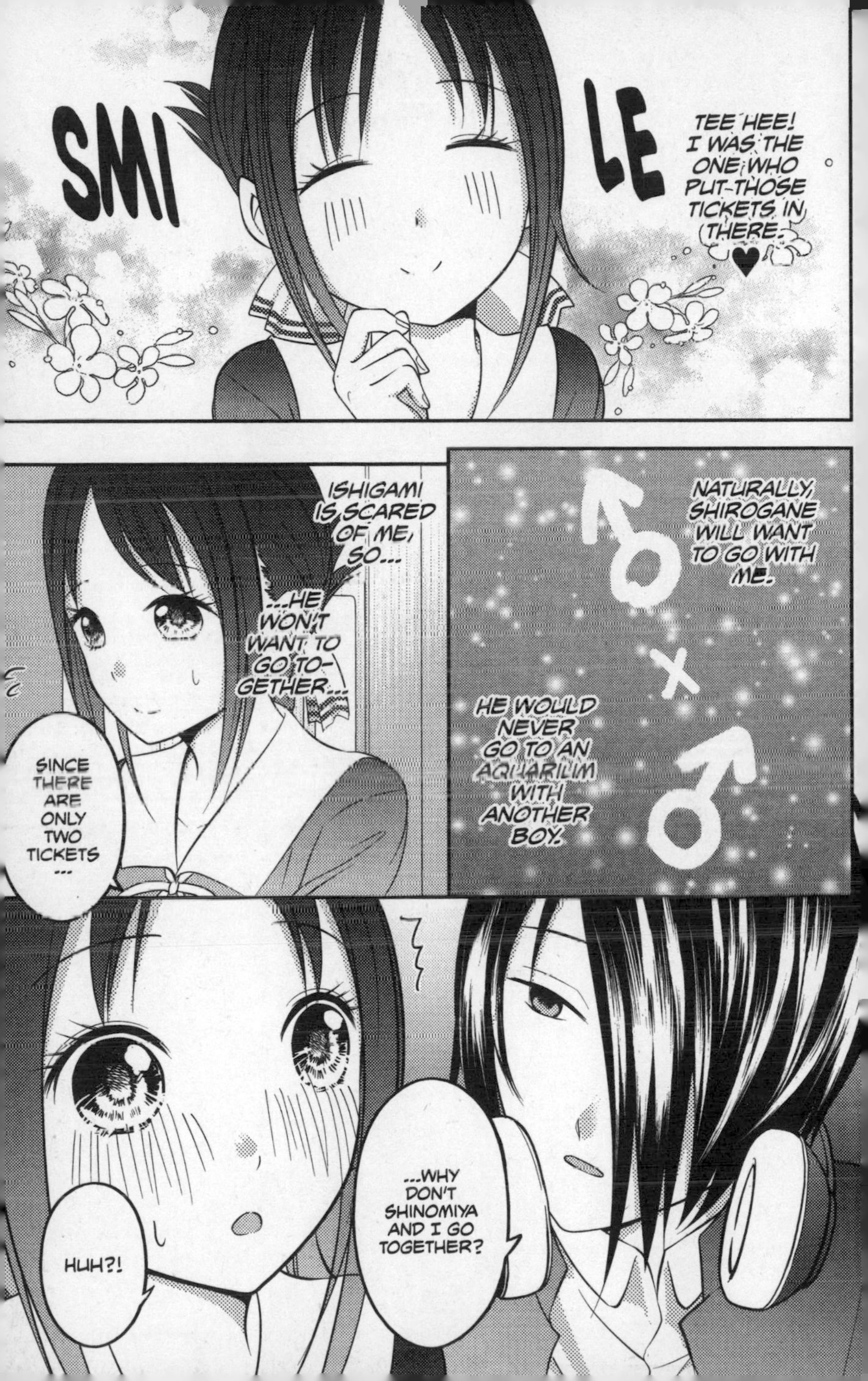
SMI LE
TEE HEE! I WAS THE ONE WHO PUT THOSE TICKETS IN THERE. ♥
NATURALLY, SHIROGANE WILL WANT TO GO WITH ME.
♂ × ♂
HE WOULD NEVER GO TO AN AQUARIUM WITH ANOTHER BOY.
ISHIGAMI IS SCARED OF ME, SO...
...HE WON'T WANT TO GO TOGETHER...
SINCE THERE ARE ONLY TWO TICKETS...
...WHY DON'T SHINOMIYA AND I GO TOGETHER?
HUH?!

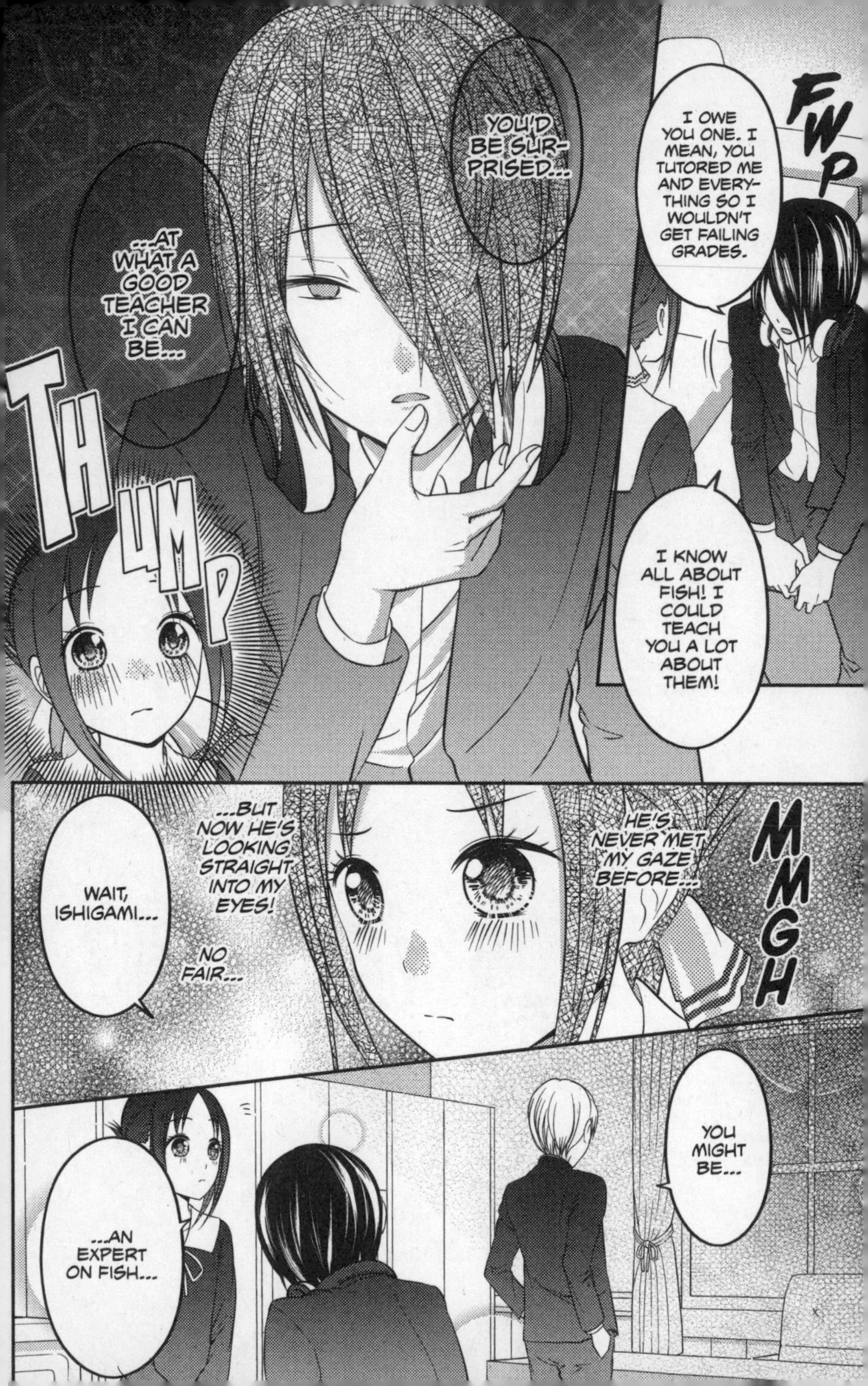
FWP
I OWE YOU ONE. I MEAN, YOU TUTORED ME AND EVERYTHING SO I WOULDN'T GET FAILING GRADES.
I KNOW ALL ABOUT FISH! I COULD TEACH YOU A LOT ABOUT THEM!
YOU'D BE SURPRISED...
...AT WHAT A GOOD TEACHER I CAN BE...
THUMP
MMGH
HE'S NEVER MET MY GAZE BEFORE...
...BUT NOW HE'S LOOKING STRAIGHT INTO MY EYES!
NO FAIR...
WAIT, ISHIGAMI...
YOU MIGHT BE...
...AN EXPERT ON FISH...

Aka Report

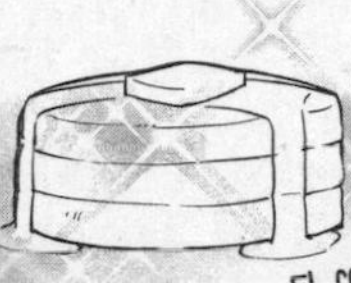

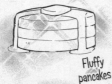

Fluffy pancakes

Hello! Aka here! ♡♡

I went to see ●Ki Theatre Company's musical♪ with my friend Y.

How can I put it... It was amaaazing. ♡ (I can't find the words to describe it...LOL.)

On the way home, we went to Shimokitazawa to eat pancakes... But I was so hungry that... I ended up ordering ground chicken flavored with soy sauce and sugar.

Because when I looked at the photos on the menu, the carbs looked too cute to eat...

I'd like to be more girly!

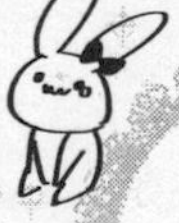

I missed out on the pancake fluffiness...

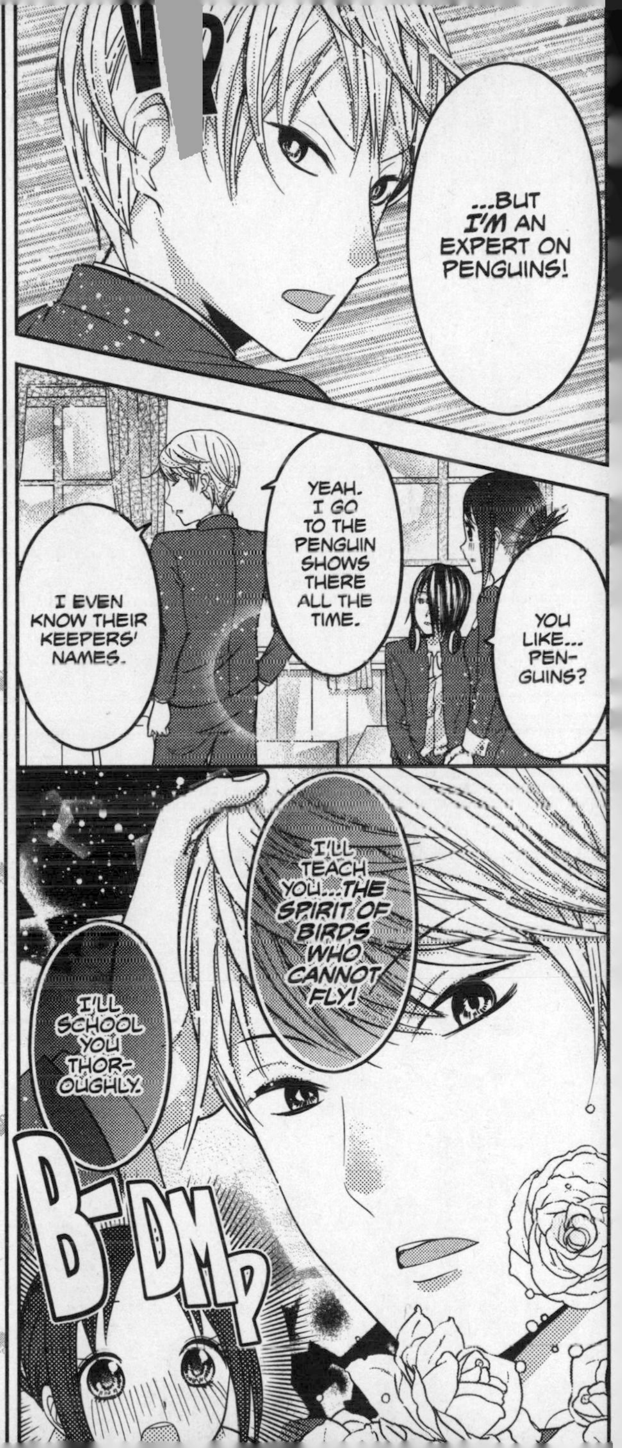
...BUT I'M AN EXPERT ON PENGUINS!
YOU LIKE... PEN-GUINS?
YEAH. I GO TO THE PENGUIN SHOWS THERE ALL THE TIME.
I EVEN KNOW THEIR KEEPERS' NAMES.
I'LL TEACH YOU...THE SPIRIT OF BIRDS WHO CANNOT FLY!
I'LL SCHOOL YOU THOR-OUGHLY.
B-DMP

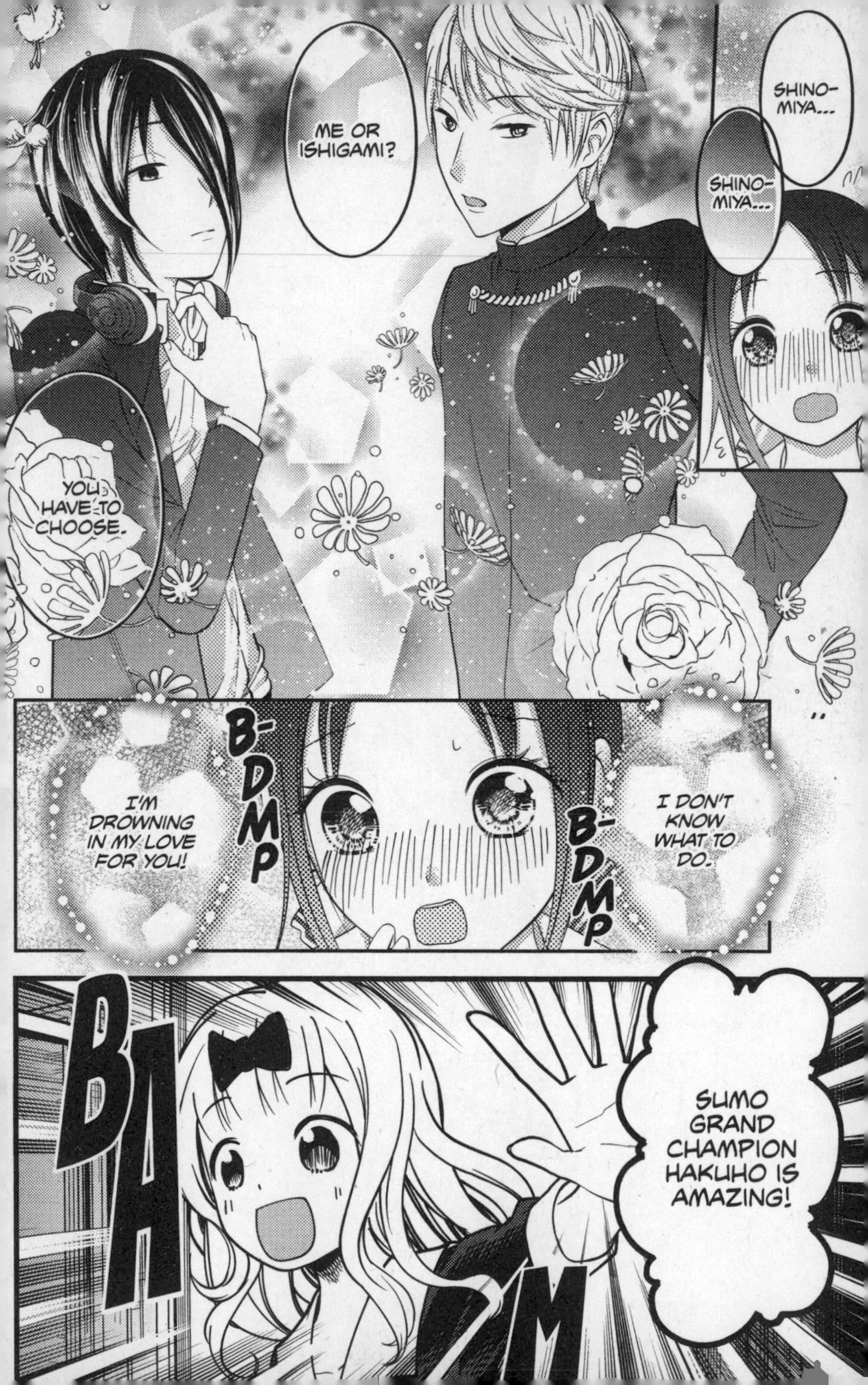
SHINO-MIYA...
SHINO-MIYA...
ME OR ISHIGAMI?
YOU HAVE TO CHOOSE.
I DON'T KNOW WHAT TO DO.
B-BDMP
B-BDMP
I'M DROWNING IN MY LOVE FOR YOU!
SUMO GRAND CHAMPION HAKUHO IS AMAZING!
BAM

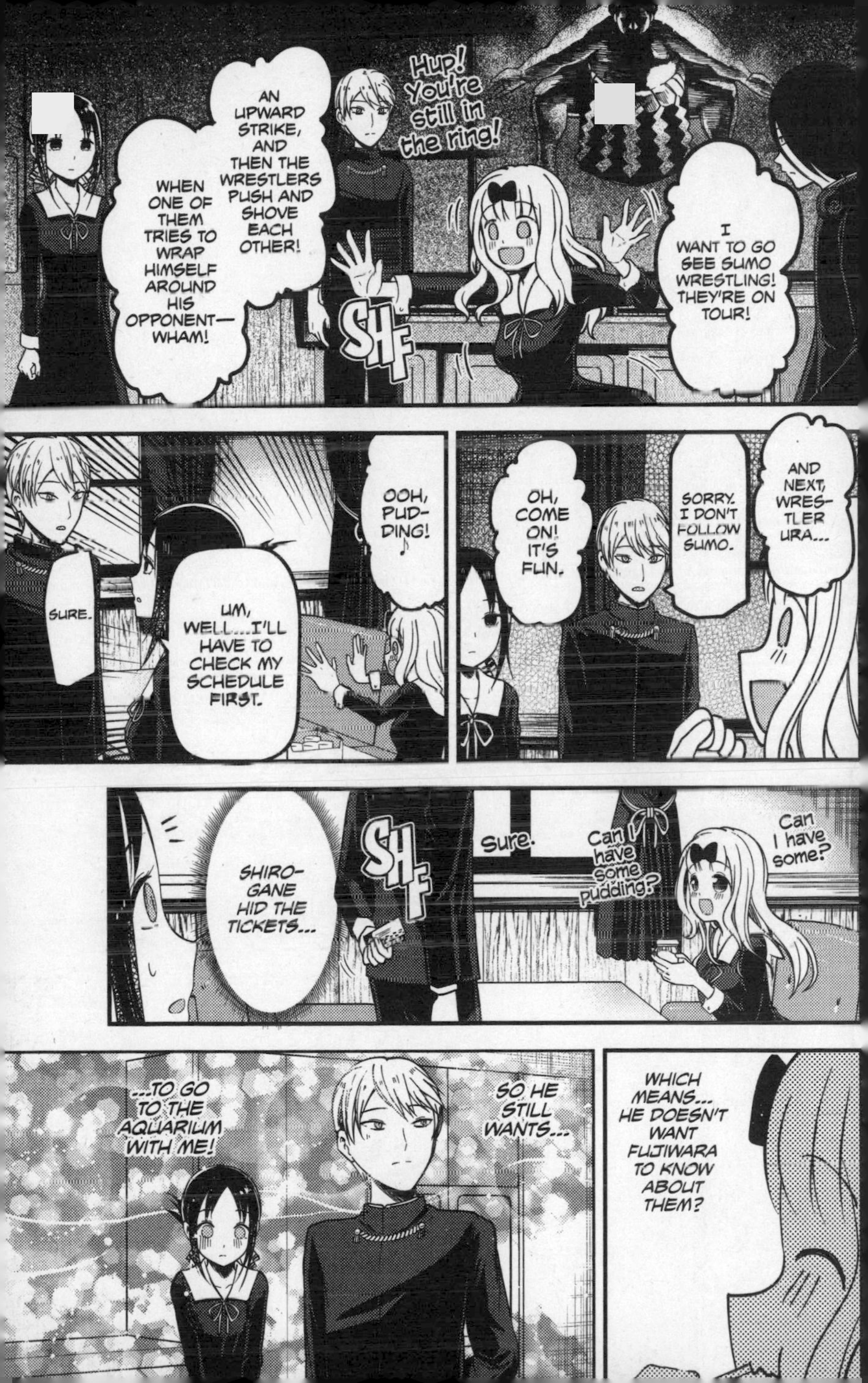
I WANT TO GO SEE SUMO WRESTLING! THEY'RE ON TOUR!
Hup! You're still in the ring!
AN UPWARD STRIKE, AND THEN THE WRESTLERS PUSH AND SHOVE EACH OTHER!
WHEN ONE OF THEM TRIES TO WRAP HIMSELF AROUND HIS OPPONENT—WHAM!
SHF
AND NEXT, WRESTLER URA...
SORRY. I DON'T FOLLOW SUMO.
OH, COME ON! IT'S FUN.
OOH, PUDDING! ♪
UM, WELL...I'LL HAVE TO CHECK MY SCHEDULE FIRST.
SURE.
Can I have some?
Can I have some pudding?
Sure.
SHF
SHIROGANE HID THE TICKETS...
WHICH MEANS... HE DOESN'T WANT FUJIWARA TO KNOW ABOUT THEM?
SO HE STILL WANTS...
...TO GO TO THE AQUARIUM WITH ME!

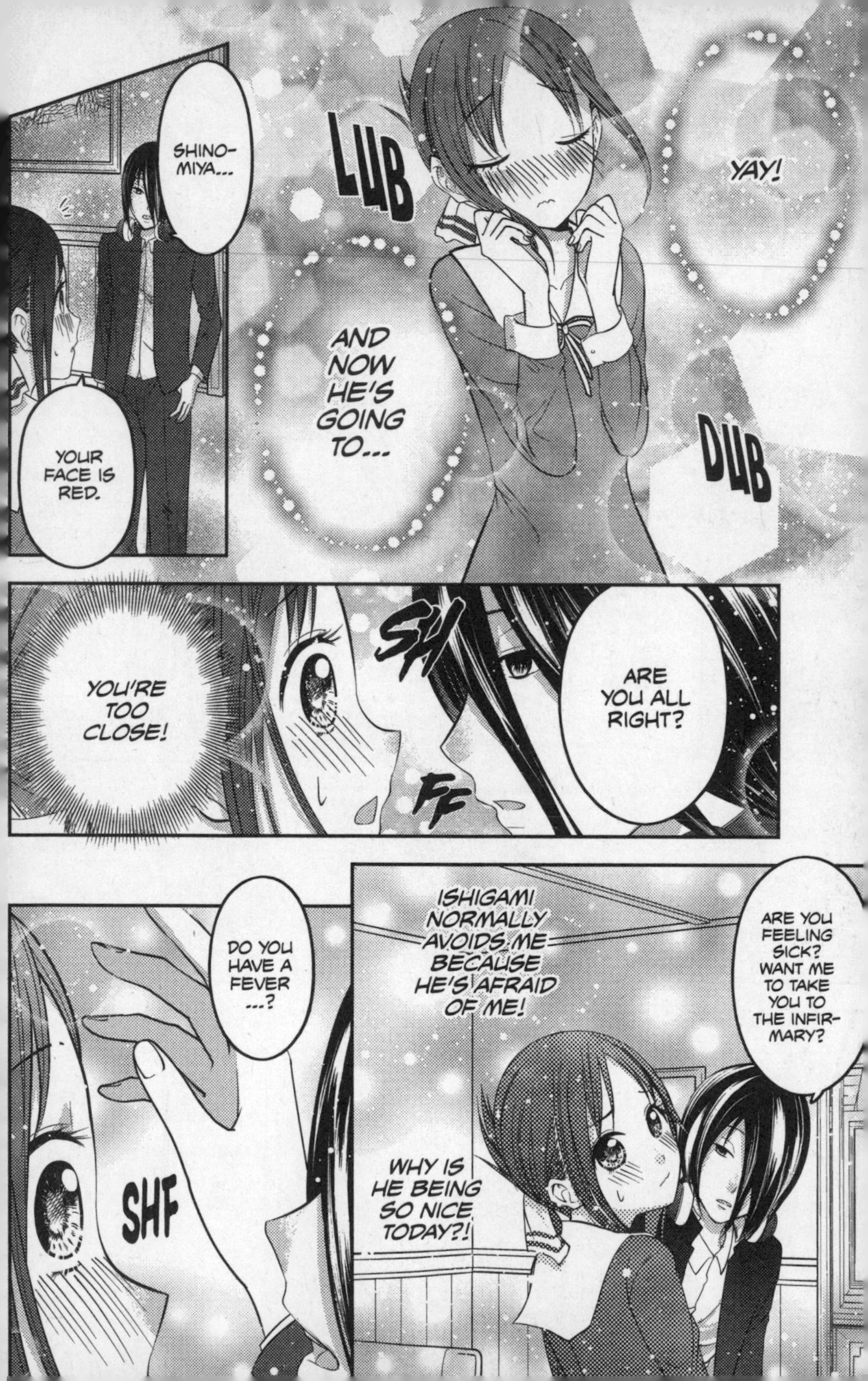
YAY!
LUB
AND NOW HE'S GOING TO...
DUB
SHINO-MIYA...
YOUR FACE IS RED.
ARE YOU ALL RIGHT?
SH
FF
YOU'RE TOO CLOSE!
ARE YOU FEELING SICK? WANT ME TO TAKE YOU TO THE INFIR-MARY?
ISHIGAMI NORMALLY AVOIDS ME BECAUSE HE'S AFRAID OF ME!
WHY IS HE BEING SO NICE TODAY?!
DO YOU HAVE A FEVER ...?
SHF

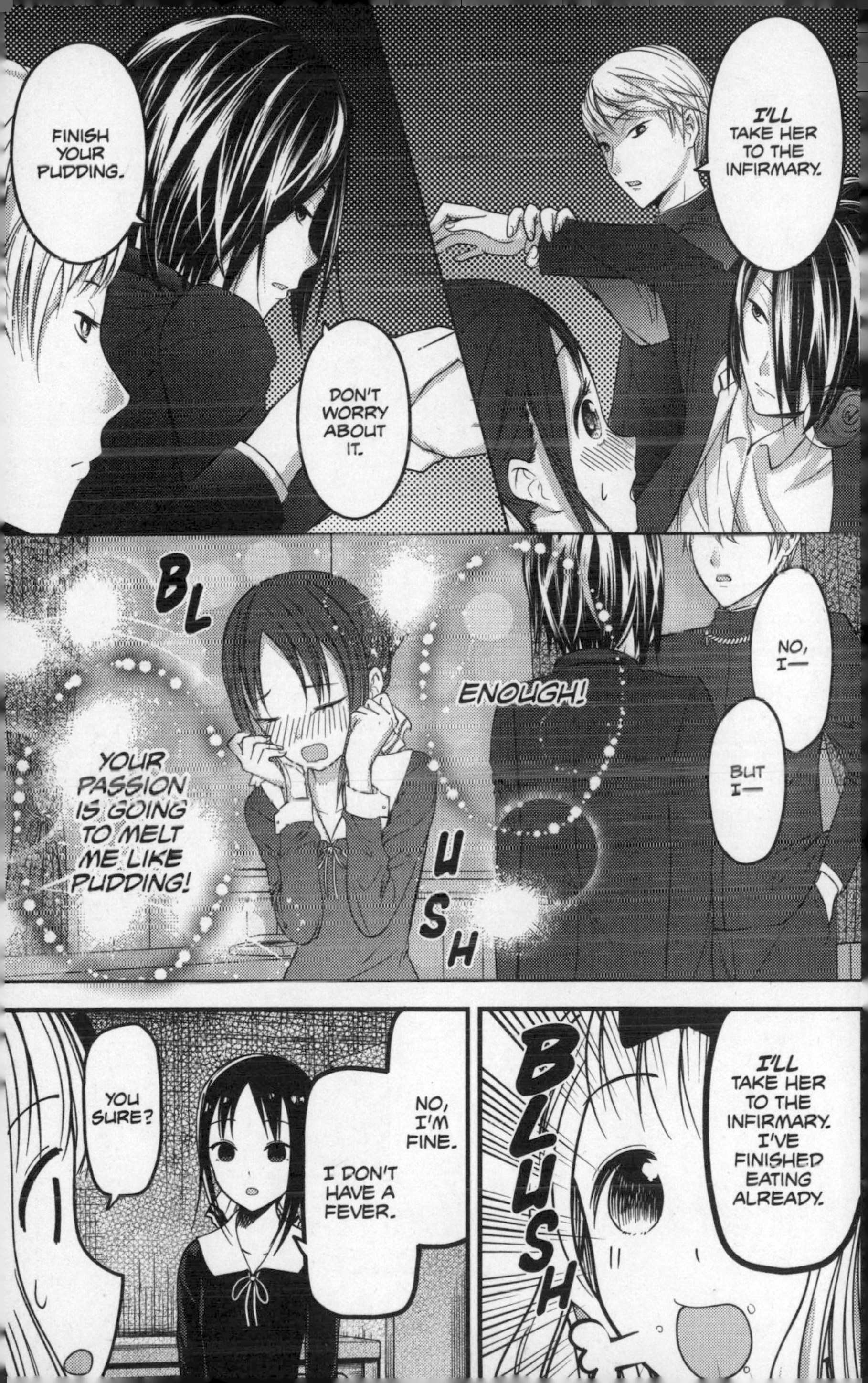
I'LL TAKE HER TO THE INFIRMARY.
DON'T WORRY ABOUT IT.
FINISH YOUR PUDDING.
NO, I—
BUT I—
ENOUGH!
BLUSH
YOUR PASSION IS GOING TO MELT ME LIKE PUDDING!
I'LL TAKE HER TO THE INFIRMARY. I'VE FINISHED EATING ALREADY.
BLUSH
NO, I'M FINE.
I DON'T HAVE A FEVER.
YOU SURE?

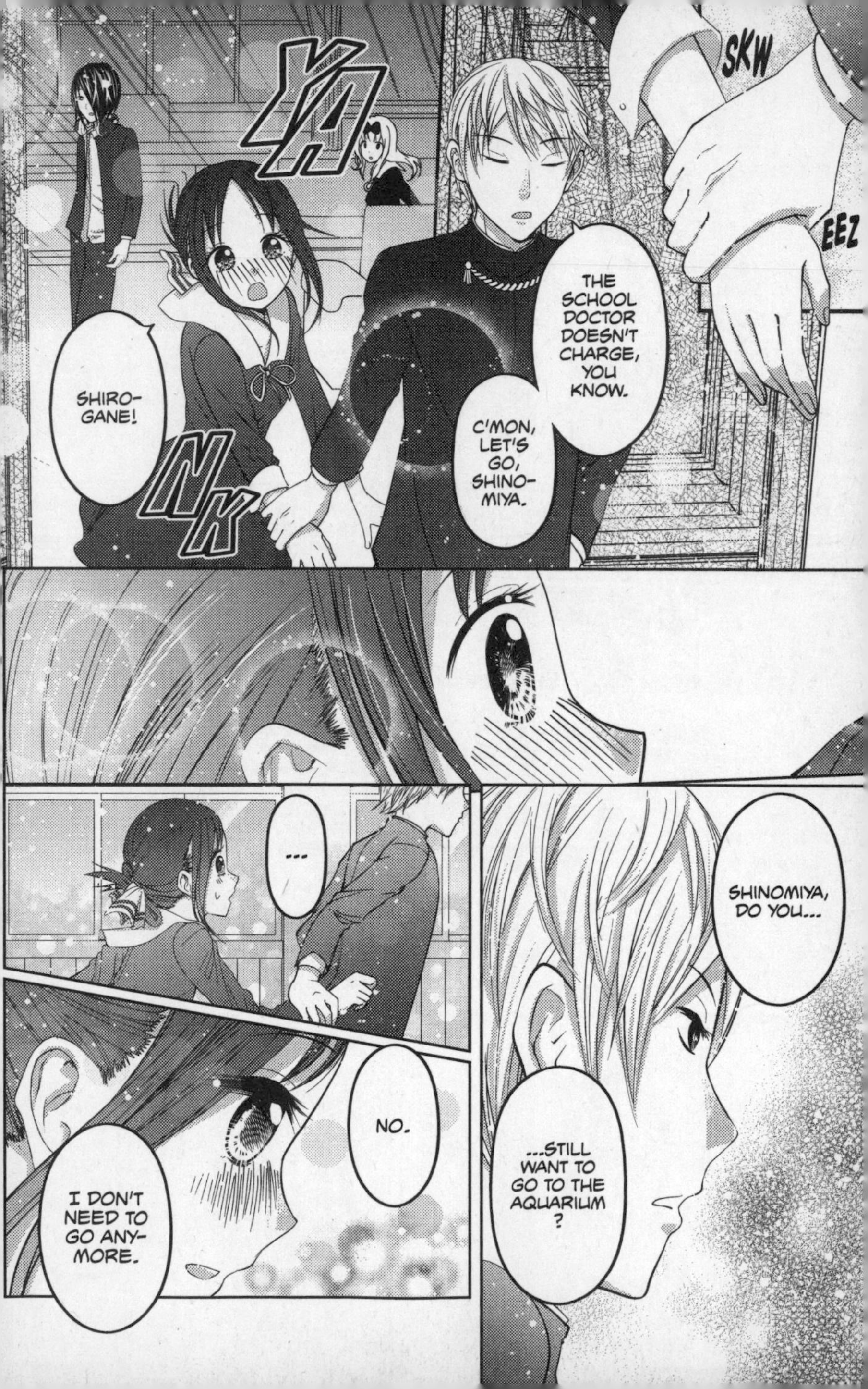
SKW
EEZ
THE SCHOOL DOCTOR DOESN'T CHARGE, YOU KNOW.
C'MON, LET'S GO, SHINOMIYA.
YA
NK
SHIRO-GANE!
SHINOMIYA, DO YOU...
...STILL WANT TO GO TO THE AQUARIUM ?
...
NO.
I DON'T NEED TO GO ANY-MORE.

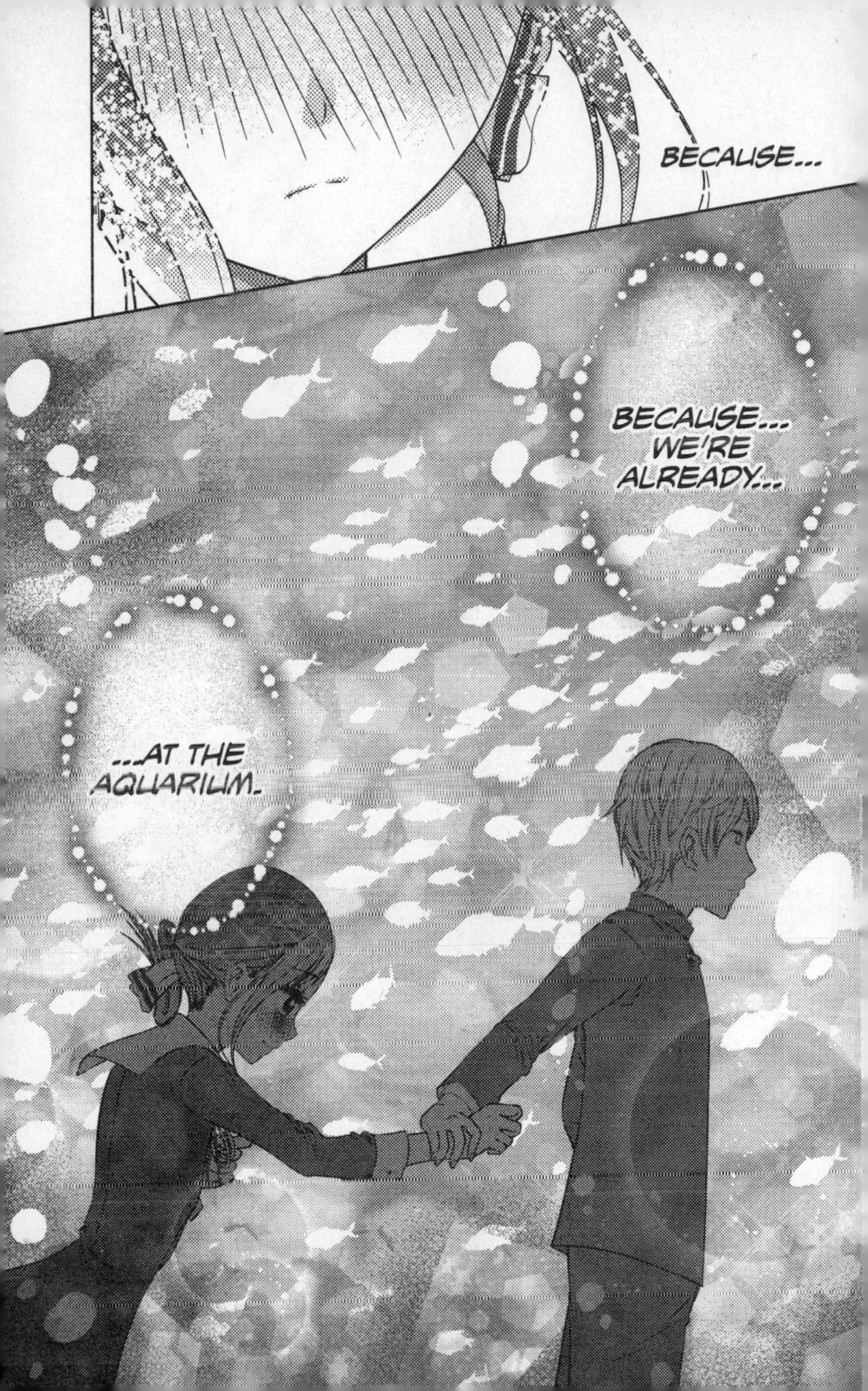
BECAUSE...
BECAUSE... WE'RE ALREADY...
...AT THE AQUARIUM.

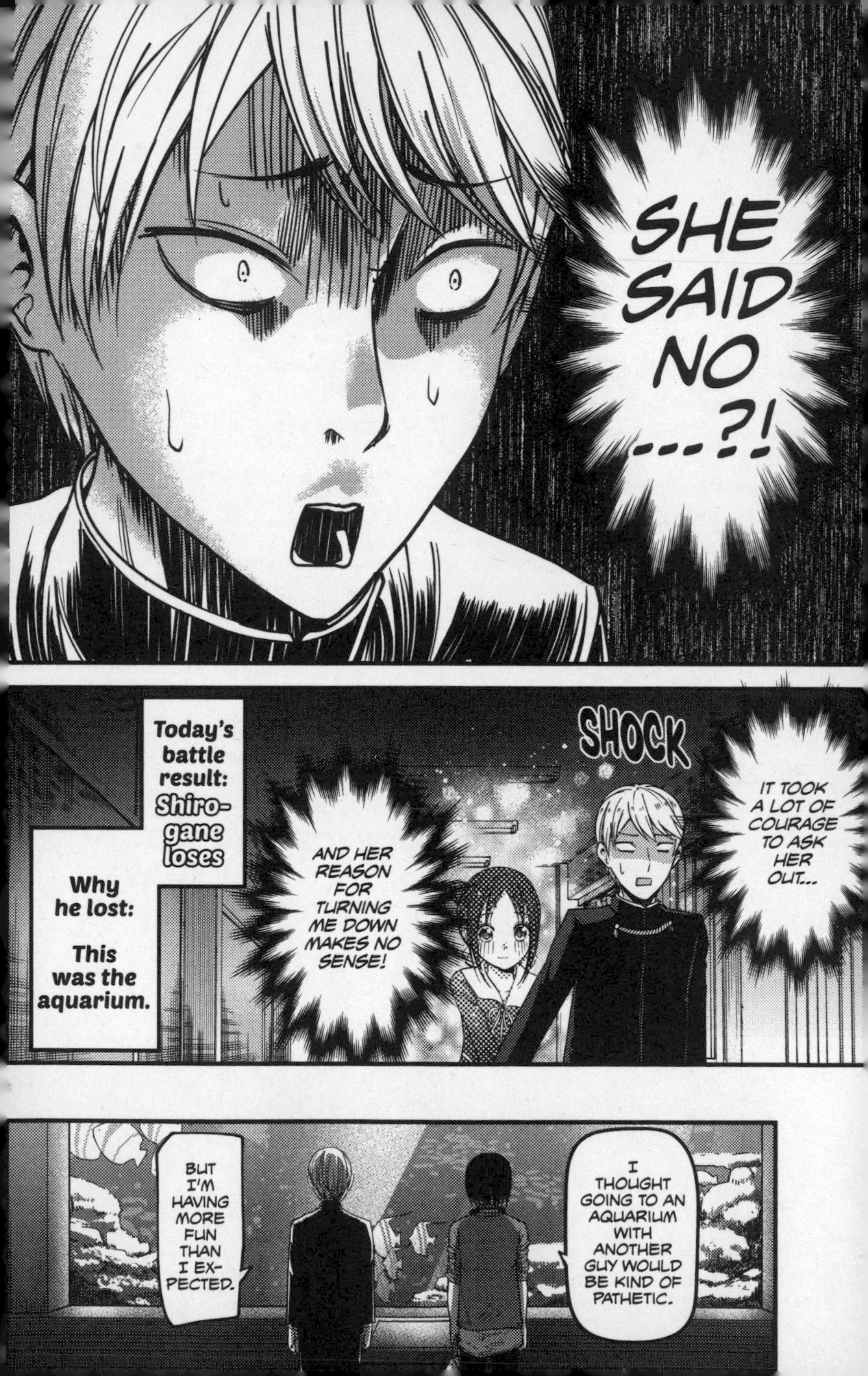
SHE SAID NO ...?!
IT TOOK A LOT OF COURAGE TO ASK HER OUT...
SHOCK
AND HER REASON FOR TURNING ME DOWN MAKES NO SENSE!
Today's battle result: Shirogane loses
Why he lost:
This was the aquarium.
I THOUGHT GOING TO AN AQUARIUM WITH ANOTHER GUY WOULD BE KIND OF PATHETIC.
BUT I'M HAVING MORE FUN THAN I EXPECTED.

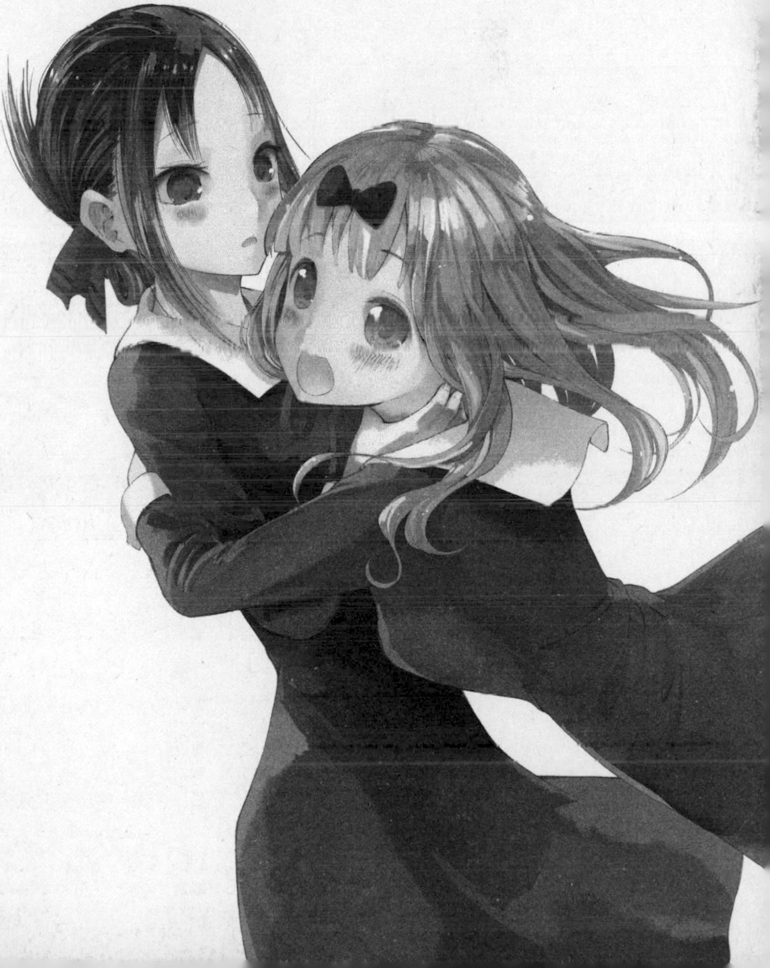

KAGUYA-SAMA
LOVE IS WAR

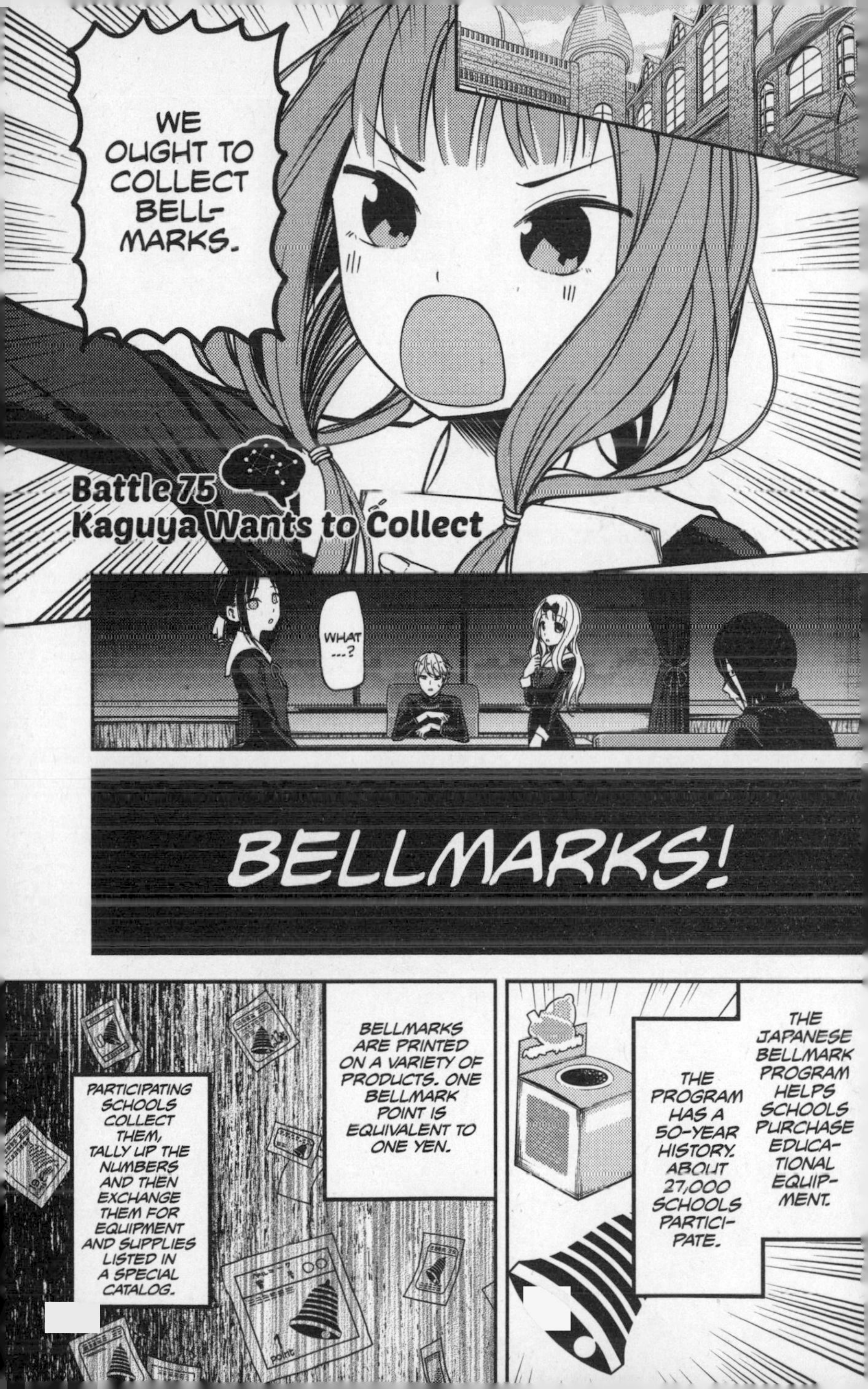
WE OUGHT TO COLLECT BELLMARKS.
Battle 75 Kaguya Wants to Collect
WHAT ...?
BELLMARKS!
THE JAPANESE BELLMARK PROGRAM HELPS SCHOOLS PURCHASE EDUCATIONAL EQUIPMENT.
THE PROGRAM HAS A 50-YEAR HISTORY. ABOUT 27,000 SCHOOLS PARTICIPATE.
BELLMARKS ARE PRINTED ON A VARIETY OF PRODUCTS. ONE BELLMARK POINT IS EQUIVALENT TO ONE YEN.
PARTICIPATING SCHOOLS COLLECT THEM, TALLY UP THE NUMBERS AND THEN EXCHANGE THEM FOR EQUIPMENT AND SUPPLIES LISTED IN A SPECIAL CATALOG.

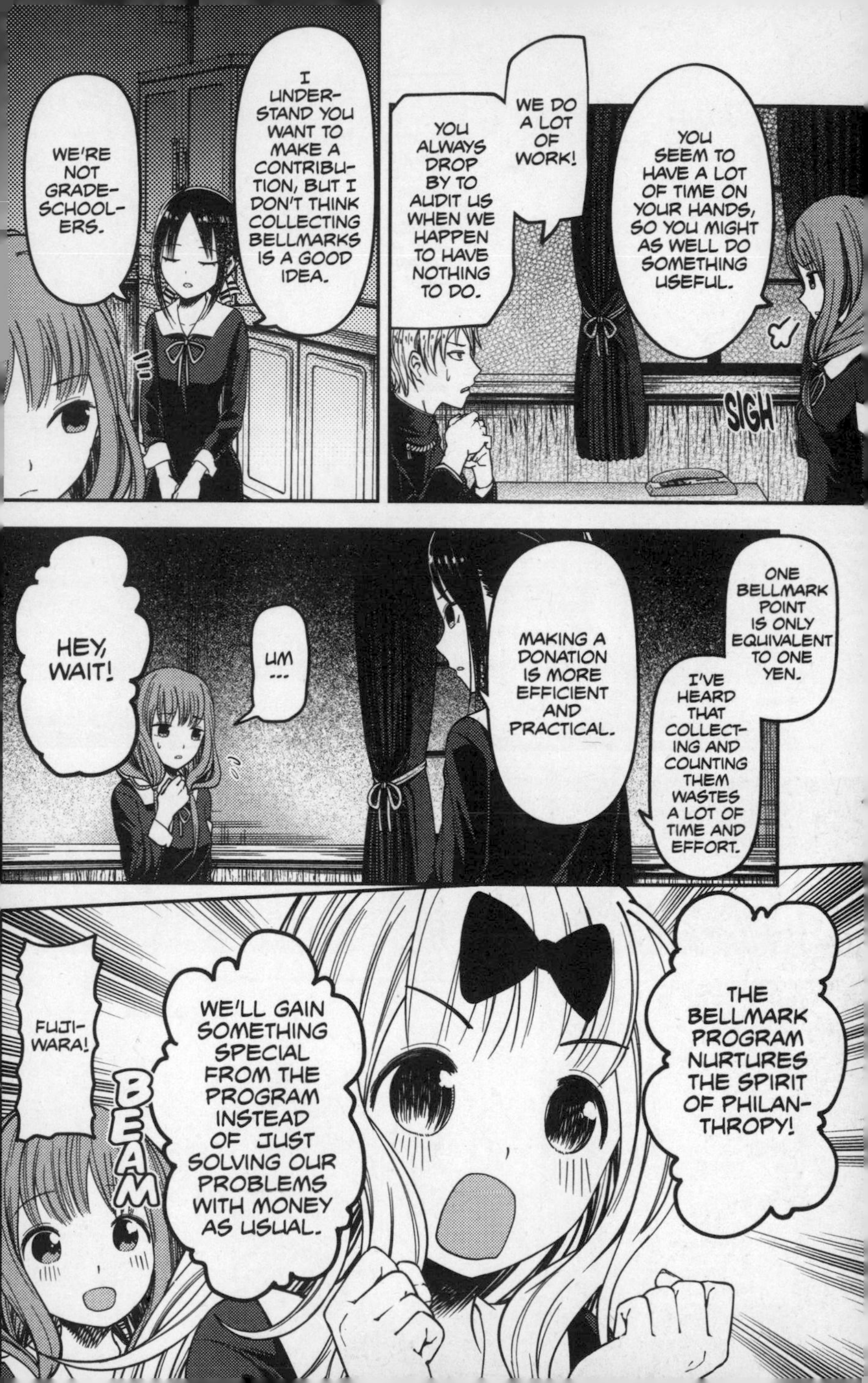
YOU SEEM TO HAVE A LOT OF TIME ON YOUR HANDS, SO YOU MIGHT AS WELL DO SOMETHING USEFUL.
SIGH
WE DO A LOT OF WORK!
YOU ALWAYS DROP BY TO AUDIT US WHEN WE HAPPEN TO HAVE NOTHING TO DO.
I UNDERSTAND YOU WANT TO MAKE A CONTRIBUTION, BUT I DON'T THINK COLLECTING BELLMARKS IS A GOOD IDEA.
WE'RE NOT GRADE-SCHOOLERS.
ONE BELLMARK POINT IS ONLY EQUIVALENT TO ONE YEN.
I'VE HEARD THAT COLLECTING AND COUNTING THEM WASTES A LOT OF TIME AND EFFORT.
MAKING A DONATION IS MORE EFFICIENT AND PRACTICAL.
UM...
HEY, WAIT!
THE BELLMARK PROGRAM NURTURES THE SPIRIT OF PHILANTHROPY!
WE'LL GAIN SOMETHING SPECIAL FROM THE PROGRAM INSTEAD OF JUST SOLVING OUR PROBLEMS WITH MONEY AS USUAL.
BEAM
FUJIWARA!

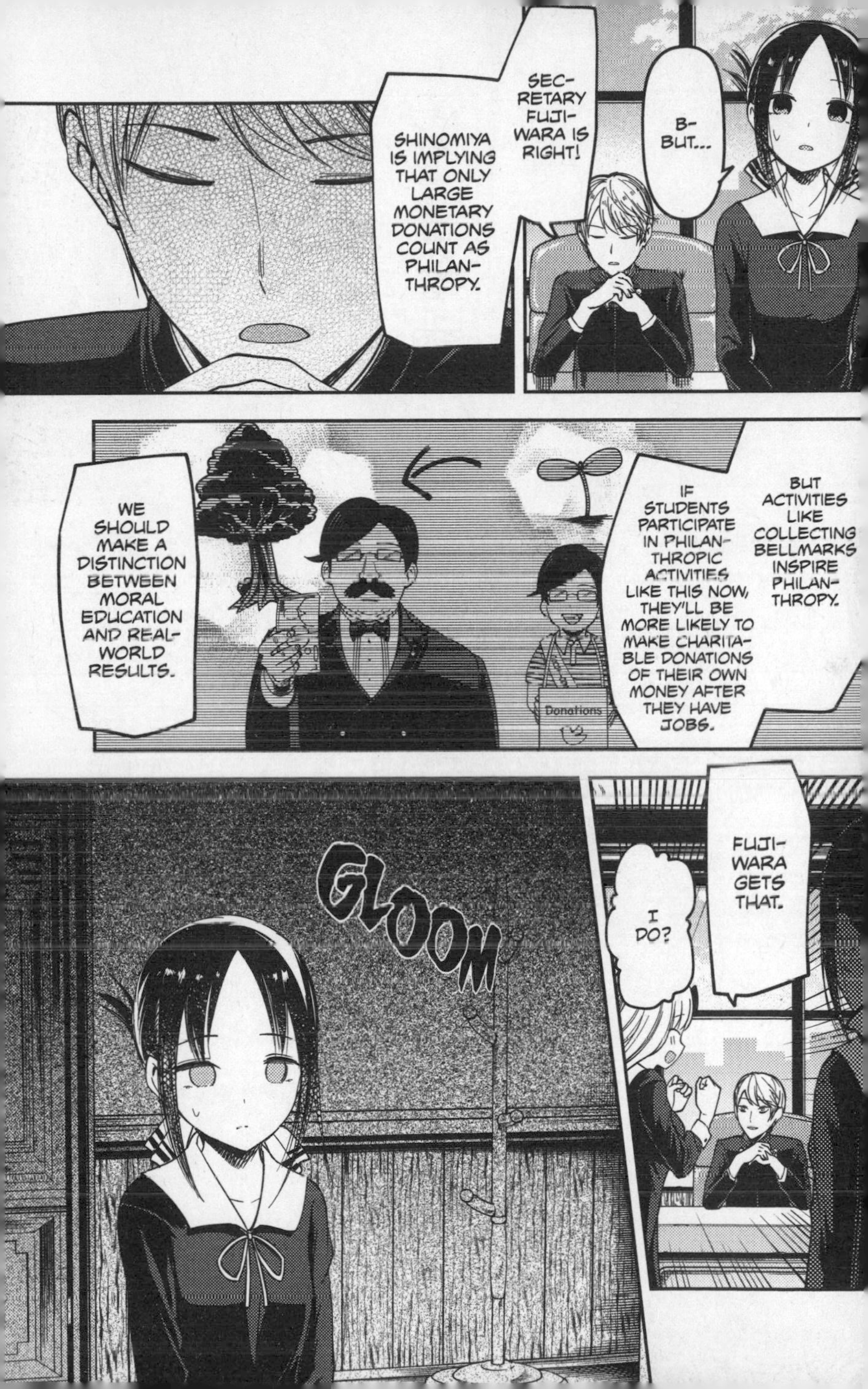
B-BUT...
SECRETARY FUJIWARA IS RIGHT!
SHINOMIYA IS IMPLYING THAT ONLY LARGE MONETARY DONATIONS COUNT AS PHILANTHROPY.
BUT ACTIVITIES LIKE COLLECTING BELLMARKS INSPIRE PHILANTHROPY.
IF STUDENTS PARTICIPATE IN PHILANTHROPIC ACTIVITIES LIKE THIS NOW, THEY'LL BE MORE LIKELY TO MAKE CHARITABLE DONATIONS OF THEIR OWN MONEY AFTER THEY HAVE JOBS.
Donations
WE SHOULD MAKE A DISTINCTION BETWEEN MORAL EDUCATION AND REAL-WORLD RESULTS.
FUJIWARA GETS THAT.
I DO?
GLOOM

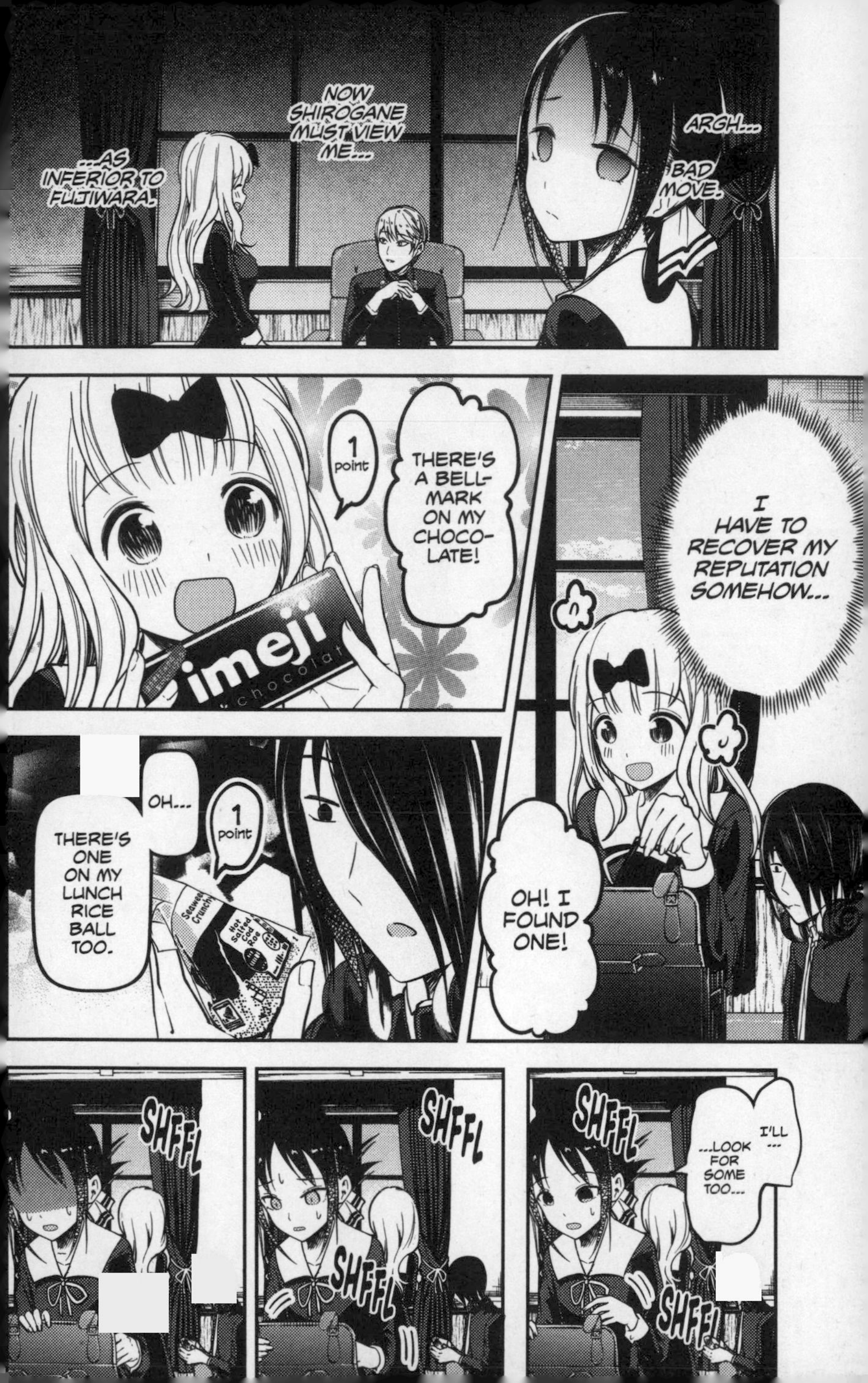
ARGH...
BAD MOVE.
NOW SHIROGANE MUST VIEW ME...
...AS INFERIOR TO FUJIWARA.
I HAVE TO RECOVER MY REPUTATION SOMEHOW...
OH! I FOUND ONE!
1 point
THERE'S A BELL-MARK ON MY CHOCOLATE!
imeji
1 point
OH...
THERE'S ONE ON MY LUNCH RICE BALL TOO.
Seaweed Crunchy
Hot Salted Cod Roe
SHFFL
I'LL...
...LOOK FOR SOME TOO...
SHFFL
SHFFL
SHFFL
SHFFL

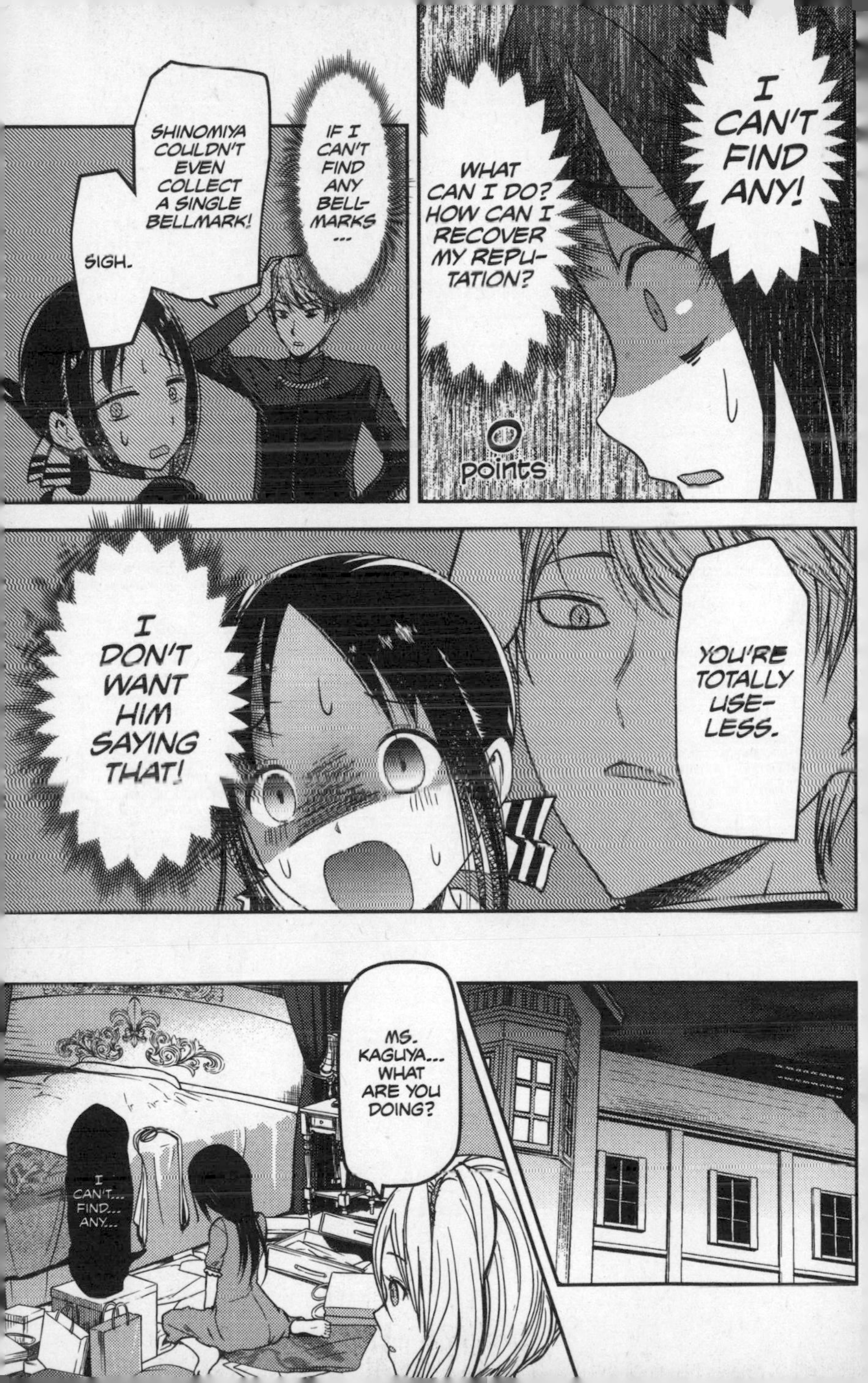
I CAN'T FIND ANY!
WHAT CAN I DO? HOW CAN I RECOVER MY REPUTATION?
0 points
IF I CAN'T FIND ANY BELL-MARKS...
SHINOMIYA COULDN'T EVEN COLLECT A SINGLE BELLMARK!
SIGH.
YOU'RE TOTALLY USE-LESS.
I DON'T WANT HIM SAYING THAT!
MS. KAGUYA... WHAT ARE YOU DOING?
I CAN'T... FIND... ANY...

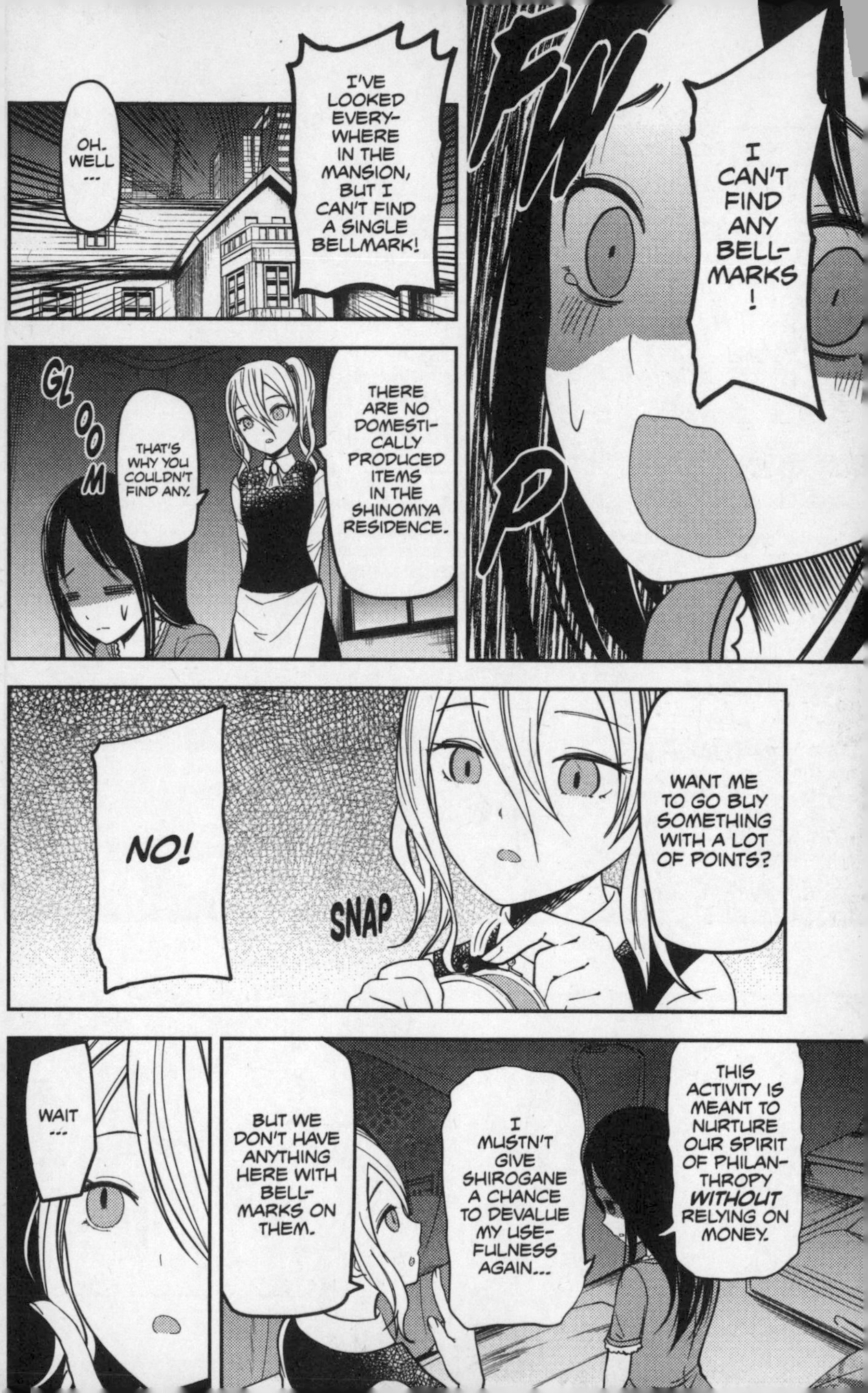
I CAN'T FIND ANY BELL-MARKS!
I'VE LOOKED EVERY-WHERE IN THE MANSION, BUT I CAN'T FIND A SINGLE BELLMARK!
OH. WELL ---
THERE ARE NO DOMESTI-CALLY PRODUCED ITEMS IN THE SHINOMIYA RESIDENCE.
THAT'S WHY YOU COULDN'T FIND ANY.
GLOOM
WANT ME TO GO BUY SOMETHING WITH A LOT OF POINTS?
SNAP
NO!
THIS ACTIVITY IS MEANT TO NURTURE OUR SPIRIT OF PHILAN-THROPY WITHOUT RELYING ON MONEY.
I MUSTN'T GIVE SHIROGANE A CHANCE TO DEVALUE MY USE-FULNESS AGAIN...
BUT WE DON'T HAVE ANYTHING HERE WITH BELL-MARKS ON THEM.
WAIT ---

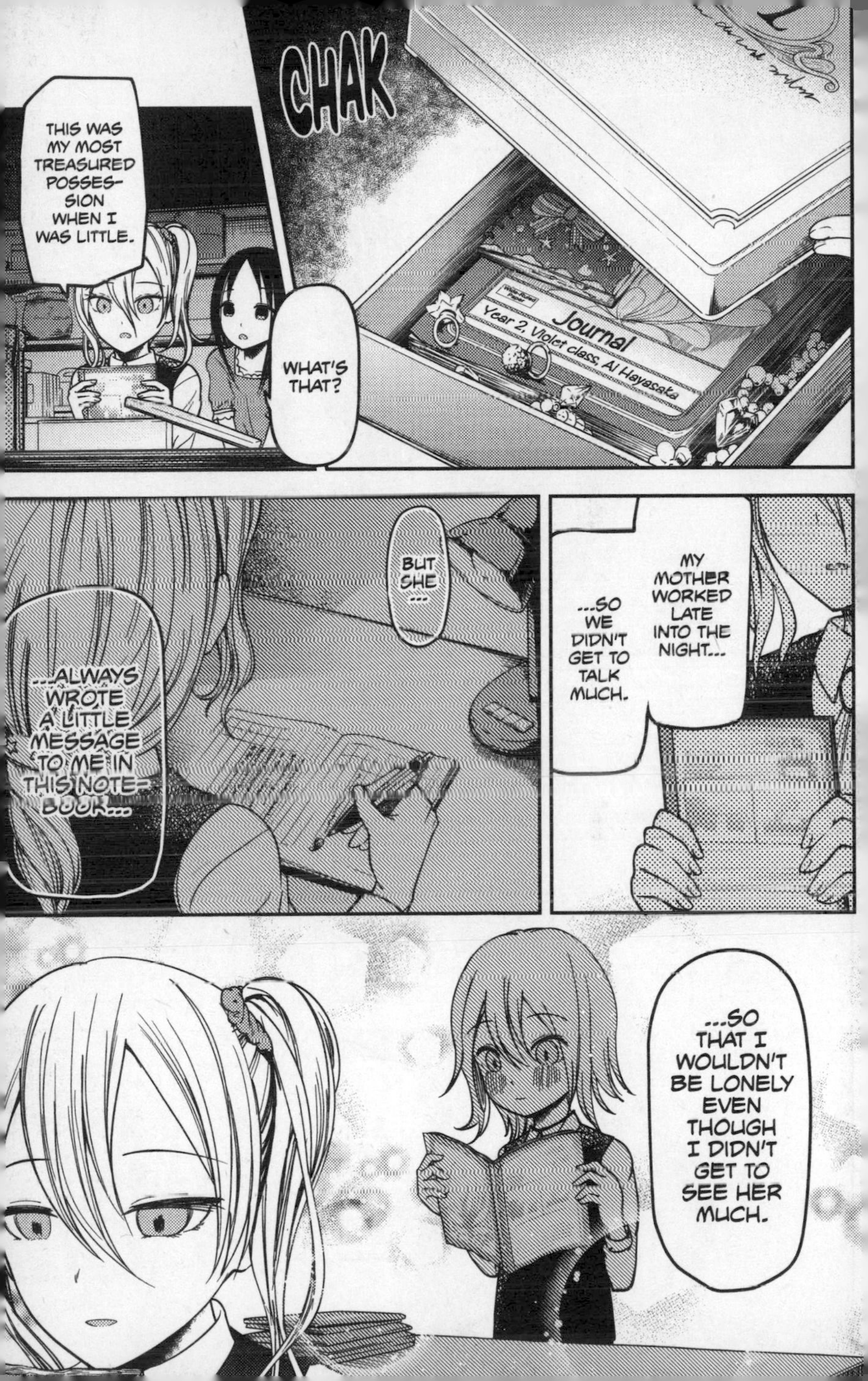
CHAK
Journal
Year 2, Violet class, Ai Hayasaka
THIS WAS MY MOST TREASURED POSSESSION WHEN I WAS LITTLE.
WHAT'S THAT?
MY MOTHER WORKED LATE INTO THE NIGHT...
...SO WE DIDN'T GET TO TALK MUCH.
BUT SHE...
...ALWAYS WROTE A LITTLE MESSAGE TO ME IN THIS NOTEBOOK...
...SO THAT I WOULDN'T BE LONELY EVEN THOUGH I DIDN'T GET TO SEE HER MUCH.

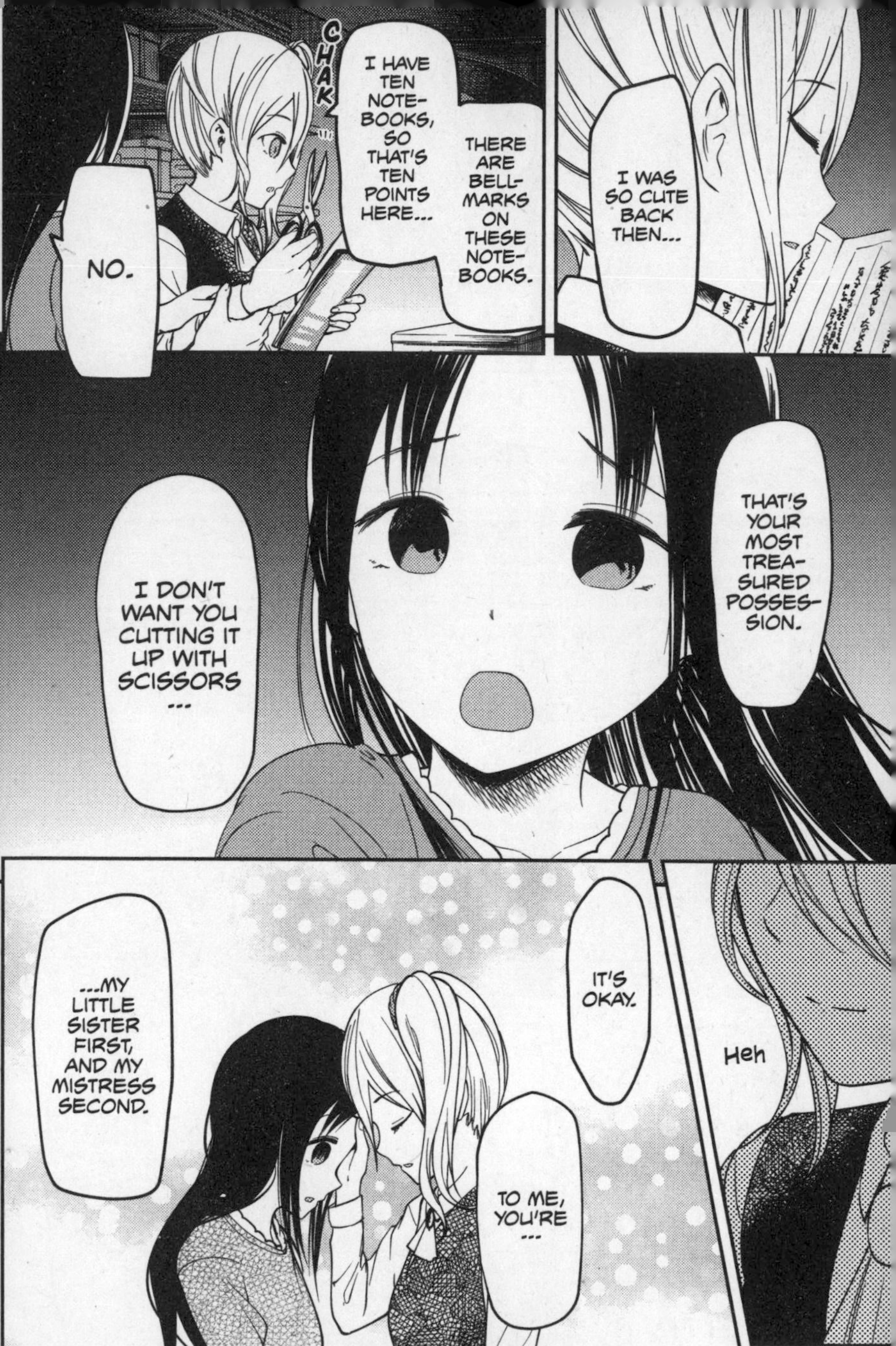
I WAS SO CUTE BACK THEN...
CHAK
THERE ARE BELL-MARKS ON THESE NOTE-BOOKS.
I HAVE TEN NOTE-BOOKS, SO THAT'S TEN POINTS HERE...
NO.
THAT'S YOUR MOST TREA-SURED POSSES-SION.
I DON'T WANT YOU CUTTING IT UP WITH SCISSORS ...
Heh
IT'S OKAY.
TO ME, YOU'RE ...
...MY LITTLE SISTER FIRST, AND MY MISTRESS SECOND.

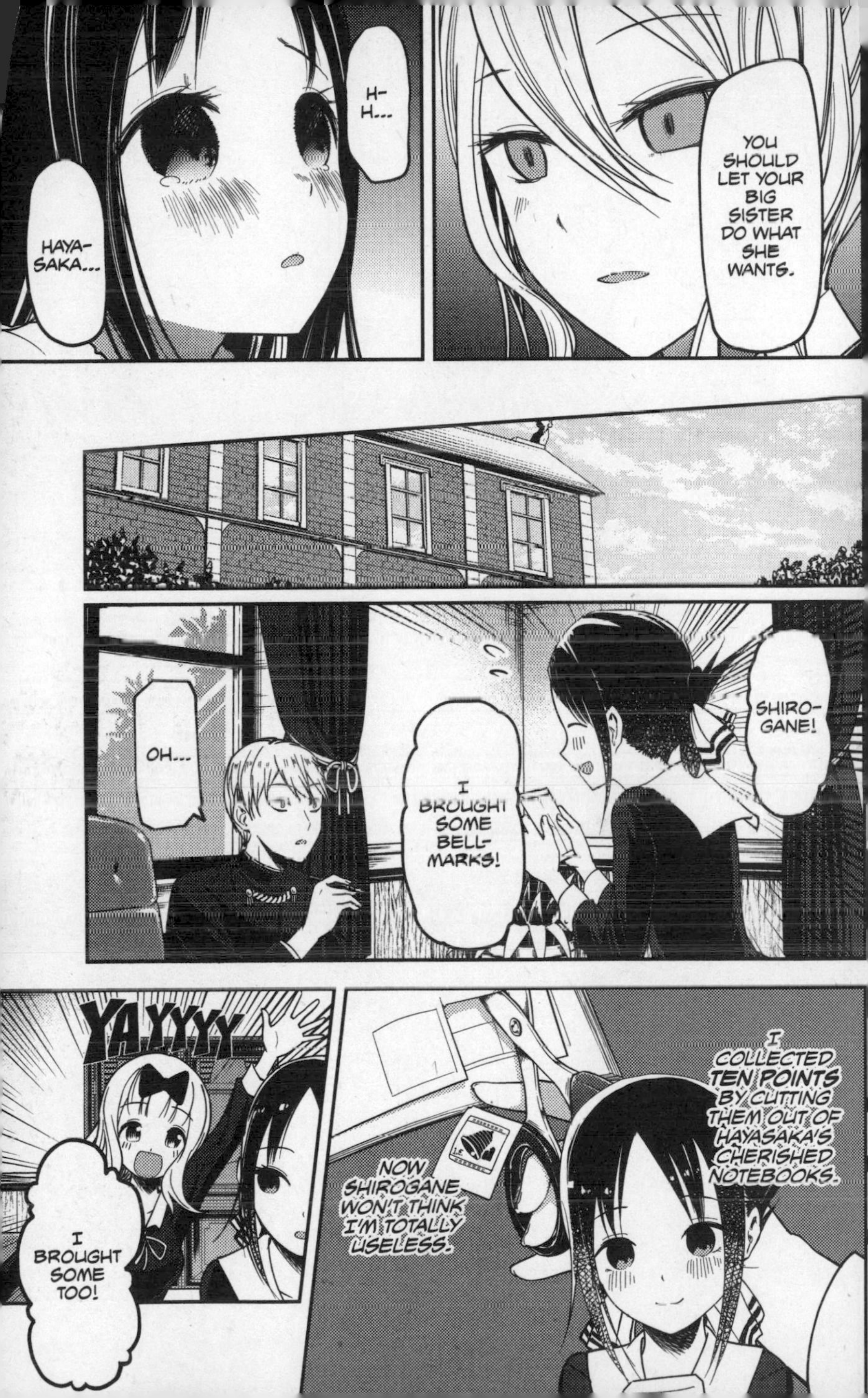
YOU SHOULD LET YOUR BIG SISTER DO WHAT SHE WANTS.
H-H...
HAYA-SAKA...
SHIRO-GANE!
I BROUGHT SOME BELL-MARKS!
OH...
I COLLECTED TEN POINTS BY CUTTING THEM OUT OF HAYASAKA'S CHERISHED NOTEBOOKS.
NOW SHIROGANE WON'T THINK I'M TOTALLY USELESS.
YAYYYY
I BROUGHT SOME TOO!

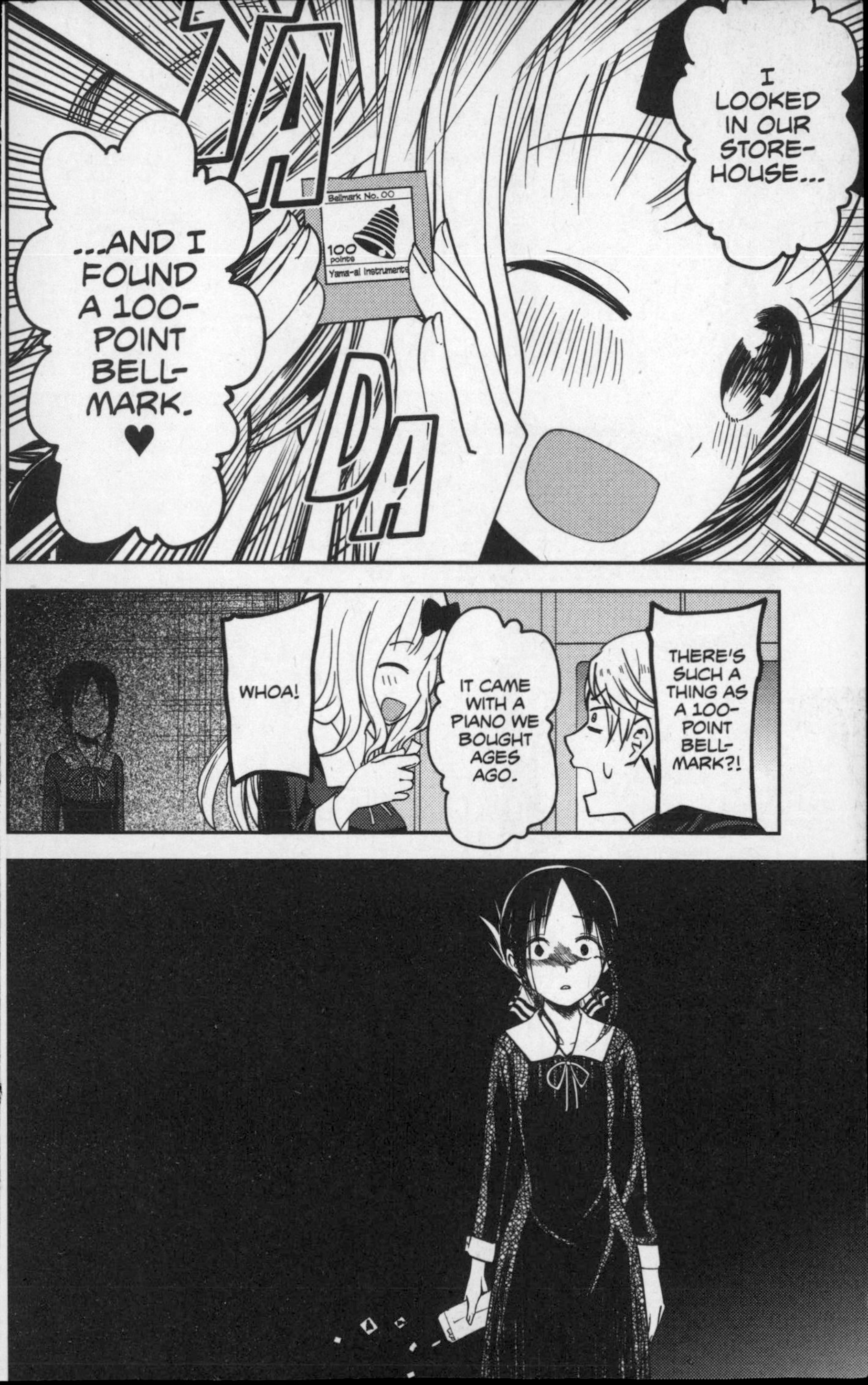
I LOOKED IN OUR STOREHOUSE...
Bellmark No. 00
100 points
Yama-ai Instruments
...AND I FOUND A 100-POINT BELLMARK. ♥
DA
THERE'S SUCH A THING AS A 100-POINT BELLMARK?!
IT CAME WITH A PIANO WE BOUGHT AGES AGO.
WHOA!

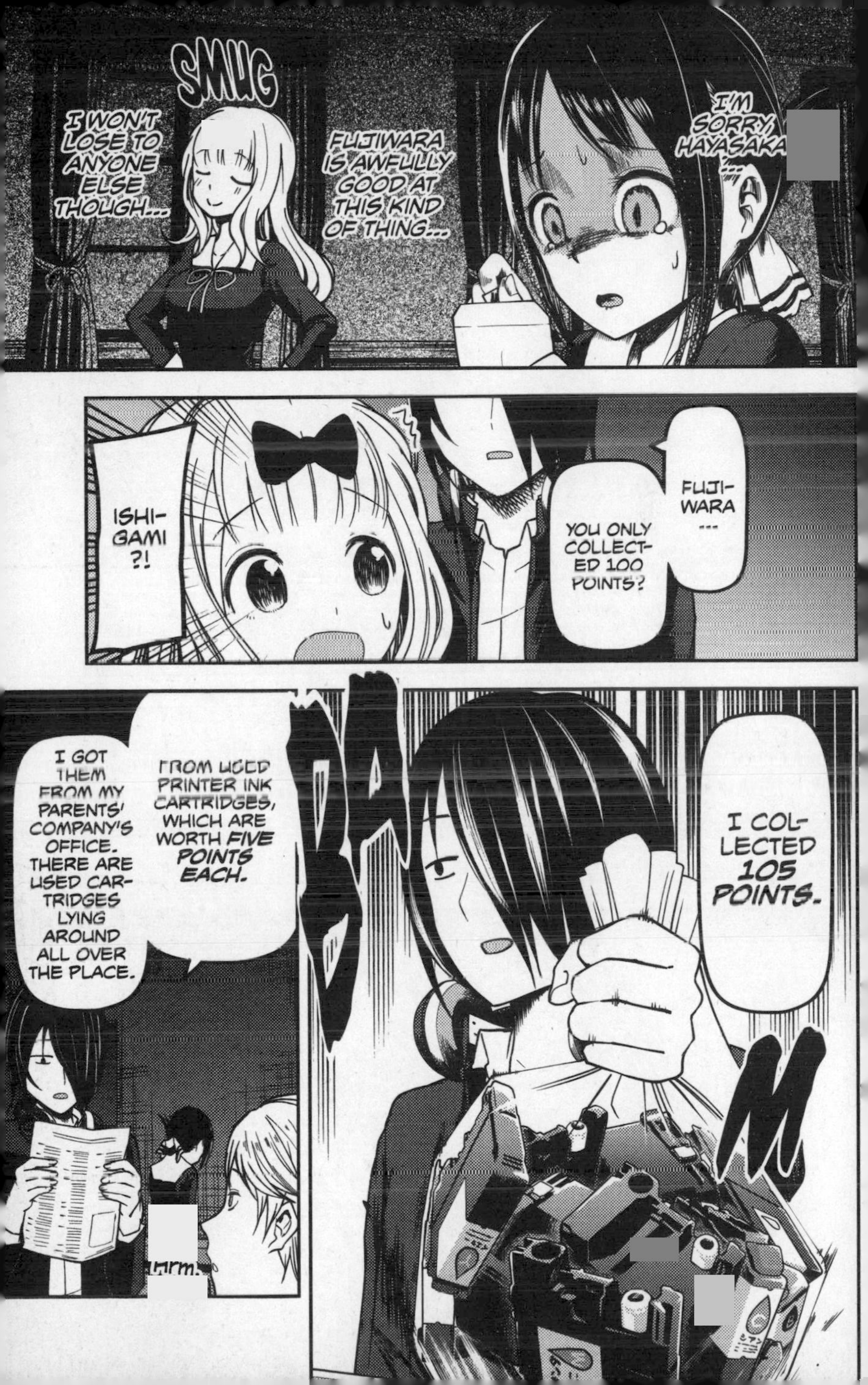
I'M SORRY, HAYASAKA...
FUJIWARA IS AWFULLY GOOD AT THIS KIND OF THING...
SMUG
I WON'T LOSE TO ANYONE ELSE THOUGH...
FUJI-WARA...
YOU ONLY COLLECT-ED 100 POINTS?
ISHI-GAMI?!
I COL-LECTED 105 POINTS.
FROM USED PRINTER INK CARTRIDGES, WHICH ARE WORTH FIVE POINTS EACH.
I GOT THEM FROM MY PARENTS' COMPANY'S OFFICE. THERE ARE USED CAR-TRIDGES LYING AROUND ALL OVER THE PLACE.
Hrm.

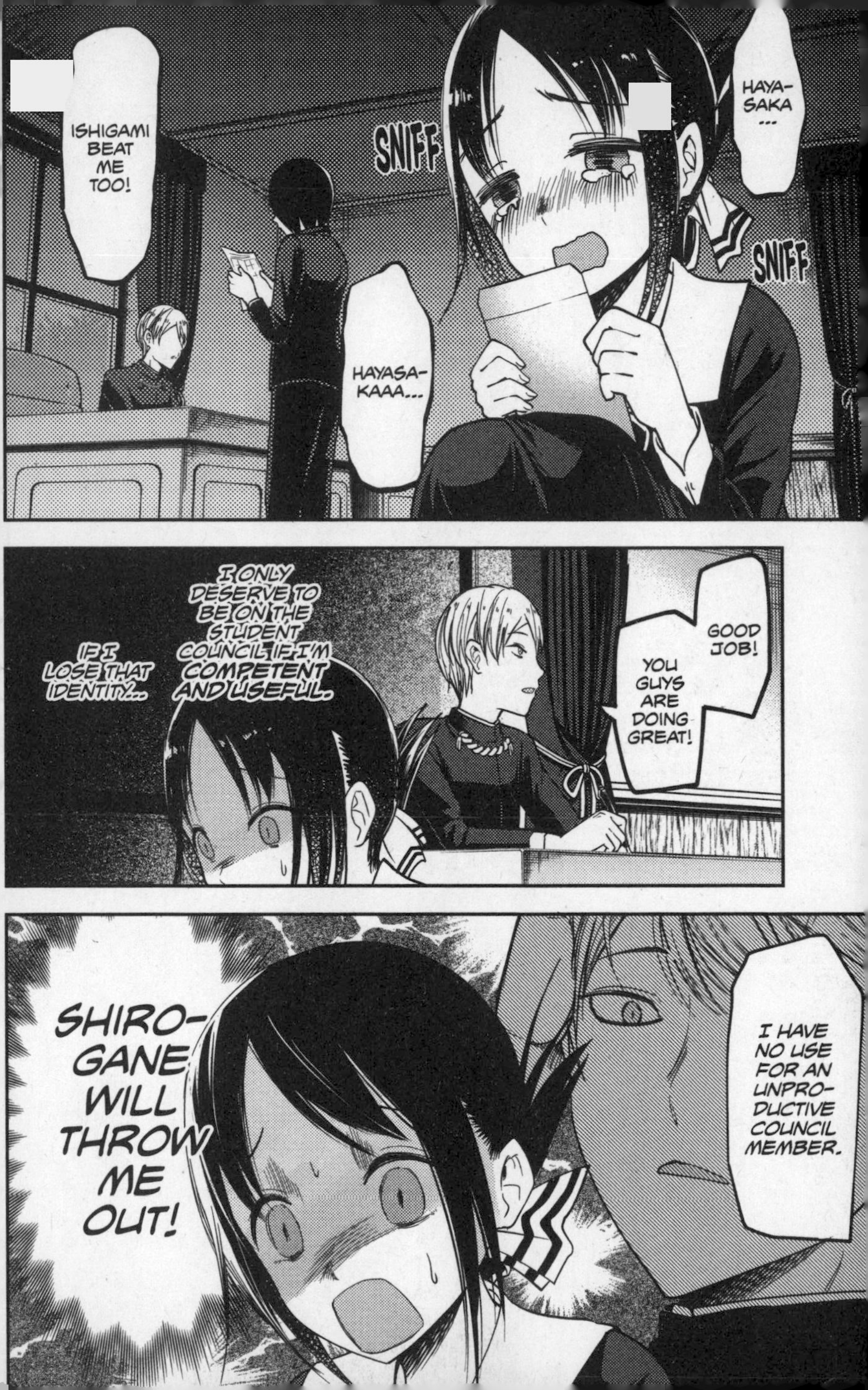
HAYA-SAKA...
SNIFF
SNIFF
ISHIGAMI BEAT ME TOO!
HAYASA-KAAA...
GOOD JOB!
YOU GUYS ARE DOING GREAT!
I ONLY DESERVE TO BE ON THE STUDENT COUNCIL IF I'M COMPETENT AND USEFUL.
IF I LOSE THAT IDENTITY...
I HAVE NO USE FOR AN UNPRO-DUCTIVE COUNCIL MEMBER.
SHIRO-GANE WILL THROW ME OUT!

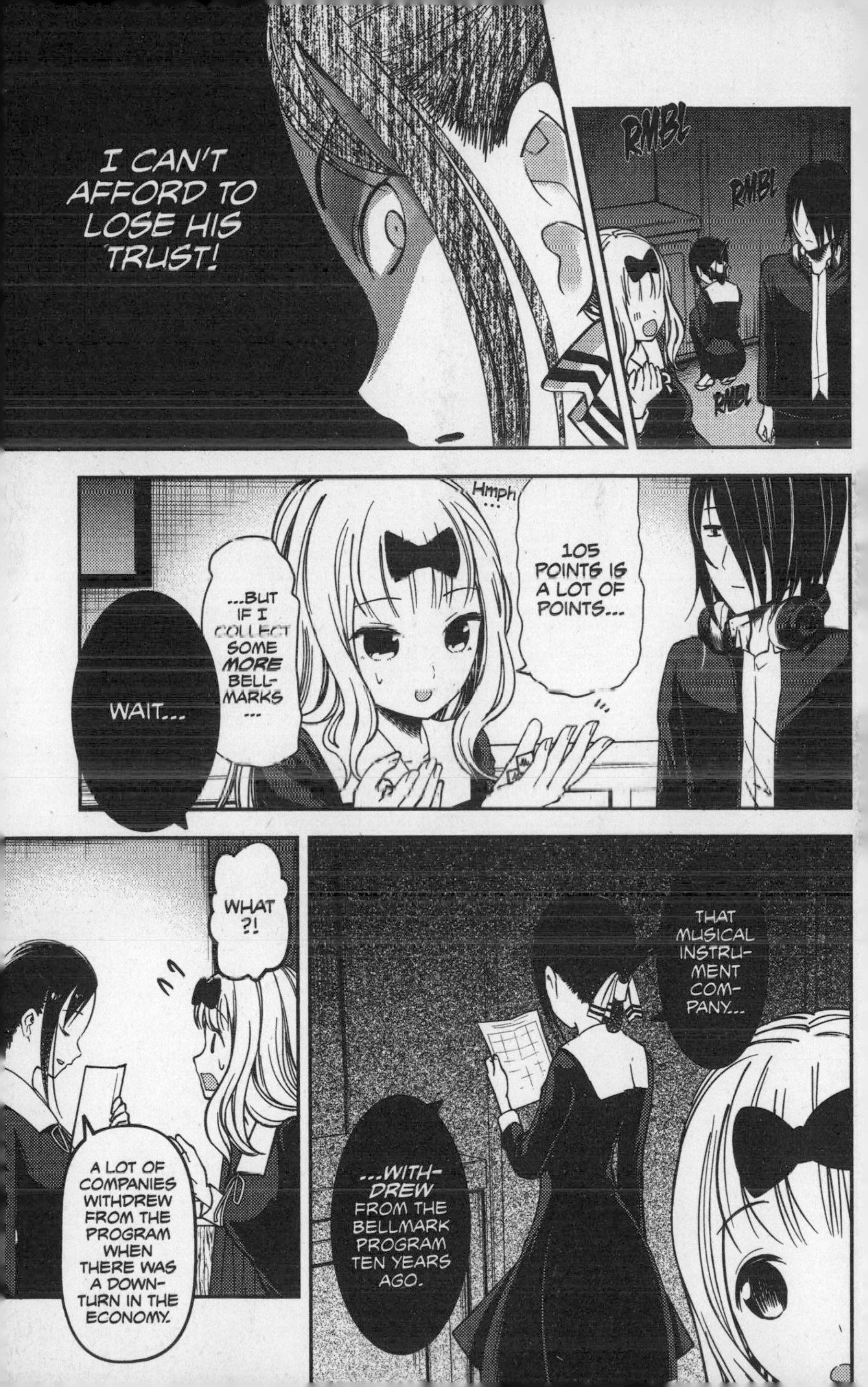
RMBL
RMBL
RMBL
I CAN'T AFFORD TO LOSE HIS TRUST!
Hmph...
105 POINTS IS A LOT OF POINTS...
...BUT IF I COLLECT SOME MORE BELL-MARKS...
WAIT...
THAT MUSICAL INSTRU-MENT COM-PANY...
...WITH-DREW FROM THE BELLMARK PROGRAM TEN YEARS AGO.
WHAT?!
A LOT OF COMPANIES WITHDREW FROM THE PROGRAM WHEN THERE WAS A DOWN-TURN IN THE ECONOMY.

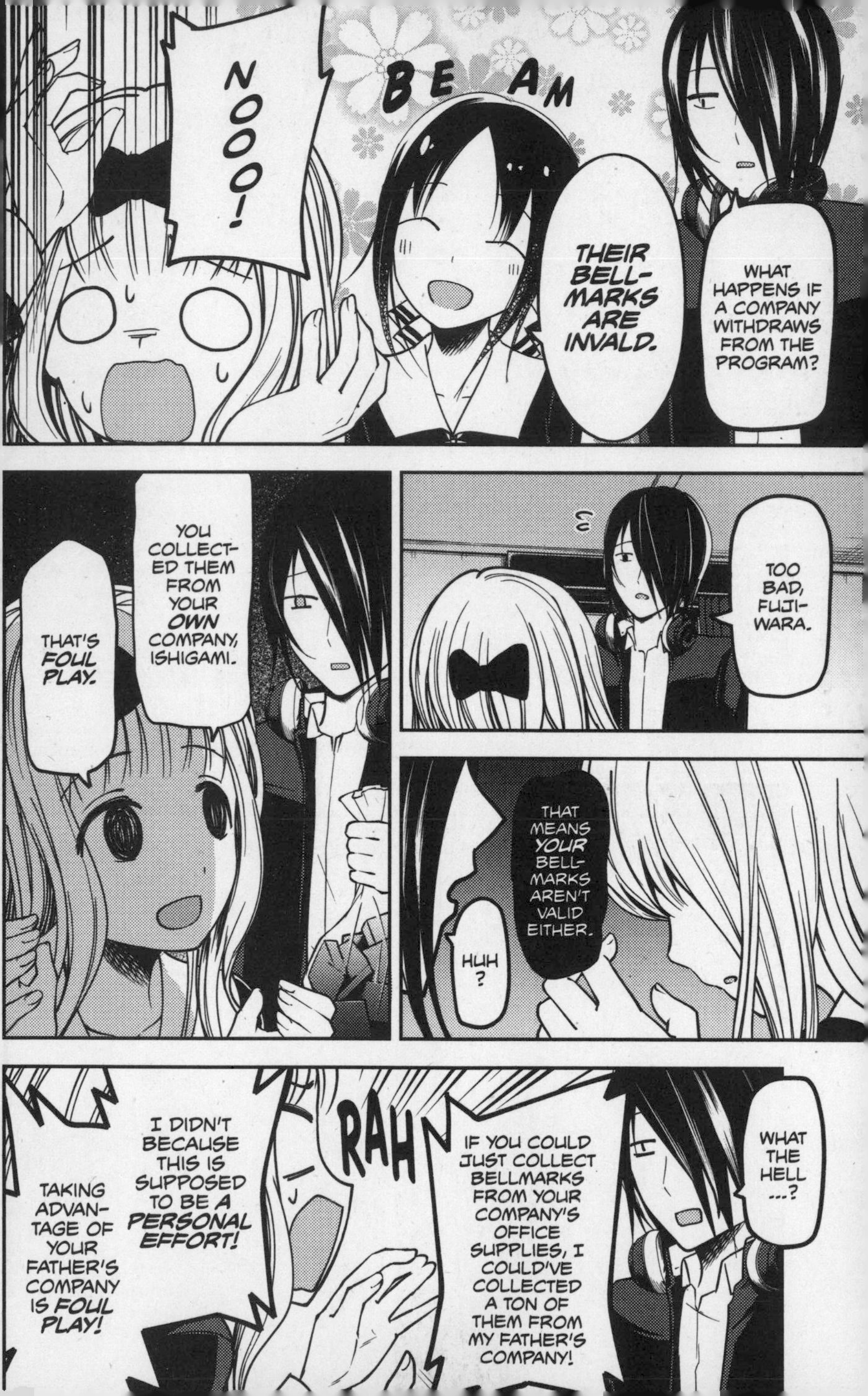
WHAT HAPPENS IF A COMPANY WITHDRAWS FROM THE PROGRAM?
THEIR BELLMARKS ARE INVALD.
BE AM
NOOOO!
TOO BAD, FUJIWARA.
THAT MEANS YOUR BELLMARKS AREN'T VALID EITHER.
HUH?
YOU COLLECTED THEM FROM YOUR OWN COMPANY, ISHIGAMI.
THAT'S FOUL PLAY.
WHAT THE HELL...?
IF YOU COULD JUST COLLECT BELLMARKS FROM YOUR COMPANY'S OFFICE SUPPLIES, I COULD'VE COLLECTED A TON OF THEM FROM MY FATHER'S COMPANY!
RAH
I DIDN'T BECAUSE THIS IS SUPPOSED TO BE A PERSONAL EFFORT!
TAKING ADVANTAGE OF YOUR FATHER'S COMPANY IS FOUL PLAY!

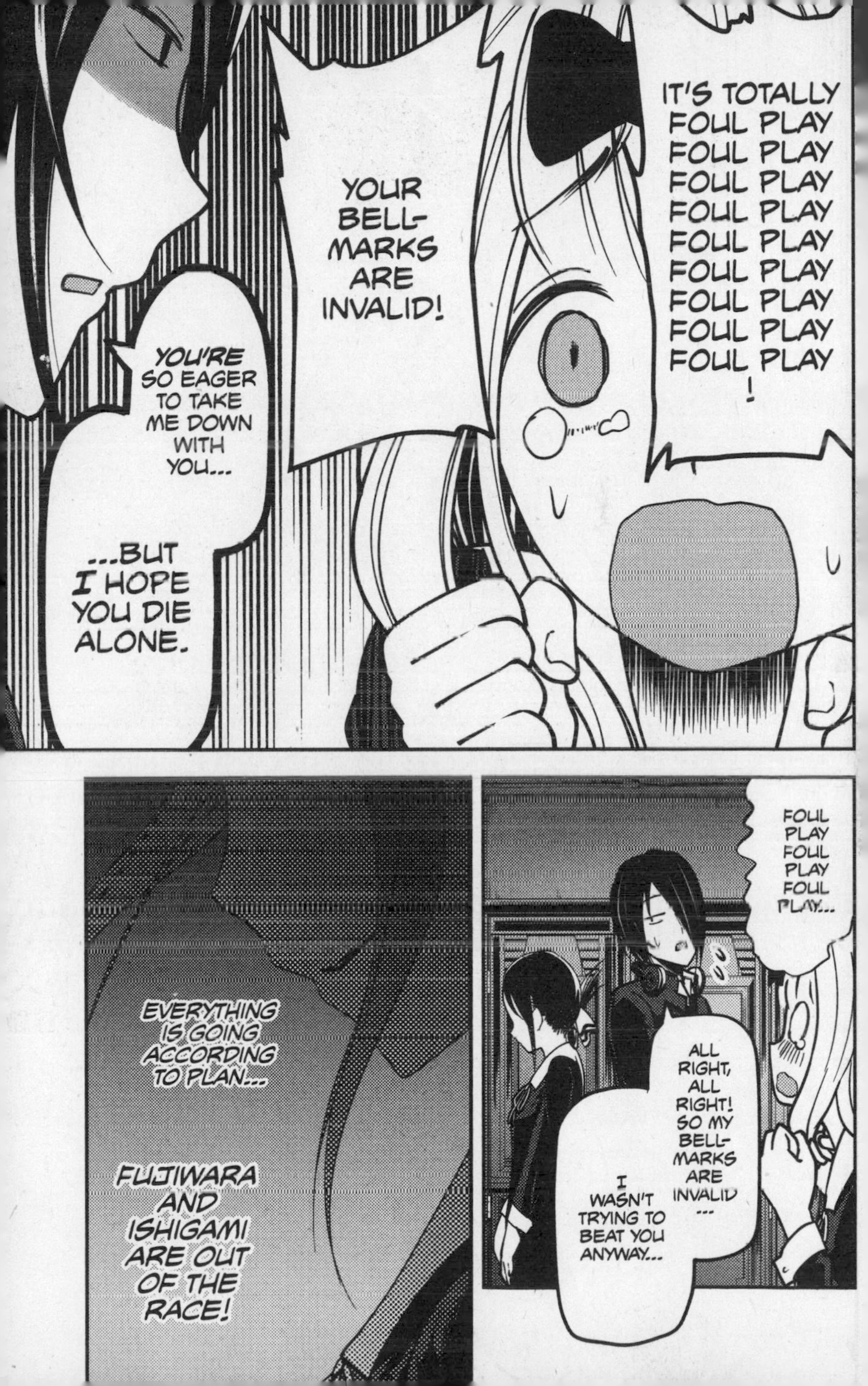
IT'S TOTALLY FOUL PLAY FOUL PLAY FOUL PLAY FOUL PLAY FOUL PLAY FOUL PLAY FOUL PLAY FOUL PLAY FOUL PLAY!
YOUR BELL-MARKS ARE INVALID!
YOU'RE SO EAGER TO TAKE ME DOWN WITH YOU...
...BUT I HOPE YOU DIE ALONE.
FOUL PLAY FOUL PLAY FOUL PLAY...
ALL RIGHT, ALL RIGHT! SO MY BELL-MARKS ARE INVALID...
I WASN'T TRYING TO BEAT YOU ANYWAY...
EVERYTHING IS GOING ACCORDING TO PLAN...
FUJIWARA AND ISHIGAMI ARE OUT OF THE RACE!

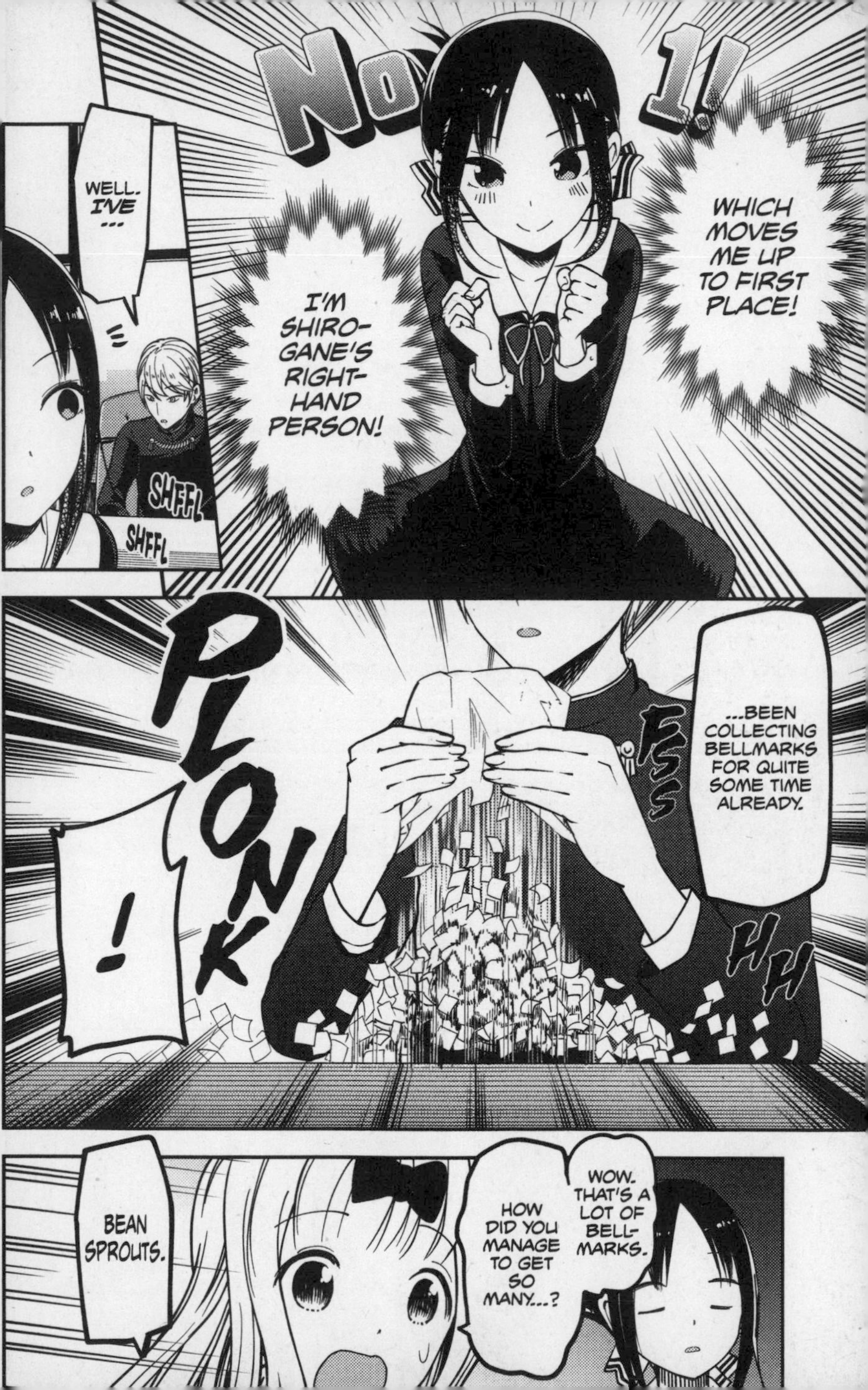
No. 1!
WHICH MOVES ME UP TO FIRST PLACE!
I'M SHIRO-GANE'S RIGHT-HAND PERSON!
WELL, I'VE...
SHFFL
SHFFL
...BEEN COLLECTING BELLMARKS FOR QUITE SOME TIME ALREADY.
FSS
PLONK
HH
!
WOW. THAT'S A LOT OF BELL-MARKS.
HOW DID YOU MANAGE TO GET SO MANY...?
BEAN SPROUTS.

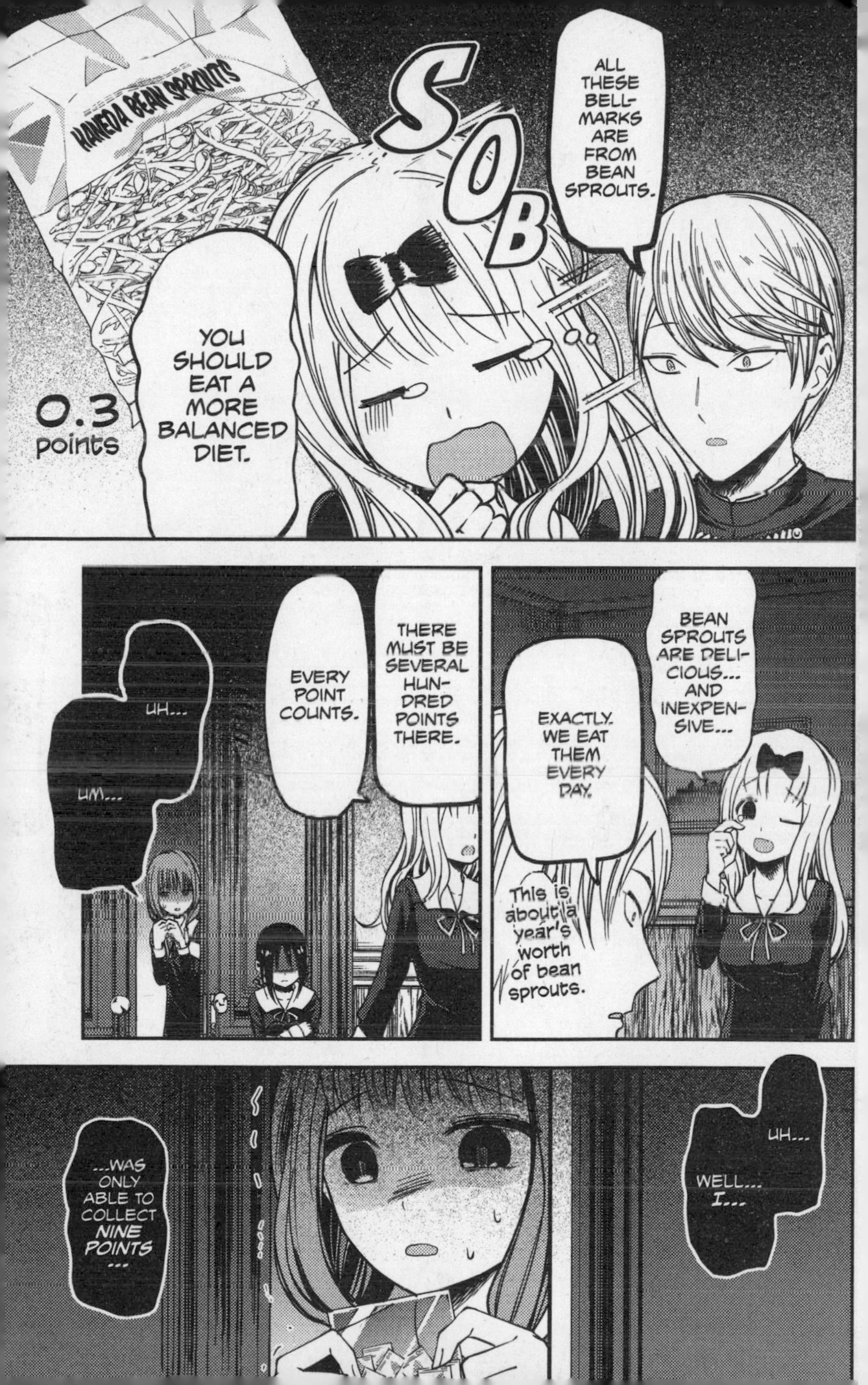
ALL THESE BELL-MARKS ARE FROM BEAN SPROUTS.
SOB
HANEDA BEAN SPROUTS
YOU SHOULD EAT A MORE BALANCED DIET.
0.3 points
BEAN SPROUTS ARE DELICIOUS... AND INEXPENSIVE...
EXACTLY. WE EAT THEM EVERY DAY.
This is about a year's worth of bean sprouts.
THERE MUST BE SEVERAL HUNDRED POINTS THERE.
EVERY POINT COUNTS.
UH...
UM...
UH... WELL... I...
...WAS ONLY ABLE TO COLLECT NINE POINTS...

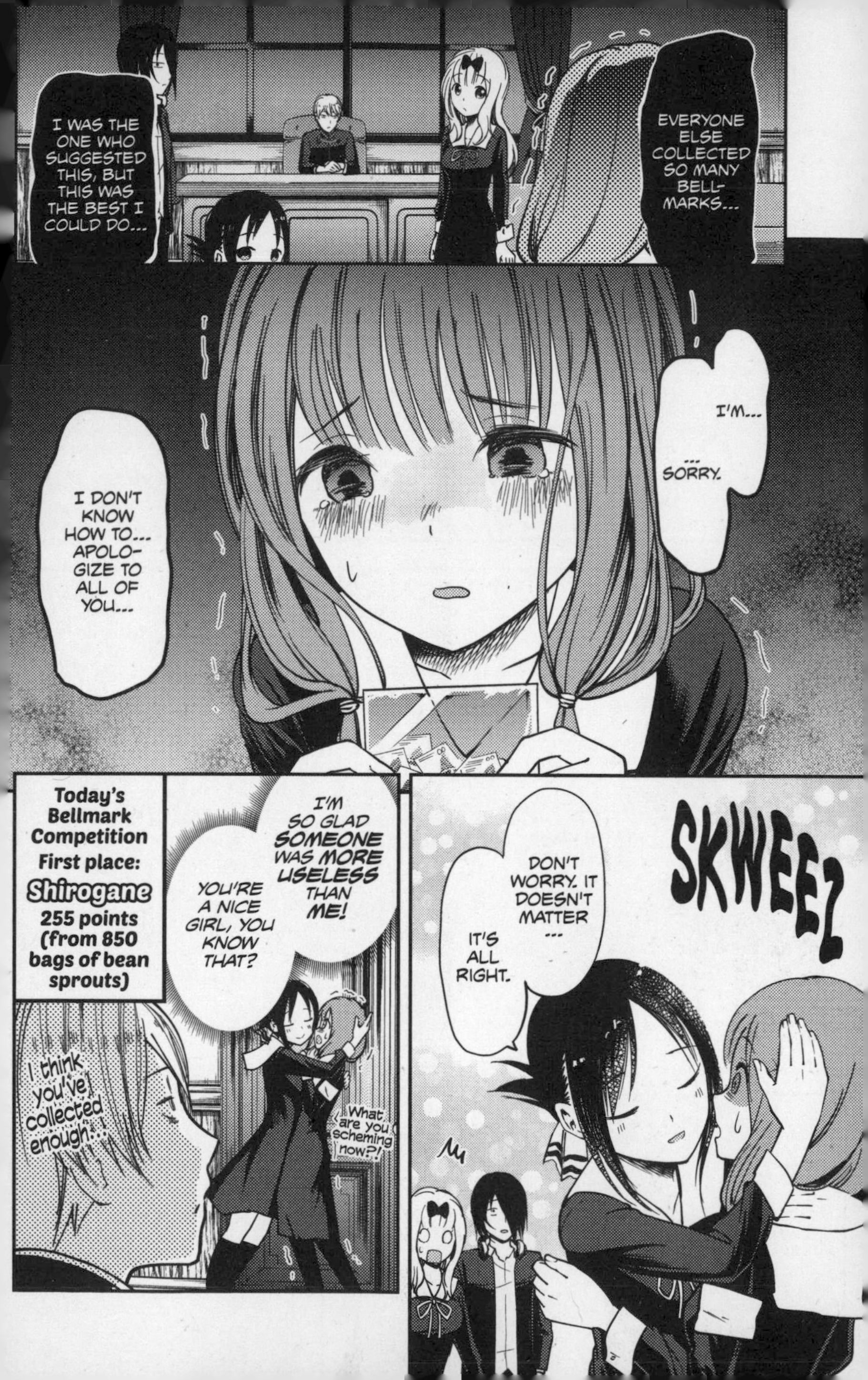
EVERYONE ELSE COLLECTED SO MANY BELL-MARKS...
I WAS THE ONE WHO SUGGESTED THIS, BUT THIS WAS THE BEST I COULD DO...
I'M... ...SORRY.
I DON'T KNOW HOW TO... APOLOGIZE TO ALL OF YOU...
SKWEEZ
DON'T WORRY. IT DOESN'T MATTER...
IT'S ALL RIGHT.
I'M SO GLAD SOMEONE WAS MORE USELESS THAN ME!
YOU'RE A NICE GIRL, YOU KNOW THAT?
What are you scheming now?!
I think you've collected enough...
Today's Bellmark Competition First place: Shirogane 255 points (from 850 bags of bean sprouts)

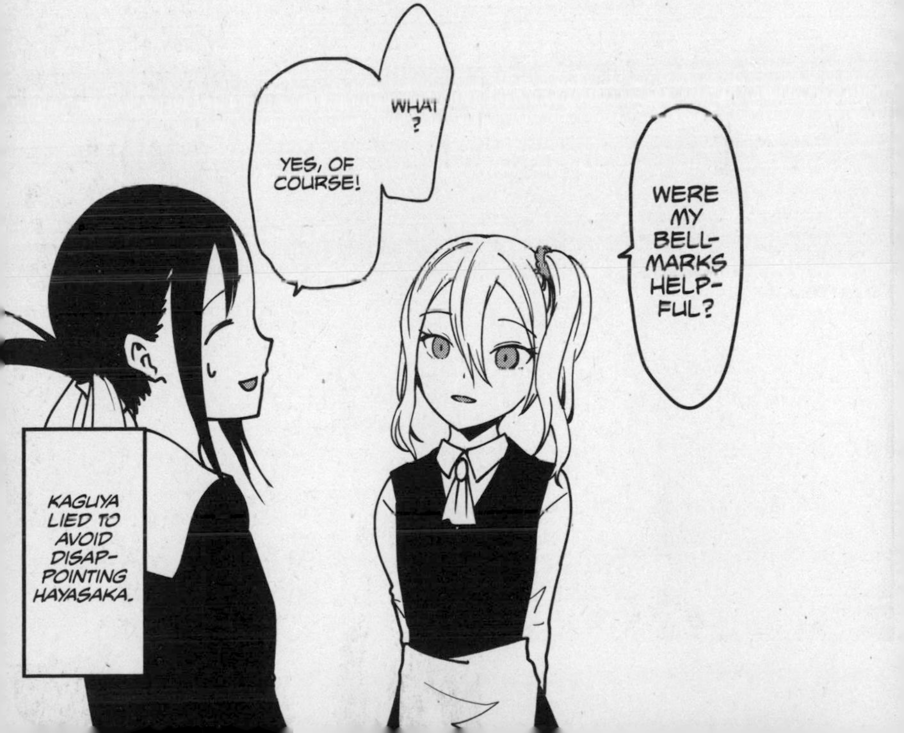
WERE MY BELL-MARKS HELPFUL?
WHAT?
YES, OF COURSE!
KAGUYA LIED TO AVOID DISAPPOINTING HAYASAKA.

KAGUYA-SAMA
LOVE IS WAR

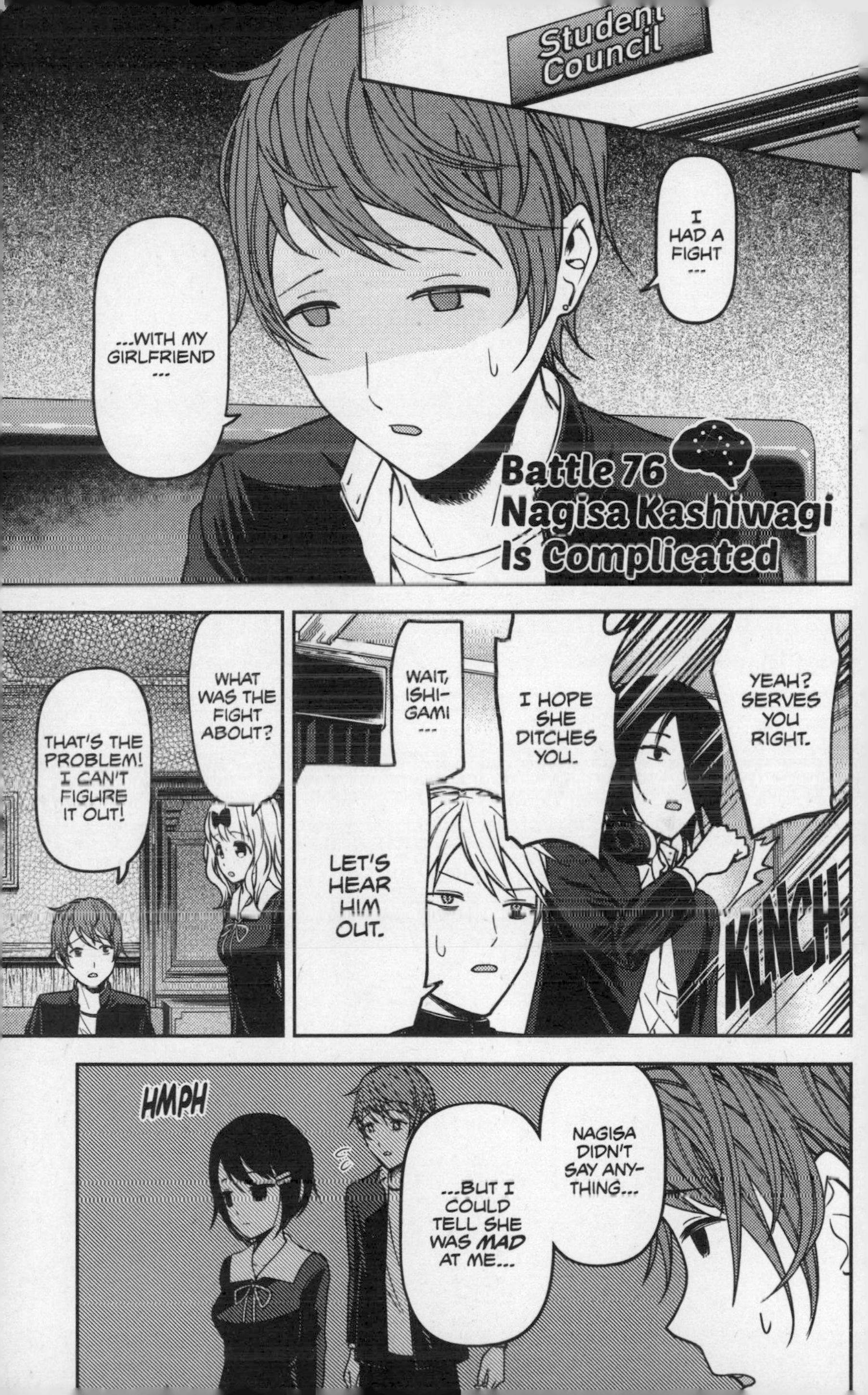
Student Council
I HAD A FIGHT ...
...WITH MY GIRLFRIEND ...
Battle 76 Nagisa Kashiwagi Is Complicated
YEAH? SERVES YOU RIGHT.
I HOPE SHE DITCHES YOU.
WAIT, ISHIGAMI ...
LET'S HEAR HIM OUT.
WHAT WAS THE FIGHT ABOUT?
THAT'S THE PROBLEM! I CAN'T FIGURE IT OUT!
NAGISA DIDN'T SAY ANYTHING...
...BUT I COULD TELL SHE WAS MAD AT ME...
HMPH

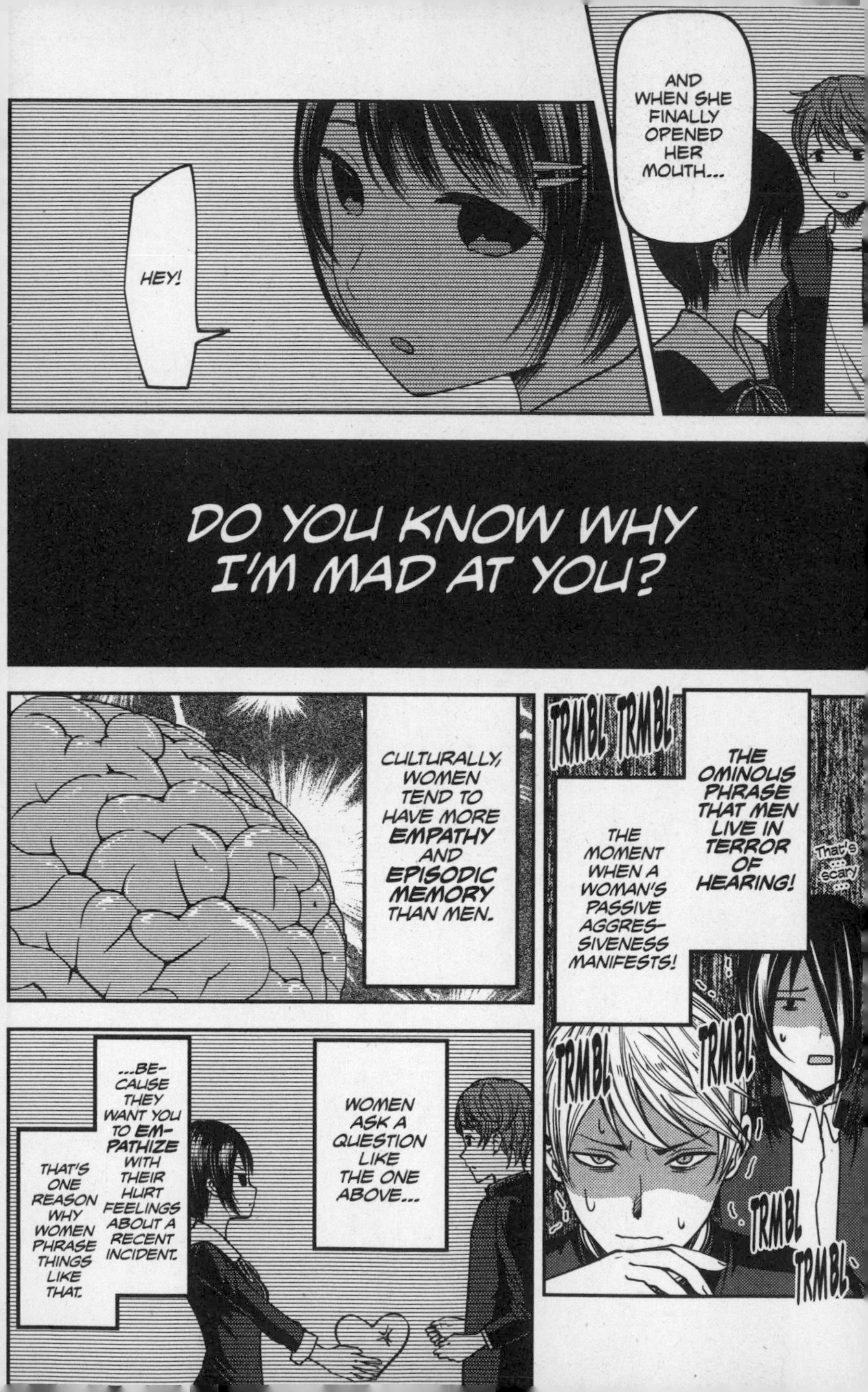
AND WHEN SHE FINALLY OPENED HER MOUTH...
HEY!
DO YOU KNOW WHY I'M MAD AT YOU?
TRMBL TRMBL
THE OMINOUS PHRASE THAT MEN LIVE IN TERROR OF HEARING!
THE MOMENT WHEN A WOMAN'S PASSIVE AGGRESSIVENESS MANIFESTS!
That's scary...
TRMBL
TRMBL
TRMBL
TRMBL
CULTURALLY, WOMEN TEND TO HAVE MORE EMPATHY AND EPISODIC MEMORY THAN MEN.
WOMEN ASK A QUESTION LIKE THE ONE ABOVE...
...BECAUSE THEY WANT YOU TO EMPATHIZE WITH THEIR HURT FEELINGS ABOUT A RECENT INCIDENT.
THAT'S ONE REASON WHY WOMEN PHRASE THINGS LIKE THAT.

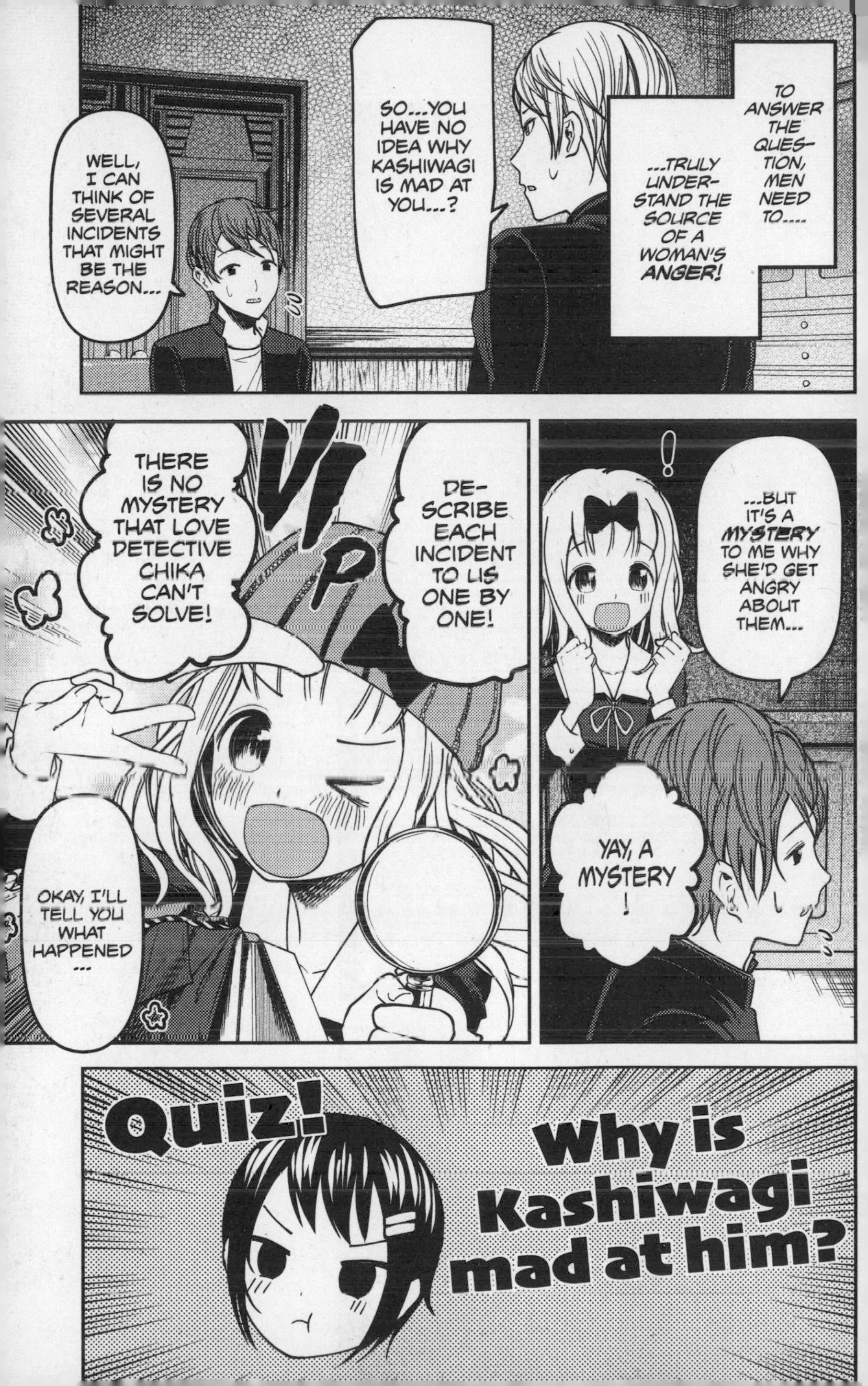
TO ANSWER THE QUESTION, MEN NEED TO...
...TRULY UNDERSTAND THE SOURCE OF A WOMAN'S ANGER!
SO...YOU HAVE NO IDEA WHY KASHIWAGI IS MAD AT YOU...?
WELL, I CAN THINK OF SEVERAL INCIDENTS THAT MIGHT BE THE REASON...
...BUT IT'S A MYSTERY TO ME WHY SHE'D GET ANGRY ABOUT THEM...
!
YAY, A MYSTERY!
DESCRIBE EACH INCIDENT TO US ONE BY ONE!
THERE IS NO MYSTERY THAT LOVE DETECTIVE CHIKA CAN'T SOLVE!
OKAY, I'LL TELL YOU WHAT HAPPENED...
Quiz!
Why is Kashiwagi mad at him?

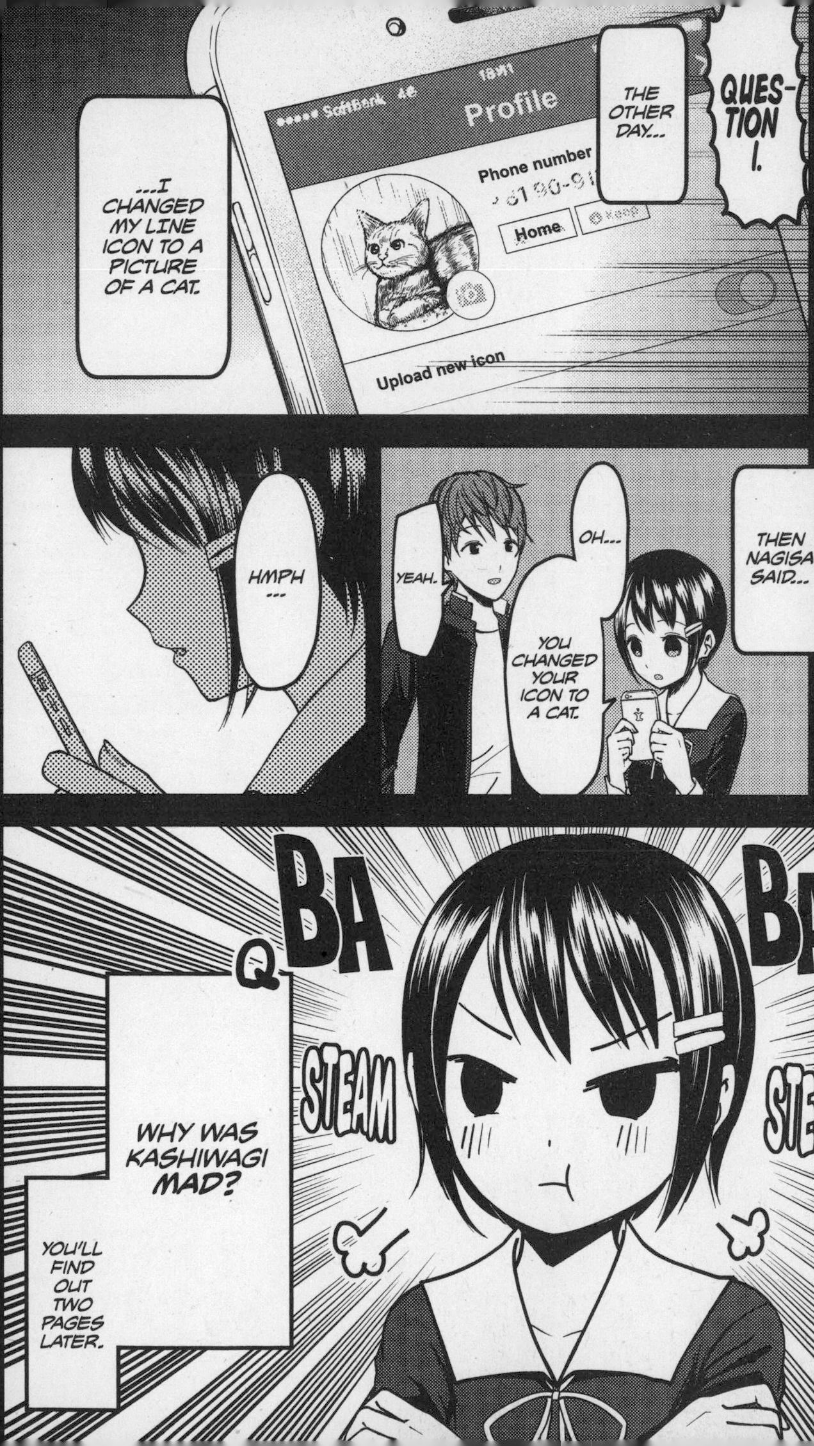
QUESTION 1.
THE OTHER DAY...
Profile
Phone number
Home
Upload new icon
...I CHANGED MY LINE ICON TO A PICTURE OF A CAT.
THEN NAGISA SAID...
OH...
YOU CHANGED YOUR ICON TO A CAT.
YEAH.
HMPH...
BA
BAM
Q
STEAM
STEAM
WHY WAS KASHIWAGI MAD?
YOU'LL FIND OUT TWO PAGES LATER.

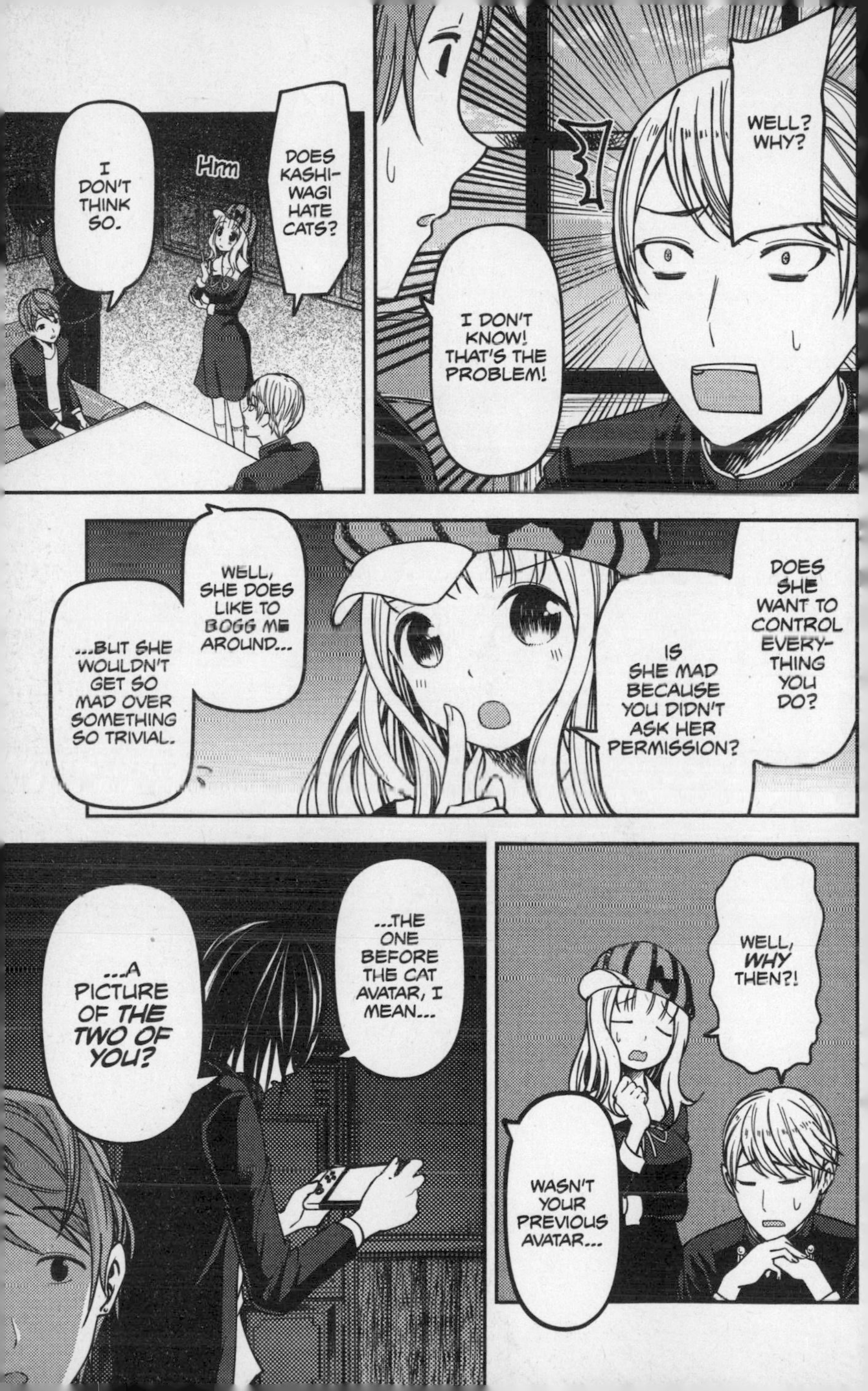
WELL? WHY?
I DON'T KNOW! THAT'S THE PROBLEM!
DOES KASHIWAGI HATE CATS?
Hrm
I DON'T THINK SO.
DOES SHE WANT TO CONTROL EVERYTHING YOU DO?
IS SHE MAD BECAUSE YOU DIDN'T ASK HER PERMISSION?
WELL, SHE DOES LIKE TO BOSS ME AROUND...
...BUT SHE WOULDN'T GET SO MAD OVER SOMETHING SO TRIVIAL.
WELL, *WHY* THEN?!
WASN'T YOUR PREVIOUS AVATAR...
...THE ONE BEFORE THE CAT AVATAR, I MEAN...
...A PICTURE OF *THE TWO OF YOU?*

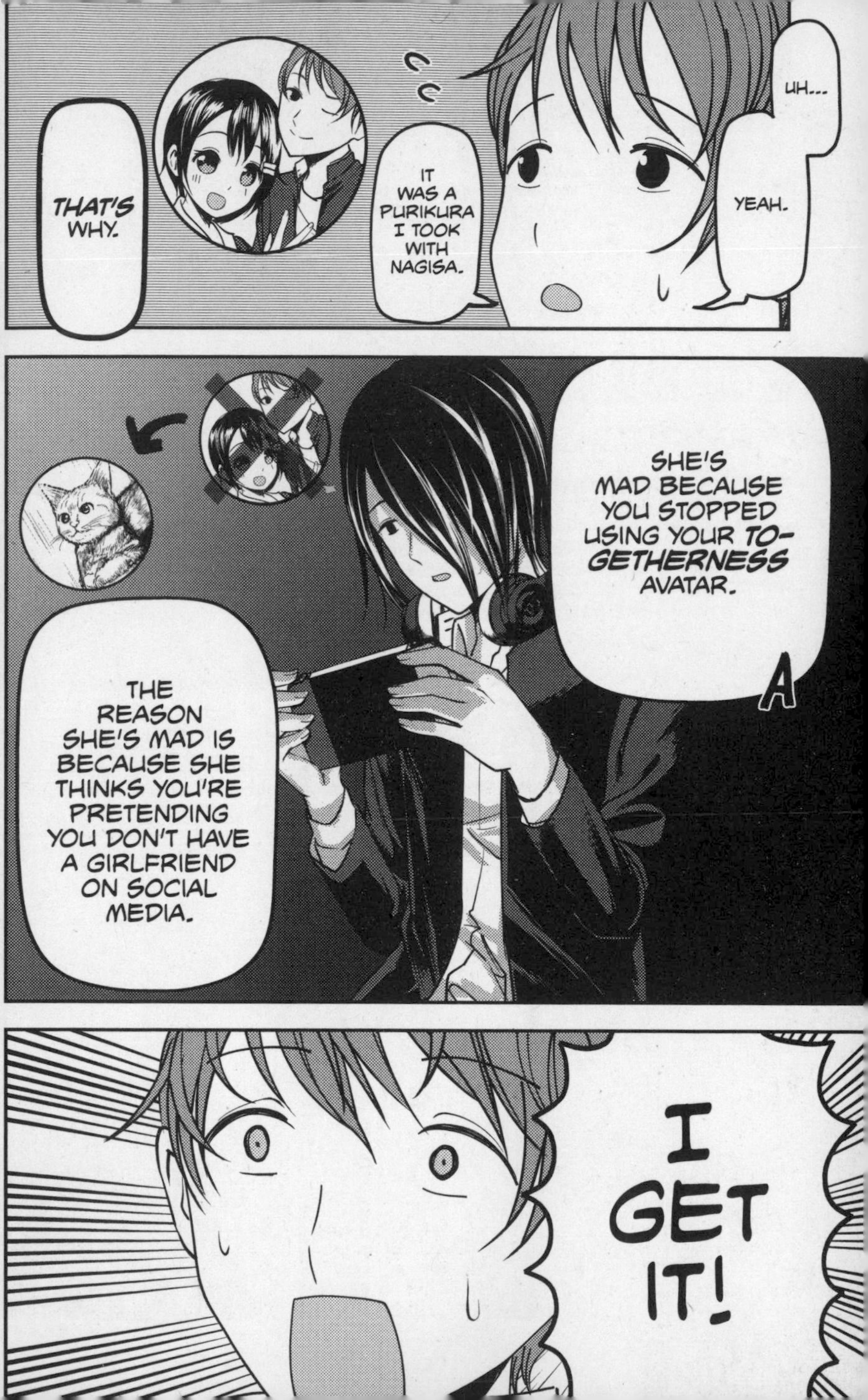
UH... YEAH.
IT WAS A PURIKURA I TOOK WITH NAGISA.
THAT'S WHY.
SHE'S MAD BECAUSE YOU STOPPED USING YOUR *TOGETHERNESS* AVATAR.
A
THE REASON SHE'S MAD IS BECAUSE SHE THINKS YOU'RE PRETENDING YOU DON'T HAVE A GIRLFRIEND ON SOCIAL MEDIA.
I GET IT!

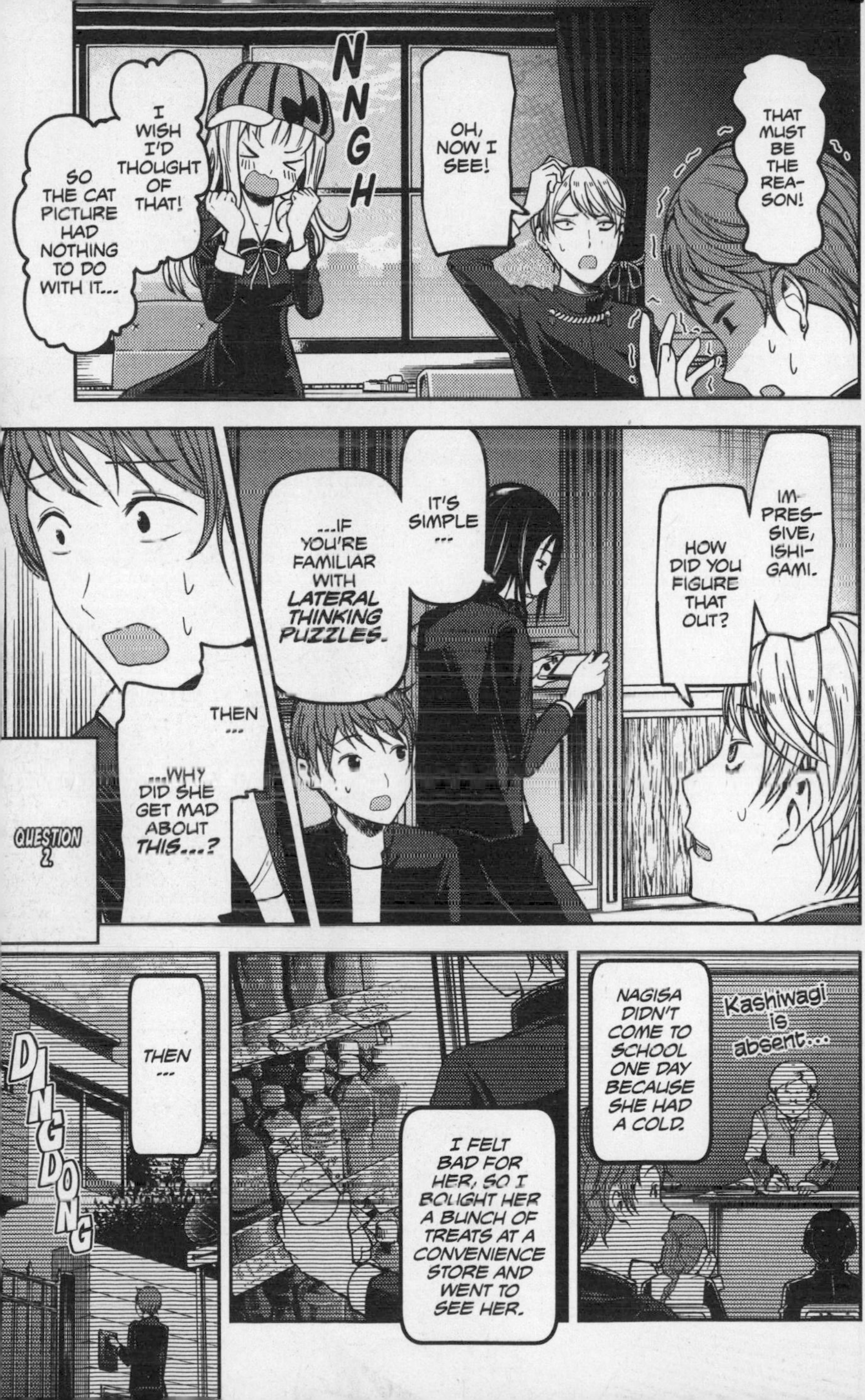
THAT MUST BE THE REASON!
OH, NOW I SEE!
NNGH
I WISH I'D THOUGHT OF THAT!
SO THE CAT PICTURE HAD NOTHING TO DO WITH IT...
IMPRESSIVE, ISHIGAMI.
HOW DID YOU FIGURE THAT OUT?
IT'S SIMPLE...
...IF YOU'RE FAMILIAR WITH LATERAL THINKING PUZZLES.
THEN...
...WHY DID SHE GET MAD ABOUT THIS...?
QUESTION 2.
Kashiwagi is absent...
NAGISA DIDN'T COME TO SCHOOL ONE DAY BECAUSE SHE HAD A COLD.
I FELT BAD FOR HER, SO I BOUGHT HER A BUNCH OF TREATS AT A CONVENIENCE STORE AND WENT TO SEE HER.
THEN...
DING DONG

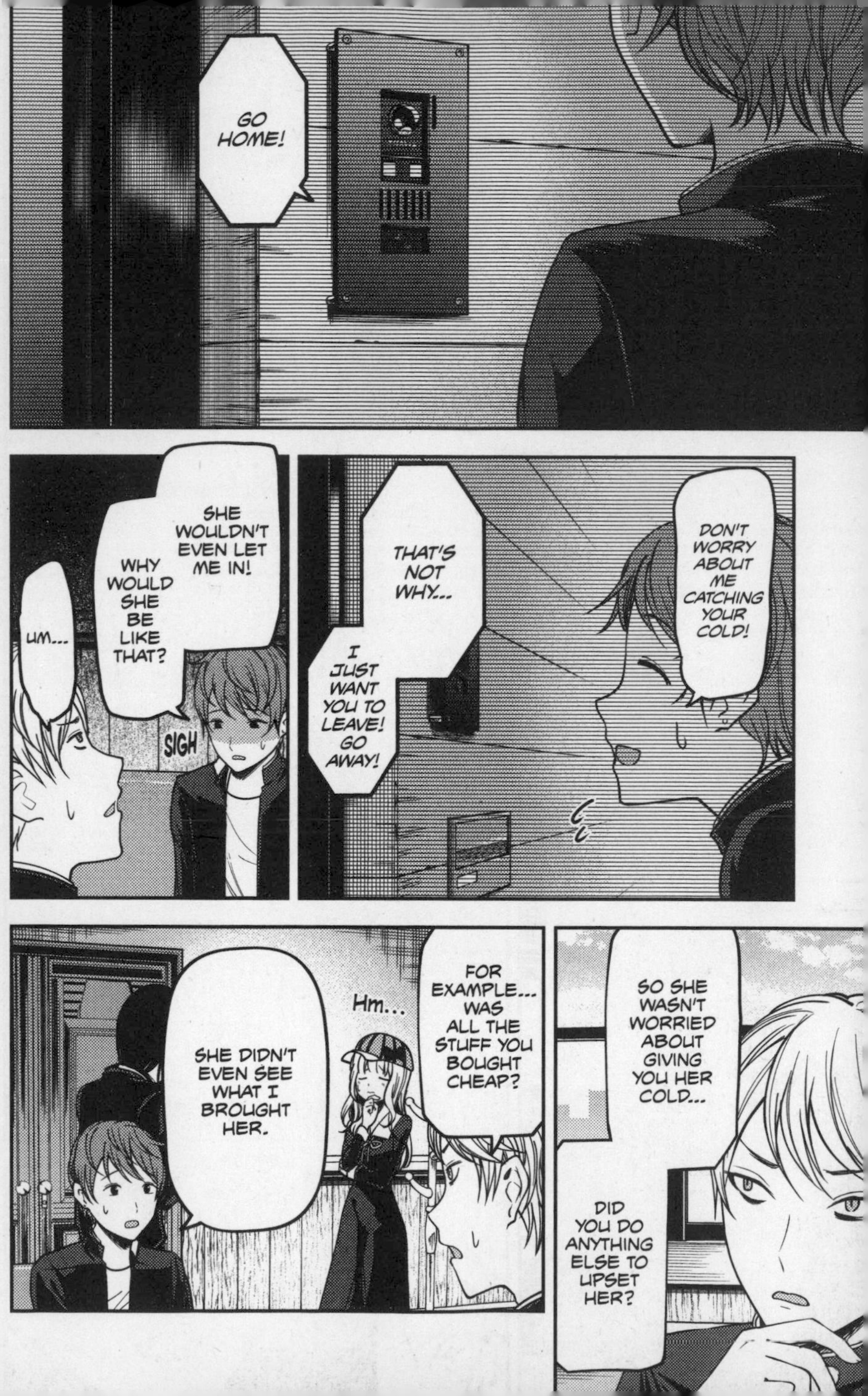
GO HOME!
DON'T WORRY ABOUT ME CATCHING YOUR COLD!
THAT'S NOT WHY...
I JUST WANT YOU TO LEAVE! GO AWAY!
SHE WOULDN'T EVEN LET ME IN!
WHY WOULD SHE BE LIKE THAT?
SIGH
UM...
SO SHE WASN'T WORRIED ABOUT GIVING YOU HER COLD...
DID YOU DO ANYTHING ELSE TO UPSET HER?
FOR EXAMPLE... WAS ALL THE STUFF YOU BOUGHT CHEAP?
Hm...
SHE DIDN'T EVEN SEE WHAT I BROUGHT HER.

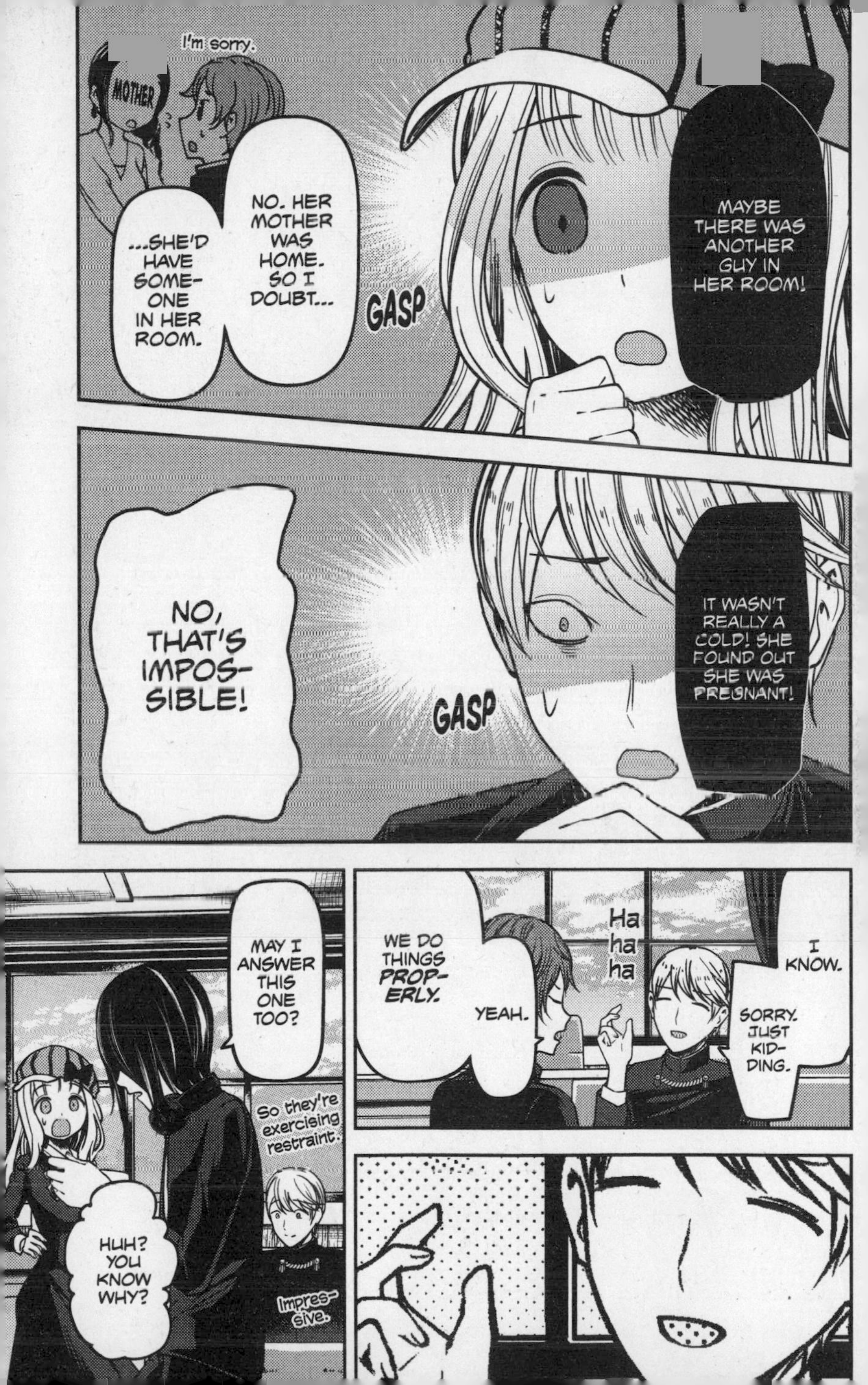
MAYBE THERE WAS ANOTHER GUY IN HER ROOM!
GASP
NO. HER MOTHER WAS HOME. SO I DOUBT...
...SHE'D HAVE SOME-ONE IN HER ROOM.
I'm sorry.
MOTHER
IT WASN'T REALLY A COLD! SHE FOUND OUT SHE WAS PREGNANT!
GASP
NO, THAT'S IMPOS-SIBLE!
I KNOW.
SORRY. JUST KID-DING.
Ha ha ha
YEAH.
WE DO THINGS *PROP-ERLY.*
MAY I ANSWER THIS ONE TOO?
So they're exercising restraint.
HUH? YOU KNOW WHY?
Impres-sive.

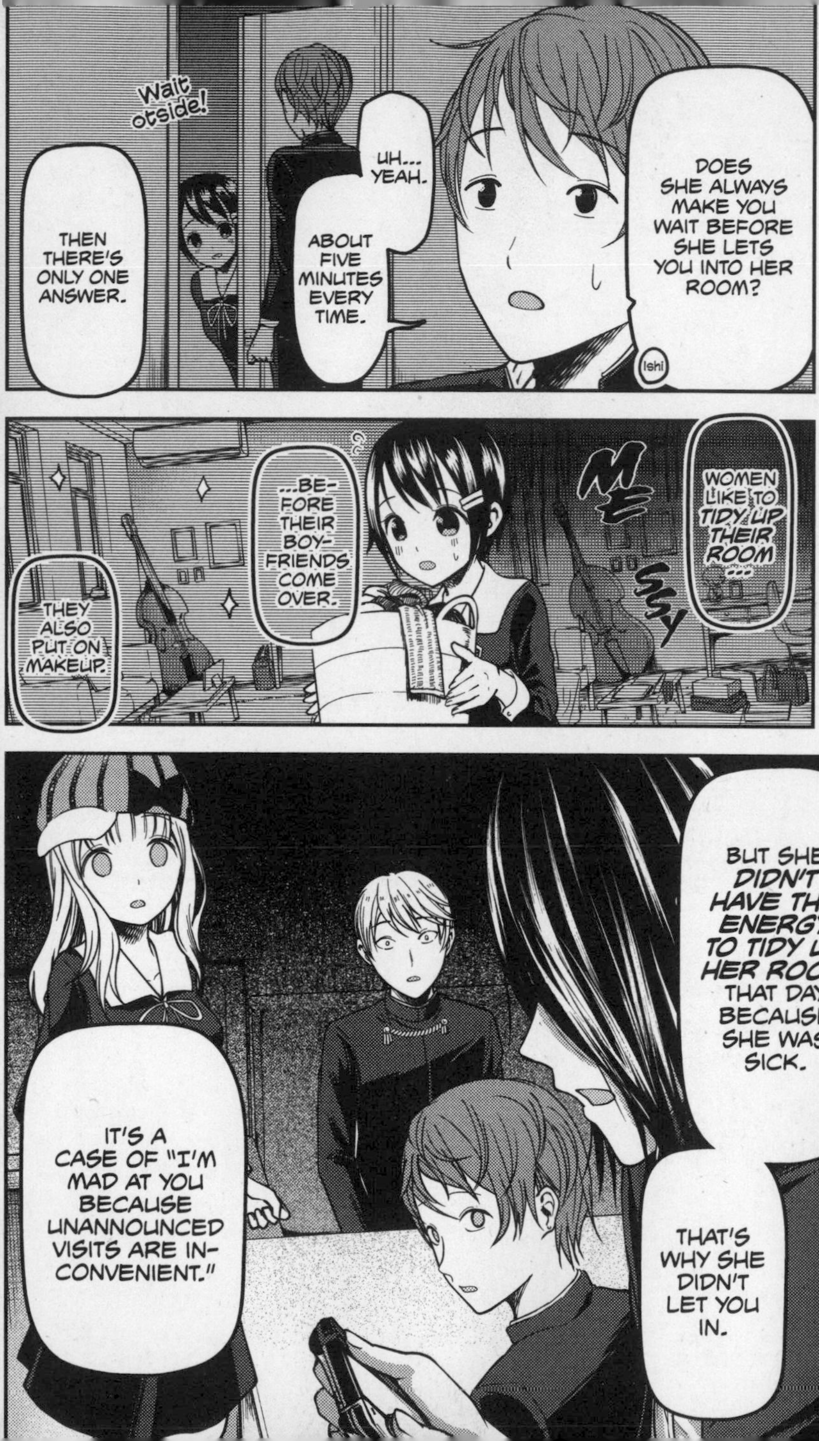
DOES SHE ALWAYS MAKE YOU WAIT BEFORE SHE LETS YOU INTO HER ROOM?
Ishi
UH... YEAH.
ABOUT FIVE MINUTES EVERY TIME.
Wait otside!
THEN THERE'S ONLY ONE ANSWER.
WOMEN LIKE TO TIDY UP THEIR ROOM...
MESSY
...BEFORE THEIR BOYFRIENDS COME OVER.
THEY ALSO PUT ON MAKEUP.
BUT SHE DIDN'T HAVE THE ENERGY TO TIDY UP HER ROOM THAT DAY BECAUSE SHE WAS SICK.
THAT'S WHY SHE DIDN'T LET YOU IN.
IT'S A CASE OF "I'M MAD AT YOU BECAUSE UNANNOUNCED VISITS ARE INCONVENIENT."

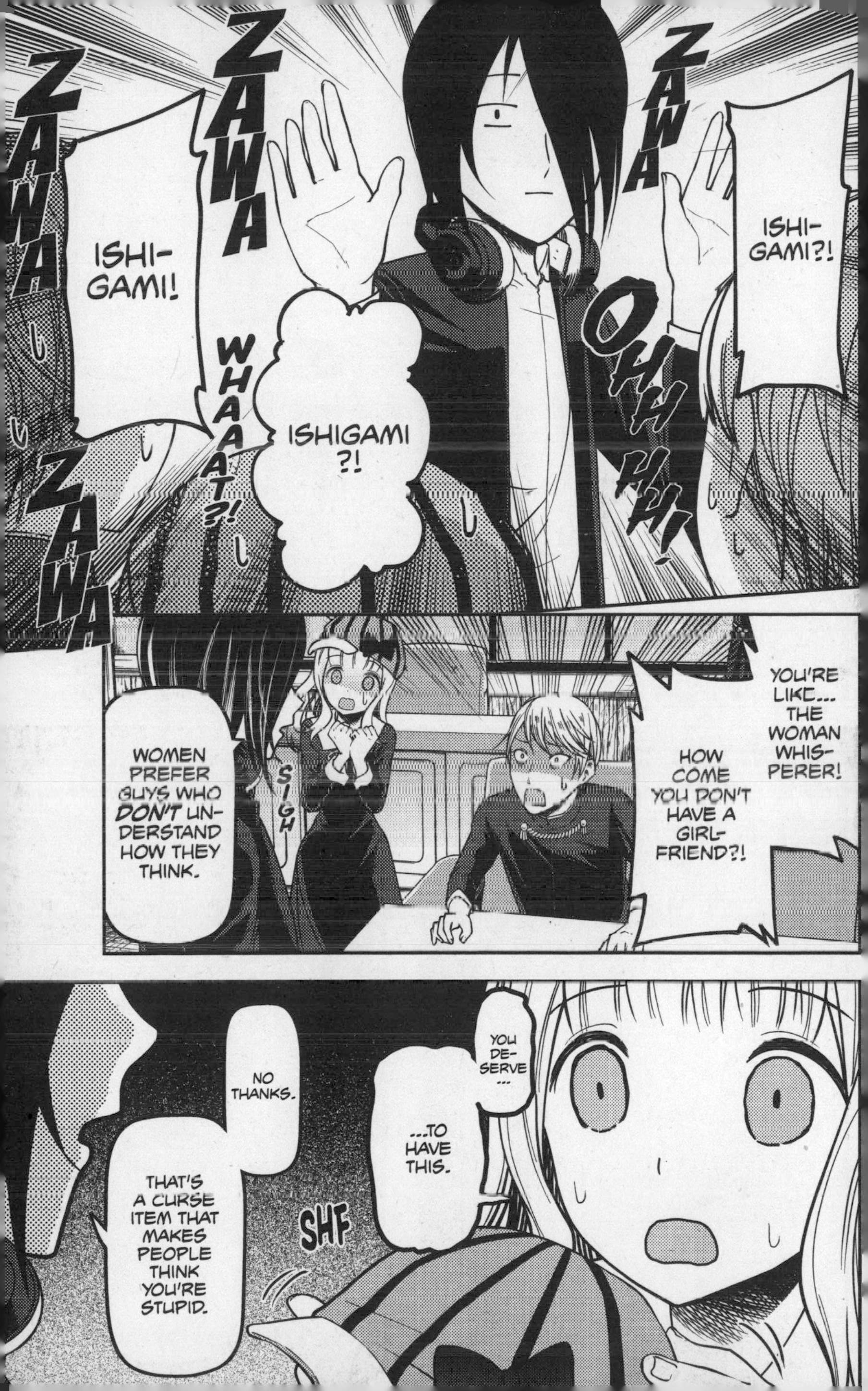
ZAWA
ISHI-GAMI?!
OHHHHH!
ISHIGAMI?!
WHAAAAT?!
ZAWA ZAWA
ISHI-GAMI!
ZAWA ZAWA
ZAWA ZAWA
YOU'RE LIKE... THE WOMAN WHISPERER!
HOW COME YOU DON'T HAVE A GIRL-FRIEND?!
SIGH
WOMEN PREFER GUYS WHO *DON'T* UN-DERSTAND HOW THEY THINK.
YOU DE-SERVE...
...TO HAVE THIS.
SHF
NO THANKS.
THAT'S A CURSE ITEM THAT MAKES PEOPLE THINK YOU'RE STUPID.

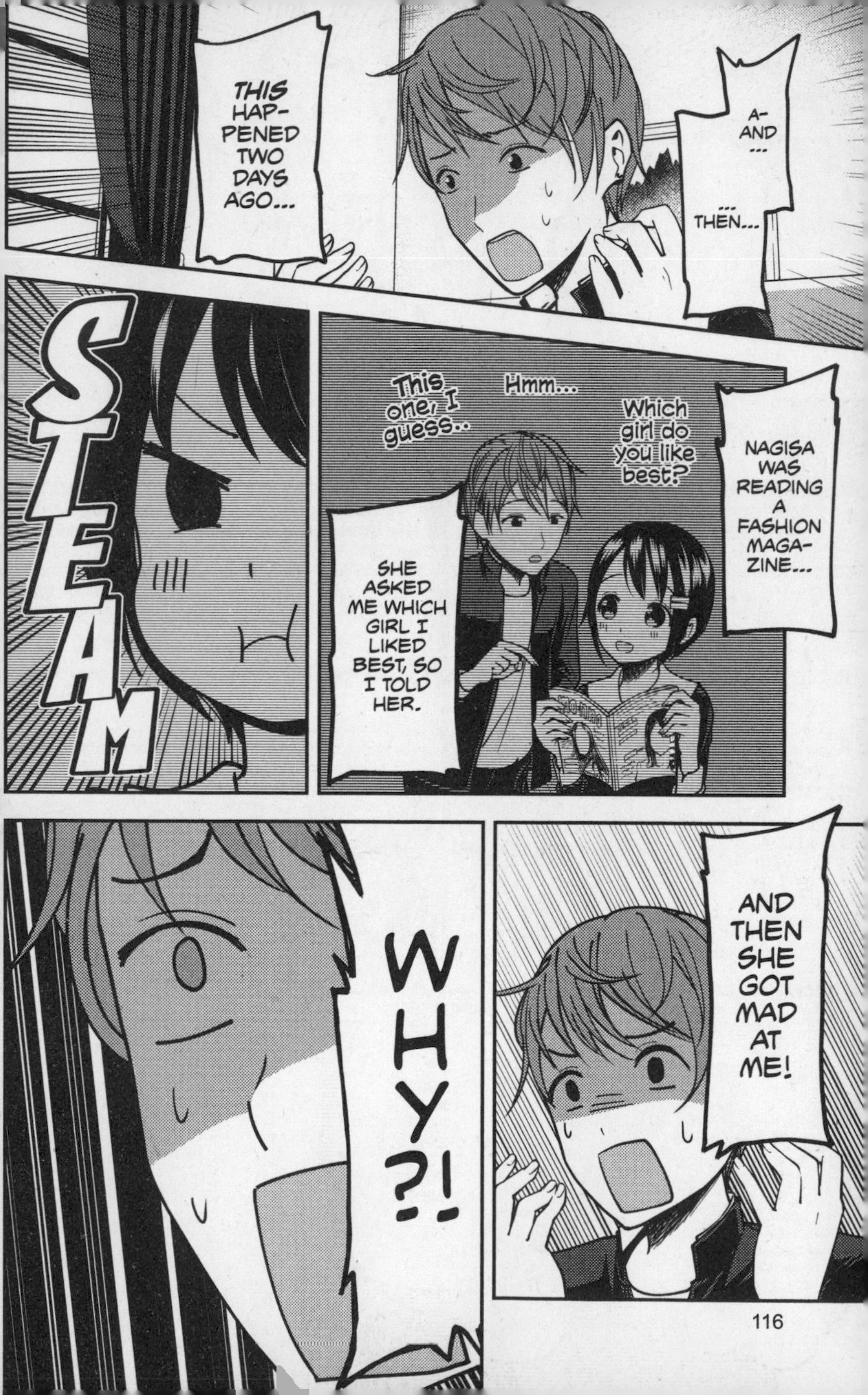
A- AND... ...THEN...
THIS HAP-PENED TWO DAYS AGO...
NAGISA WAS READING A FASHION MAGA-ZINE...
Which girl do you like best?
Hmm...
This one, I guess..
SHE ASKED ME WHICH GIRL I LIKED BEST, SO I TOLD HER.
STEAM
AND THEN SHE GOT MAD AT ME!
WHY?!

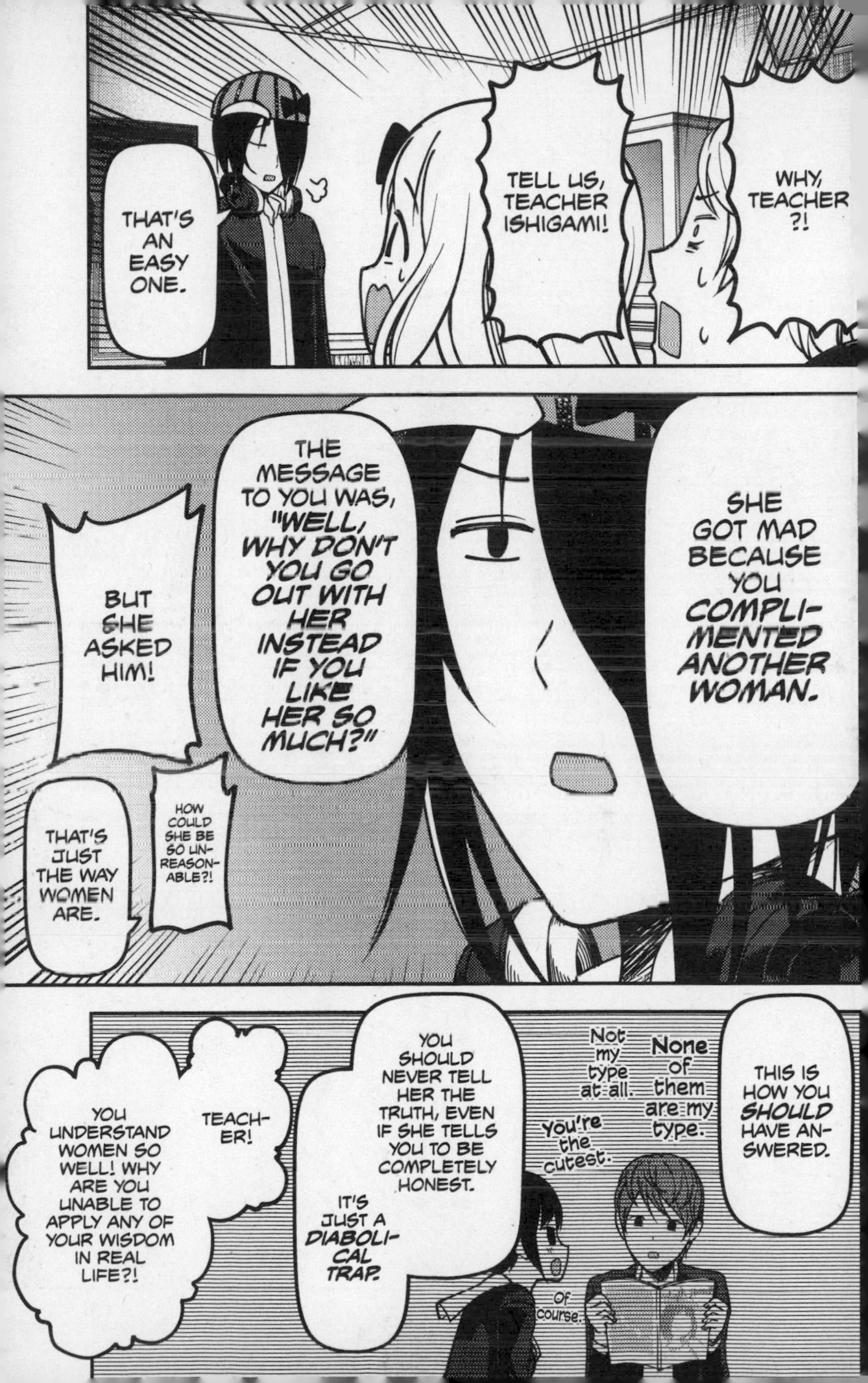
WHY, TEACHER?!
TELL US, TEACHER ISHIGAMI!
THAT'S AN EASY ONE.
SHE GOT MAD BECAUSE YOU COMPLIMENTED ANOTHER WOMAN.
THE MESSAGE TO YOU WAS, "WELL, WHY DON'T YOU GO OUT WITH HER INSTEAD IF YOU LIKE HER SO MUCH?"
BUT SHE ASKED HIM!
HOW COULD SHE BE SO UNREASONABLE?!
THAT'S JUST THE WAY WOMEN ARE.
THIS IS HOW YOU SHOULD HAVE ANSWERED.
None of them are my type.
Not my type at all.
You're the cutest.
Of course.
YOU SHOULD NEVER TELL HER THE TRUTH, EVEN IF SHE TELLS YOU TO BE COMPLETELY HONEST.
IT'S JUST A DIABOLICAL TRAP.
TEACHER!
YOU UNDERSTAND WOMEN SO WELL! WHY ARE YOU UNABLE TO APPLY ANY OF YOUR WISDOM IN REAL LIFE?!

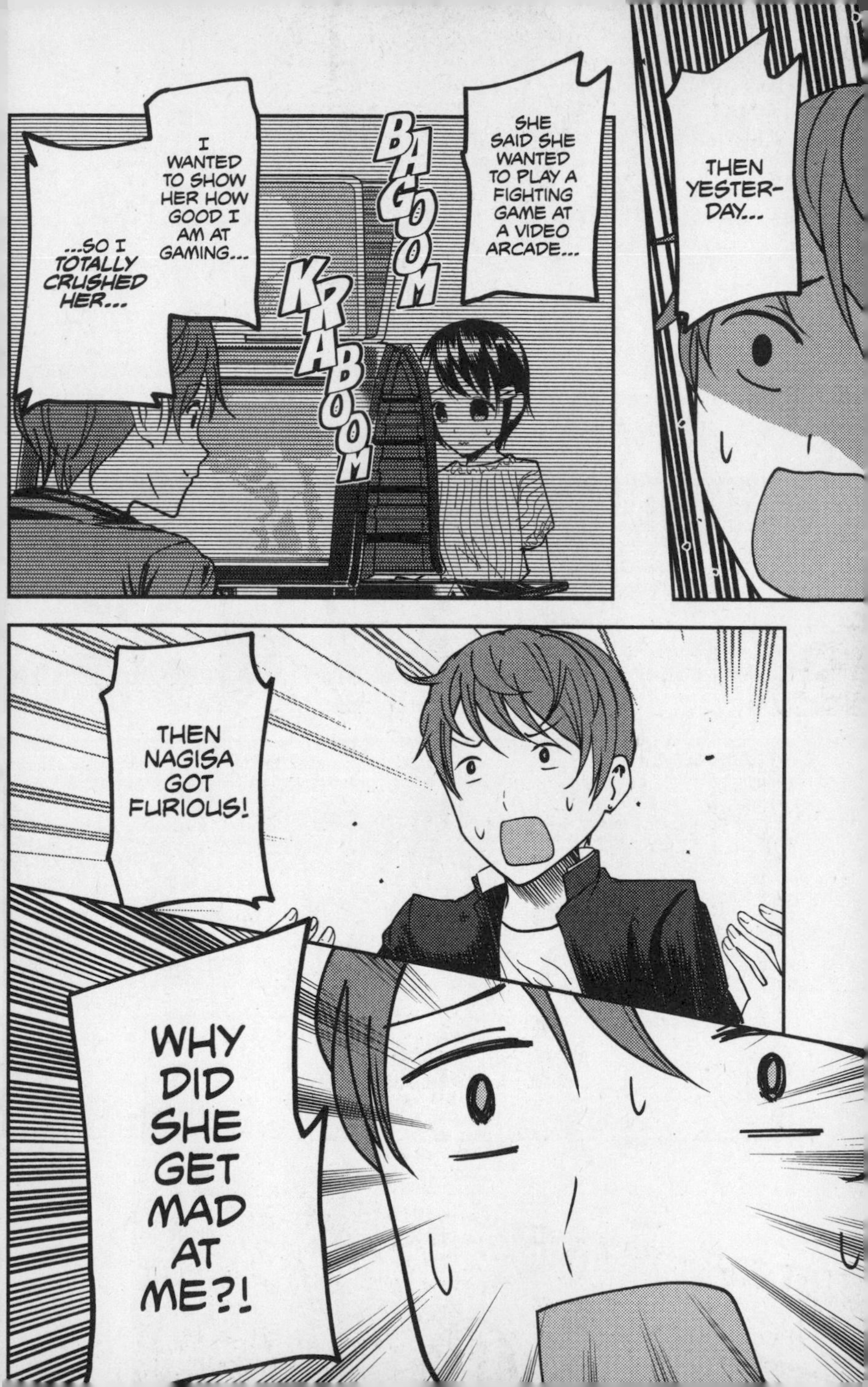
THEN YESTER-DAY...
SHE SAID SHE WANTED TO PLAY A FIGHTING GAME AT A VIDEO ARCADE...
BAGOOM
KRABOOM
I WANTED TO SHOW HER HOW GOOD I AM AT GAMING...
...SO I TOTALLY CRUSHED HER...
THEN NAGISA GOT FURIOUS!
WHY DID SHE GET MAD AT ME?!

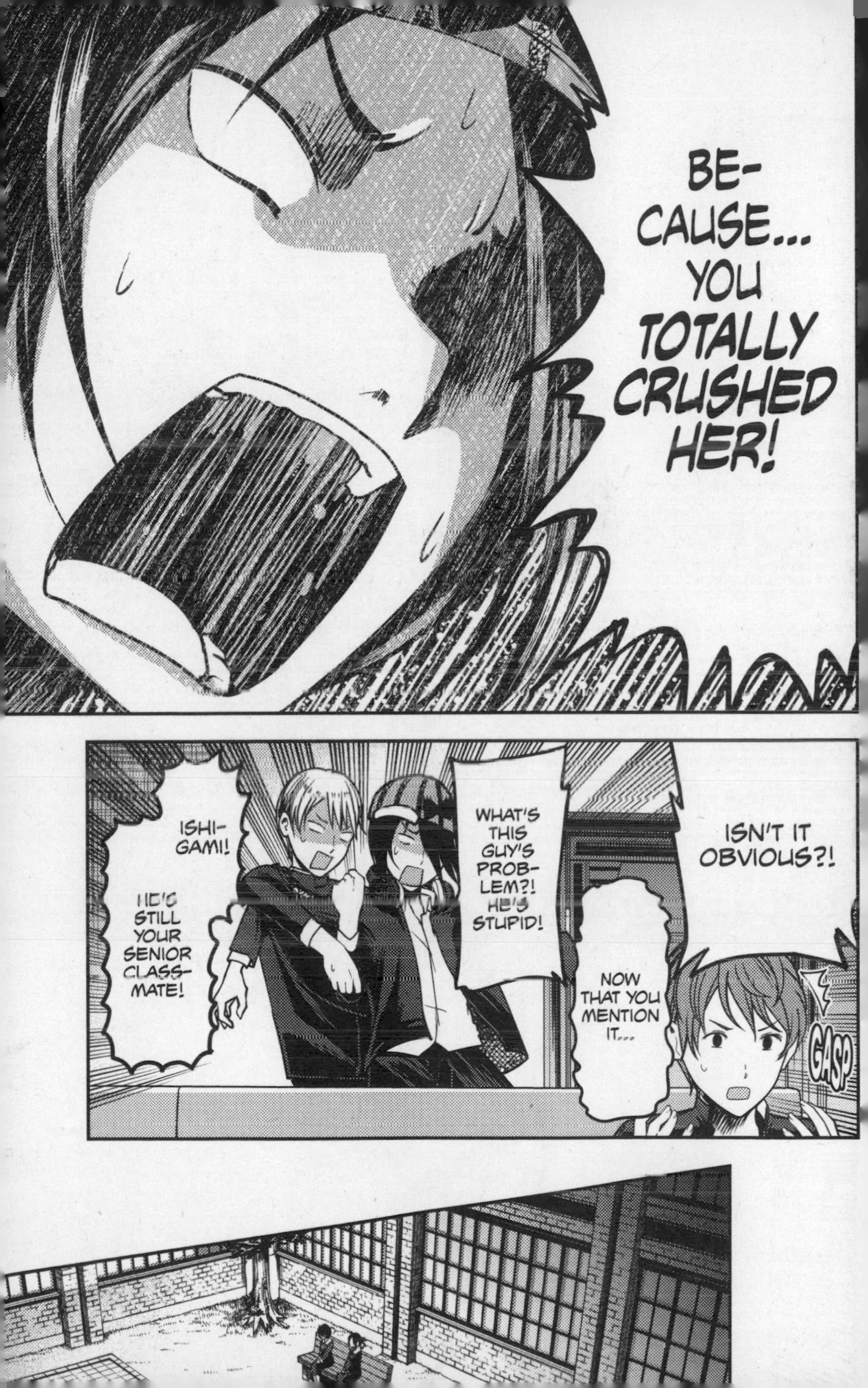
BE-CAUSE... YOU TOTALLY CRUSHED HER!
ISN'T IT OBVIOUS?!
WHAT'S THIS GUY'S PROBLEM?! HE'S STUPID!
ISHI-GAMI!
HE'S STILL YOUR SENIOR CLASS-MATE!
GASP
NOW THAT YOU MENTION IT...

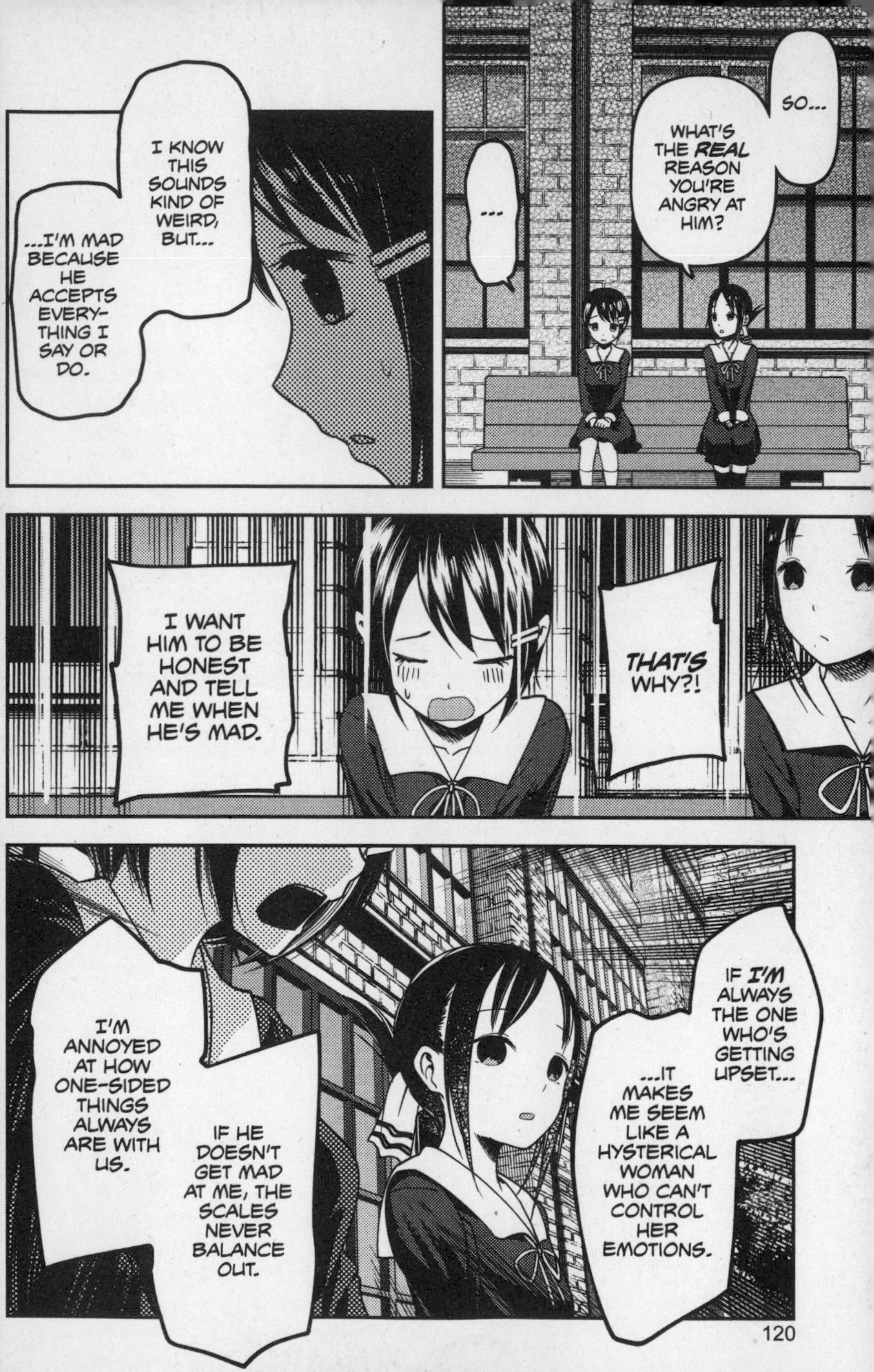
SO...
WHAT'S THE *REAL* REASON YOU'RE ANGRY AT HIM?
...
I KNOW THIS SOUNDS KIND OF WEIRD, BUT...
...I'M MAD BECAUSE HE ACCEPTS EVERYTHING I SAY OR DO.
THAT'S WHY?!
I WANT HIM TO BE HONEST AND TELL ME WHEN HE'S MAD.
IF *I'M* ALWAYS THE ONE WHO'S GETTING UPSET...
...IT MAKES ME SEEM LIKE A HYSTERICAL WOMAN WHO CAN'T CONTROL HER EMOTIONS.
I'M ANNOYED AT HOW ONE-SIDED THINGS ALWAYS ARE WITH US.
IF HE DOESN'T GET MAD AT ME, THE SCALES NEVER BALANCE OUT.

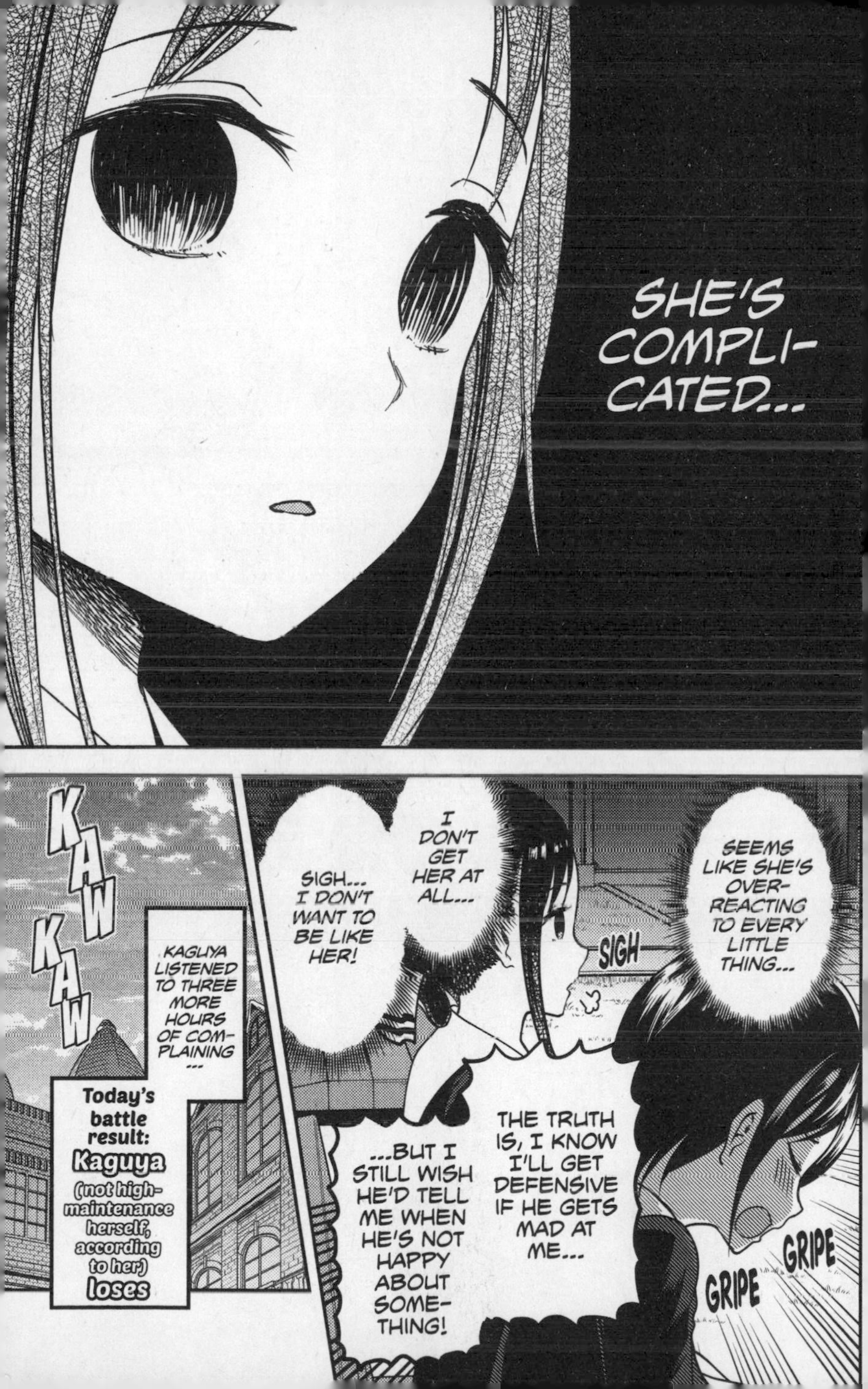
SHE'S COMPLICATED...
SEEMS LIKE SHE'S OVER-REACTING TO EVERY LITTLE THING...
SIGH
I DON'T GET HER AT ALL...
SIGH... I DON'T WANT TO BE LIKE HER!
GRIPE GRIPE
THE TRUTH IS, I KNOW I'LL GET DEFENSIVE IF HE GETS MAD AT ME...
...BUT I STILL WISH HE'D TELL ME WHEN HE'S NOT HAPPY ABOUT SOME-THING!
KAW KAW KAW
KAGUYA LISTENED TO THREE MORE HOURS OF COM-PLAINING...
Today's battle result: Kaguya (not high-maintenance herself, according to her) loses

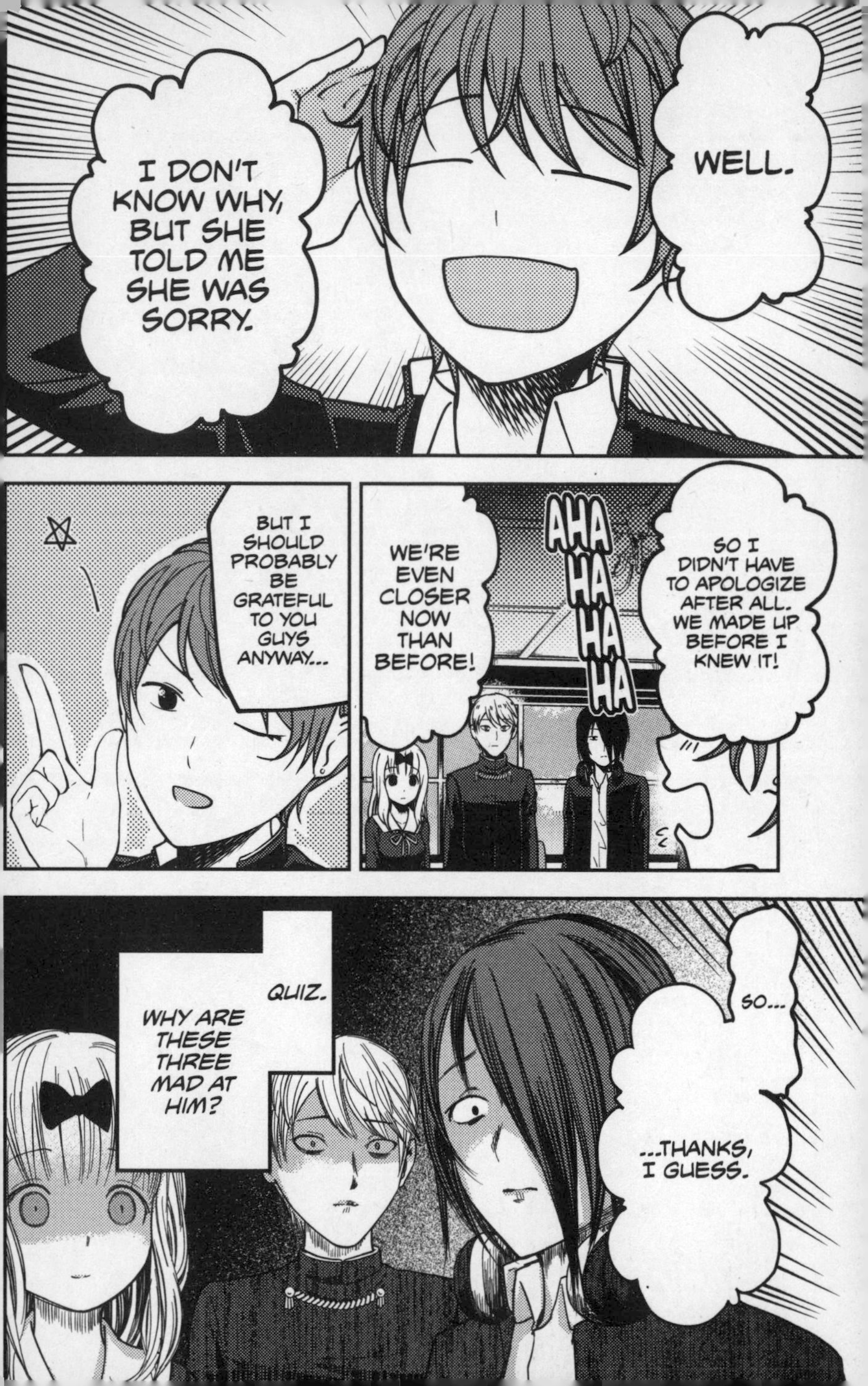

WELL.
I DON'T KNOW WHY, BUT SHE TOLD ME SHE WAS SORRY.
SO I DIDN'T HAVE TO APOLOGIZE AFTER ALL. WE MADE UP BEFORE I KNEW IT!
AHA HA HA HA HA
WE'RE EVEN CLOSER NOW THAN BEFORE!
BUT I SHOULD PROBABLY BE GRATEFUL TO YOU GUYS ANYWAY...
SO...
...THANKS, I GUESS.
QUIZ.
WHY ARE THESE THREE MAD AT HIM?

Question...

Will I
ever be
that
happy...?

KAGUYA-SAMA
LOVE IS WAR

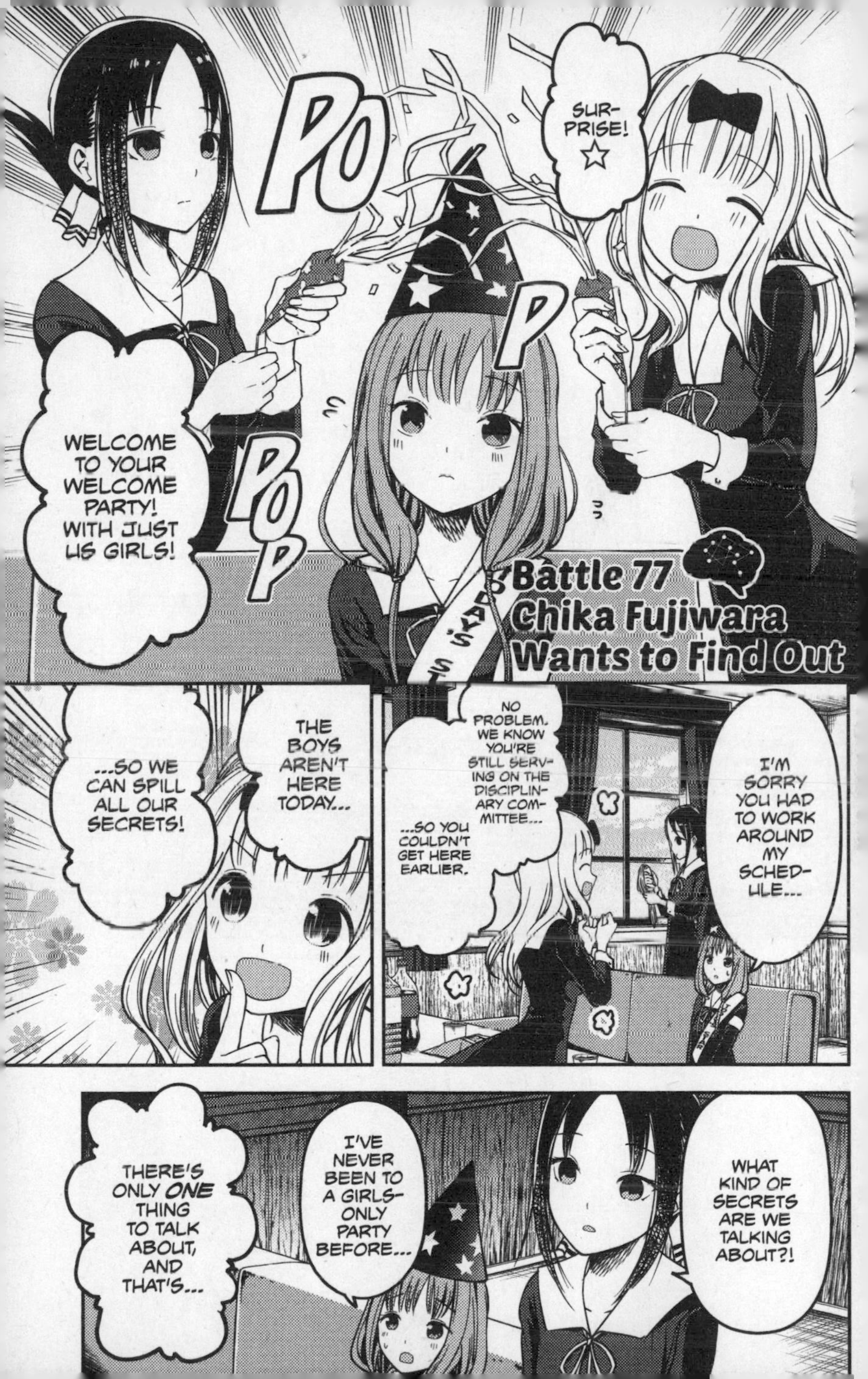
SUR-PRISE! ☆
POP
POP
WELCOME TO YOUR WELCOME PARTY! WITH JUST US GIRLS!
Battle 77
Chika Fujiwara Wants to Find Out
I'M SORRY YOU HAD TO WORK AROUND MY SCHED-ULE...
NO PROBLEM. WE KNOW YOU'RE STILL SERV-ING ON THE DISCIPLIN-ARY COM-MITTEE...
...SO YOU COULDN'T GET HERE EARLIER.
THE BOYS AREN'T HERE TODAY...
...SO WE CAN SPILL ALL OUR SECRETS!
WHAT KIND OF SECRETS ARE WE TALKING ABOUT?!
I'VE NEVER BEEN TO A GIRLS-ONLY PARTY BEFORE...
THERE'S ONLY *ONE* THING TO TALK ABOUT, AND THAT'S...

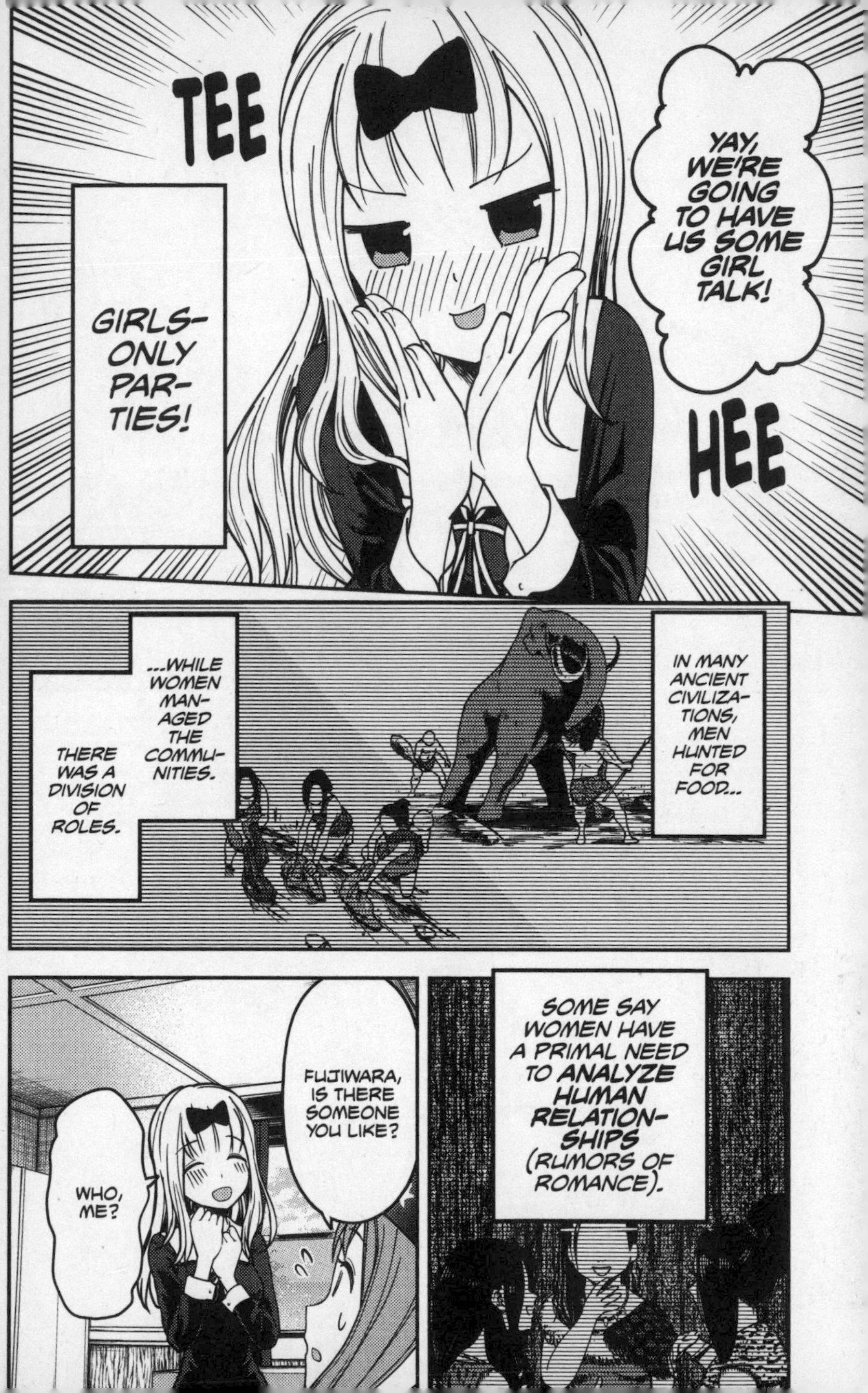
YAY, WE'RE GOING TO HAVE US SOME GIRL TALK!
TEE
HEE
GIRLS-ONLY PARTIES!
IN MANY ANCIENT CIVILIZATIONS, MEN HUNTED FOR FOOD...
...WHILE WOMEN MANAGED THE COMMUNITIES.
THERE WAS A DIVISION OF ROLES.
SOME SAY WOMEN HAVE A PRIMAL NEED TO **ANALYZE HUMAN RELATIONSHIPS** (RUMORS OF ROMANCE).
FUJIWARA, IS THERE SOMEONE YOU LIKE?
WHO, ME?

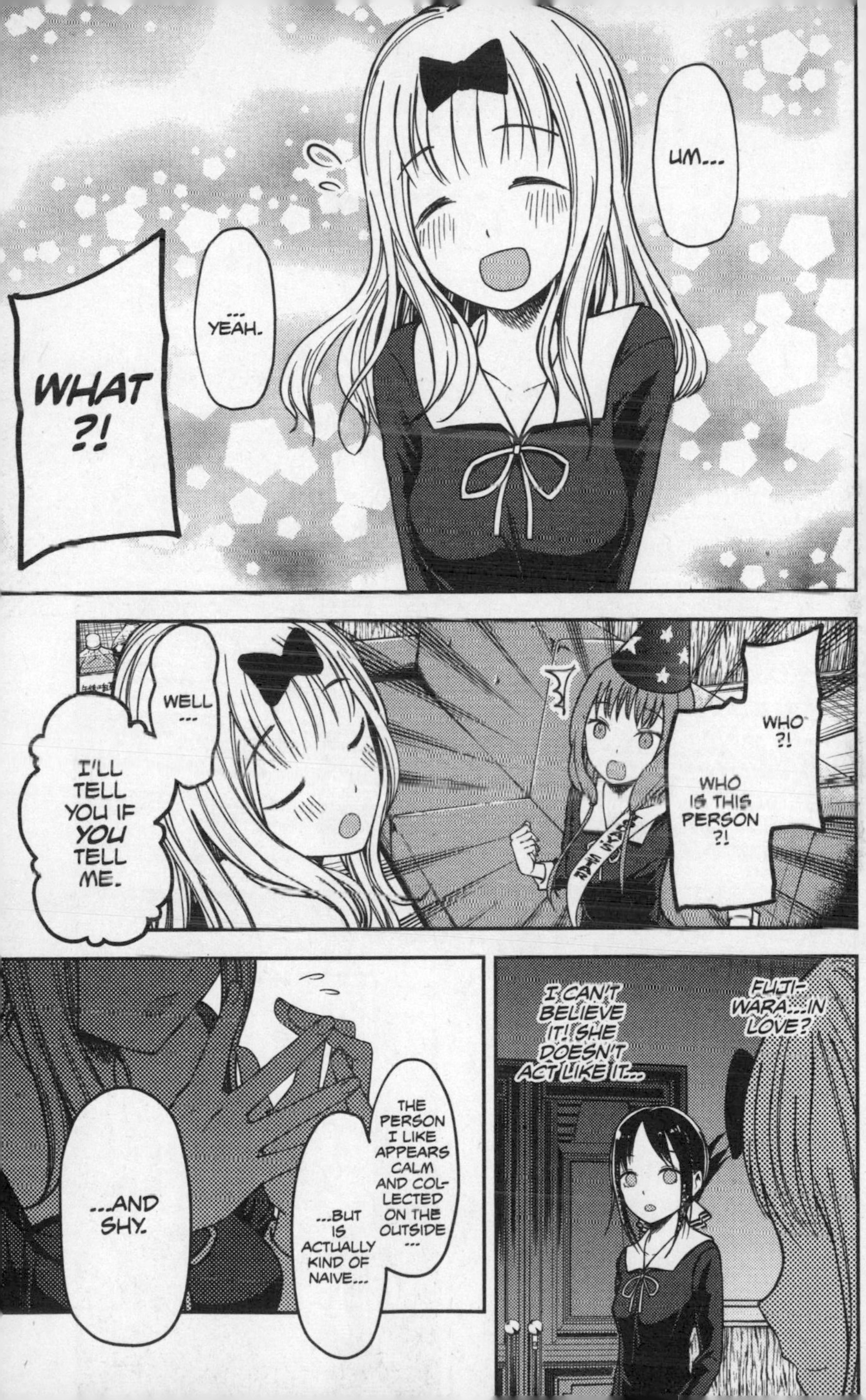
UM...
...YEAH.
WHAT?!
WHO?!
WHO IS THIS PERSON?!
WELL...
I'LL TELL YOU IF *YOU* TELL ME.
FUJIWARA...IN LOVE?
I CAN'T BELIEVE IT! SHE DOESN'T ACT LIKE IT...
THE PERSON I LIKE APPEARS CALM AND COLLECTED ON THE OUTSIDE...
...BUT IS ACTUALLY KIND OF NAIVE...
...AND SHY.

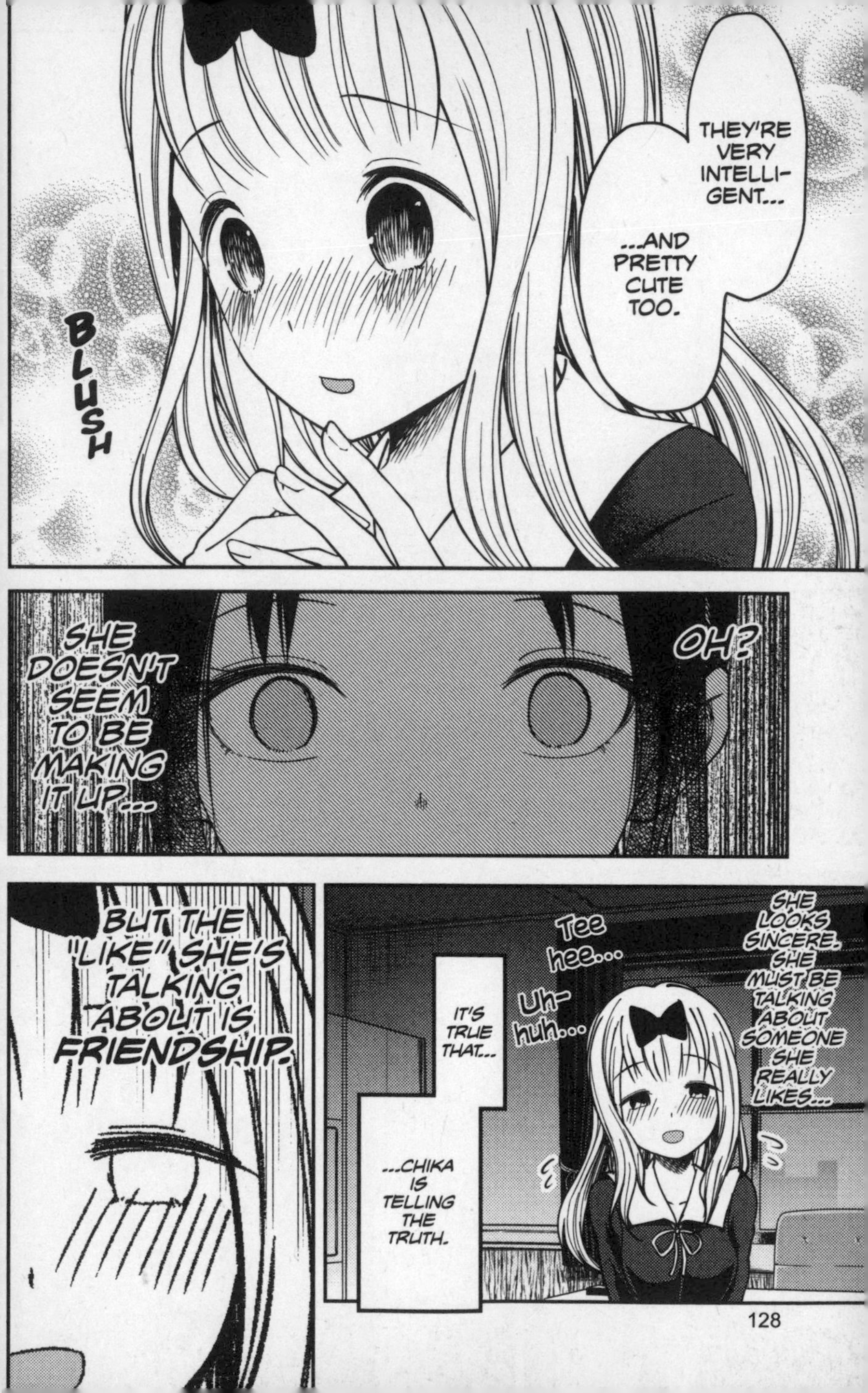
THEY'RE VERY INTELLI- GENT...
...AND PRETTY CUTE TOO.
BLUSH
OH?
SHE DOESN'T SEEM TO BE MAKING IT UP...
SHE LOOKS SINCERE. SHE MUST BE TALKING ABOUT SOMEONE SHE REALLY LIKES...
Tee hee...
Uh-huh...
IT'S TRUE THAT...
...CHIKA IS TELLING THE TRUTH.
BUT THE "LIKE" SHE'S TALKING ABOUT IS FRIENDSHIP.

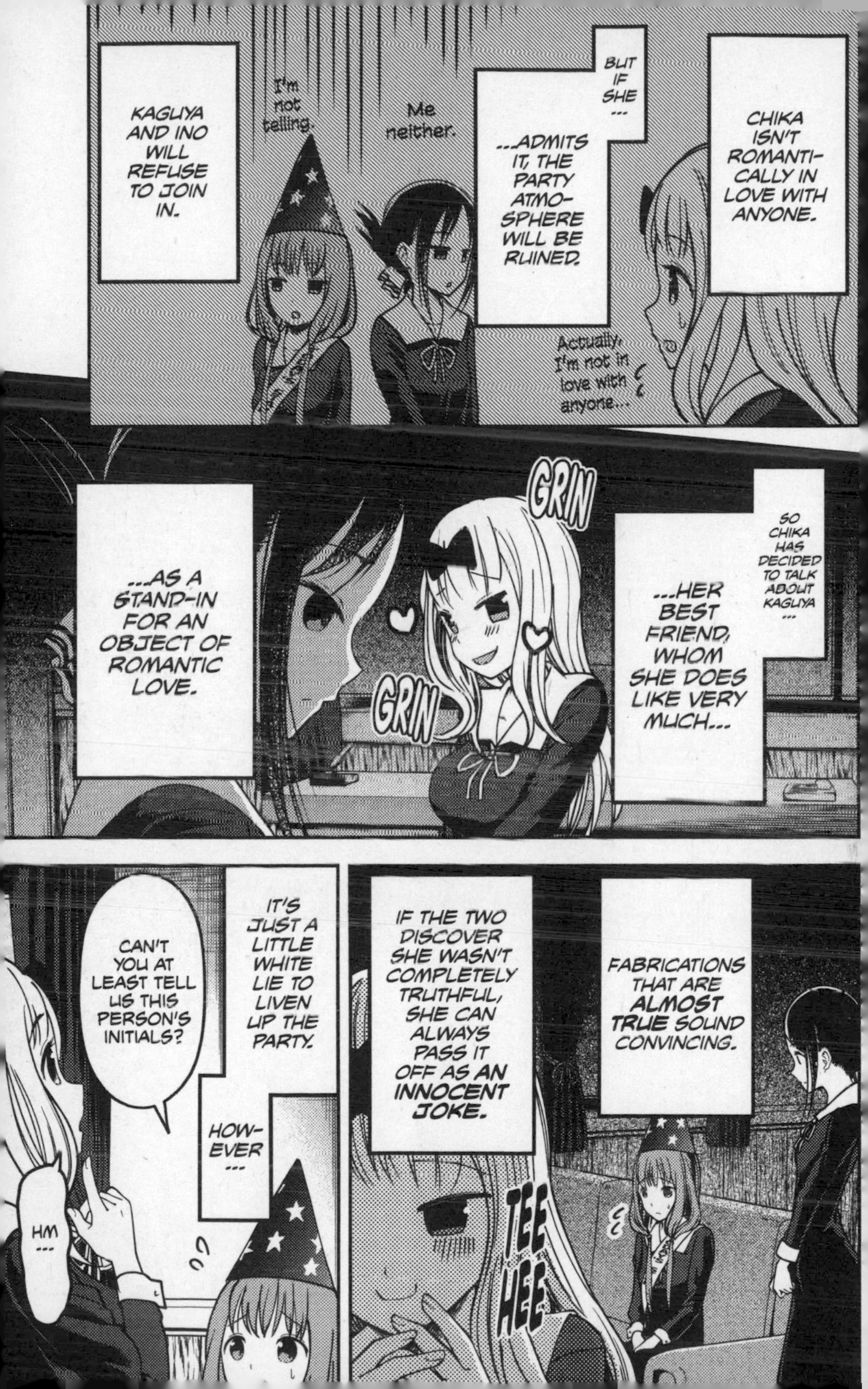
CHIKA ISN'T ROMANTICALLY IN LOVE WITH ANYONE.
Actually, I'm not in love with anyone...
BUT IF SHE...
...ADMITS IT, THE PARTY ATMOSPHERE WILL BE RUINED.
Me neither.
I'm not telling.
KAGUYA AND INO WILL REFUSE TO JOIN IN.
SO CHIKA HAS DECIDED TO TALK ABOUT KAGUYA...
...HER BEST FRIEND, WHOM SHE DOES LIKE VERY MUCH...
GRIN
GRIN
...AS A STAND-IN FOR AN OBJECT OF ROMANTIC LOVE.
FABRICATIONS THAT ARE ALMOST TRUE SOUND CONVINCING.
IF THE TWO DISCOVER SHE WASN'T COMPLETELY TRUTHFUL, SHE CAN ALWAYS PASS IT OFF AS AN INNOCENT JOKE.
TEE HEE
IT'S JUST A LITTLE WHITE LIE TO LIVEN UP THE PARTY.
HOWEVER...
CAN'T YOU AT LEAST TELL US THIS PERSON'S INITIALS?
HM...

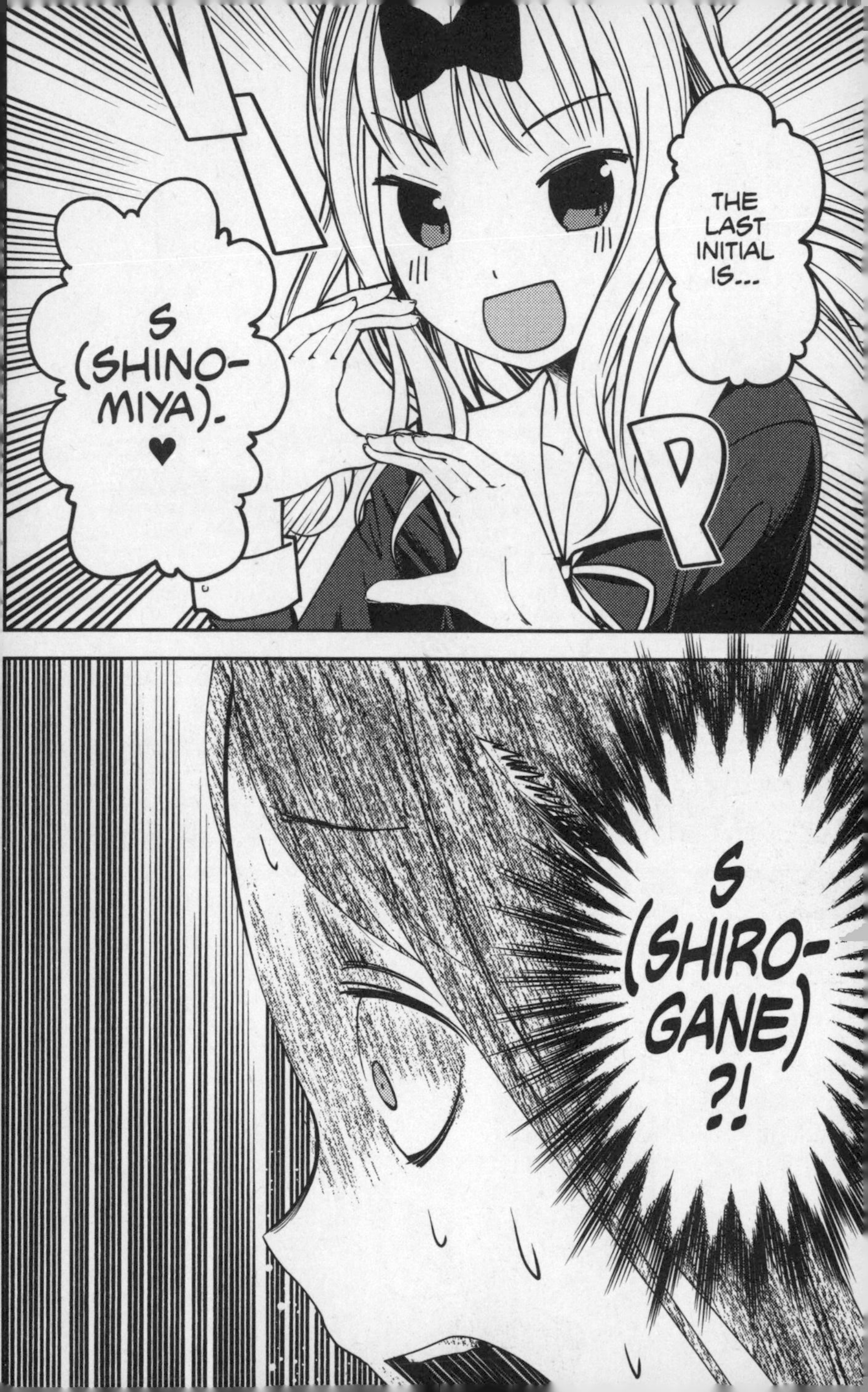
THE LAST INITIAL IS...
S (SHINO-MIYA). ♥
S (SHIRO-GANE)?!

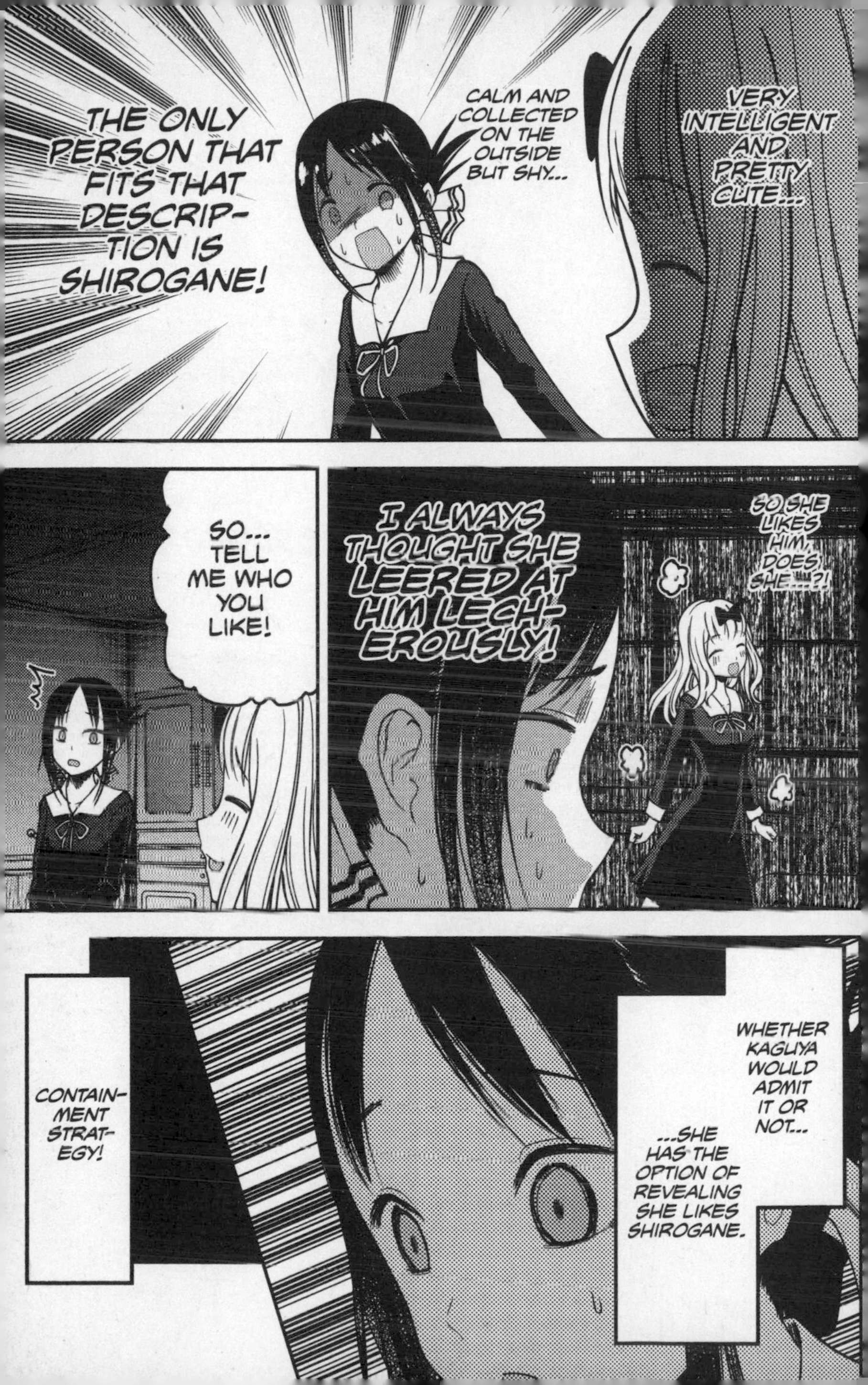
VERY INTELLIGENT AND PRETTY CUTE...
CALM AND COLLECTED ON THE OUTSIDE BUT SHY...
THE ONLY PERSON THAT FITS THAT DESCRIPTION IS SHIROGANE!
SO SHE LIKES HIM, DOES SHE...?!
I ALWAYS THOUGHT SHE LEERED AT HIM LECHEROUSLY!
SO... TELL ME WHO YOU LIKE!
WHETHER KAGUYA WOULD ADMIT IT OR NOT...
...SHE HAS THE OPTION OF REVEALING SHE LIKES SHIROGANE.
CONTAINMENT STRATEGY!

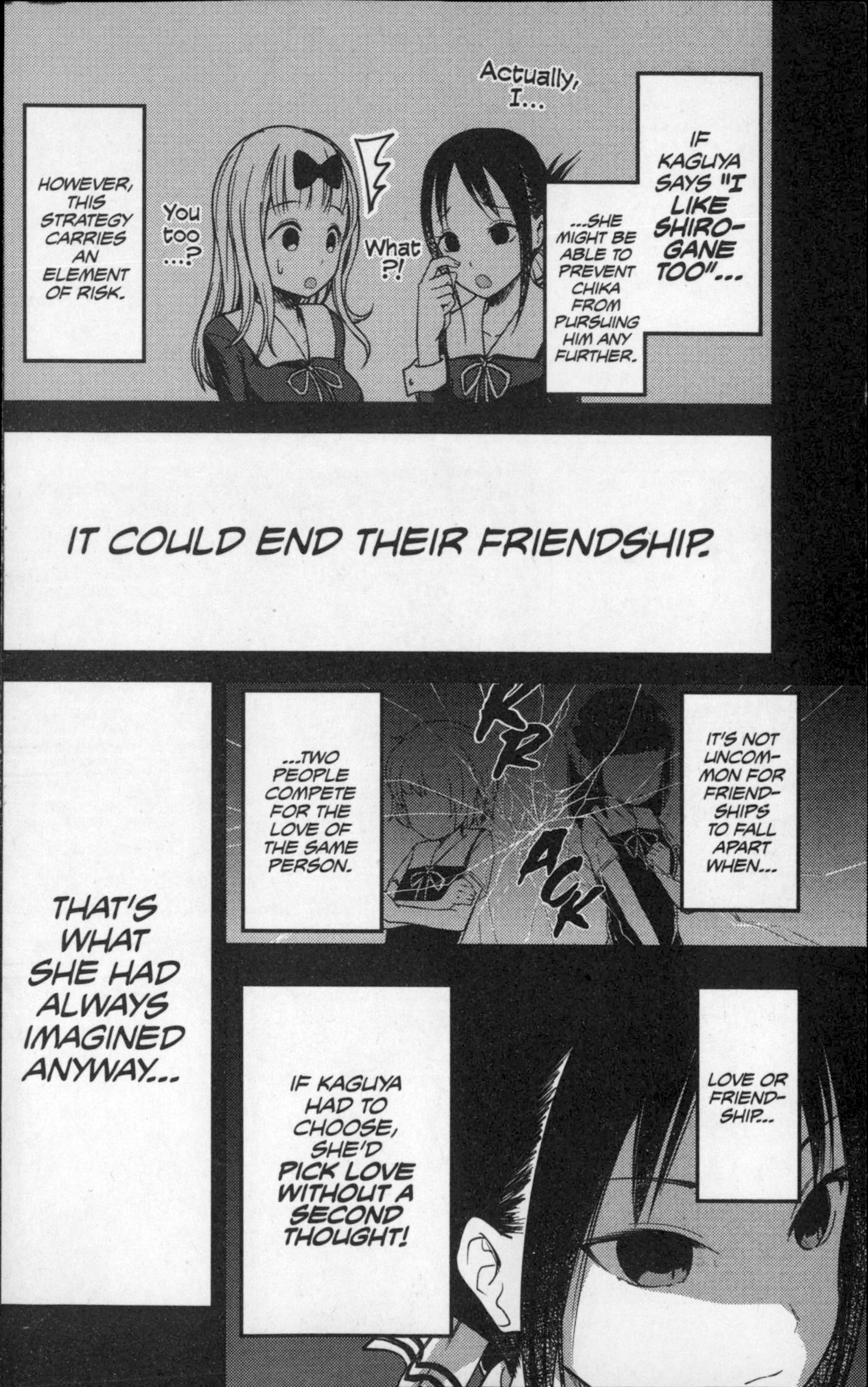
IF KAGUYA SAYS "I LIKE SHIROGANE TOO"...
...SHE MIGHT BE ABLE TO PREVENT CHIKA FROM PURSUING HIM ANY FURTHER.
Actually, I...
What?!
You too...?
HOWEVER, THIS STRATEGY CARRIES AN ELEMENT OF RISK.
IT COULD END THEIR FRIENDSHIP.
IT'S NOT UNCOMMON FOR FRIENDSHIPS TO FALL APART WHEN...
KRACK
...TWO PEOPLE COMPETE FOR THE LOVE OF THE SAME PERSON.
LOVE OR FRIENDSHIP...
IF KAGUYA HAD TO CHOOSE, SHE'D PICK LOVE WITHOUT A SECOND THOUGHT!
THAT'S WHAT SHE HAD ALWAYS IMAGINED ANYWAY...

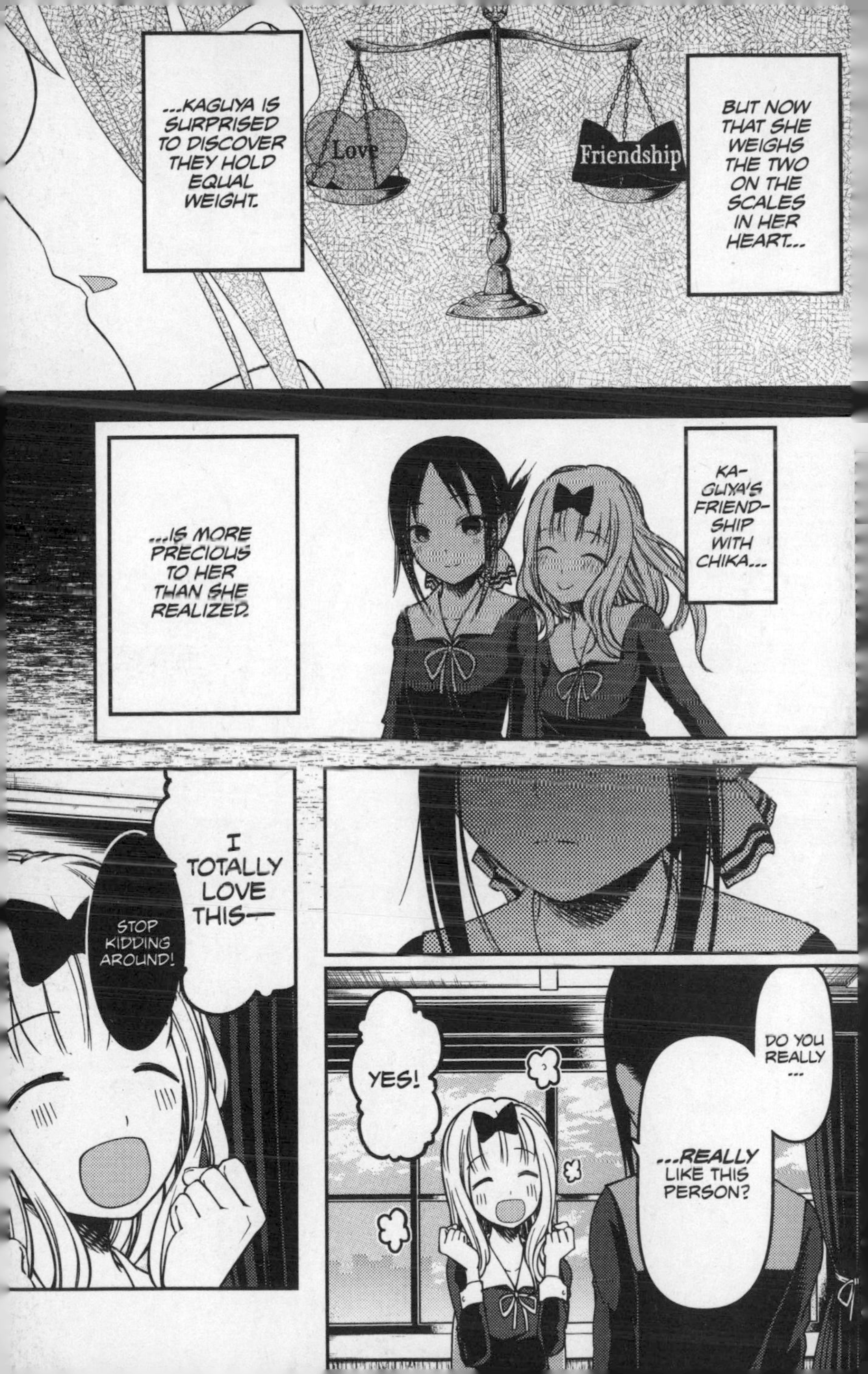
BUT NOW THAT SHE WEIGHS THE TWO ON THE SCALES IN HER HEART...
Friendship
Love
...KAGUYA IS SURPRISED TO DISCOVER THEY HOLD EQUAL WEIGHT.
KAGUYA'S FRIENDSHIP WITH CHIKA...
...IS MORE PRECIOUS TO HER THAN SHE REALIZED.
DO YOU REALLY...
...REALLY LIKE THIS PERSON?
YES!
I TOTALLY LOVE THIS—
STOP KIDDING AROUND!

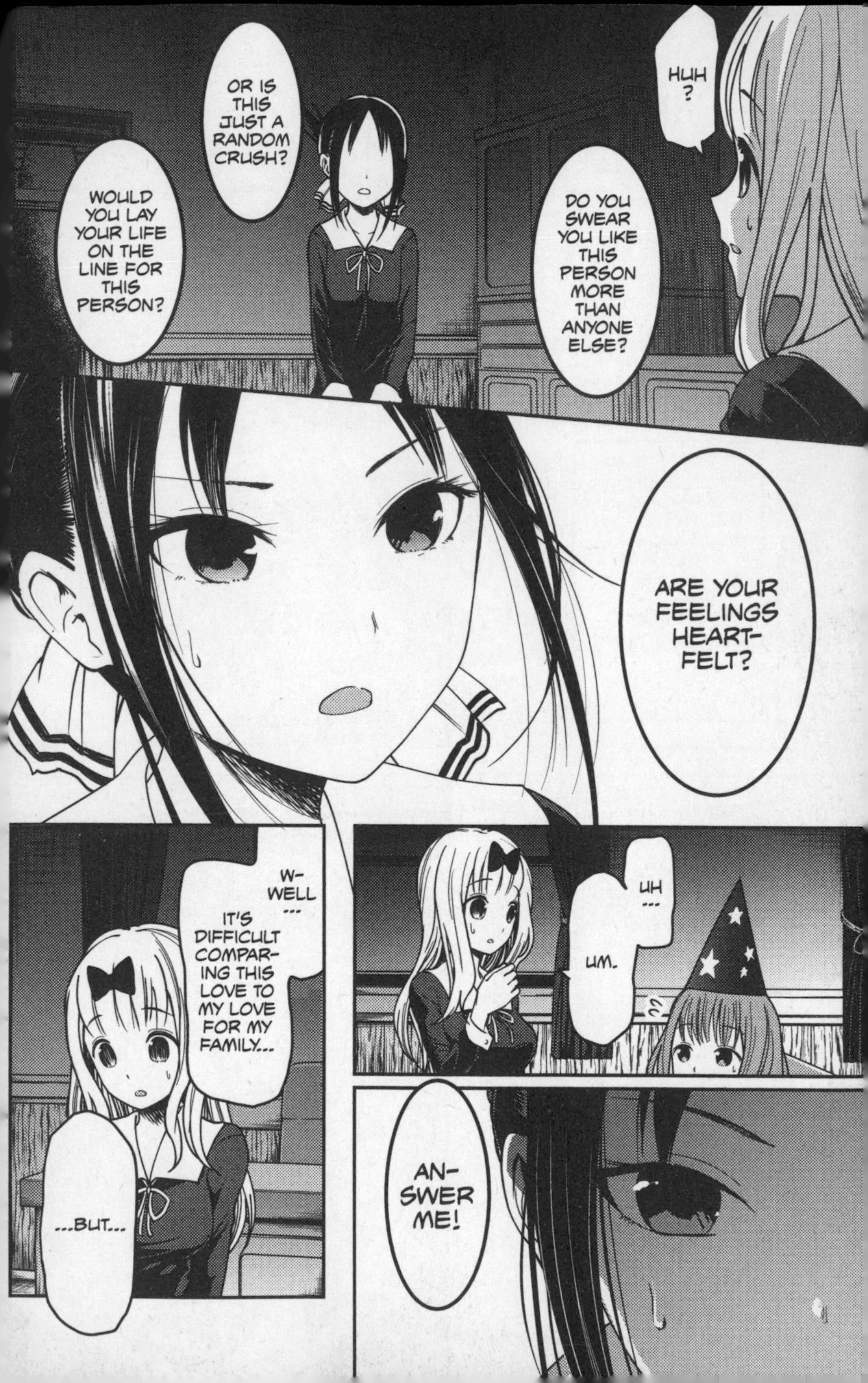
HUH?
DO YOU SWEAR YOU LIKE THIS PERSON MORE THAN ANYONE ELSE?
OR IS THIS JUST A RANDOM CRUSH?
WOULD YOU LAY YOUR LIFE ON THE LINE FOR THIS PERSON?
ARE YOUR FEELINGS HEART-FELT?
UH...
UM.
AN-SWER ME!
W-WELL...
IT'S DIFFICULT COMPARING THIS LOVE TO MY LOVE FOR MY FAMILY...
...BUT...

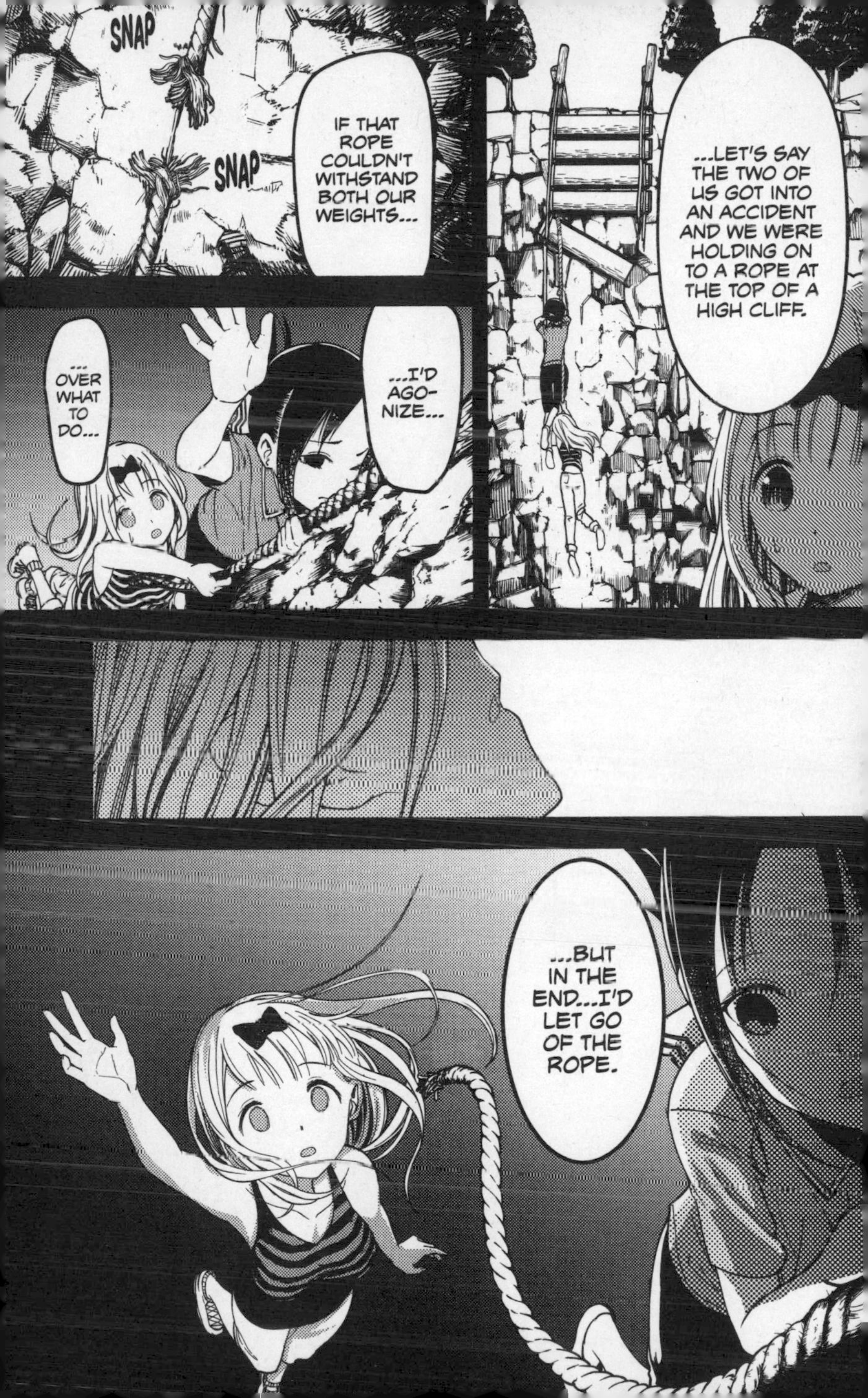
...LET'S SAY THE TWO OF US GOT INTO AN ACCIDENT AND WE WERE HOLDING ON TO A ROPE AT THE TOP OF A HIGH CLIFF.
IF THAT ROPE COULDN'T WITHSTAND BOTH OUR WEIGHTS...
SNAP
SNAP
...I'D AGONIZE...
...OVER WHAT TO DO...
...BUT IN THE END...I'D LET GO OF THE ROPE.

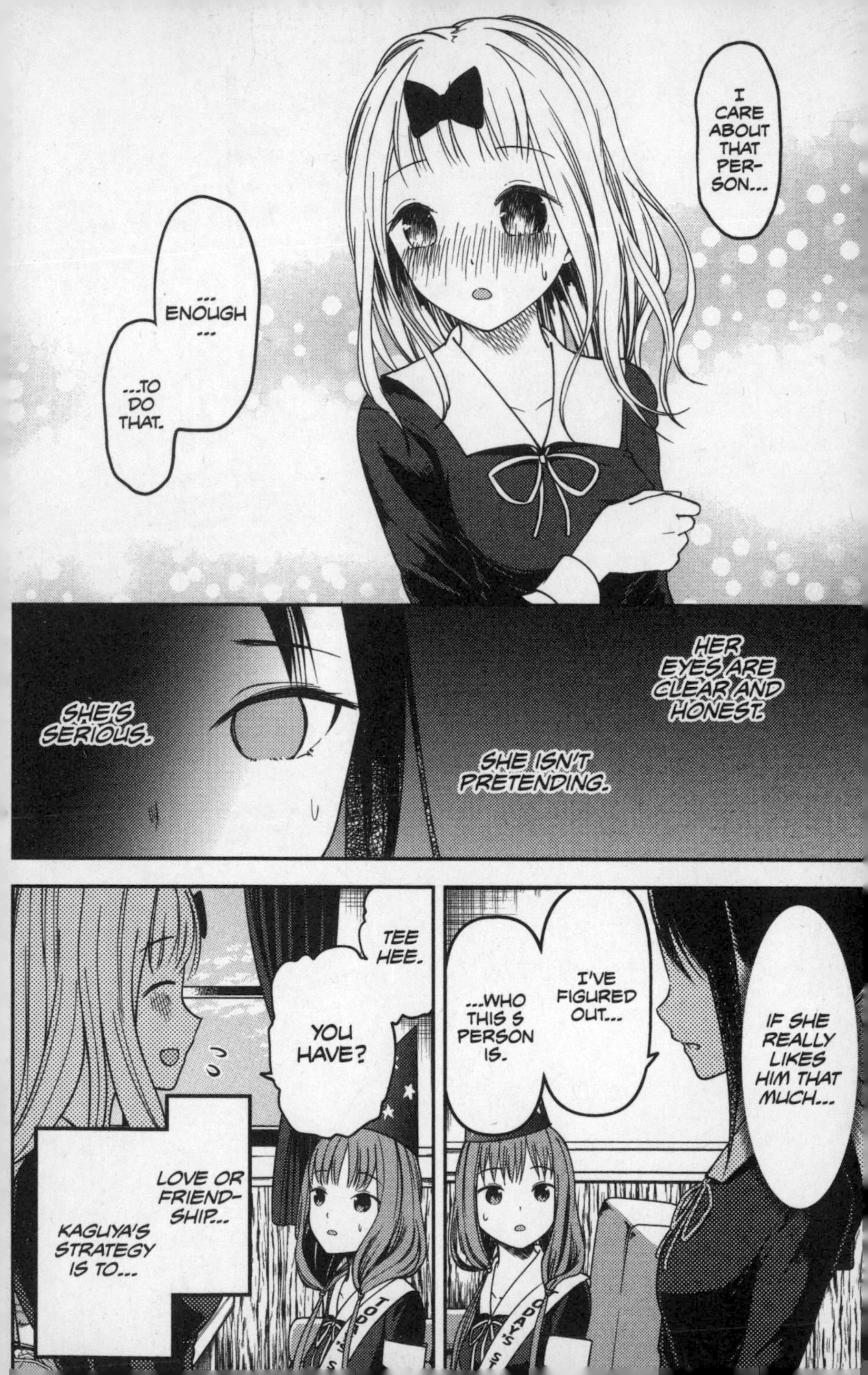
I CARE ABOUT THAT PER-SON...
...ENOUGH...
...TO DO THAT.
HER EYES ARE CLEAR AND HONEST.
SHE ISN'T PRETENDING.
SHE IS SERIOUS.
IF SHE REALLY LIKES HIM THAT MUCH...
I'VE FIGURED OUT...
...WHO THIS S PERSON IS.
TEE HEE.
YOU HAVE?
LOVE OR FRIEND-SHIP...
KAGUYA'S STRATEGY IS TO...

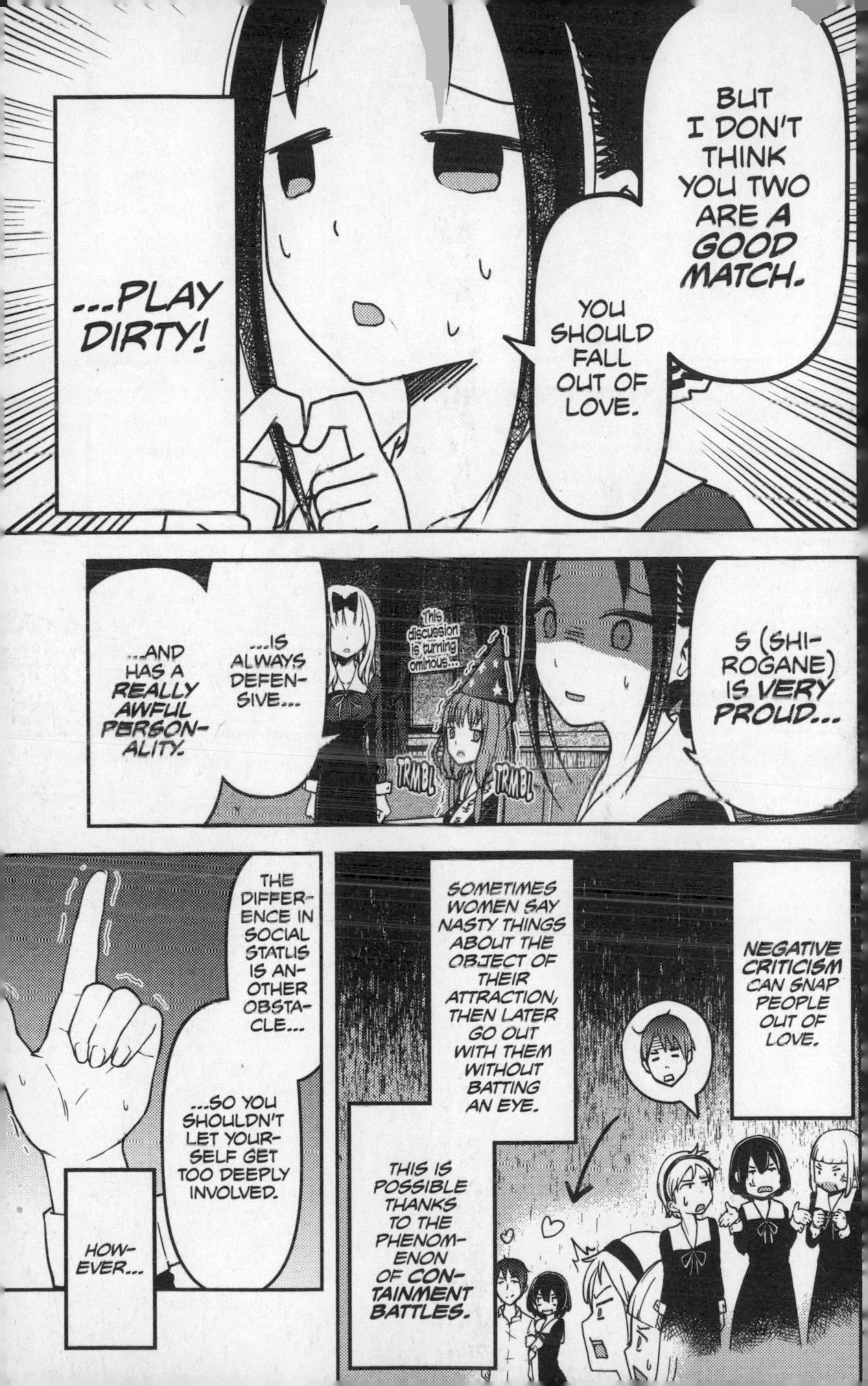

BUT I DON'T THINK YOU TWO ARE A GOOD MATCH.
YOU SHOULD FALL OUT OF LOVE.
...PLAY DIRTY!
S (SHIROGANE) IS VERY PROUD...
This discussion is turning ominous...
TRMBL
TRMBL
...IS ALWAYS DEFENSIVE...
...AND HAS A REALLY AWFUL PERSONALITY.
NEGATIVE CRITICISM CAN SNAP PEOPLE OUT OF LOVE.
SOMETIMES WOMEN SAY NASTY THINGS ABOUT THE OBJECT OF THEIR ATTRACTION, THEN LATER GO OUT WITH THEM WITHOUT BATTING AN EYE.
THIS IS POSSIBLE THANKS TO THE PHENOMENON OF CONTAINMENT BATTLES.
THE DIFFERENCE IN SOCIAL STATUS IS ANOTHER OBSTACLE...
...SO YOU SHOULDN'T LET YOURSELF GET TOO DEEPLY INVOLVED.
HOWEVER...

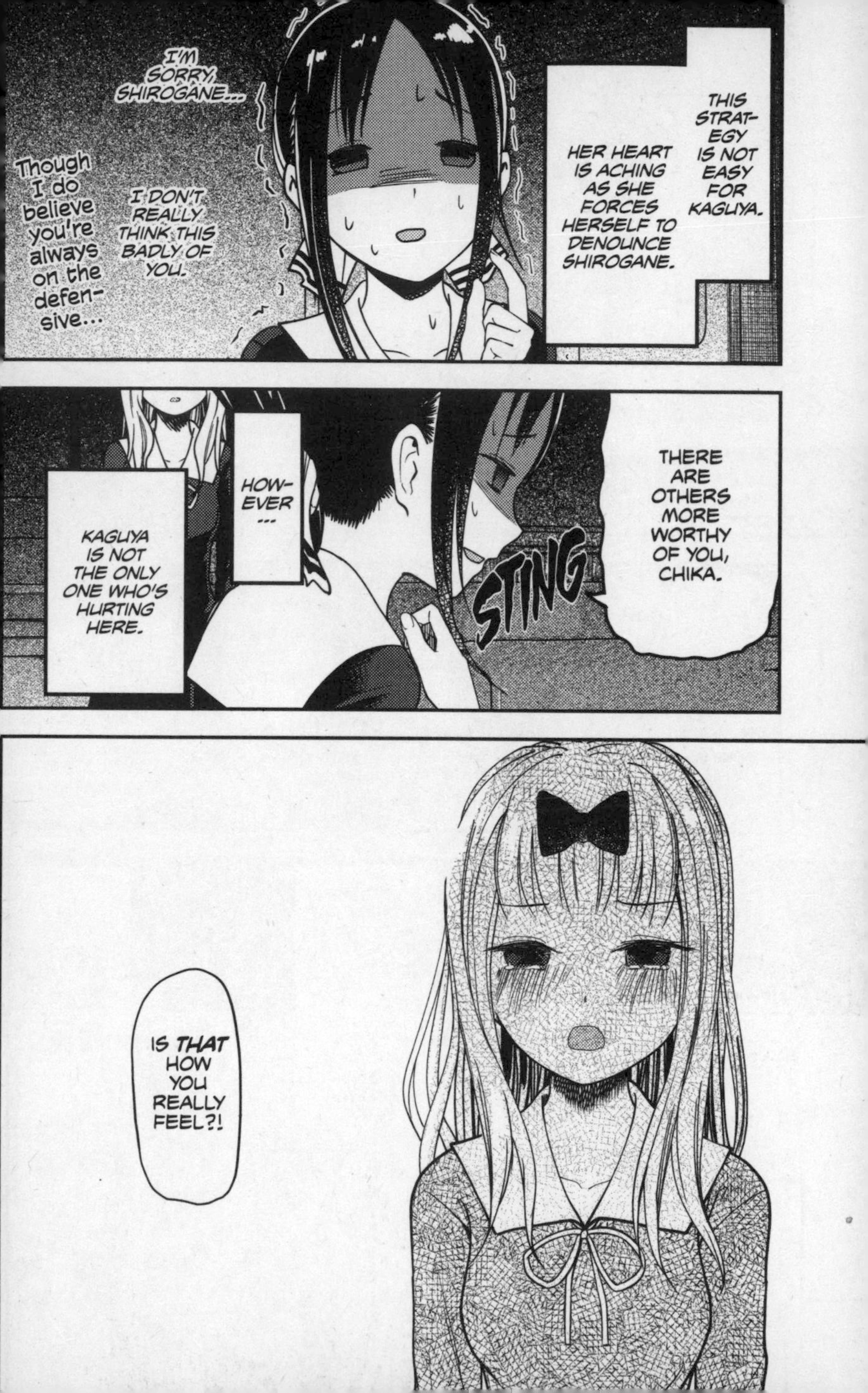
THIS STRATEGY IS NOT EASY FOR KAGUYA.
HER HEART IS ACHING AS SHE FORCES HERSELF TO DENOUNCE SHIROGANE.
I'M SORRY, SHIROGANE...
I DON'T REALLY THINK THIS BADLY OF YOU.
Though I do believe you're always on the defensive...
THERE ARE OTHERS MORE WORTHY OF YOU, CHIKA.
STING
HOWEVER...
KAGUYA IS NOT THE ONLY ONE WHO'S HURTING HERE.
IS *THAT* HOW YOU REALLY FEEL?!

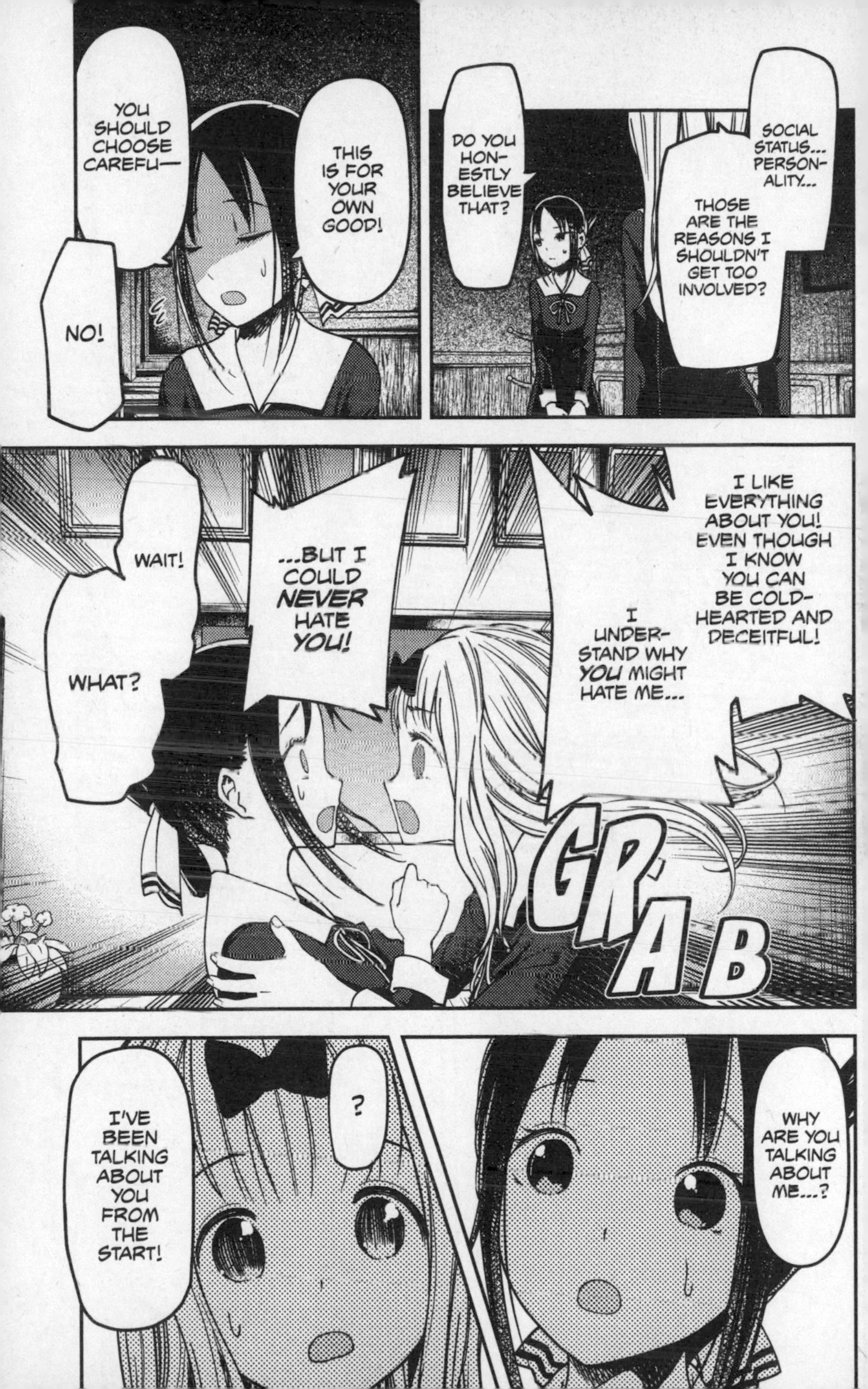
SOCIAL STATUS... PERSONALITY...
THOSE ARE THE REASONS I SHOULDN'T GET TOO INVOLVED?
DO YOU HONESTLY BELIEVE THAT?
THIS IS FOR YOUR OWN GOOD!
YOU SHOULD CHOOSE CAREFU—
NO!
I LIKE EVERYTHING ABOUT YOU! EVEN THOUGH I KNOW YOU CAN BE COLD-HEARTED AND DECEITFUL!
I UNDERSTAND WHY *YOU* MIGHT HATE ME...
...BUT I COULD *NEVER* HATE *YOU*!
GRAB
WAIT!
WHAT?
WHY ARE YOU TALKING ABOUT ME...?
?
I'VE BEEN TALKING ABOUT YOU FROM THE START!

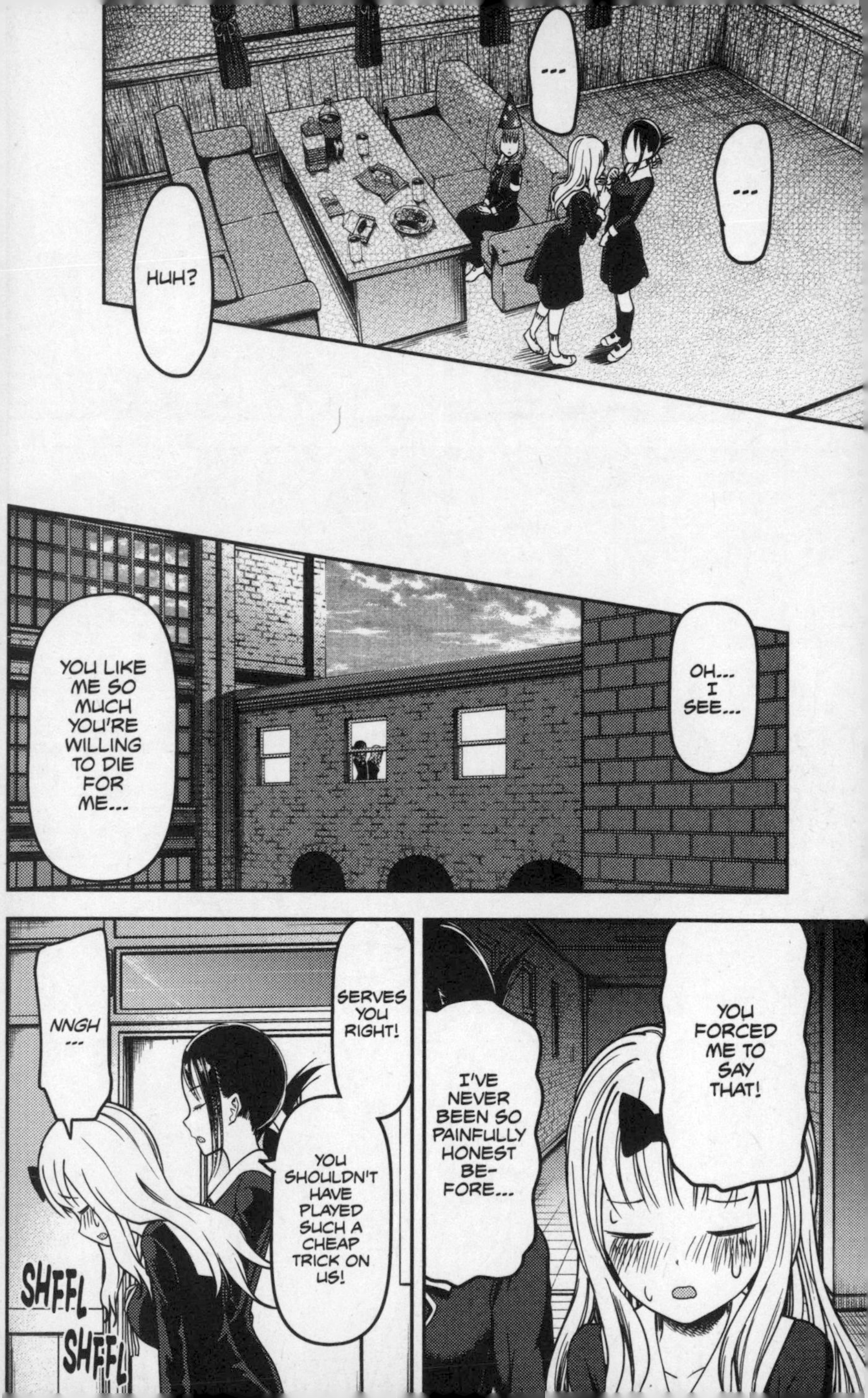
...
...
HUH?
OH... I SEE...
YOU LIKE ME SO MUCH YOU'RE WILLING TO DIE FOR ME...
YOU FORCED ME TO SAY THAT!
I'VE NEVER BEEN SO PAINFULLY HONEST BE-FORE...
SERVES YOU RIGHT!
NNGH ...
YOU SHOULDN'T HAVE PLAYED SUCH A CHEAP TRICK ON US!
SHFFL
SHFFL

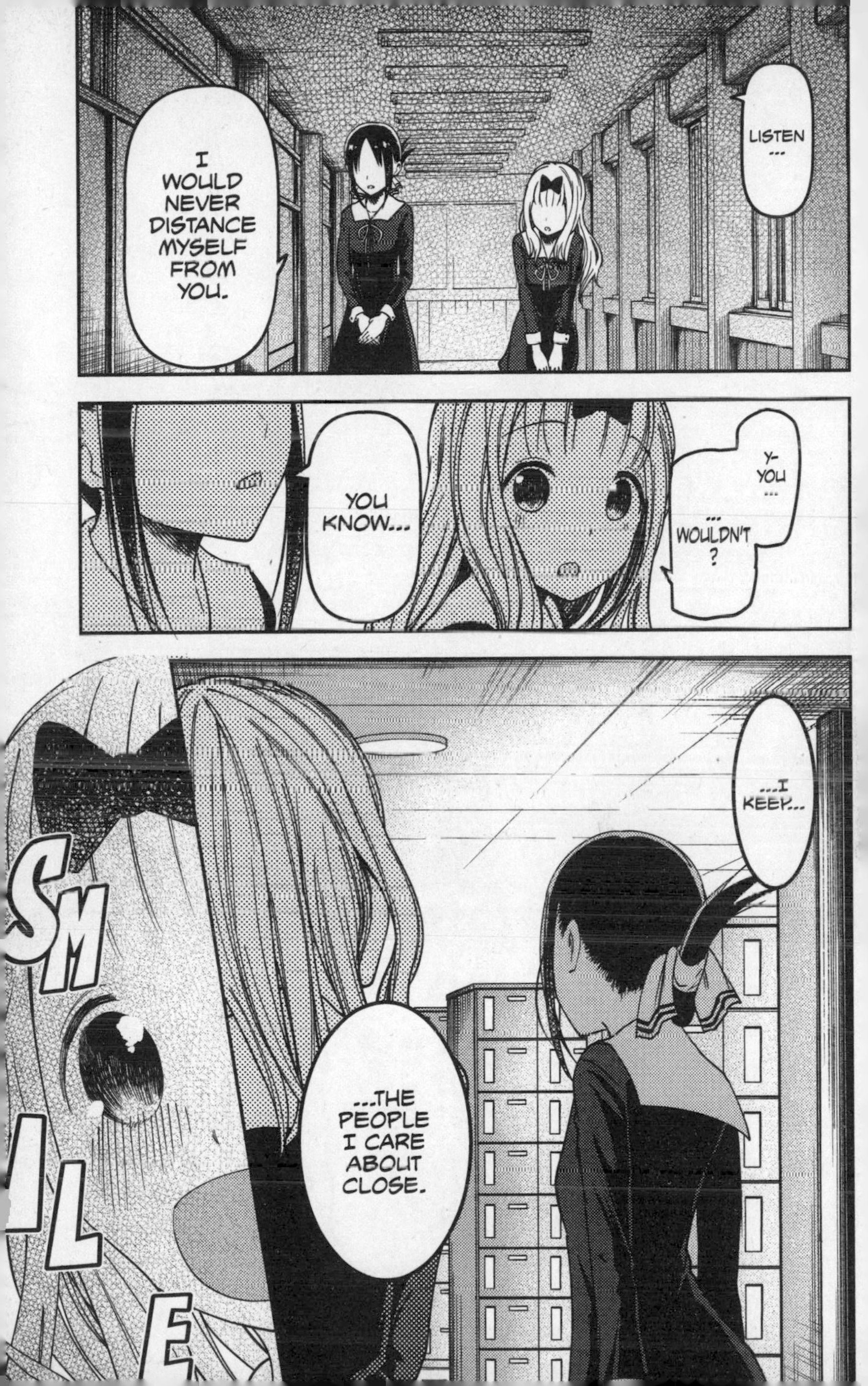
LISTEN ...
I WOULD NEVER DISTANCE MYSELF FROM YOU.
Y-YOU ... ...WOULDN'T ?
YOU KNOW...
...I KEEP...
...THE PEOPLE I CARE ABOUT CLOSE.
SMILE

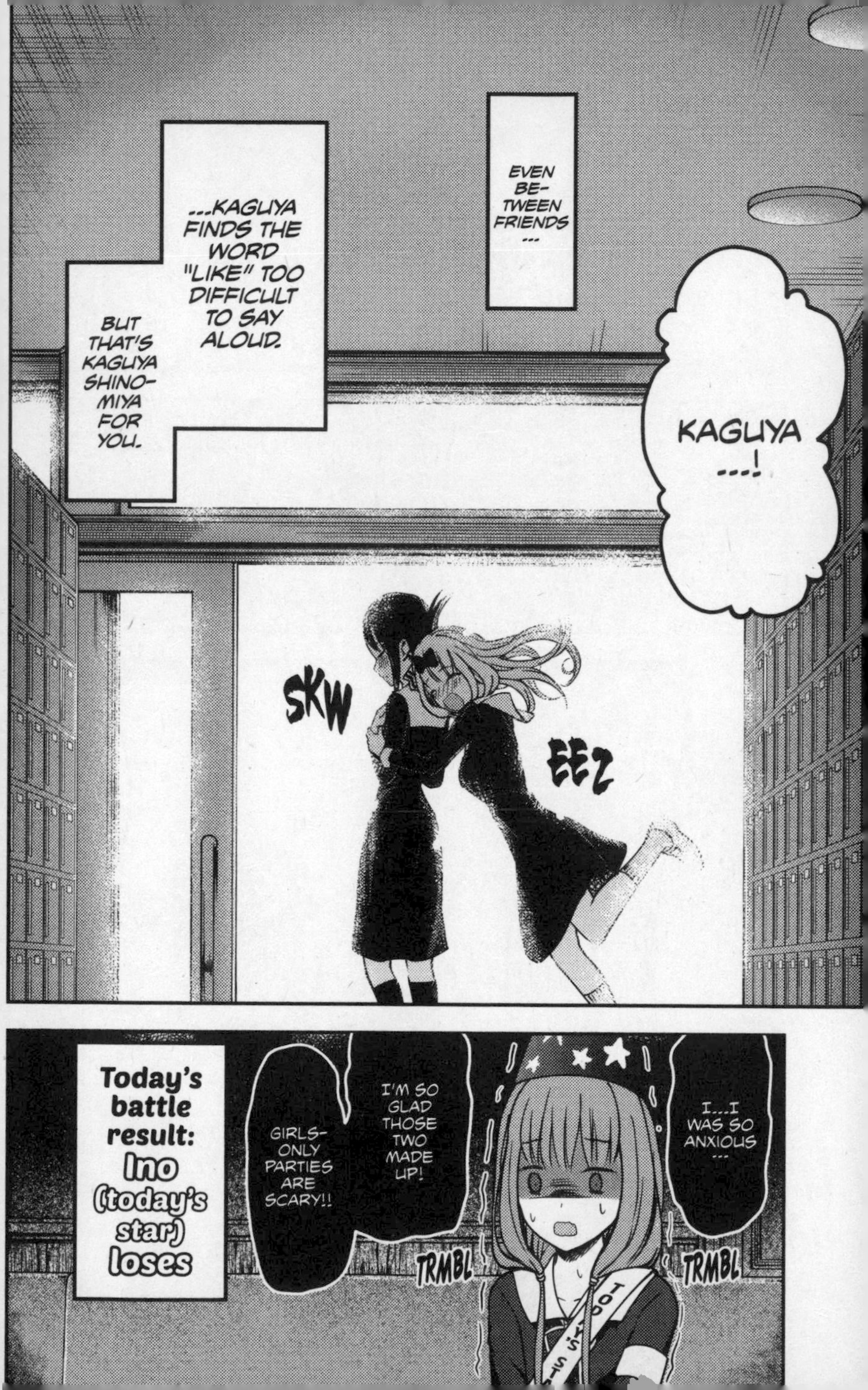
KAGUYA ...!
EVEN BE-TWEEN FRIENDS ...
...KAGUYA FINDS THE WORD "LIKE" TOO DIFFICULT TO SAY ALOUD.
BUT THAT'S KAGUYA SHINO-MIYA FOR YOU.
SKW
EEZ
I...I WAS SO ANXIOUS ...
I'M SO GLAD THOSE TWO MADE UP!
GIRLS-ONLY PARTIES ARE SCARY!!
TRMBL
TRMBL
Today's battle result: Ino (today's star) loses

KAGUYA-SAMA

LOVE IS WAR

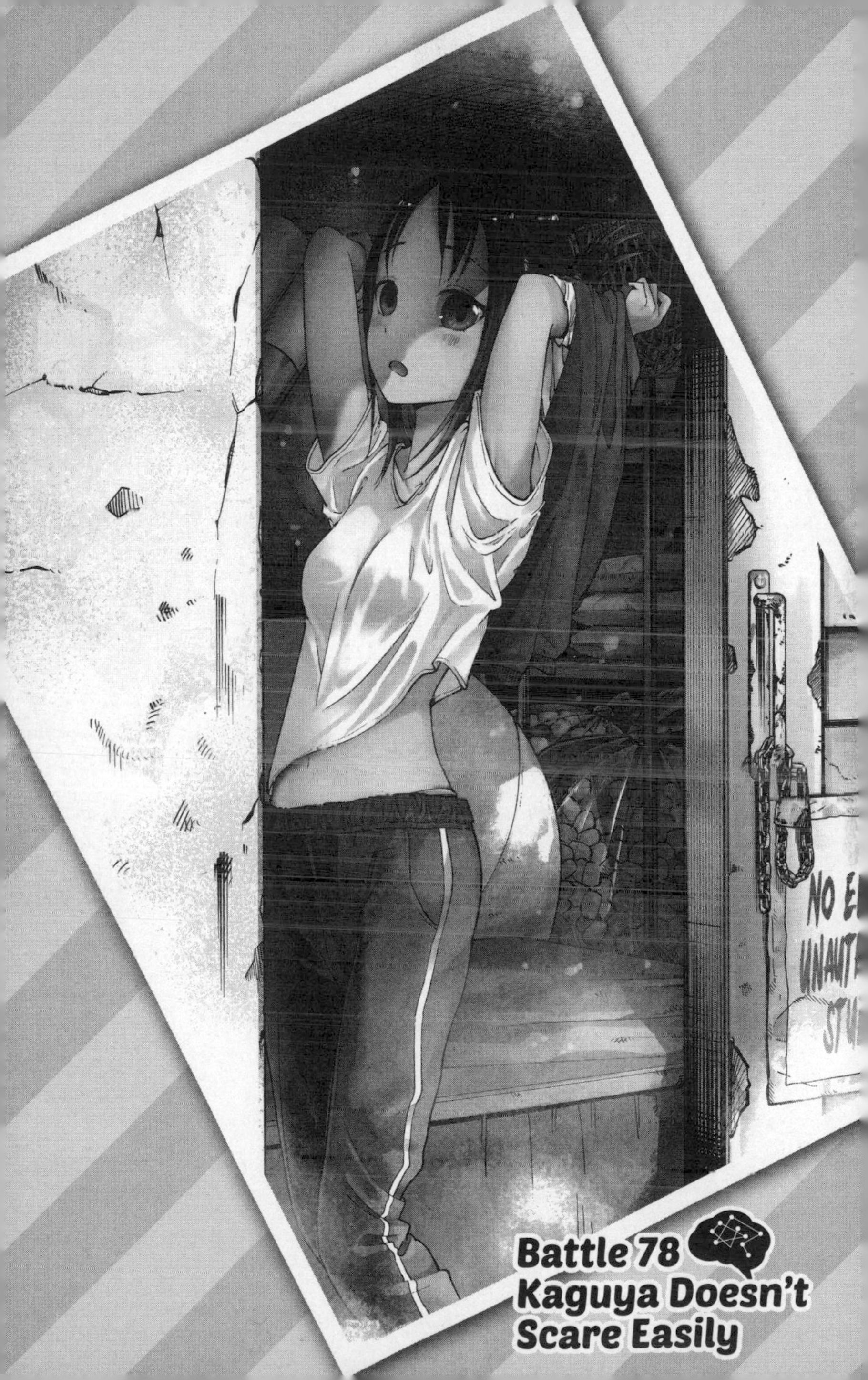

Battle 78
Kaguya Doesn't Scare Easily

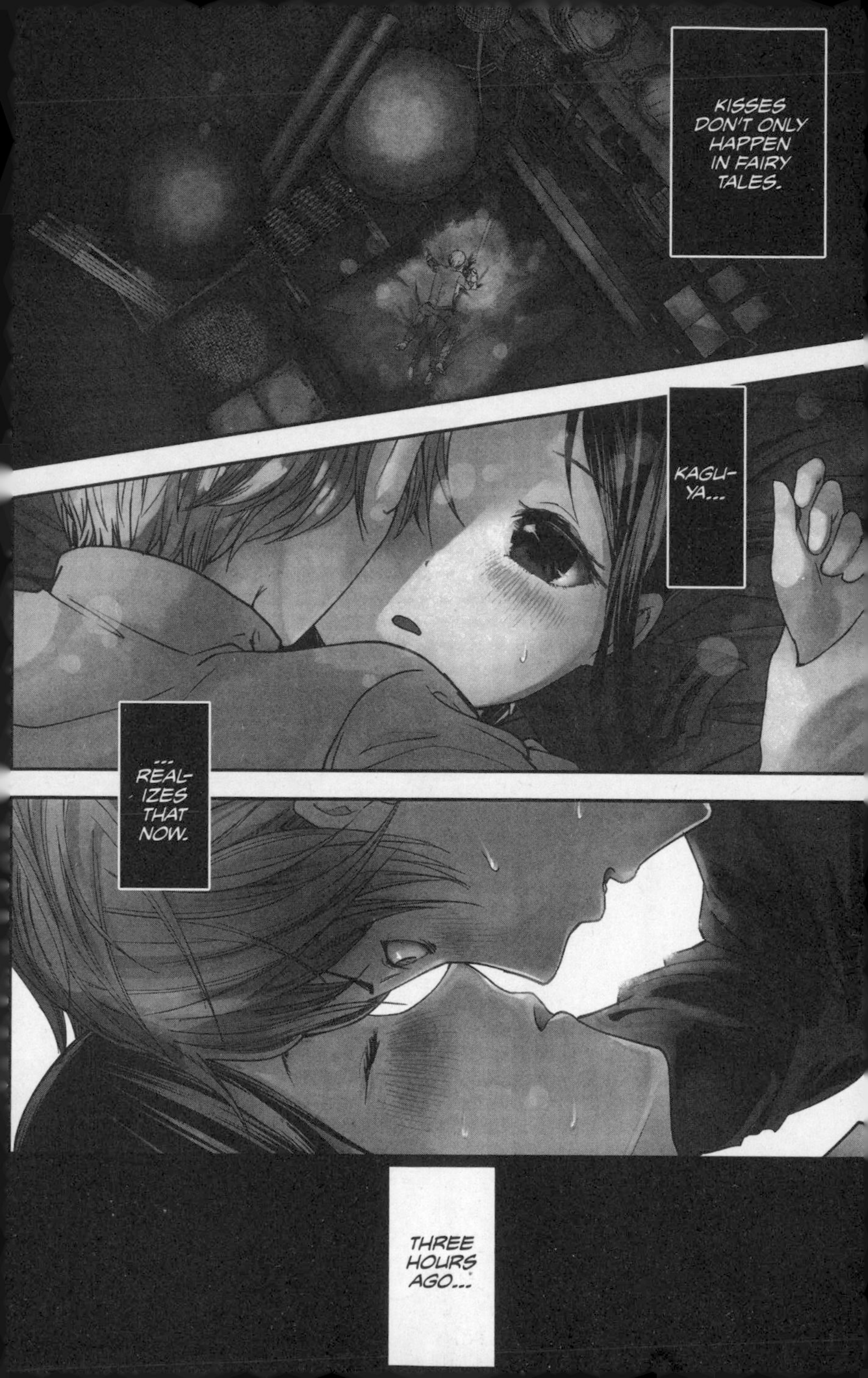
KISSES DON'T ONLY HAPPEN IN FAIRY TALES.
KAGU-YA...
...REAL-IZES THAT NOW.
THREE HOURS AGO...

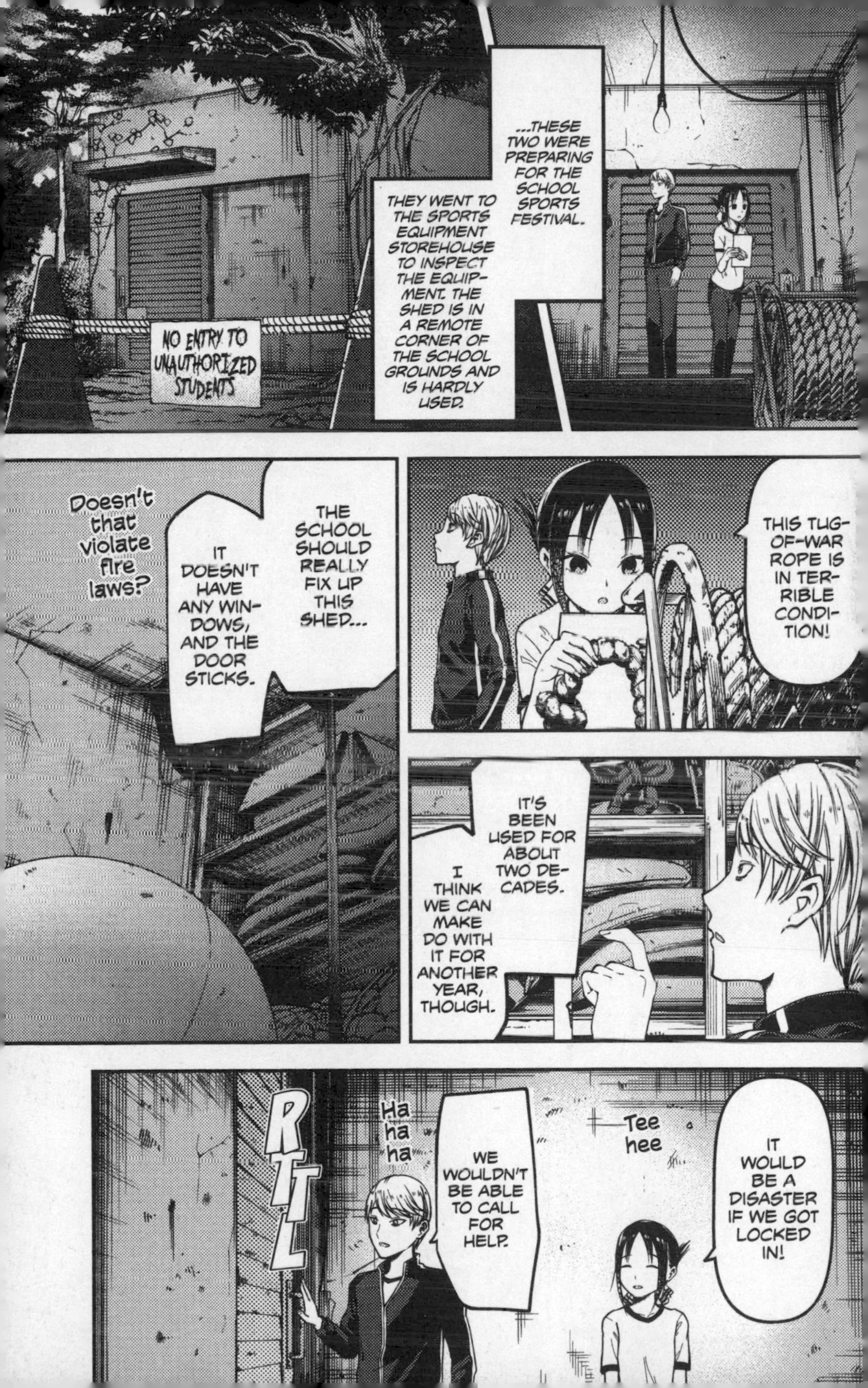
...THESE TWO WERE PREPARING FOR THE SCHOOL SPORTS FESTIVAL.
THEY WENT TO THE SPORTS EQUIPMENT STOREHOUSE TO INSPECT THE EQUIPMENT. THE SHED IS IN A REMOTE CORNER OF THE SCHOOL GROUNDS AND IS HARDLY USED.
NO ENTRY TO UNAUTHORIZED STUDENTS
THIS TUG-OF-WAR ROPE IS IN TERRIBLE CONDITION!
IT'S BEEN USED FOR ABOUT TWO DECADES.
I THINK WE CAN MAKE DO WITH IT FOR ANOTHER YEAR, THOUGH.
THE SCHOOL SHOULD REALLY FIX UP THIS SHED...
IT DOESN'T HAVE ANY WINDOWS, AND THE DOOR STICKS.
Doesn't that violate fire laws?
IT WOULD BE A DISASTER IF WE GOT LOCKED IN!
Tee hee
WE WOULDN'T BE ABLE TO CALL FOR HELP.
Ha ha ha
RTTL

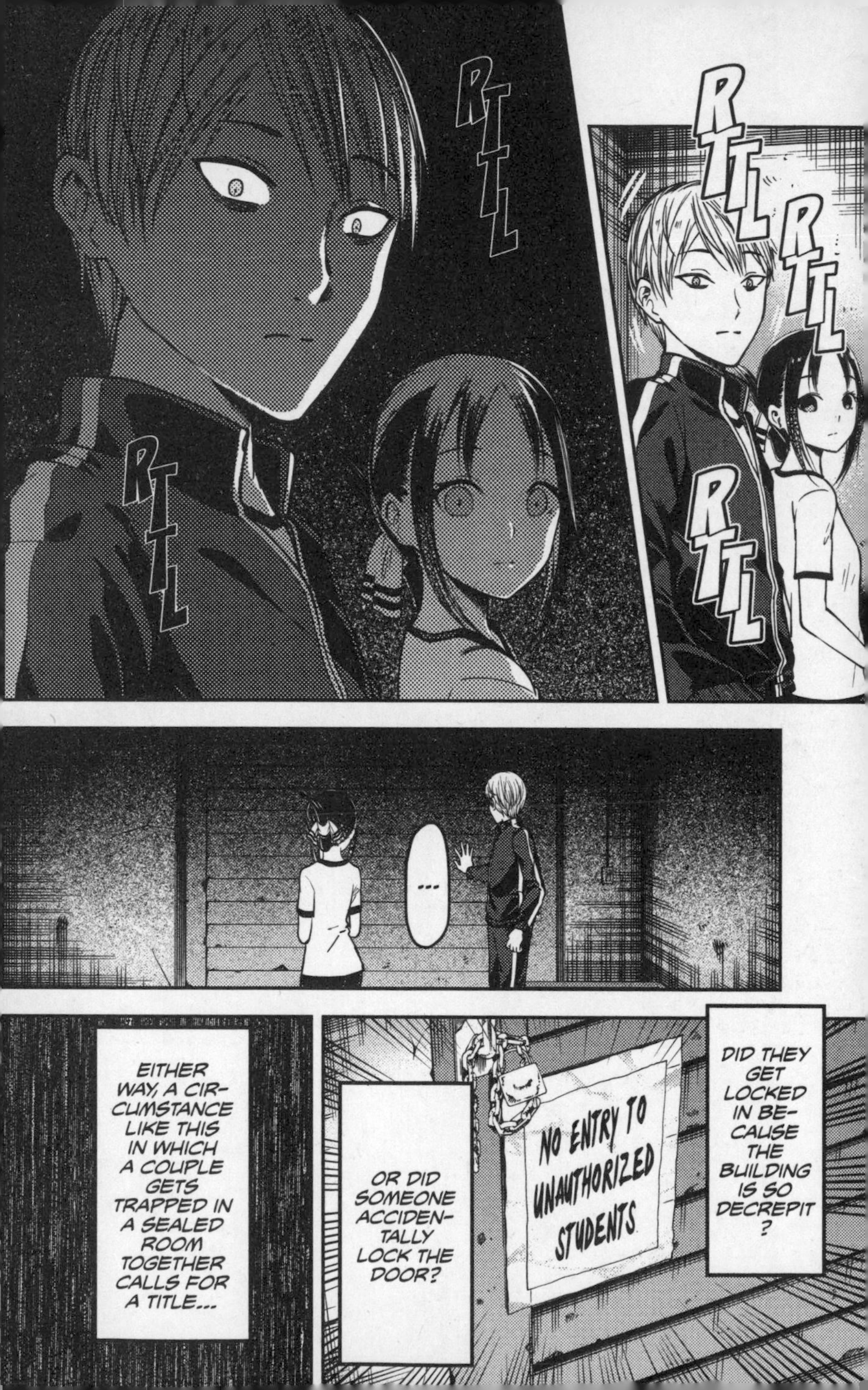
RTTL
RTTL
RTTL
RTTL
RTTL
...
DID THEY GET LOCKED IN BE-CAUSE THE BUILDING IS SO DECREPIT?
NO ENTRY TO UNAUTHORIZED STUDENTS
OR DID SOMEONE ACCIDEN-TALLY LOCK THE DOOR?
EITHER WAY, A CIR-CUMSTANCE LIKE THIS IN WHICH A COUPLE GETS TRAPPED IN A SEALED ROOM TOGETHER CALLS FOR A TITLE...

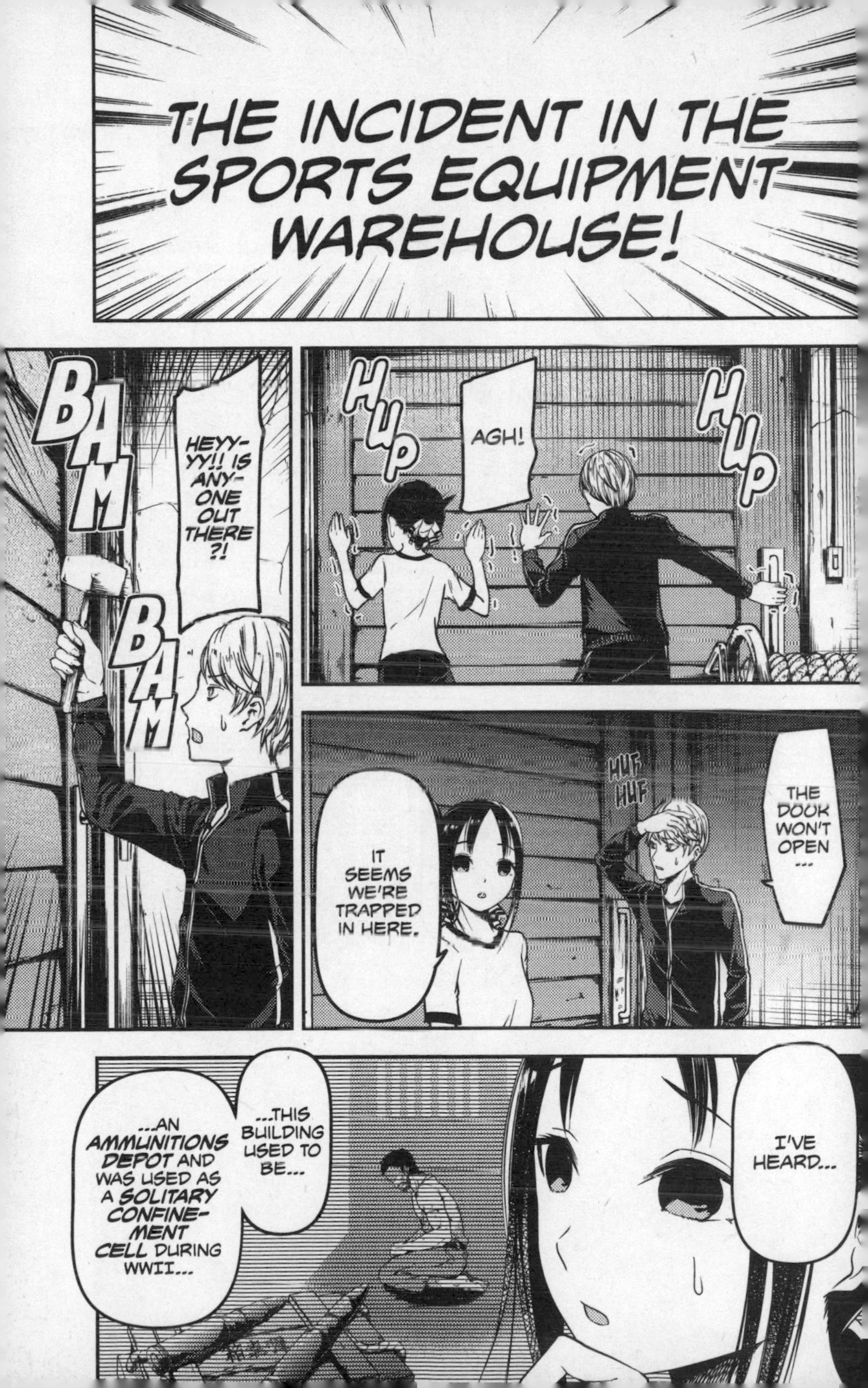
THE INCIDENT IN THE SPORTS EQUIPMENT WAREHOUSE!
HUP
AGH!
HUP
HUF HUF
THE DOOR WON'T OPEN...
IT SEEMS WE'RE TRAPPED IN HERE.
BAM
HEYYY-YY!! IS ANYONE OUT THERE?!
BAM
I'VE HEARD...
...THIS BUILDING USED TO BE...
...AN AMMUNITIONS DEPOT AND WAS USED AS A SOLITARY CONFINEMENT CELL DURING WWII...

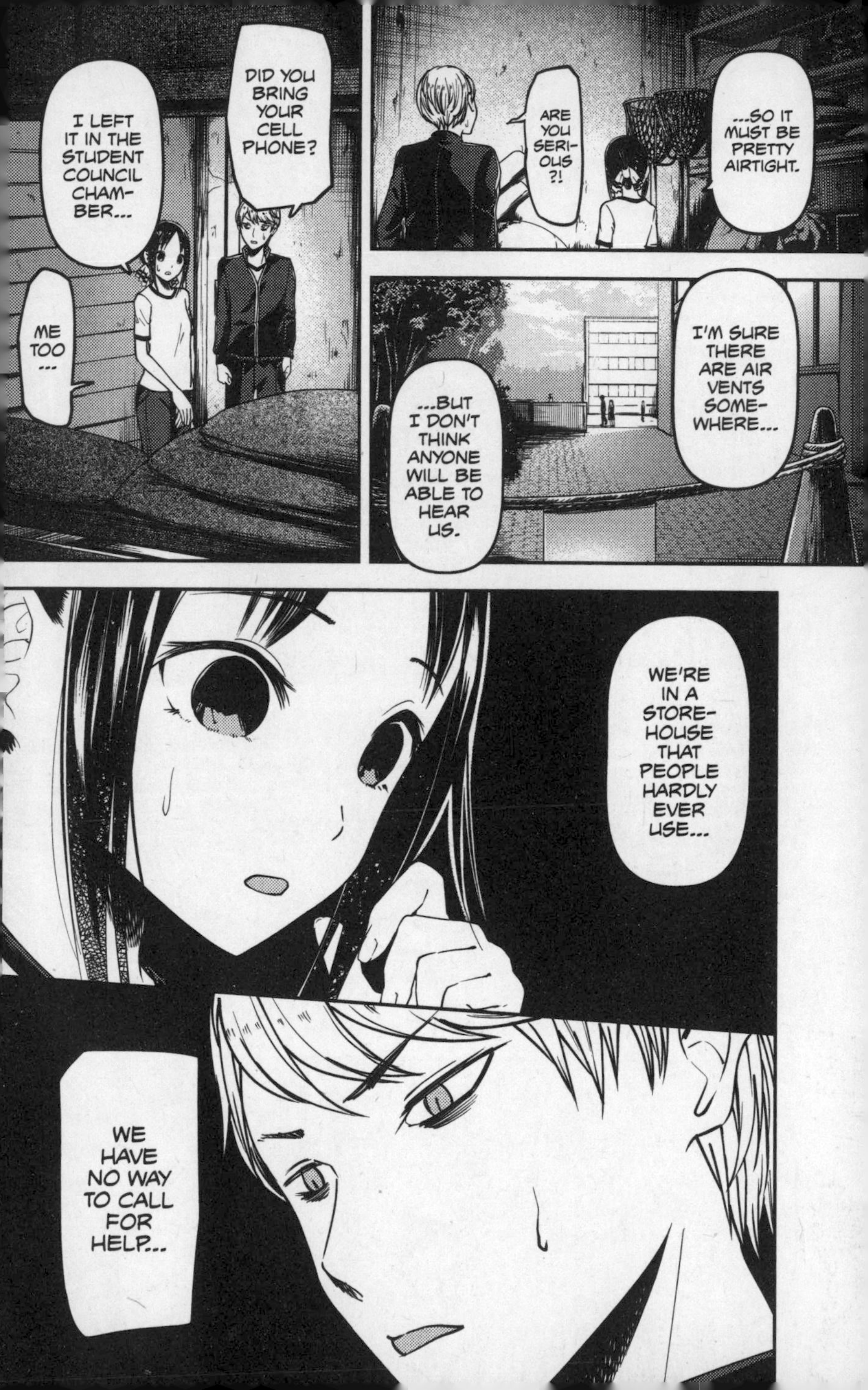
...SO IT MUST BE PRETTY AIRTIGHT.
ARE YOU SERIOUS?!
I'M SURE THERE ARE AIR VENTS SOMEWHERE...
...BUT I DON'T THINK ANYONE WILL BE ABLE TO HEAR US.
DID YOU BRING YOUR CELL PHONE?
I LEFT IT IN THE STUDENT COUNCIL CHAMBER...
ME TOO...
WE'RE IN A STOREHOUSE THAT PEOPLE HARDLY EVER USE...
WE HAVE NO WAY TO CALL FOR HELP...

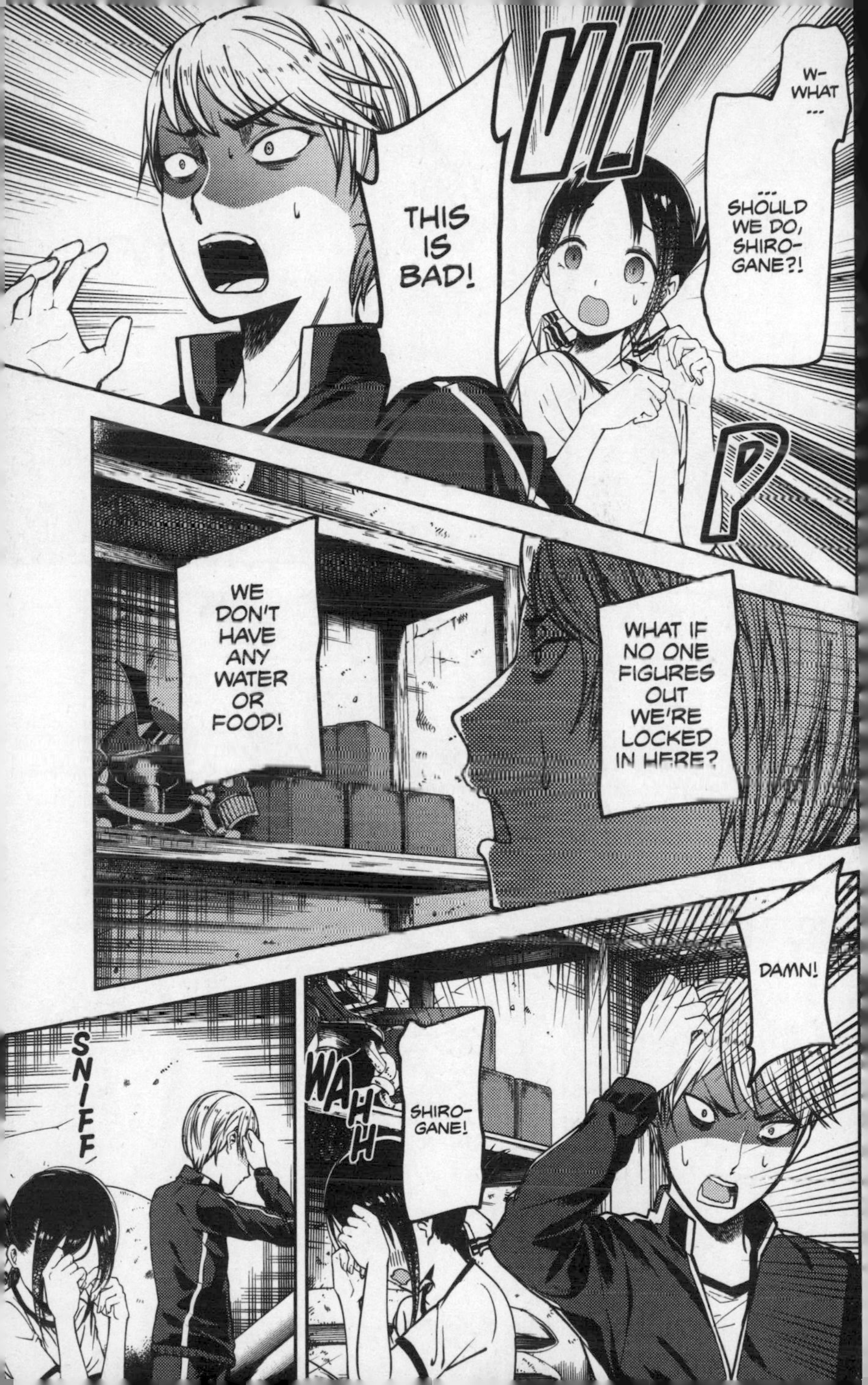
W-WHAT... ...SHOULD WE DO, SHIROGANE?!
VIP
THIS IS BAD!
WHAT IF NO ONE FIGURES OUT WE'RE LOCKED IN HERE?
WE DON'T HAVE ANY WATER OR FOOD!
DAMN!
SHIROGANE!
WAHH
SNIFF

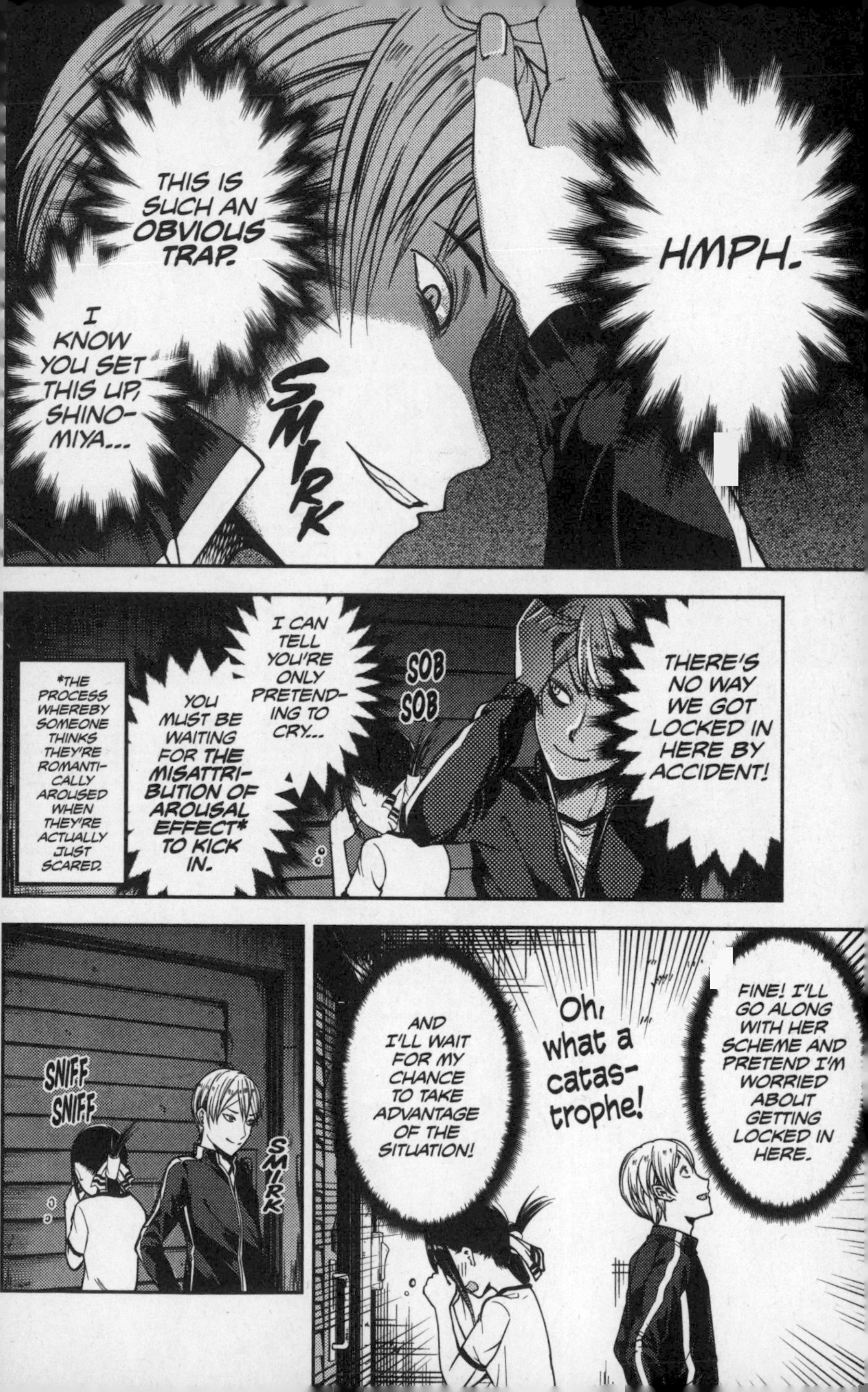
HMPH.
THIS IS SUCH AN OBVIOUS TRAP.
SMIRK
I KNOW YOU SET THIS UP, SHINOMIYA...
THERE'S NO WAY WE GOT LOCKED IN HERE BY ACCIDENT!
SOB SOB
I CAN TELL YOU'RE ONLY PRETENDING TO CRY...
YOU MUST BE WAITING FOR THE MISATTRIBUTION OF AROUSAL EFFECT* TO KICK IN.
*THE PROCESS WHEREBY SOMEONE THINKS THEY'RE ROMANTICALLY AROUSED WHEN THEY'RE ACTUALLY JUST SCARED.
FINE! I'LL GO ALONG WITH HER SCHEME AND PRETEND I'M WORRIED ABOUT GETTING LOCKED IN HERE.
Oh, what a catastrophe!
AND I'LL WAIT FOR MY CHANCE TO TAKE ADVANTAGE OF THE SITUATION!
SMIRK
SNIFF SNIFF

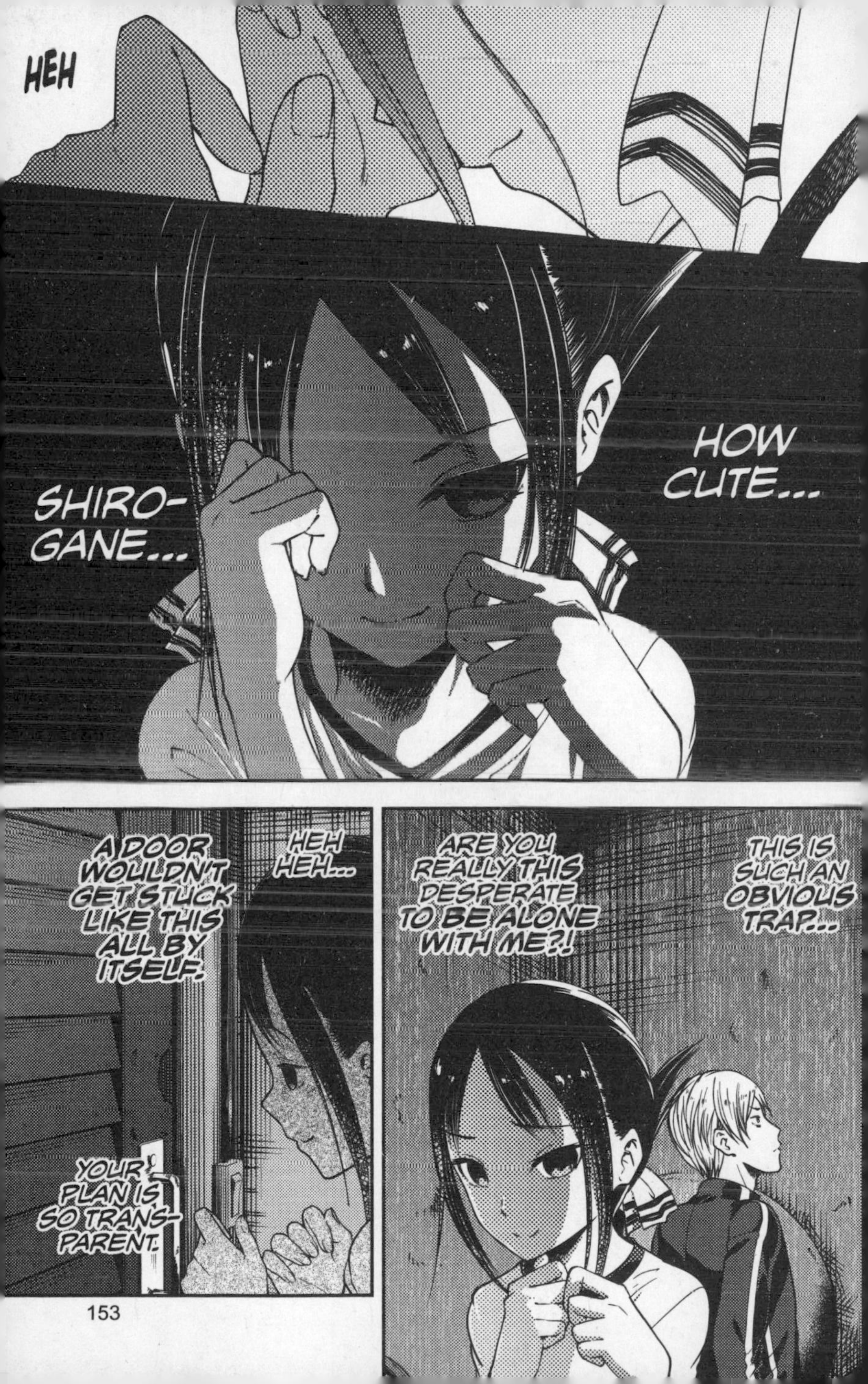
HEH
HOW CUTE...
SHIRO-GANE...
THIS IS SUCH AN OBVIOUS TRAP...
ARE YOU REALLY THIS DESPERATE TO BE ALONE WITH ME?!
HEH HEH...
A DOOR WOULDN'T GET STUCK LIKE THIS ALL BY ITSELF.
YOUR PLAN IS SO TRANS-PARENT.

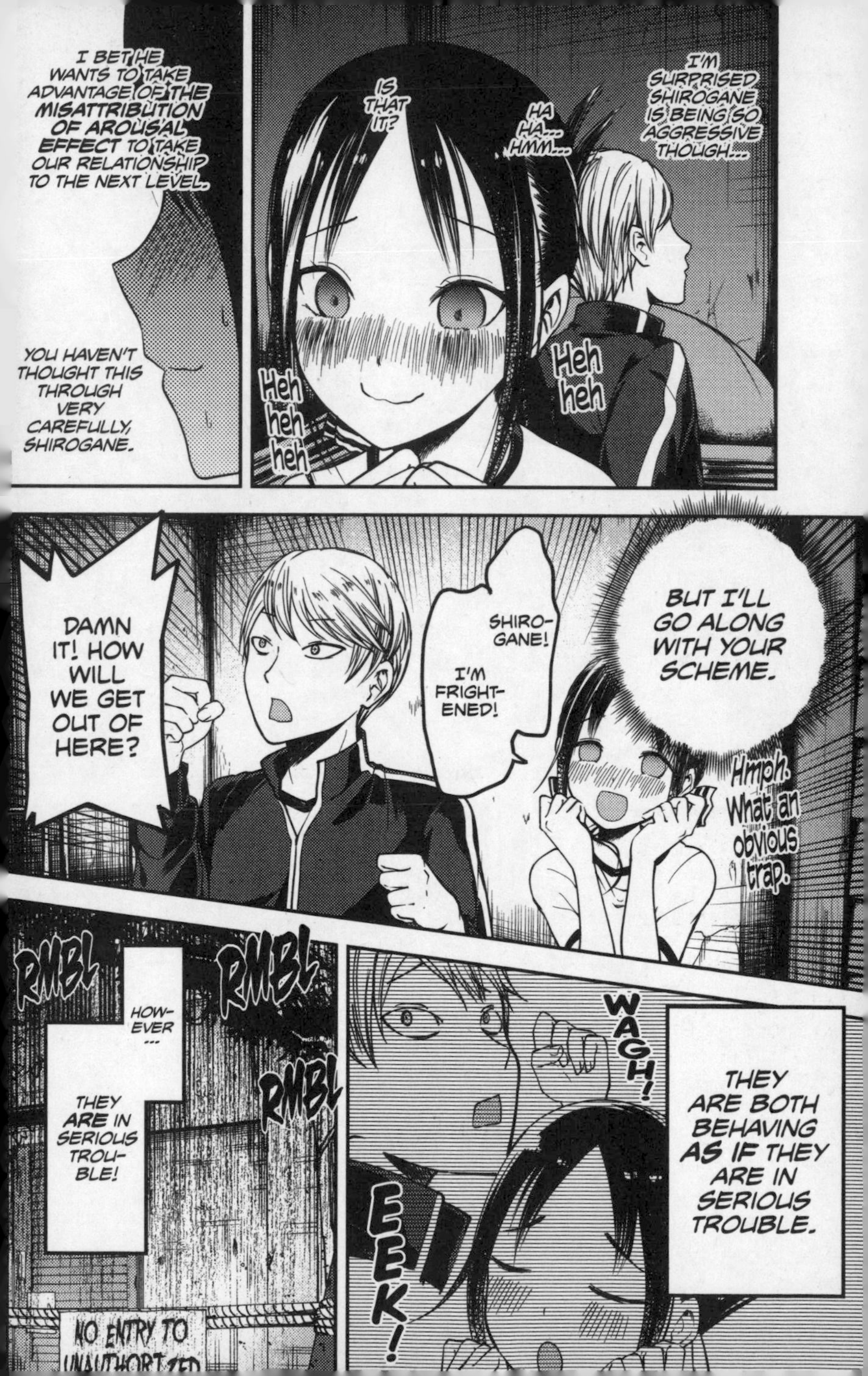

I'M SURPRISED SHIROGANE IS BEING SO AGGRESSIVE THOUGH...
HA HA... HMM...
IS THAT IT?
Heh heh
Heh heh heh
I BET HE WANTS TO TAKE ADVANTAGE OF THE MISATTRIBUTION OF AROUSAL EFFECT TO TAKE OUR RELATIONSHIP TO THE NEXT LEVEL.
YOU HAVEN'T THOUGHT THIS THROUGH VERY CAREFULLY, SHIROGANE.
BUT I'LL GO ALONG WITH YOUR SCHEME.
Hmph. What an obvious trap.
SHIRO-GANE!
I'M FRIGHT-ENED!
DAMN IT! HOW WILL WE GET OUT OF HERE?
THEY ARE BOTH BEHAVING AS IF THEY ARE IN SERIOUS TROUBLE.
WAGH!
EEK!
RMBL
RMBL
HOW-EVER ...
THEY ARE IN SERIOUS TROU-BLE!
RMBL
NO ENTRY TO

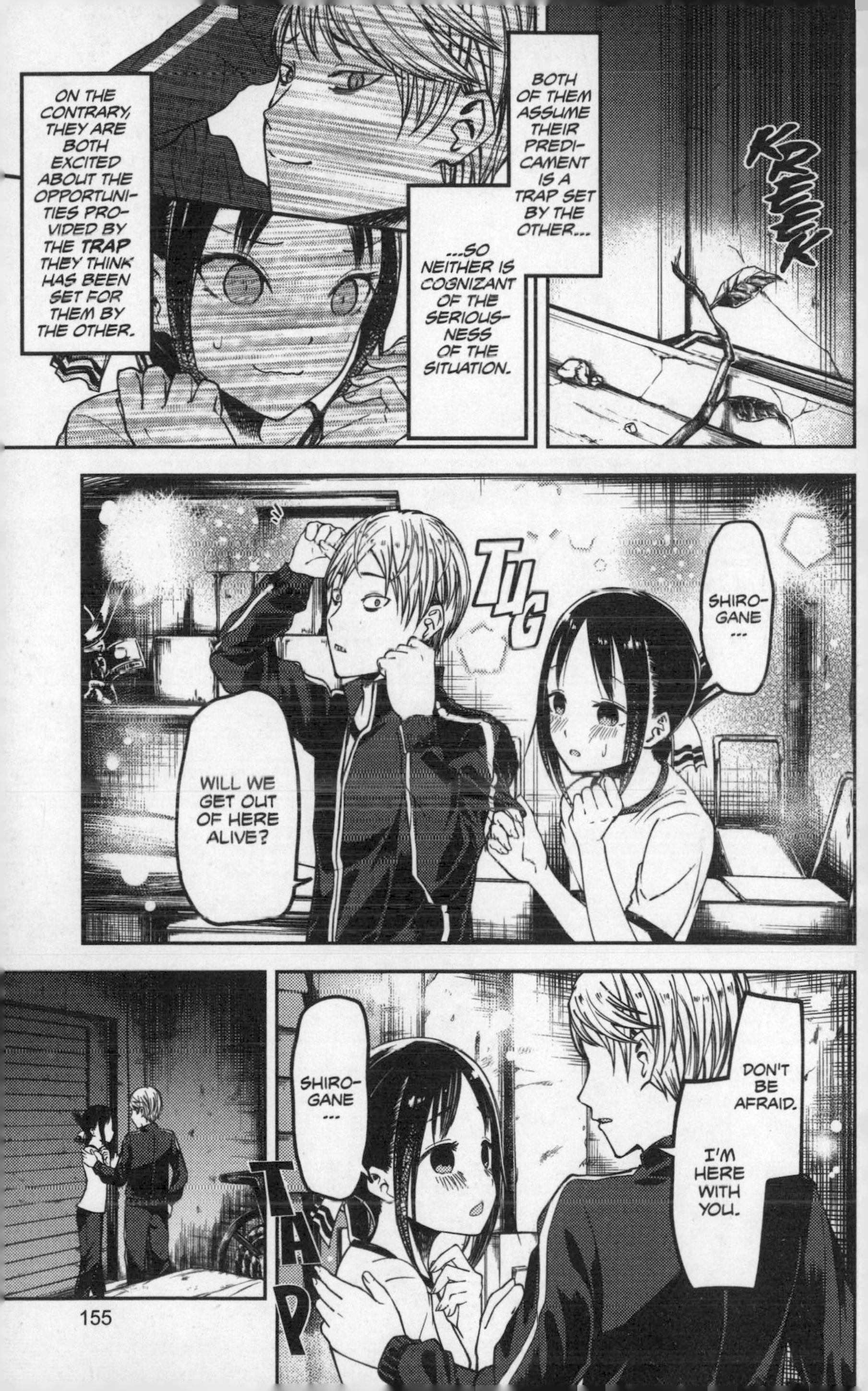
KREEEK
BOTH OF THEM ASSUME THEIR PREDICAMENT IS A TRAP SET BY THE OTHER...
...SO NEITHER IS COGNIZANT OF THE SERIOUSNESS OF THE SITUATION.
ON THE CONTRARY, THEY ARE BOTH EXCITED ABOUT THE OPPORTUNITIES PROVIDED BY THE **TRAP** THEY THINK HAS BEEN SET FOR THEM BY THE OTHER.
SHIRO-GANE...
TUG
WILL WE GET OUT OF HERE ALIVE?
DON'T BE AFRAID.
I'M HERE WITH YOU.
SHIRO-GANE...
TAP

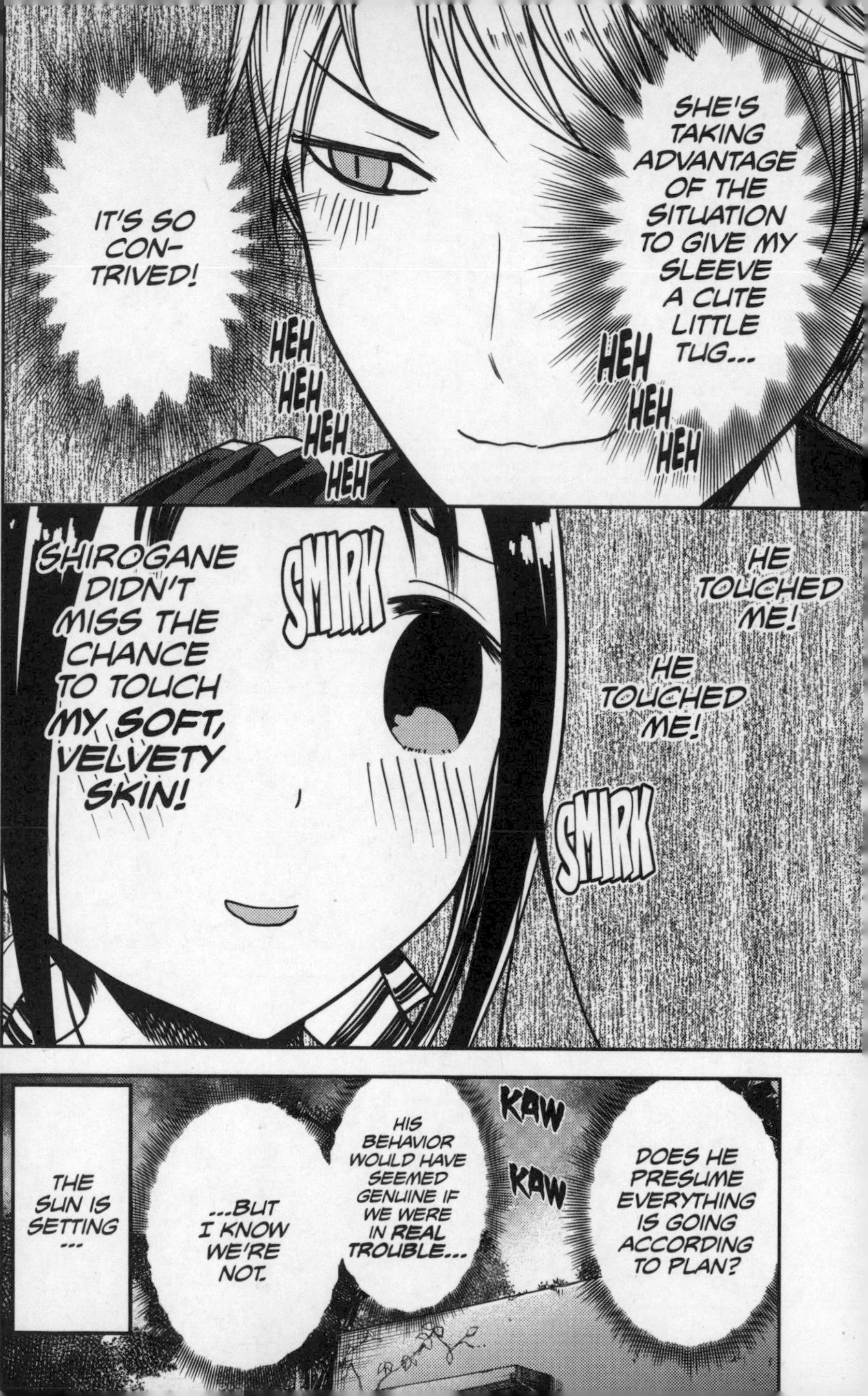
SHE'S TAKING ADVANTAGE OF THE SITUATION TO GIVE MY SLEEVE A CUTE LITTLE TUG...
HEH HEH HEH
IT'S SO CON-TRIVED!
HEH HEH HEH HEH
HE TOUCHED ME!
HE TOUCHED ME!
SMIRK
SMIRK
SHIROGANE DIDN'T MISS THE CHANCE TO TOUCH MY SOFT, VELVETY SKIN!
DOES HE PRESUME EVERYTHING IS GOING ACCORDING TO PLAN?
KAW
KAW
HIS BEHAVIOR WOULD HAVE SEEMED GENUINE IF WE WERE IN REAL TROUBLE...
...BUT I KNOW WE'RE NOT.
THE SUN IS SETTING...

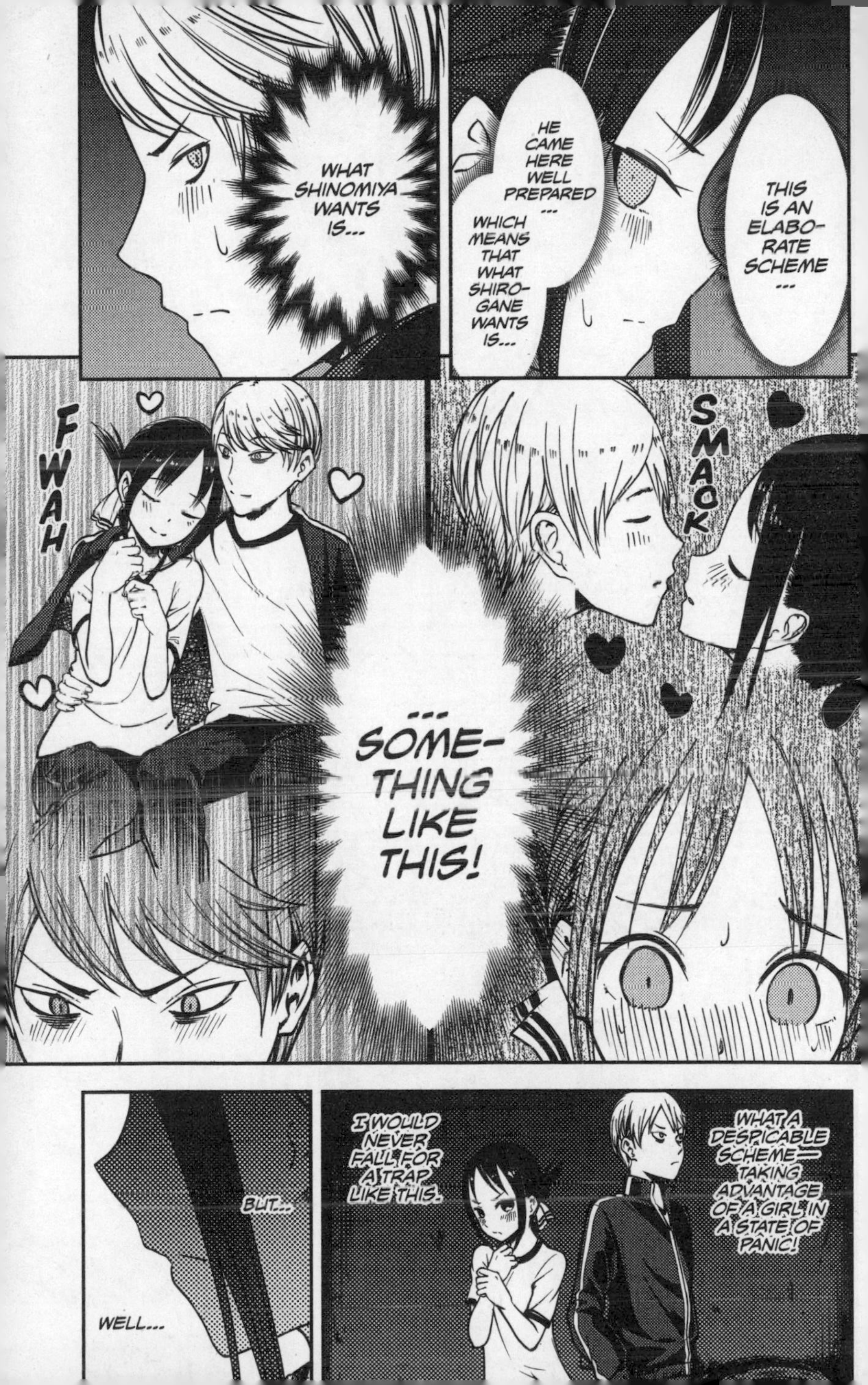
THIS IS AN ELABORATE SCHEME...
HE CAME HERE WELL PREPARED...
WHICH MEANS THAT WHAT SHIROGANE WANTS IS...
WHAT SHINOMIYA WANTS IS...
SMACK
FWAH
...SOMETHING LIKE THIS!
WHAT A DESPICABLE SCHEME—TAKING ADVANTAGE OF A GIRL IN A STATE OF PANIC!
I WOULD NEVER FALL FOR A TRAP LIKE THIS.
BUT...
WELL...

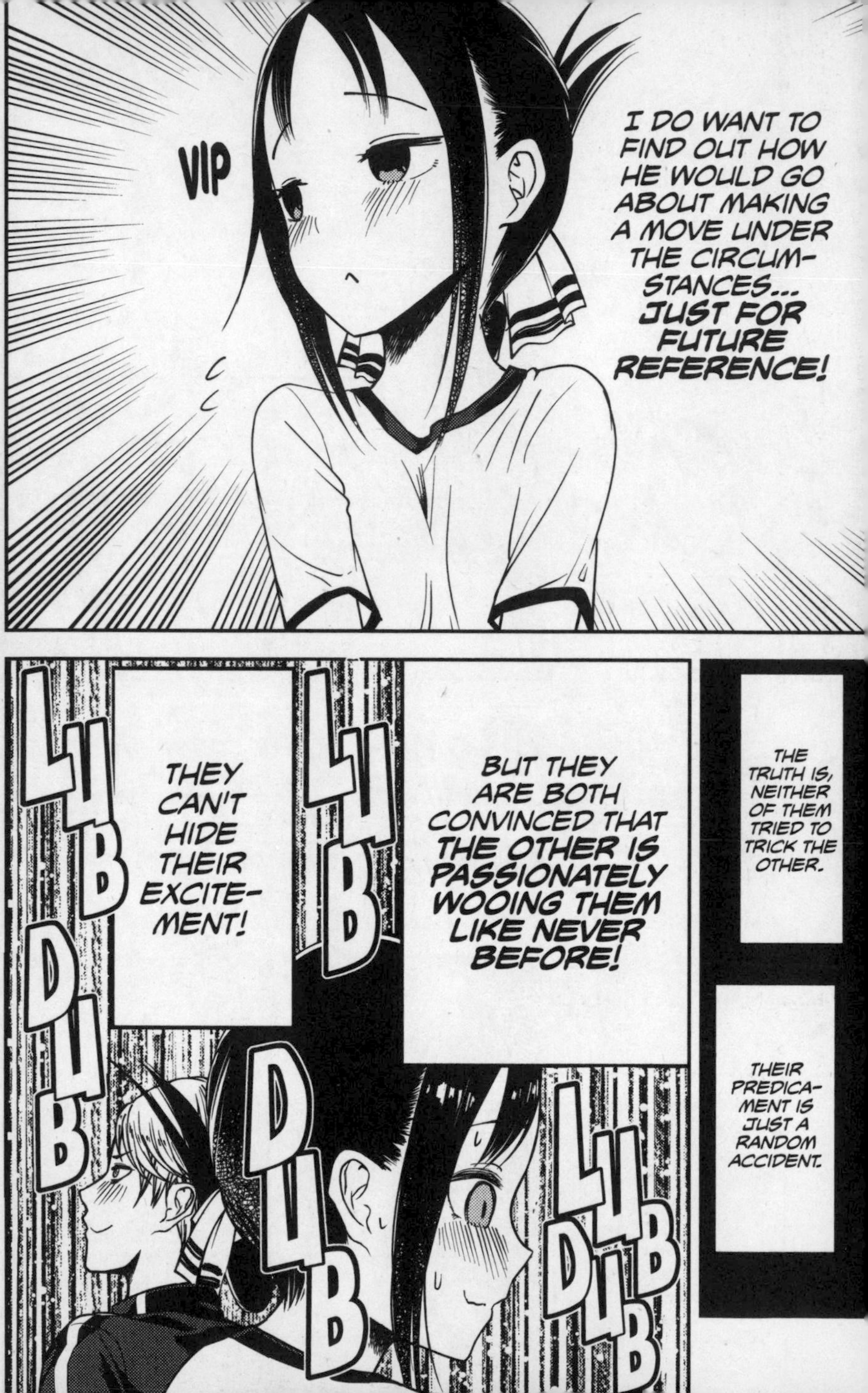
I DO WANT TO FIND OUT HOW HE WOULD GO ABOUT MAKING A MOVE UNDER THE CIRCUM-STANCES... JUST FOR FUTURE REFERENCE!
VIP
THE TRUTH IS, NEITHER OF THEM TRIED TO TRICK THE OTHER.
THEIR PREDICA-MENT IS JUST A RANDOM ACCIDENT.
BUT THEY ARE BOTH CONVINCED THAT THE OTHER IS PASSIONATELY WOOING THEM LIKE NEVER BEFORE!
THEY CAN'T HIDE THEIR EXCITE-MENT!
LUB DUB
LUB DUB
LUB DUB
LUB DUB

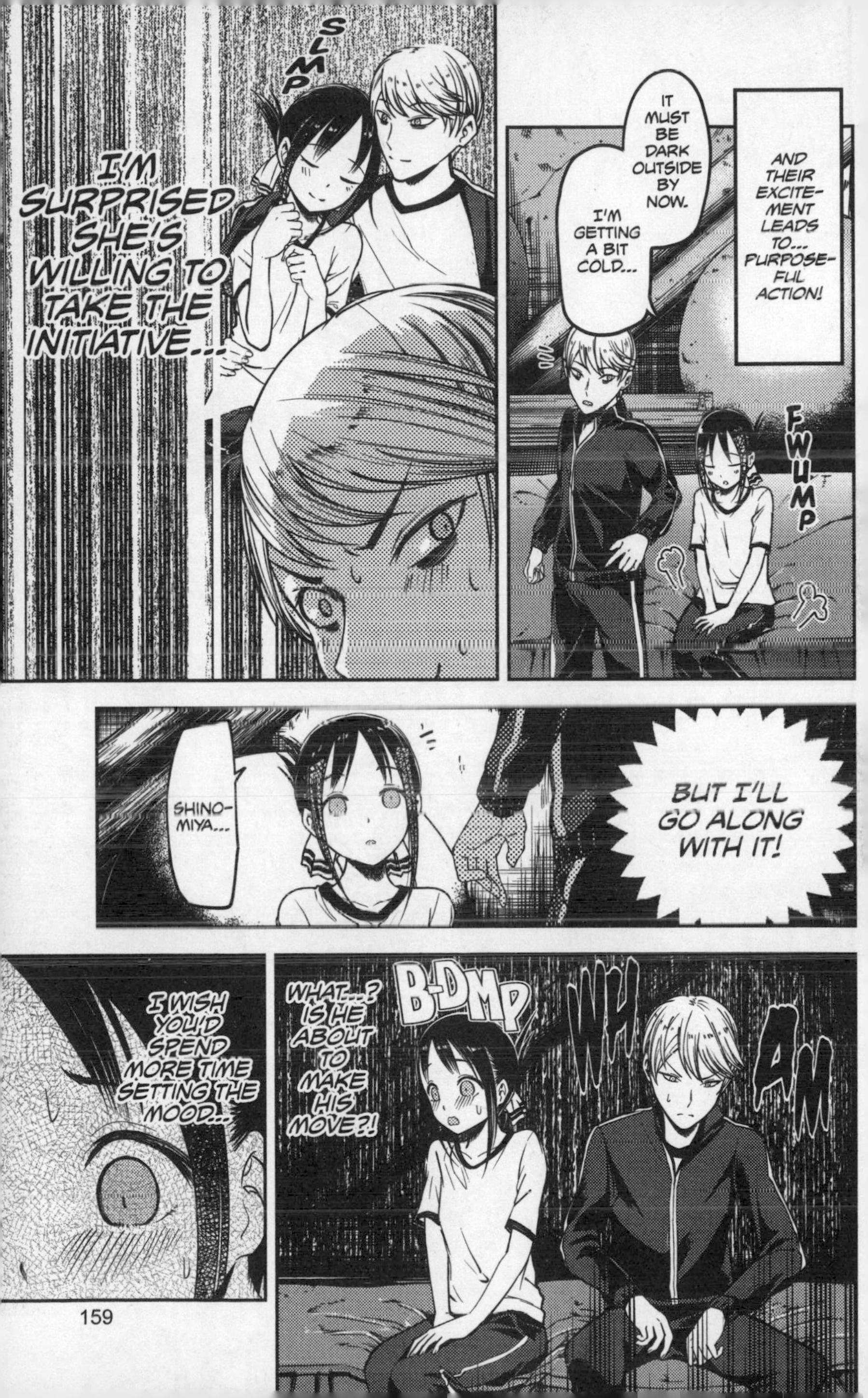
AND THEIR EXCITEMENT LEADS TO... PURPOSEFUL ACTION!
IT MUST BE DARK OUTSIDE BY NOW.
I'M GETTING A BIT COLD...
FWUMP
SLMP
I'M SURPRISED SHE'S WILLING TO TAKE THE INITIATIVE...
BUT I'LL GO ALONG WITH IT!
SHINOMIYA...
WHAM
B-DMP
WHAT...? IS HE ABOUT TO MAKE HIS MOVE?!
I WISH YOU'D SPEND MORE TIME SETTING THE MOOD...

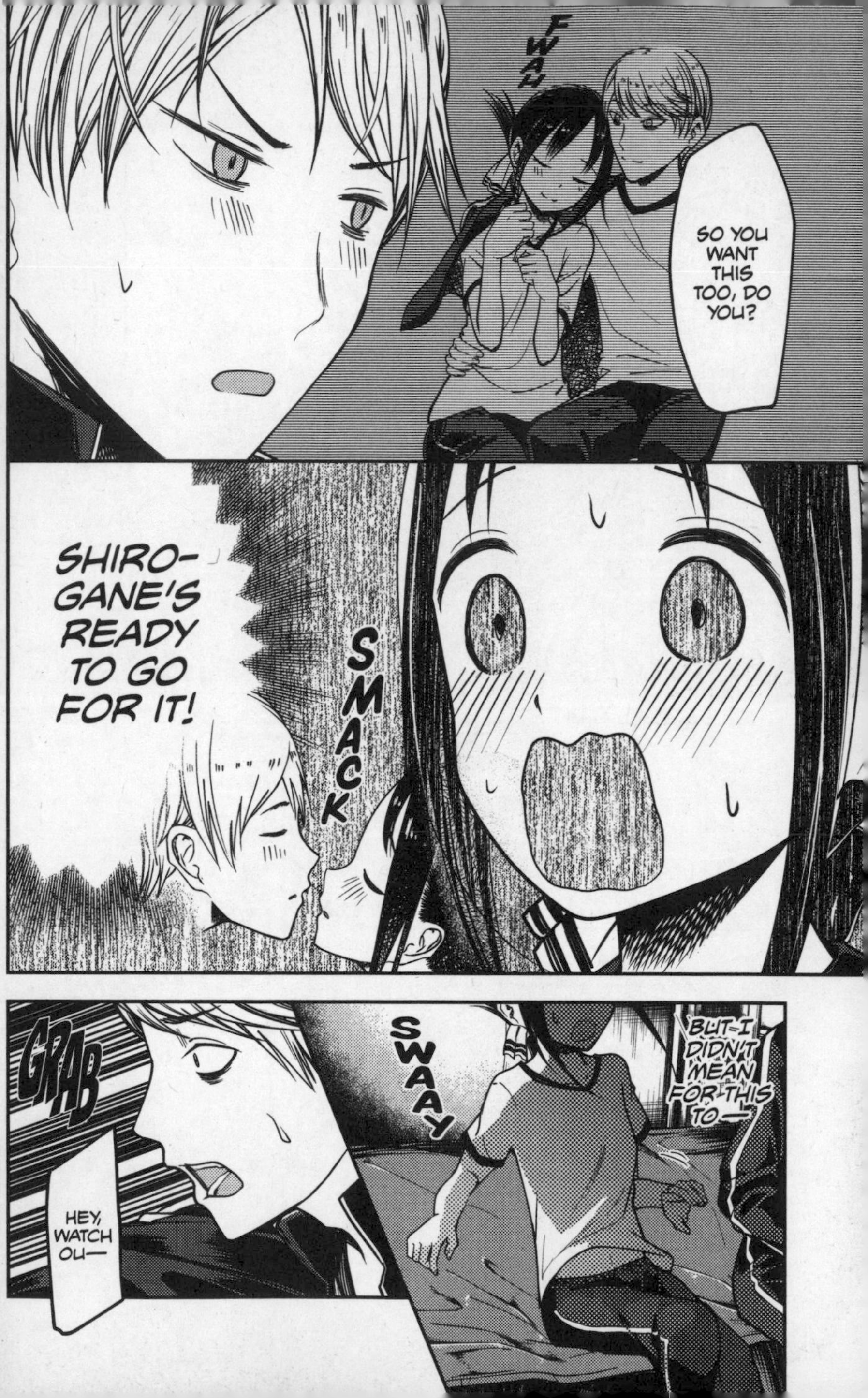
FWAH
SO YOU WANT THIS TOO, DO YOU?
SHIRO-GANE'S READY TO GO FOR IT!
SMACK
BUT I DIDN'T MEAN FOR THIS TO—
SWAAY
GRAB
HEY, WATCH OU—

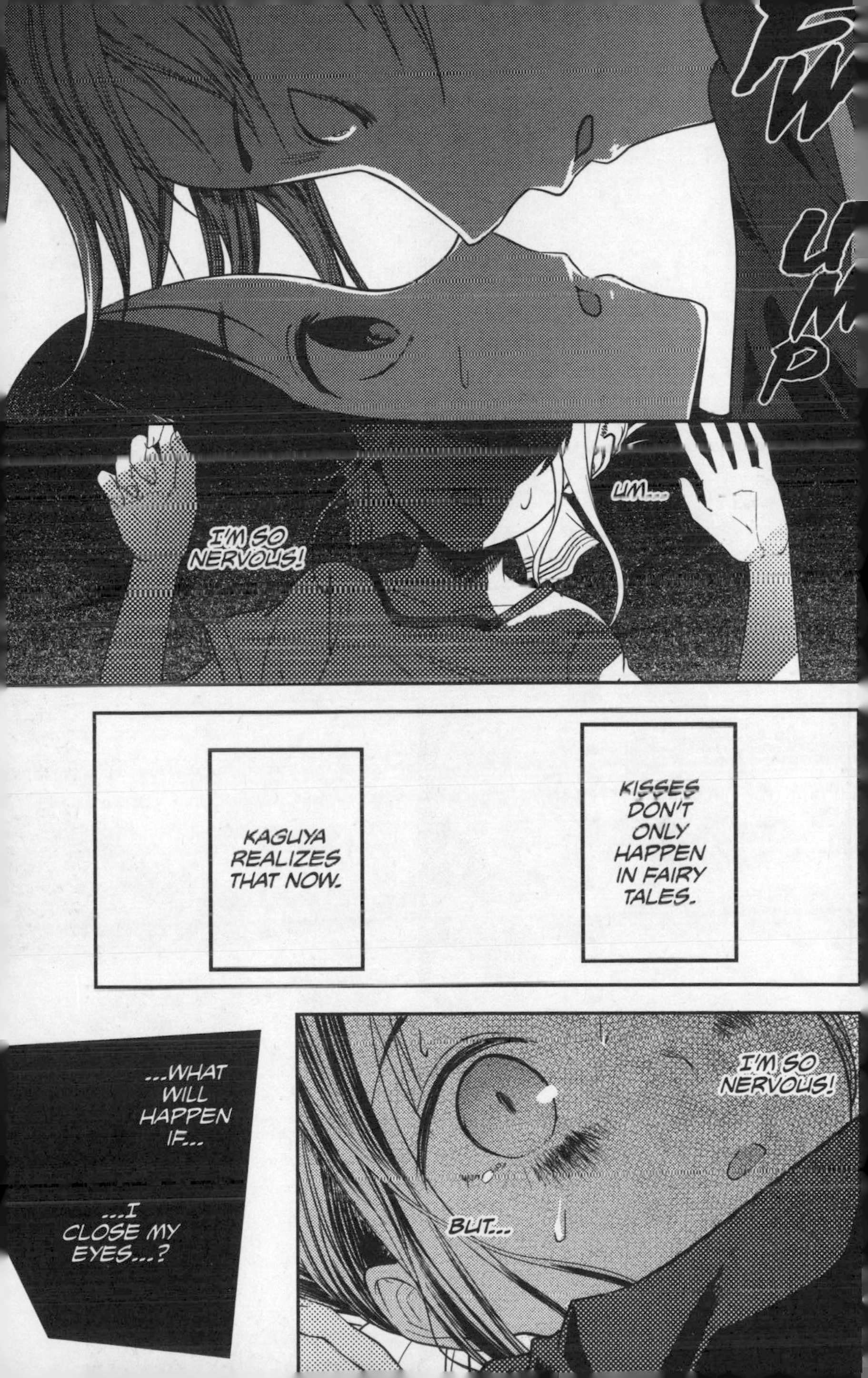
UM...
I'M SO NERVOUS!
KISSES DON'T ONLY HAPPEN IN FAIRY TALES.
KAGUYA REALIZES THAT NOW.
I'M SO NERVOUS!
BUT...
...WHAT WILL HAPPEN IF...
...I CLOSE MY EYES...?

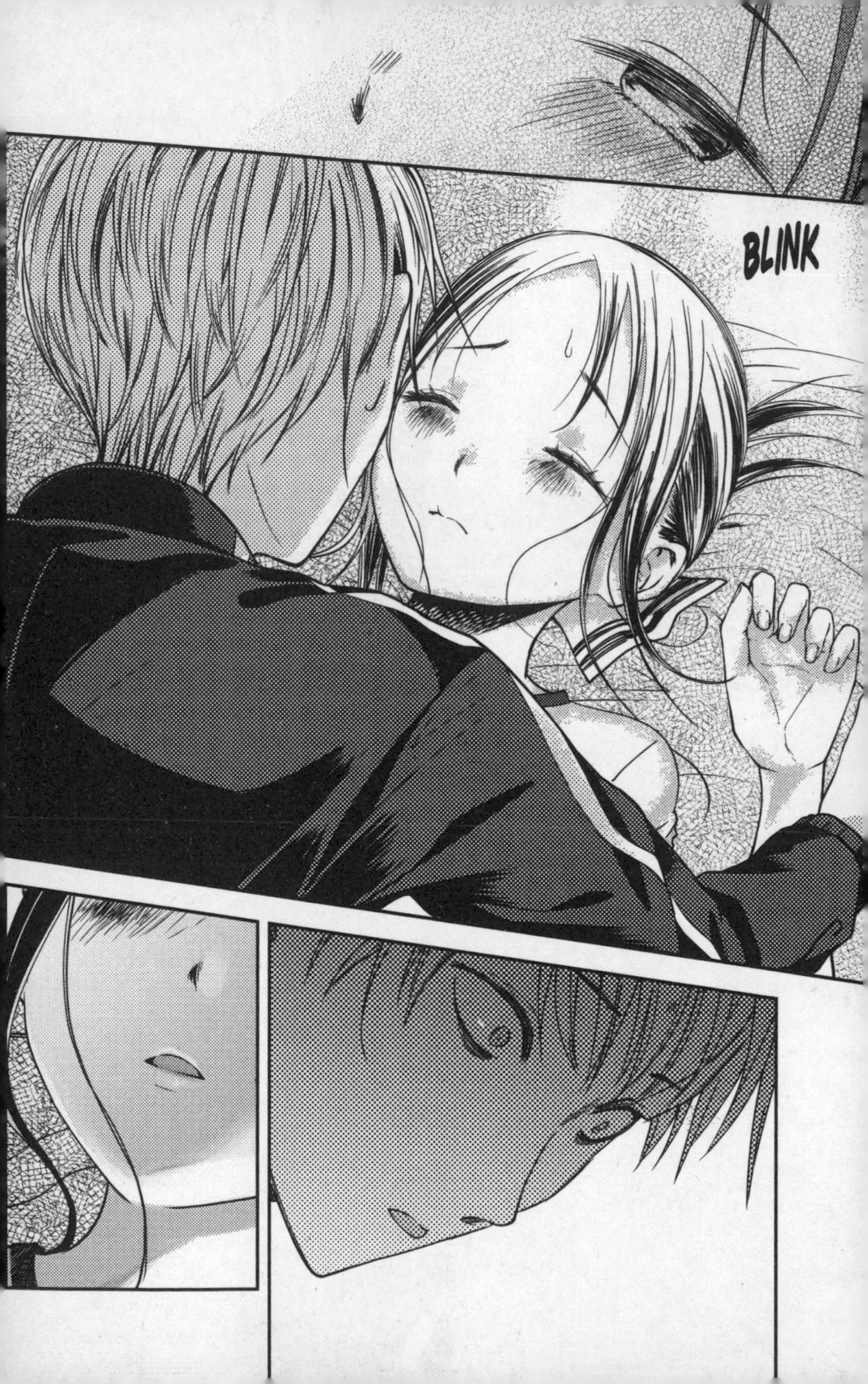
BLINK

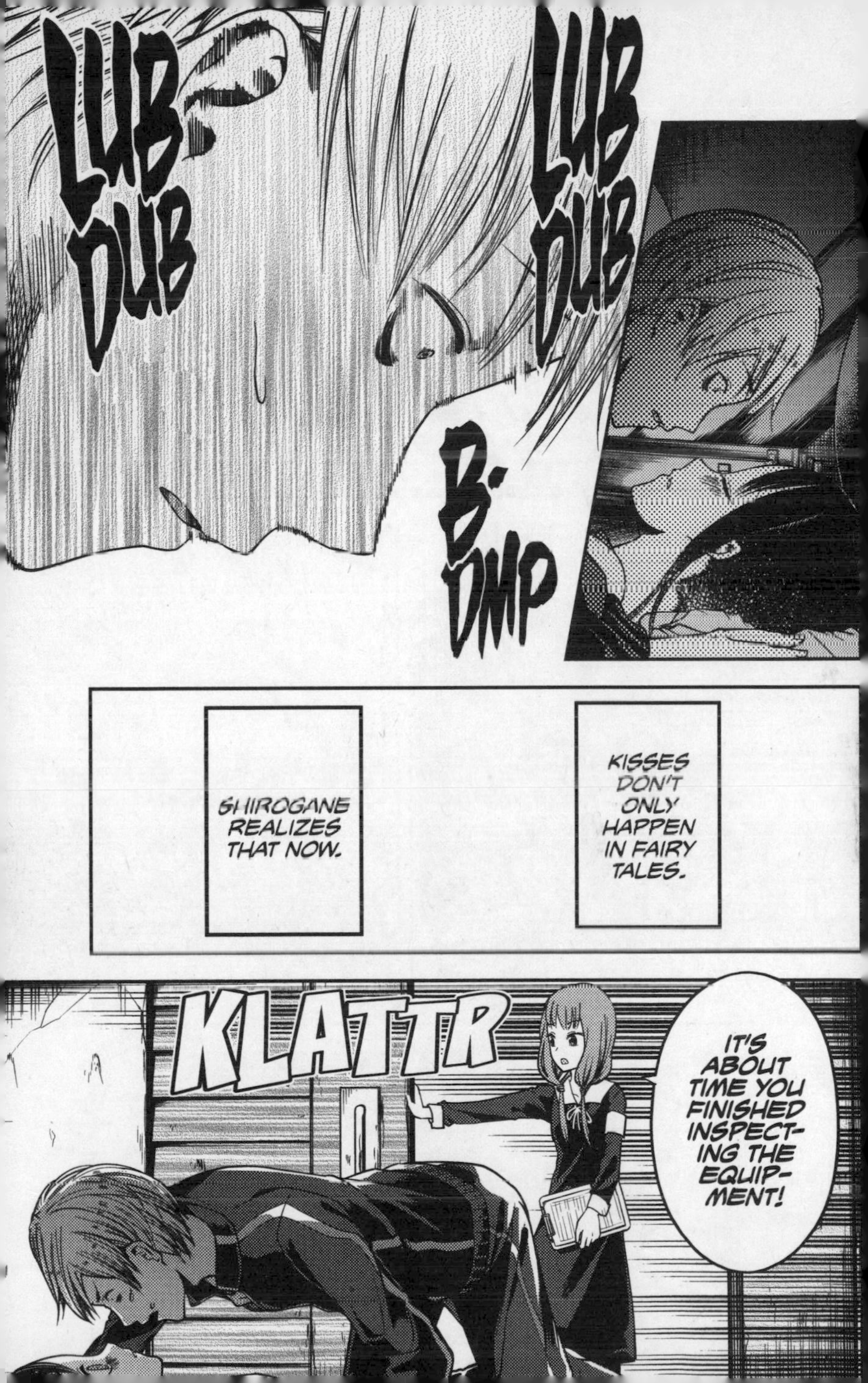
LUB DUB
B-DMP
LUB DUB
KISSES DON'T ONLY HAPPEN IN FAIRY TALES.
SHIROGANE REALIZES THAT NOW.
KLATTR
IT'S ABOUT TIME YOU FINISHED INSPECTING THE EQUIPMENT!

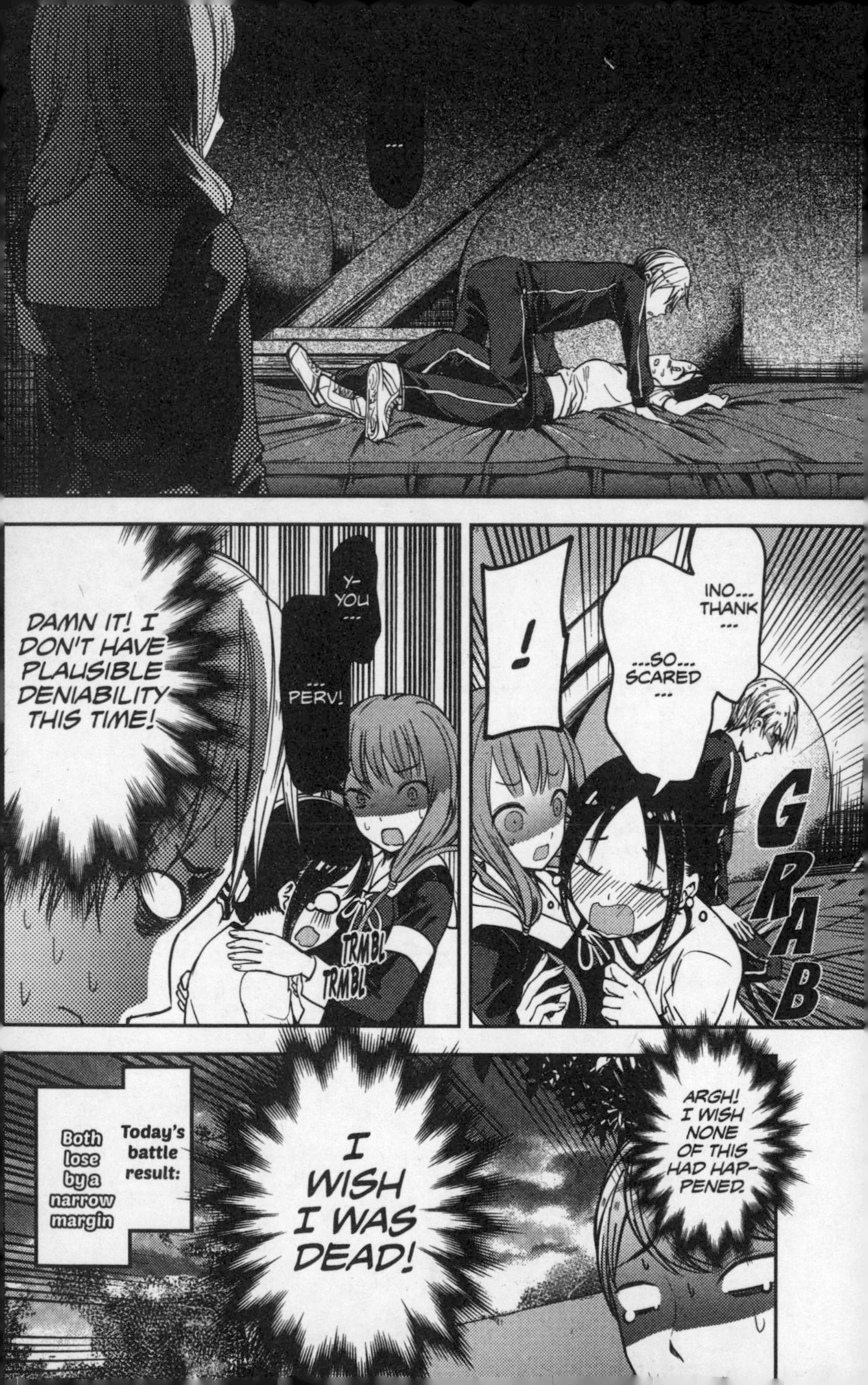
...
!
INO... THANK ...
...SO... SCARED ...
GRAB
Y-YOU ... ... PERV!
TRMBL TRMBL
DAMN IT! I DON'T HAVE PLAUSIBLE DENIABILITY THIS TIME!
ARGH! I WISH NONE OF THIS HAD HAP-PENED.
I WISH I WAS DEAD!
Today's battle result:
Both lose by a narrow margin

Looks like this branch got stuck in the door.

KAGUYA-SAMA

LOVE IS WAR

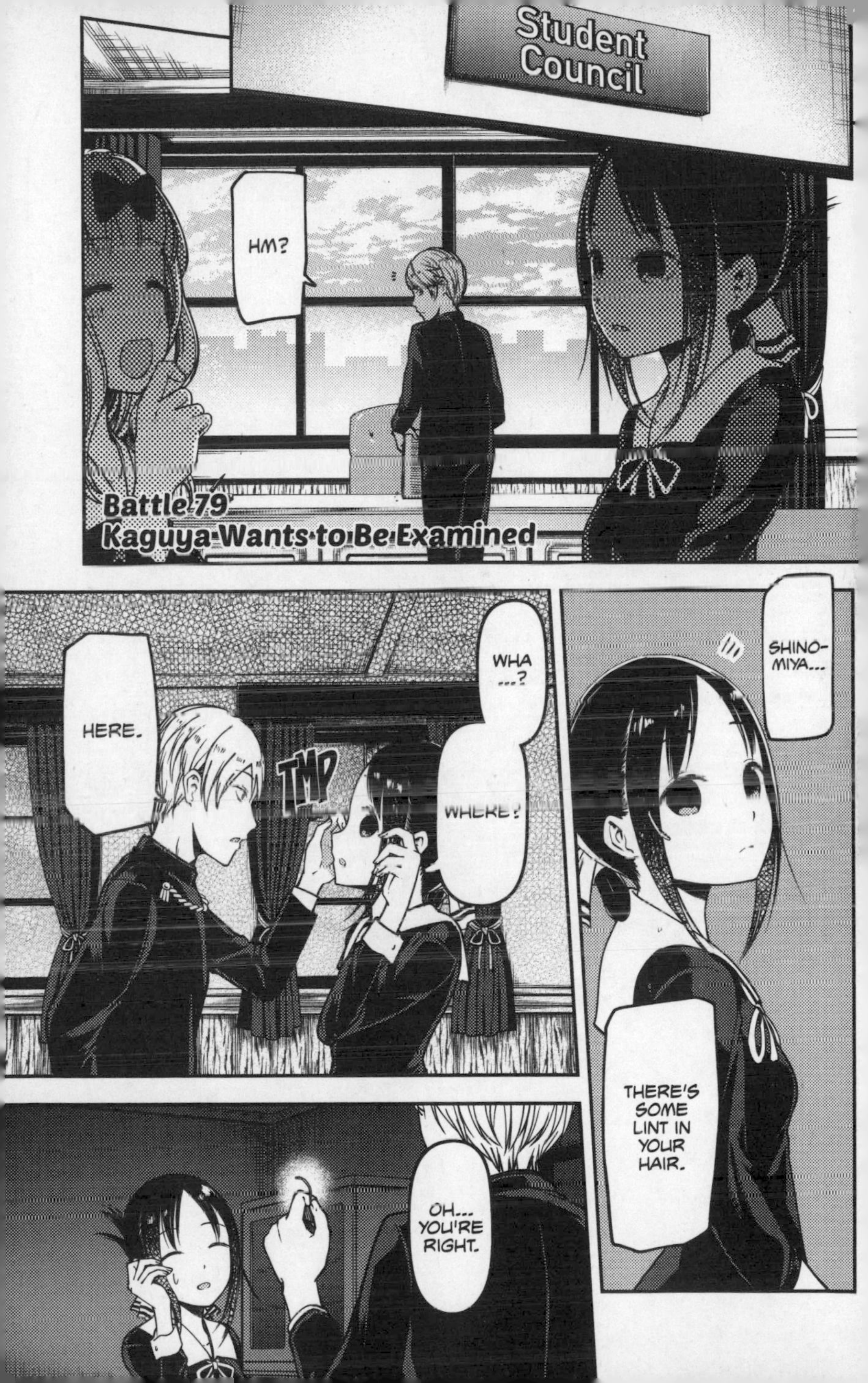
Student Council
HM?
Battle 79
Kaguya Wants to Be Examined
SHINO-MIYA...
THERE'S SOME LINT IN YOUR HAIR.
WHA...?
WHERE?
TMP
HERE.
OH... YOU'RE RIGHT.

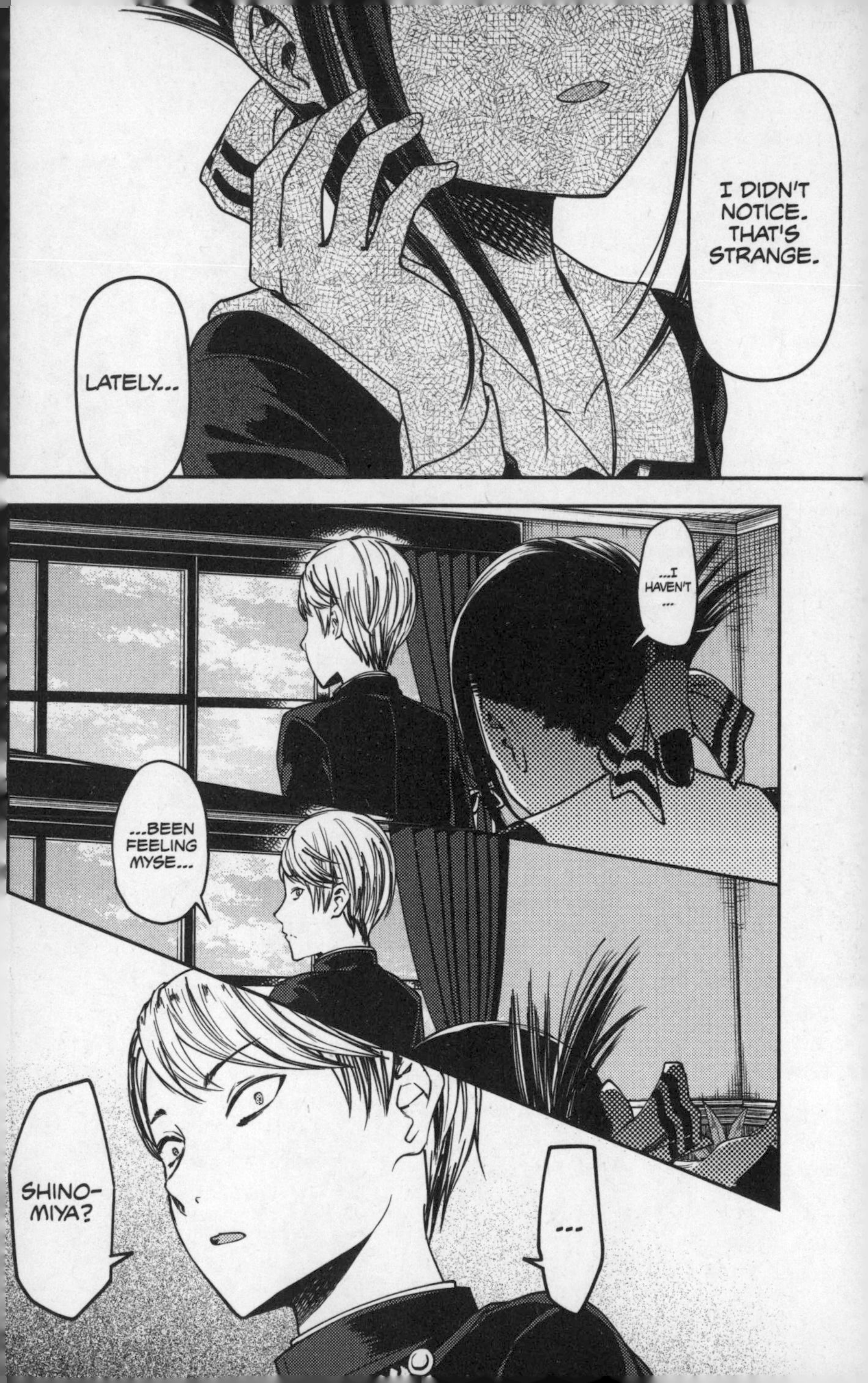
I DIDN'T NOTICE. THAT'S STRANGE.
LATELY...
...I HAVEN'T ...
...BEEN FEELING MYSE...
...
SHINO-MIYA?

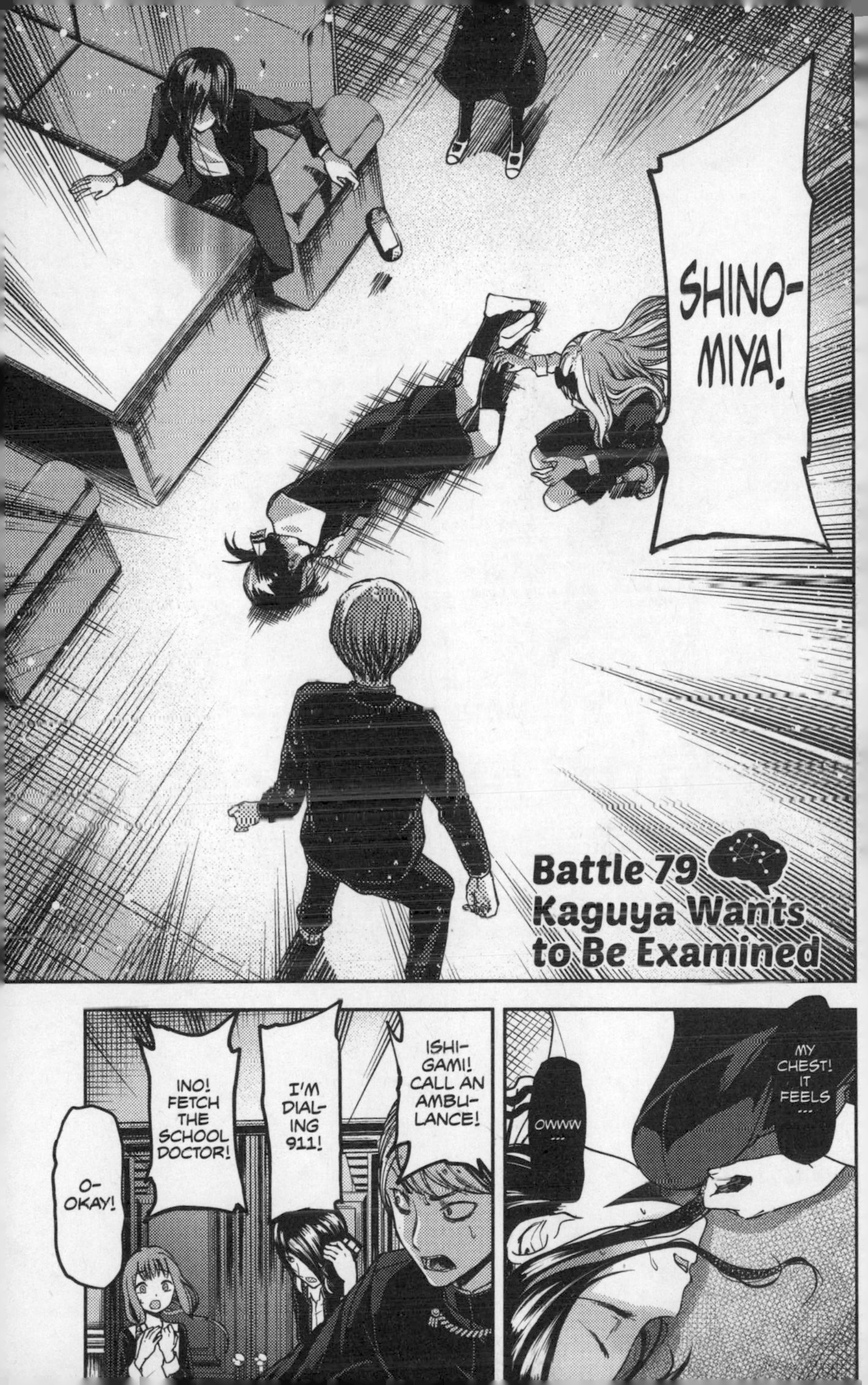
SHINO-MIYA!
Battle 79 Kaguya Wants to Be Examined
MY CHEST! IT FEELS...
OWWW...
ISHI-GAMI! CALL AN AMBU-LANCE!
I'M DIAL-ING 911!
INO! FETCH THE SCHOOL DOCTOR!
O-OKAY!

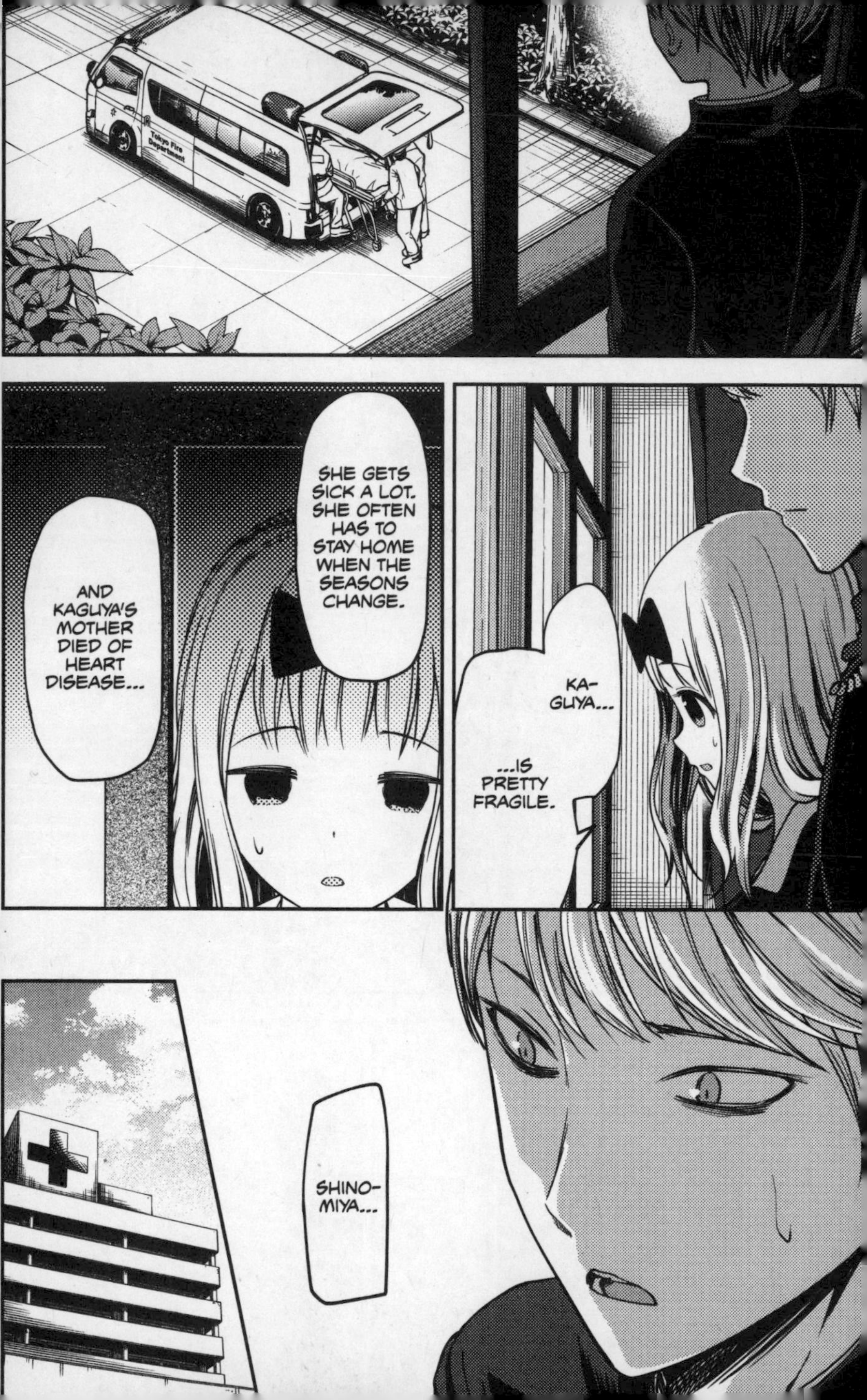
Tokyo Fire Department
KA-GUYA...
...IS PRETTY FRAGILE.
SHE GETS SICK A LOT. SHE OFTEN HAS TO STAY HOME WHEN THE SEASONS CHANGE.
AND KAGUYA'S MOTHER DIED OF HEART DISEASE...
SHINO-MIYA...

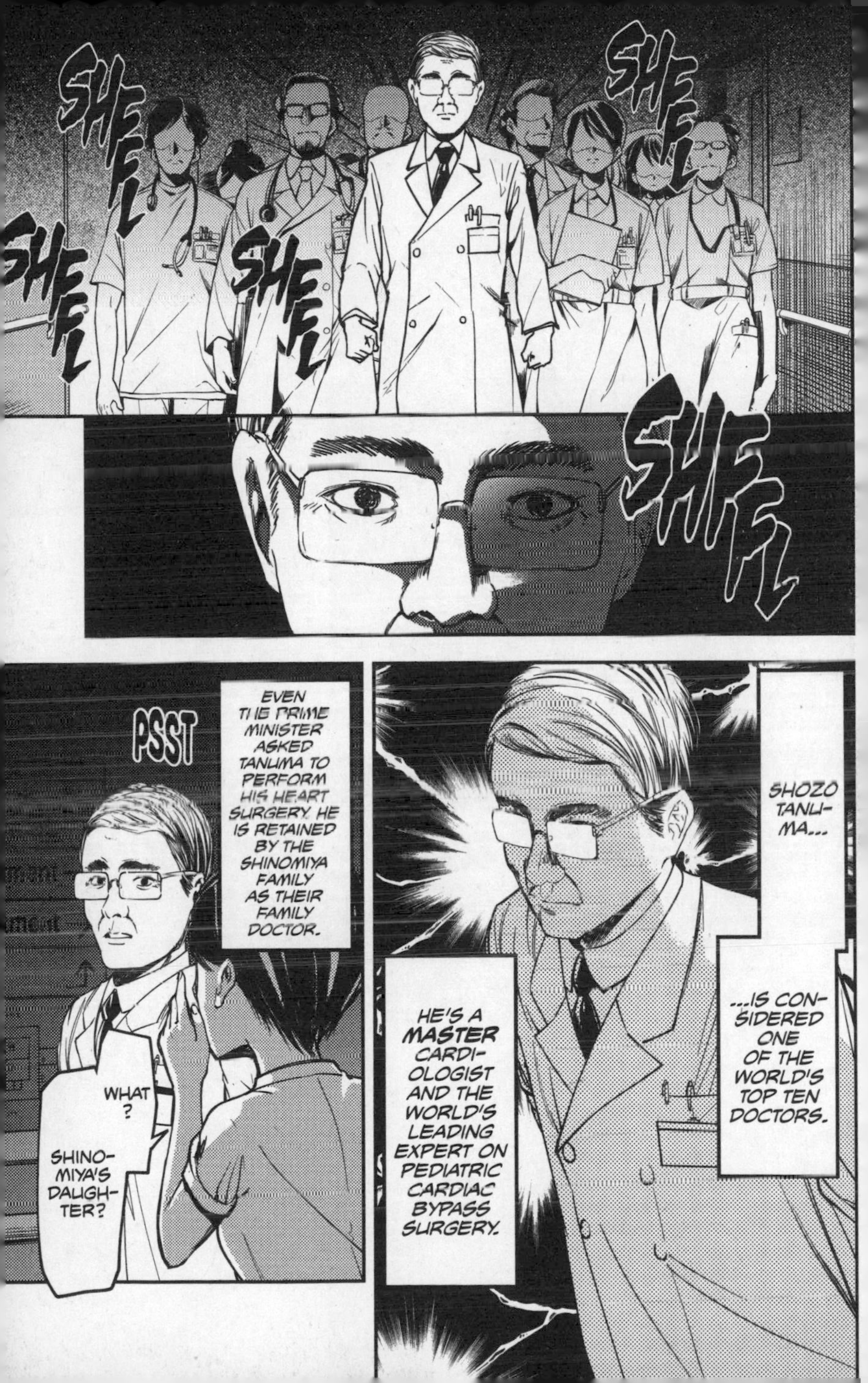
SHFFL
SHFFL
SHFFL
SHFFL
SHFFL
SHOZO TANUMA...
...IS CONSIDERED ONE OF THE WORLD'S TOP TEN DOCTORS.
HE'S A **MASTER** CARDIOLOGIST AND THE WORLD'S LEADING EXPERT ON PEDIATRIC CARDIAC BYPASS SURGERY.
EVEN THE PRIME MINISTER ASKED TANUMA TO PERFORM HIS HEART SURGERY. HE IS RETAINED BY THE SHINOMIYA FAMILY AS THEIR FAMILY DOCTOR.
PSST
WHAT?
SHINOMIYA'S DAUGHTER?

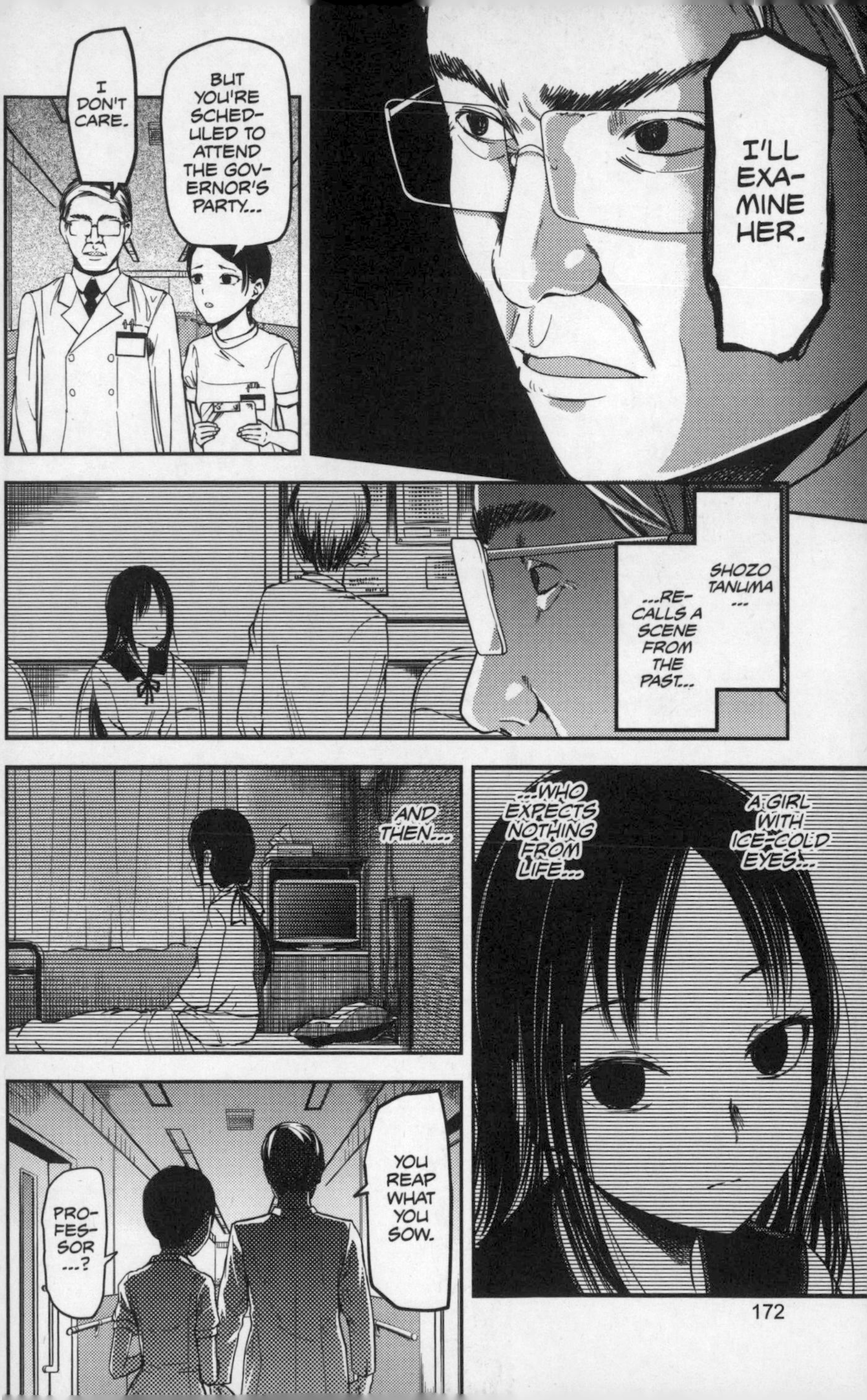
I'LL EXA-MINE HER.
BUT YOU'RE SCHED-ULED TO ATTEND THE GOV-ERNOR'S PARTY...
I DON'T CARE.
SHOZO TANUMA...
...RE-CALLS A SCENE FROM THE PAST...
A GIRL WITH ICE-COLD EYES...
...WHO EXPECTS NOTHING FROM LIFE...
AND THEN...
YOU REAP WHAT YOU SOW.
PRO-FES-SOR...?

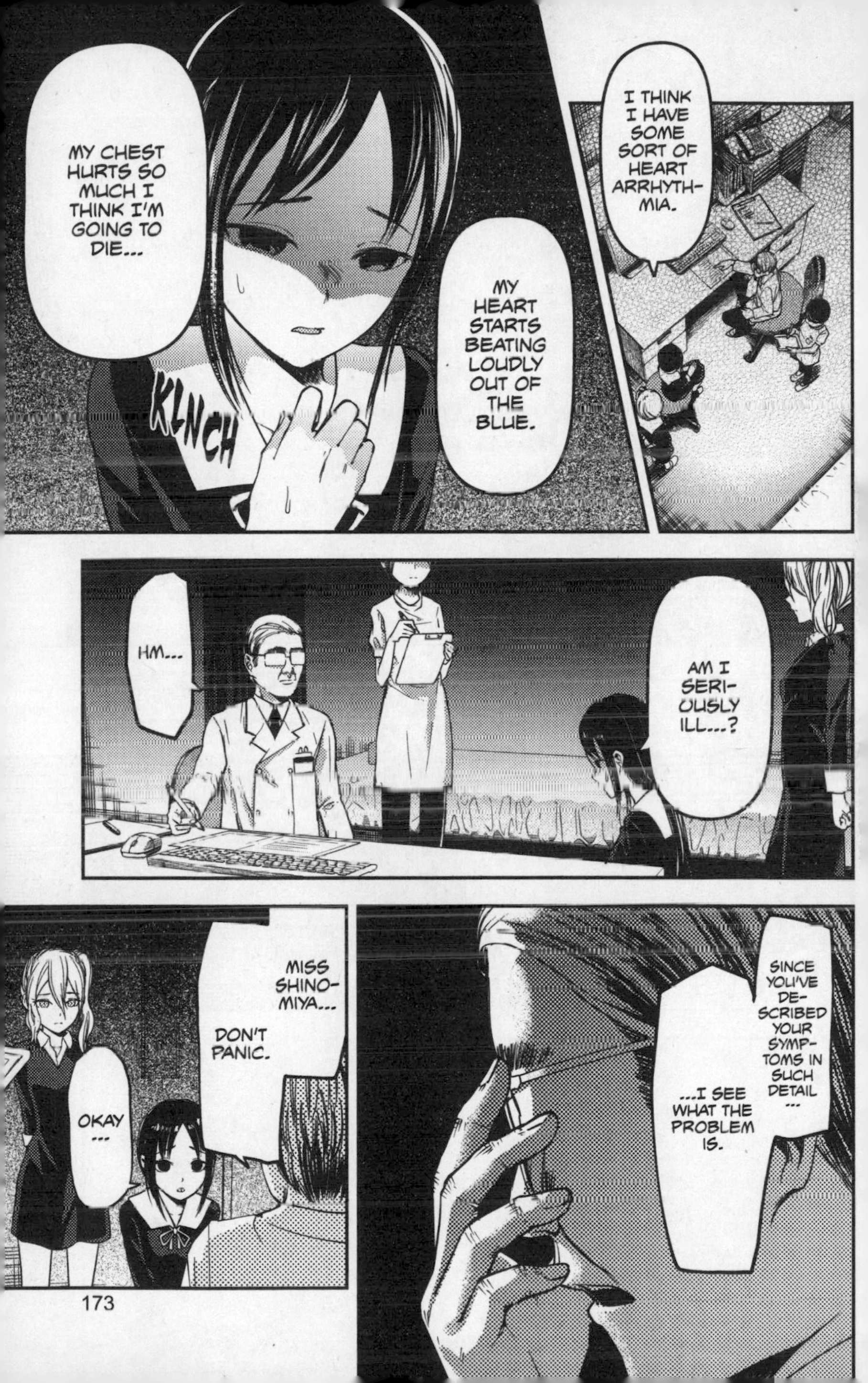

I THINK I HAVE SOME SORT OF HEART ARRHYTHMIA.
MY HEART STARTS BEATING LOUDLY OUT OF THE BLUE.
MY CHEST HURTS SO MUCH I THINK I'M GOING TO DIE...
KLNCH
AM I SERIOUSLY ILL...?
HM...
SINCE YOU'VE DESCRIBED YOUR SYMPTOMS IN SUCH DETAIL...
...I SEE WHAT THE PROBLEM IS.
MISS SHINOMIYA...
DON'T PANIC.
OKAY...

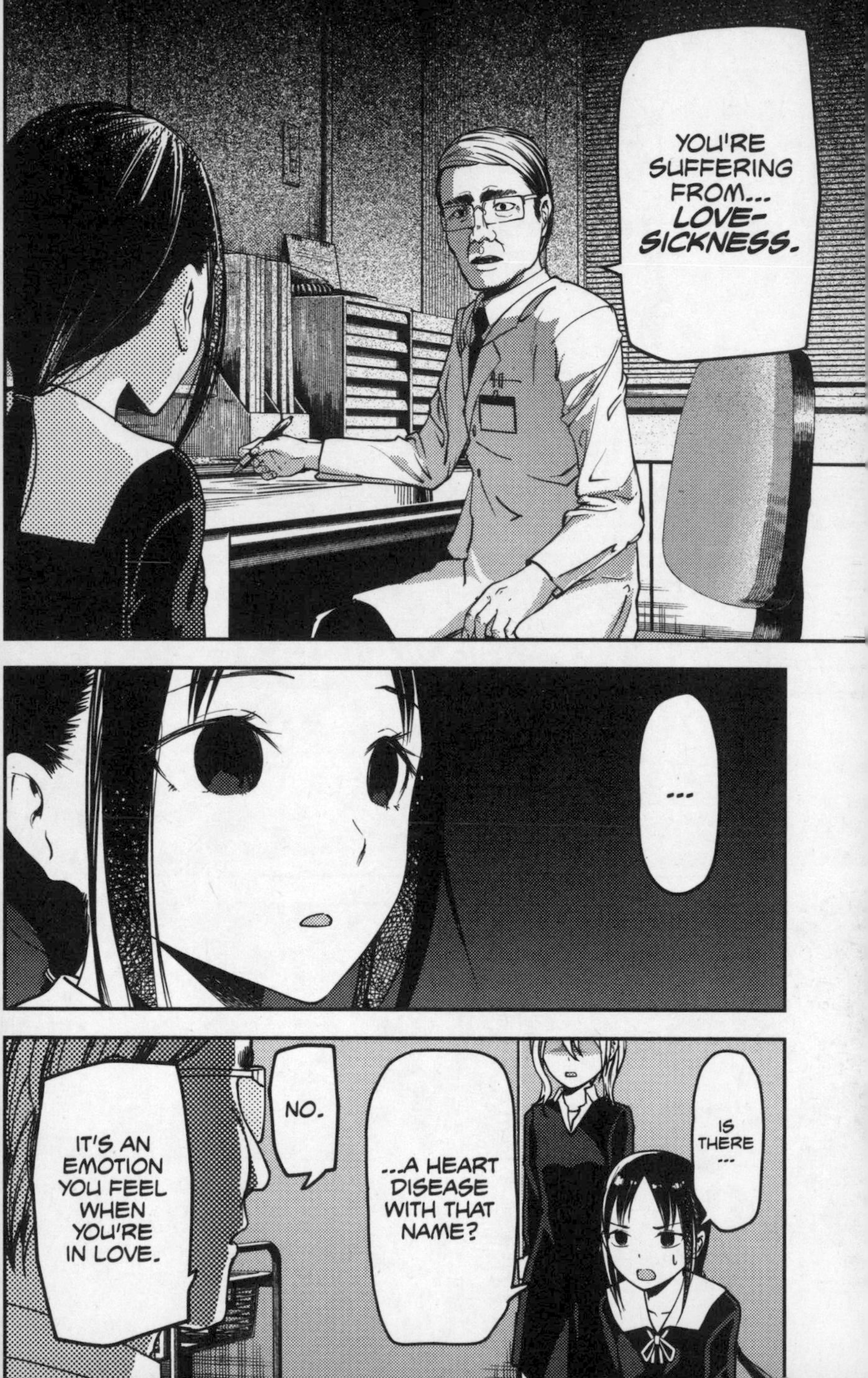
YOU'RE SUFFERING FROM... LOVE-SICKNESS.
...
IS THERE ...
...A HEART DISEASE WITH THAT NAME?
NO.
IT'S AN EMOTION YOU FEEL WHEN YOU'RE IN LOVE.

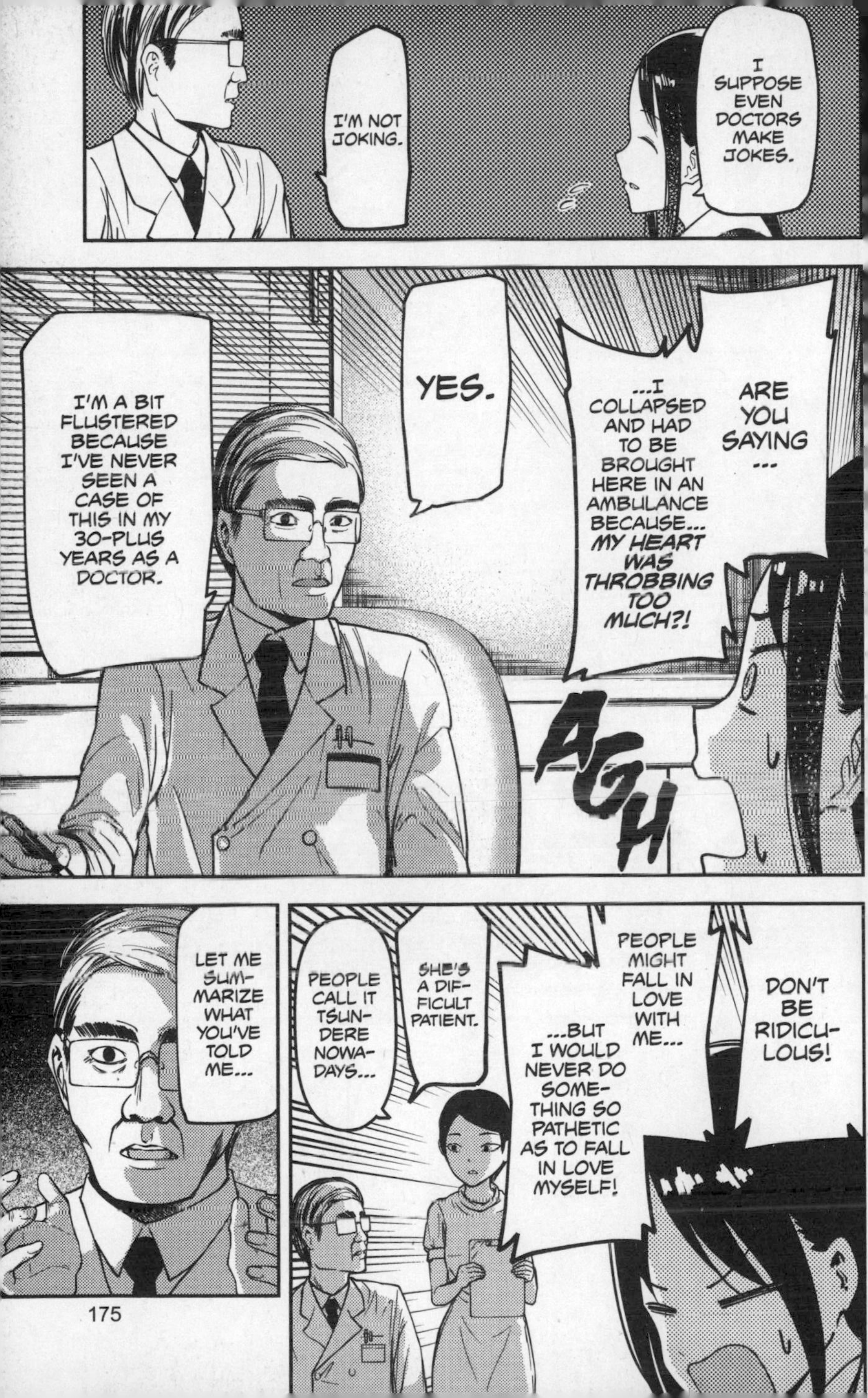
I SUPPOSE EVEN DOCTORS MAKE JOKES.
I'M NOT JOKING.
ARE YOU SAYING...
...I COLLAPSED AND HAD TO BE BROUGHT HERE IN AN AMBULANCE BECAUSE... MY HEART WAS THROBBING TOO MUCH?!
AGH
YES.
I'M A BIT FLUSTERED BECAUSE I'VE NEVER SEEN A CASE OF THIS IN MY 30-PLUS YEARS AS A DOCTOR.
DON'T BE RIDICULOUS!
PEOPLE MIGHT FALL IN LOVE WITH ME...
...BUT I WOULD NEVER DO SOMETHING SO PATHETIC AS TO FALL IN LOVE MYSELF!
SHE'S A DIFFICULT PATIENT.
PEOPLE CALL IT TSUNDERE NOWADAYS...
LET ME SUMMARIZE WHAT YOU'VE TOLD ME...

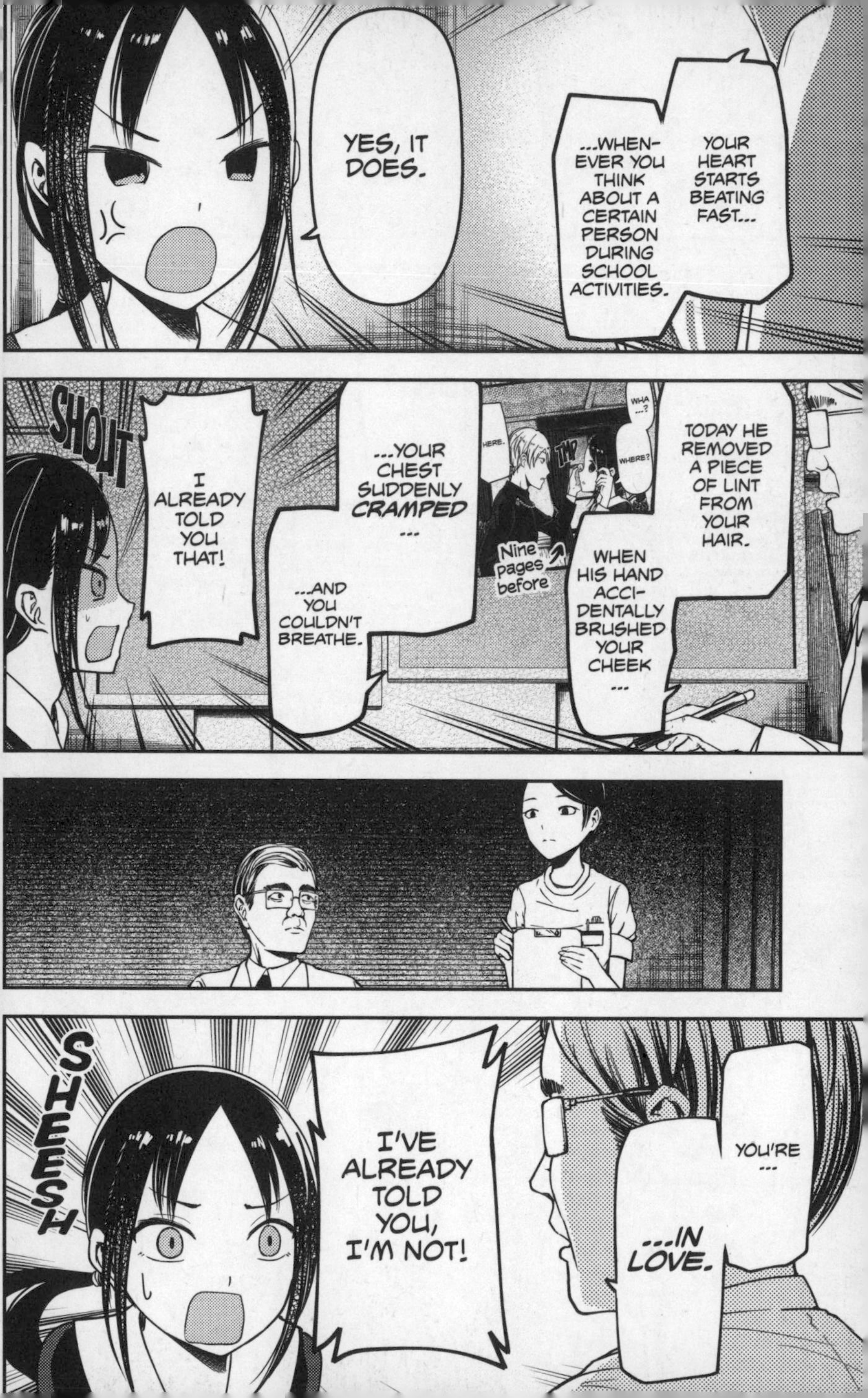
YOUR HEART STARTS BEATING FAST...
...WHENEVER YOU THINK ABOUT A CERTAIN PERSON DURING SCHOOL ACTIVITIES.
YES, IT DOES.
TODAY HE REMOVED A PIECE OF LINT FROM YOUR HAIR.
WHA...?
WHERE?
HERE.
Nine pages before
WHEN HIS HAND ACCIDENTALLY BRUSHED YOUR CHEEK...
...YOUR CHEST SUDDENLY CRAMPED...
...AND YOU COULDN'T BREATHE.
I ALREADY TOLD YOU THAT!
SHOUT
YOU'RE...
...IN LOVE.
I'VE ALREADY TOLD YOU, I'M NOT!
SHEESH

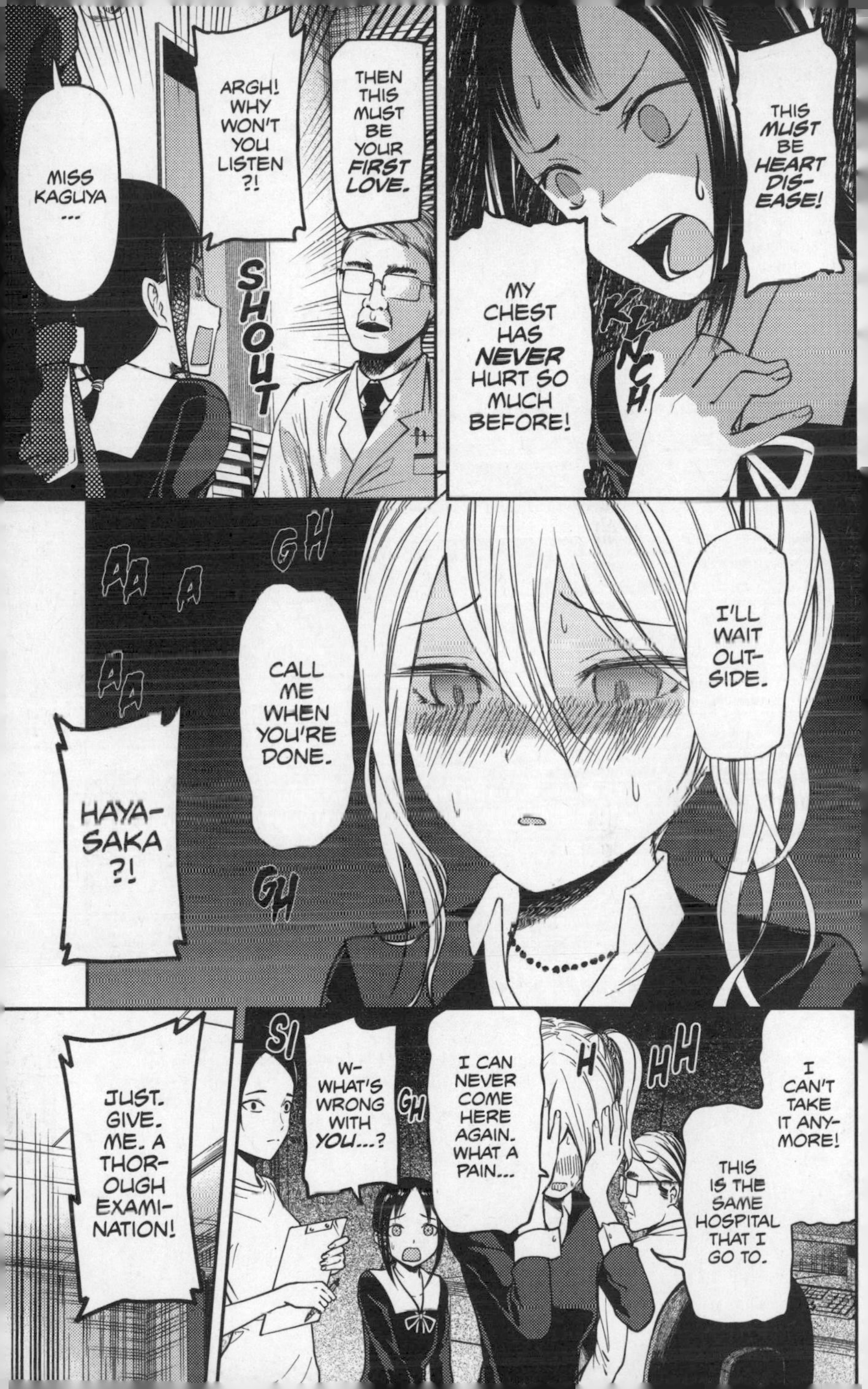
THIS MUST BE HEART DIS-EASE!
KLINCH
MY CHEST HAS NEVER HURT SO MUCH BEFORE!
THEN THIS MUST BE YOUR FIRST LOVE.
SHOUT
ARGH! WHY WON'T YOU LISTEN?!
MISS KAGUYA...
I'LL WAIT OUT-SIDE.
CALL ME WHEN YOU'RE DONE.
GH
AA A
AA
GH
HAYA-SAKA?!
I CAN'T TAKE IT ANY-MORE!
THIS IS THE SAME HOSPITAL THAT I GO TO.
HHH
I CAN NEVER COME HERE AGAIN. WHAT A PAIN...
SI GH
W-WHAT'S WRONG WITH YOU...?
JUST. GIVE. ME. A THOR-OUGH EXAMI-NATION!

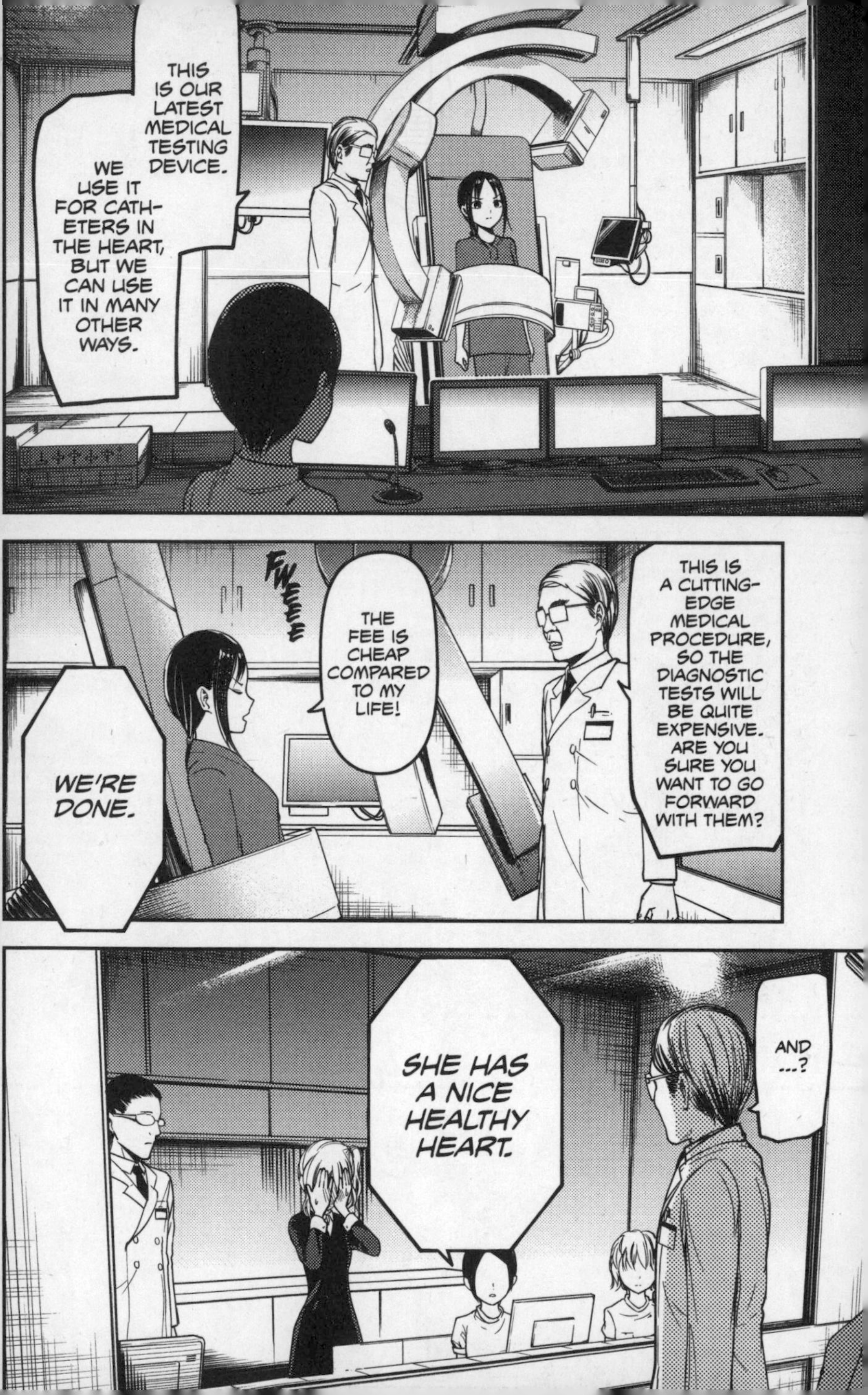
THIS IS OUR LATEST MEDICAL TESTING DEVICE.
WE USE IT FOR CATH-ETERS IN THE HEART, BUT WE CAN USE IT IN MANY OTHER WAYS.
THIS IS A CUTTING-EDGE MEDICAL PROCEDURE, SO THE DIAGNOSTIC TESTS WILL BE QUITE EXPENSIVE. ARE YOU SURE YOU WANT TO GO FORWARD WITH THEM?
THE FEE IS CHEAP COMPARED TO MY LIFE!
FWEEE
WE'RE DONE.
AND ...?
SHE HAS A NICE HEALTHY HEART.

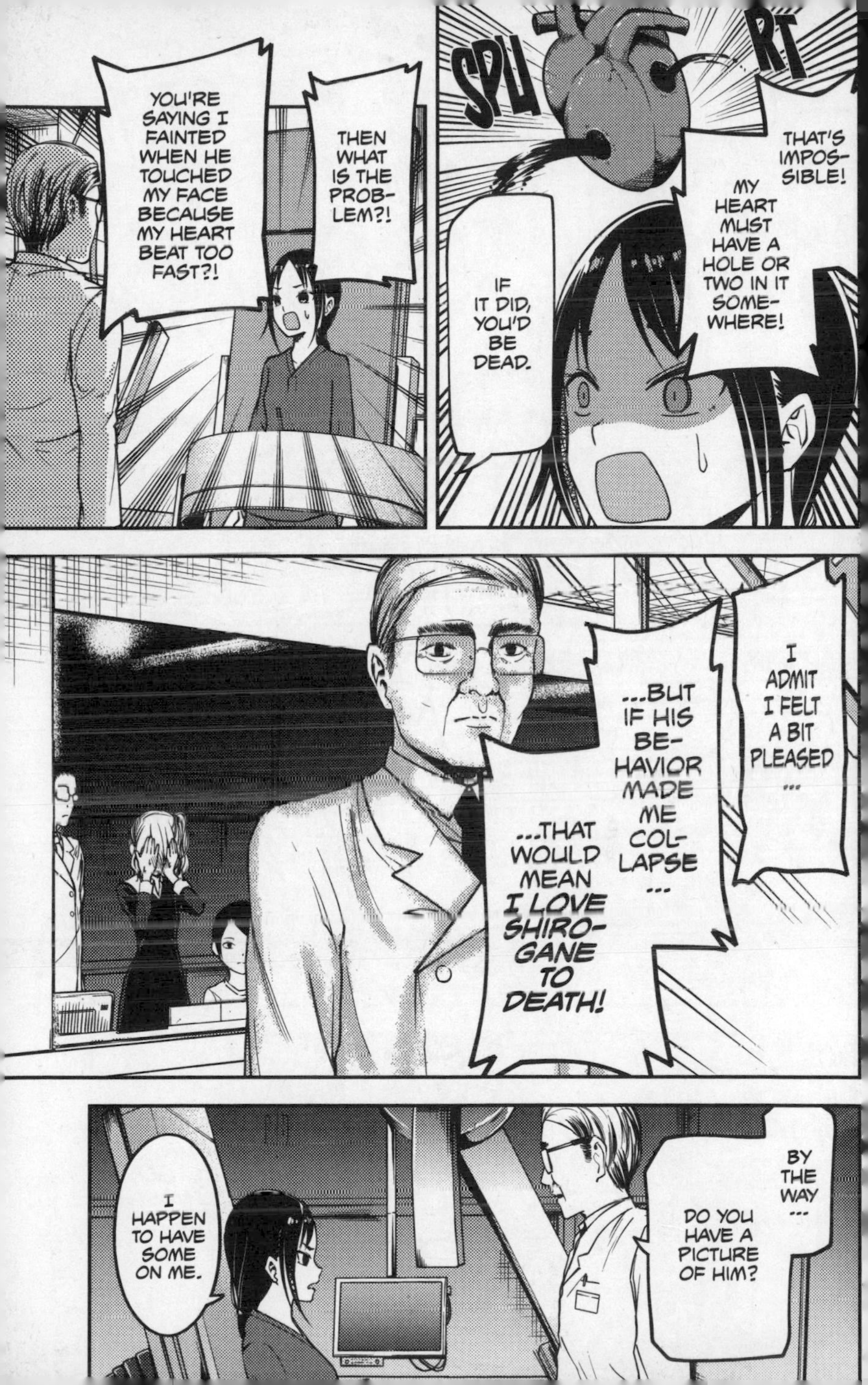
SPU
RT
THAT'S IMPOSSIBLE!
MY HEART MUST HAVE A HOLE OR TWO IN IT SOMEWHERE!
IF IT DID, YOU'D BE DEAD.
THEN WHAT IS THE PROBLEM?!
YOU'RE SAYING I FAINTED WHEN HE TOUCHED MY FACE BECAUSE MY HEART BEAT TOO FAST?!
I ADMIT I FELT A BIT PLEASED...
...BUT IF HIS BEHAVIOR MADE ME COLLAPSE...
...THAT WOULD MEAN *I LOVE SHIROGANE TO DEATH!*
BY THE WAY...
DO YOU HAVE A PICTURE OF HIM?
I HAPPEN TO HAVE SOME ON ME.

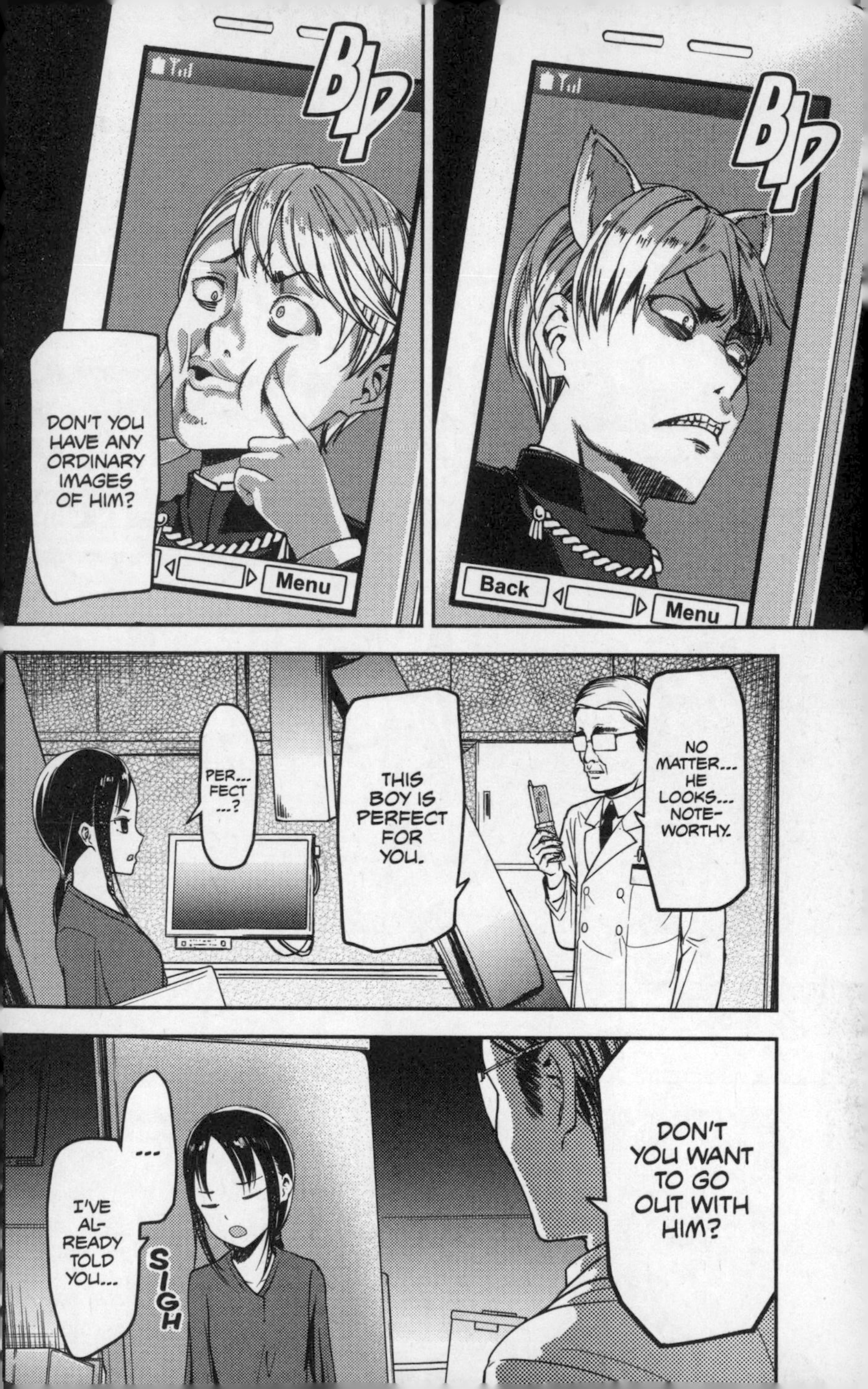
BIP
Back
Menu
BIP
DON'T YOU HAVE ANY ORDINARY IMAGES OF HIM?
Menu
NO MATTER... HE LOOKS... NOTE-WORTHY.
THIS BOY IS PERFECT FOR YOU.
PER... FECT ...?
DON'T YOU WANT TO GO OUT WITH HIM?
...
I'VE AL-READY TOLD YOU...
SIGH

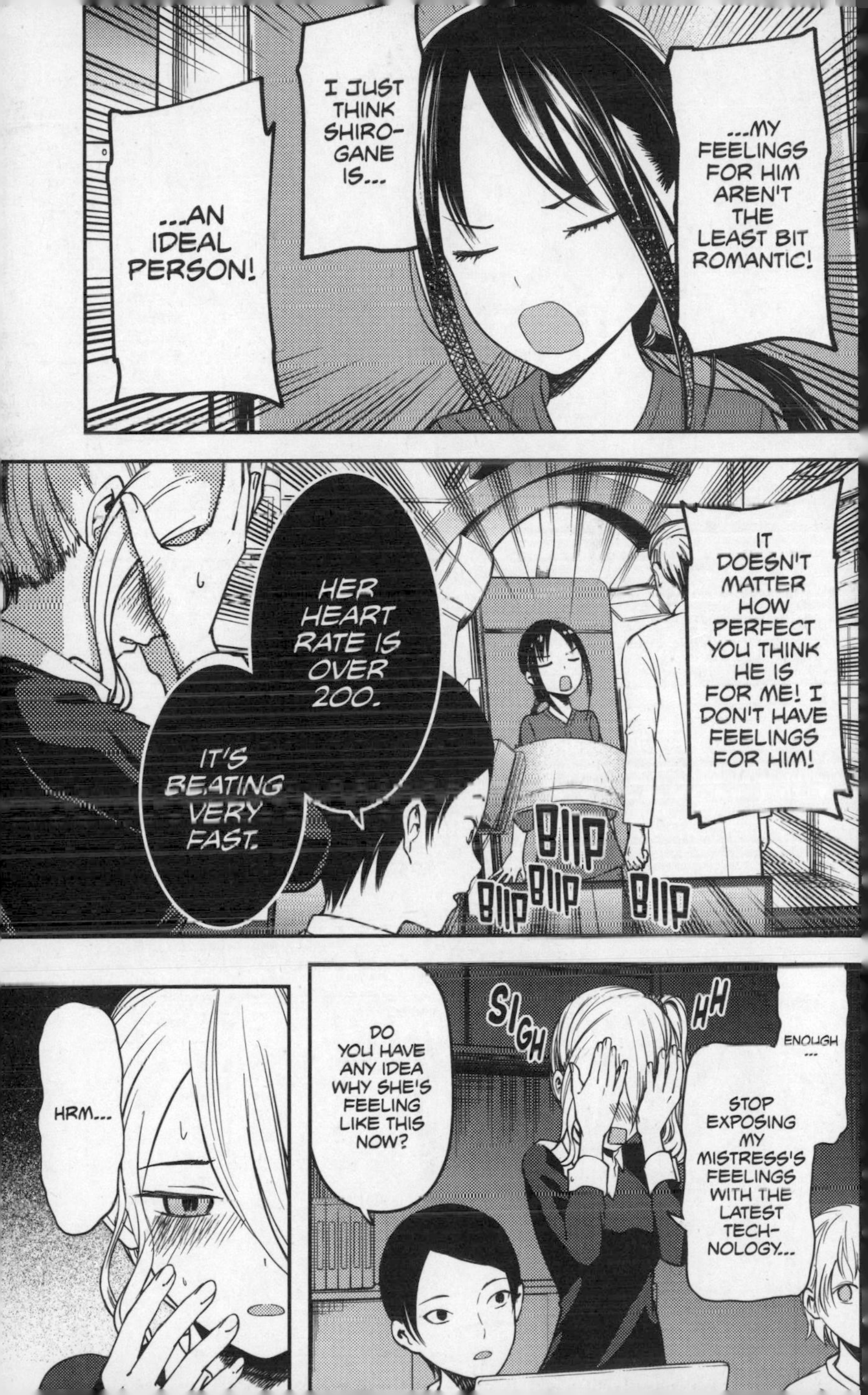
...MY FEELINGS FOR HIM AREN'T THE LEAST BIT ROMANTIC!
I JUST THINK SHIRO-GANE IS...
...AN IDEAL PERSON!
IT DOESN'T MATTER HOW PERFECT YOU THINK HE IS FOR ME! I DON'T HAVE FEELINGS FOR HIM!
BIIP BIIP BIIP BIIP
HER HEART RATE IS OVER 200.
IT'S BEATING VERY FAST.
ENOUGH...
STOP EXPOSING MY MISTRESS'S FEELINGS WITH THE LATEST TECH-NOLOGY...
SIGHHH
DO YOU HAVE ANY IDEA WHY SHE'S FEELING LIKE THIS NOW?
HRM...

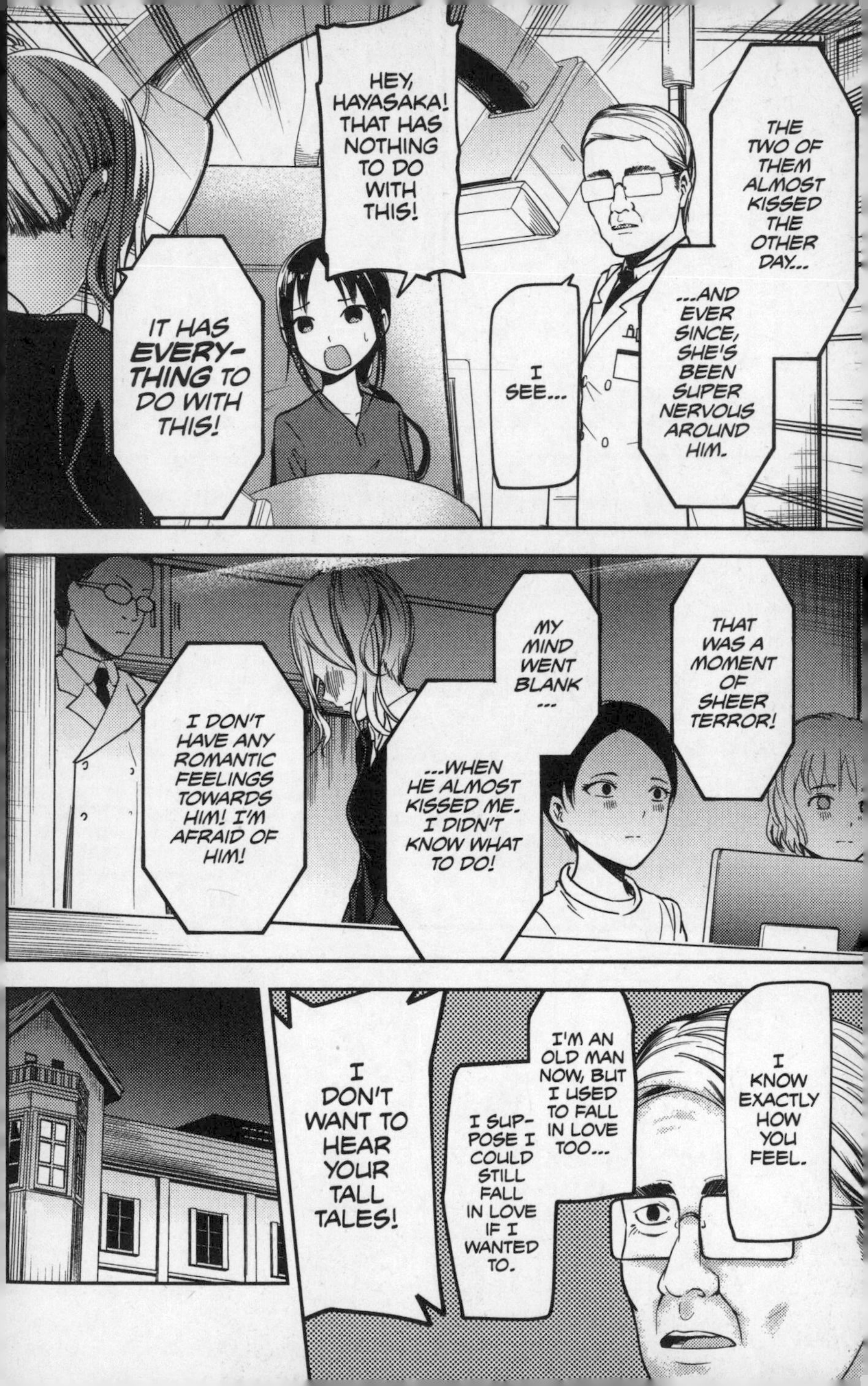
THE TWO OF THEM ALMOST KISSED THE OTHER DAY...
...AND EVER SINCE, SHE'S BEEN SUPER NERVOUS AROUND HIM.
I SEE...
HEY, HAYASAKA! THAT HAS NOTHING TO DO WITH THIS!
IT HAS EVERYTHING TO DO WITH THIS!
THAT WAS A MOMENT OF SHEER TERROR!
MY MIND WENT BLANK...
...WHEN HE ALMOST KISSED ME. I DIDN'T KNOW WHAT TO DO!
I DON'T HAVE ANY ROMANTIC FEELINGS TOWARDS HIM! I'M AFRAID OF HIM!
I KNOW EXACTLY HOW YOU FEEL.
I'M AN OLD MAN NOW, BUT I USED TO FALL IN LOVE TOO...
I SUPPOSE I COULD STILL FALL IN LOVE IF I WANTED TO.
I DON'T WANT TO HEAR YOUR TALL TALES!

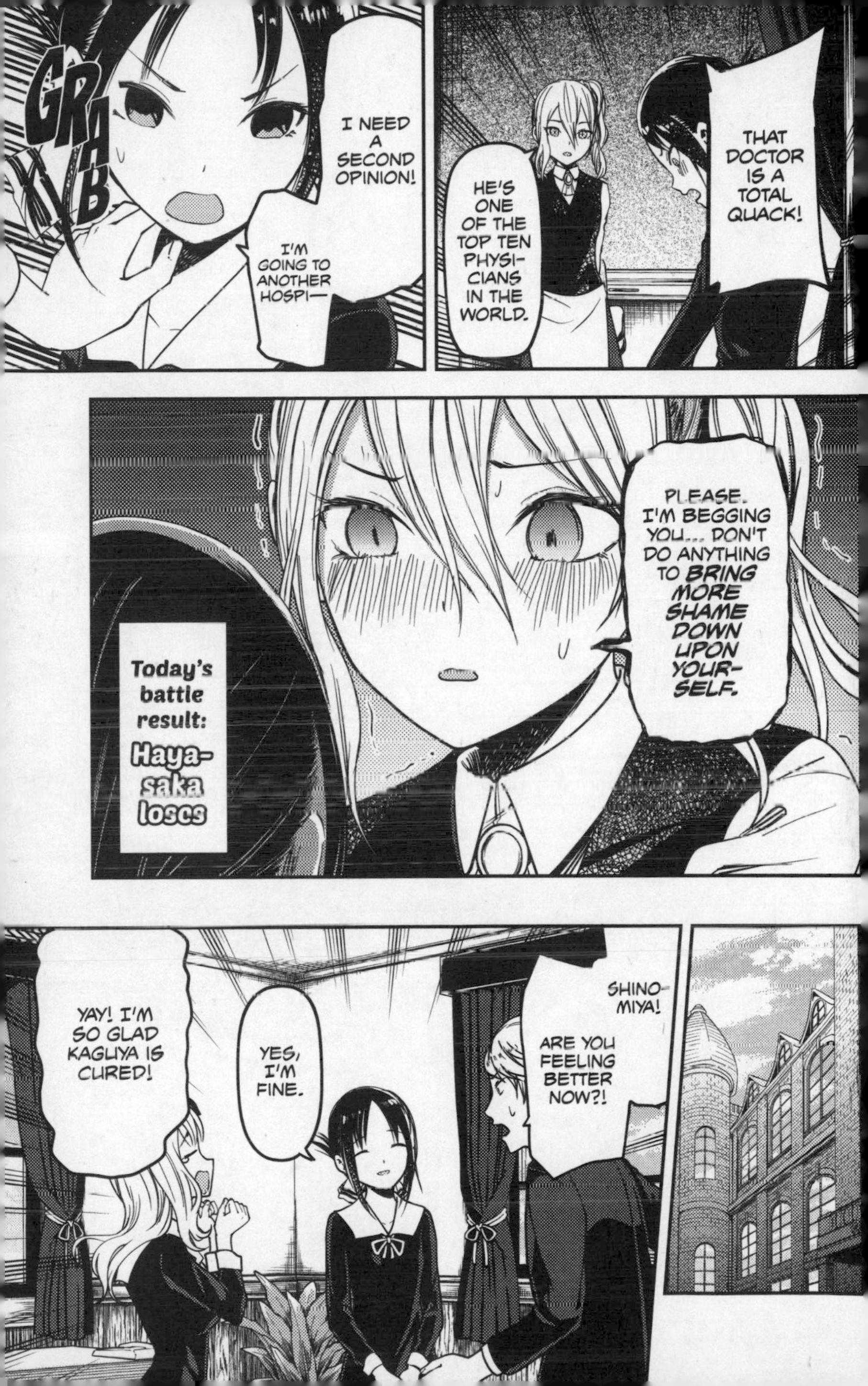
THAT DOCTOR IS A TOTAL QUACK!
HE'S ONE OF THE TOP TEN PHYSICIANS IN THE WORLD.
I NEED A SECOND OPINION!
GRAB
I'M GOING TO ANOTHER HOSPI—
PLEASE. I'M BEGGING YOU... DON'T DO ANYTHING TO BRING MORE SHAME DOWN UPON YOURSELF.
Today's battle result: Hayasaka loses
SHINOMIYA!
ARE YOU FEELING BETTER NOW?!
YES, I'M FINE.
YAY! I'M SO GLAD KAGUYA IS CURED!

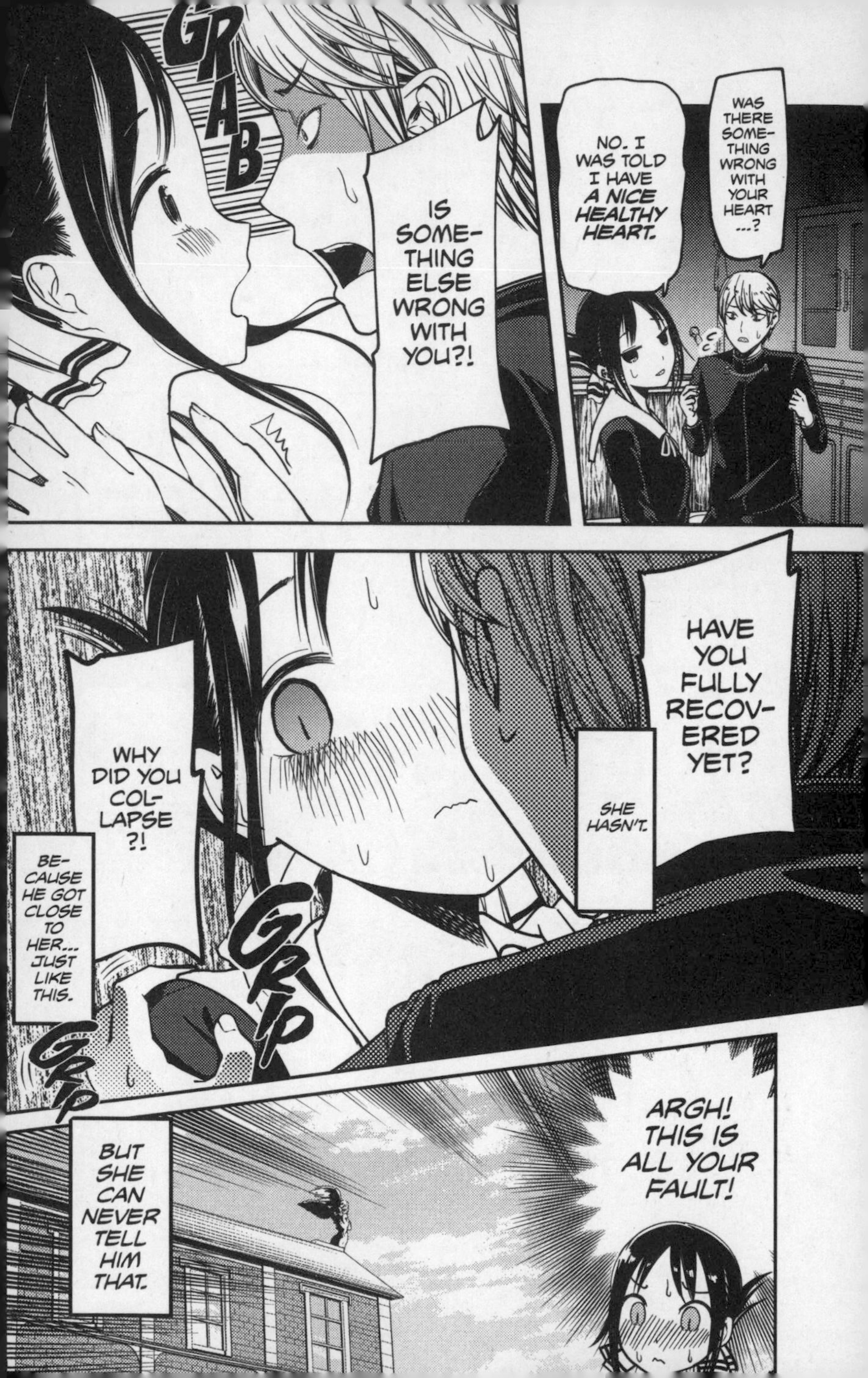
WAS THERE SOME-THING WRONG WITH YOUR HEART ...?
NO. I WAS TOLD I HAVE A NICE HEALTHY HEART.
GRAB
IS SOME-THING ELSE WRONG WITH YOU?!
HAVE YOU FULLY RECOV-ERED YET?
SHE HASN'T.
WHY DID YOU COL-LAPSE ?!
BE-CAUSE HE GOT CLOSE TO HER... JUST LIKE THIS.
GRIP
GRIP
ARGH! THIS IS ALL YOUR FAULT!
BUT SHE CAN NEVER TELL HIM THAT.

Nayotake, your daughter is doing fine...

KAGUYA-SAMA
LOVE IS WAR

THE FIFTH MEMBER OF THE SHUCHIIN ACADEMY STUDENT COUNCIL IS....

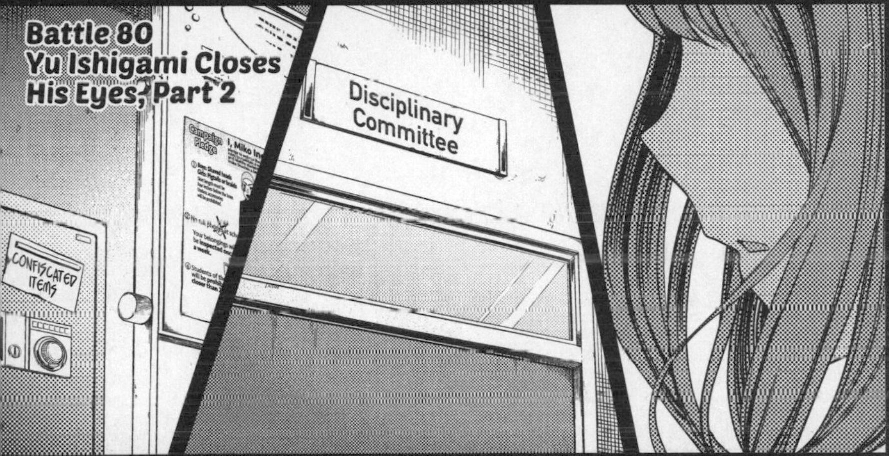
Disciplinary Committee
Campaign Pledge
I, Miko Ino
CONFISCATED ITEMS
Battle 80
Yu Ishigami Closes His Eyes, Part 2

...FINANCIAL AUDITOR MIKO INO.

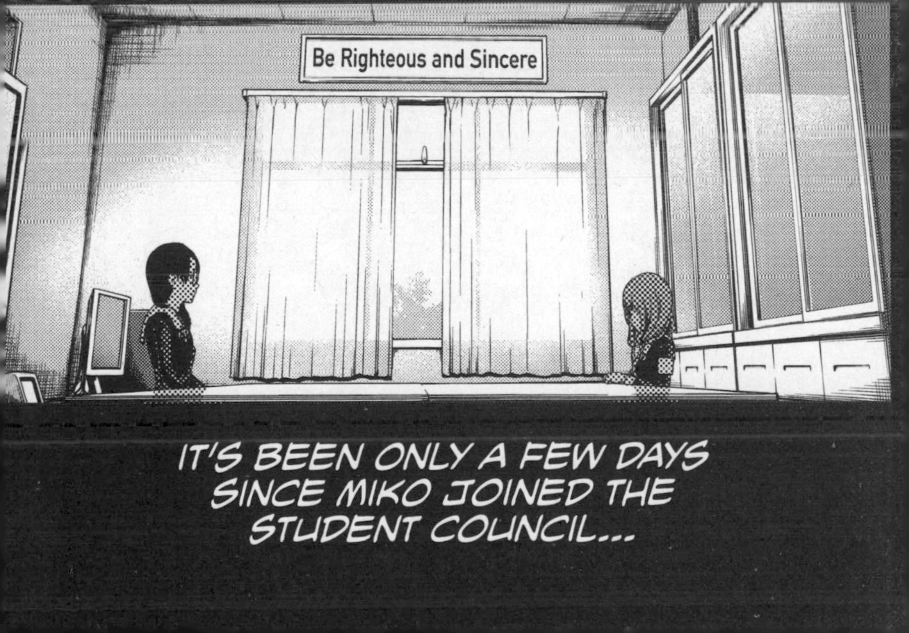
Be Righteous and Sincere

IT'S BEEN ONLY A FEW DAYS SINCE MIKO JOINED THE STUDENT COUNCIL...

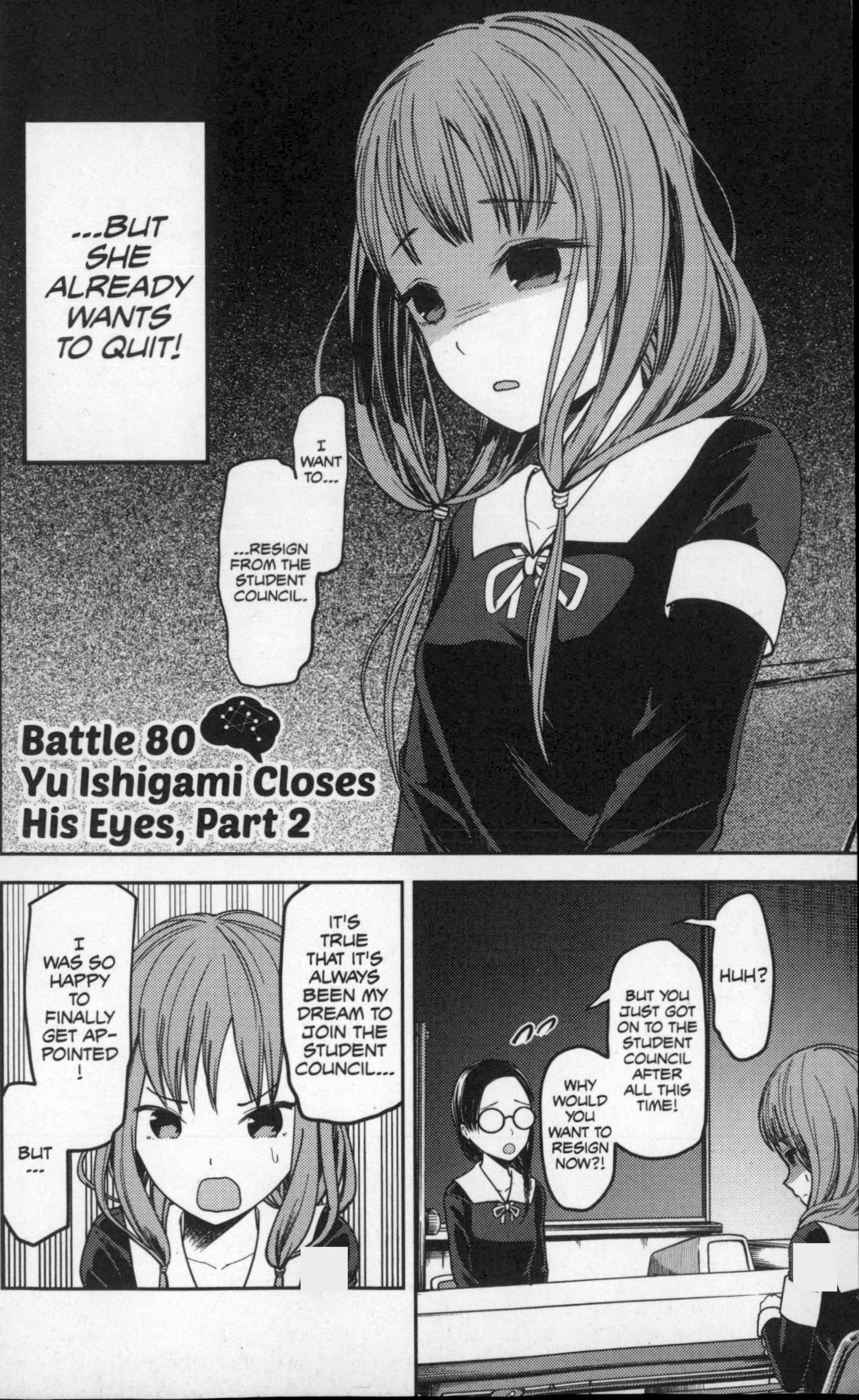
I WANT TO...
...RESIGN FROM THE STUDENT COUNCIL.
...BUT SHE ALREADY WANTS TO QUIT!
Battle 80 Yu Ishigami Closes His Eyes, Part 2
HUH?
BUT YOU JUST GOT ON TO THE STUDENT COUNCIL AFTER ALL THIS TIME!
WHY WOULD YOU WANT TO RESIGN NOW?!
IT'S TRUE THAT IT'S ALWAYS BEEN MY DREAM TO JOIN THE STUDENT COUNCIL...
I WAS SO HAPPY TO FINALLY GET AP-POINTED!
BUT...

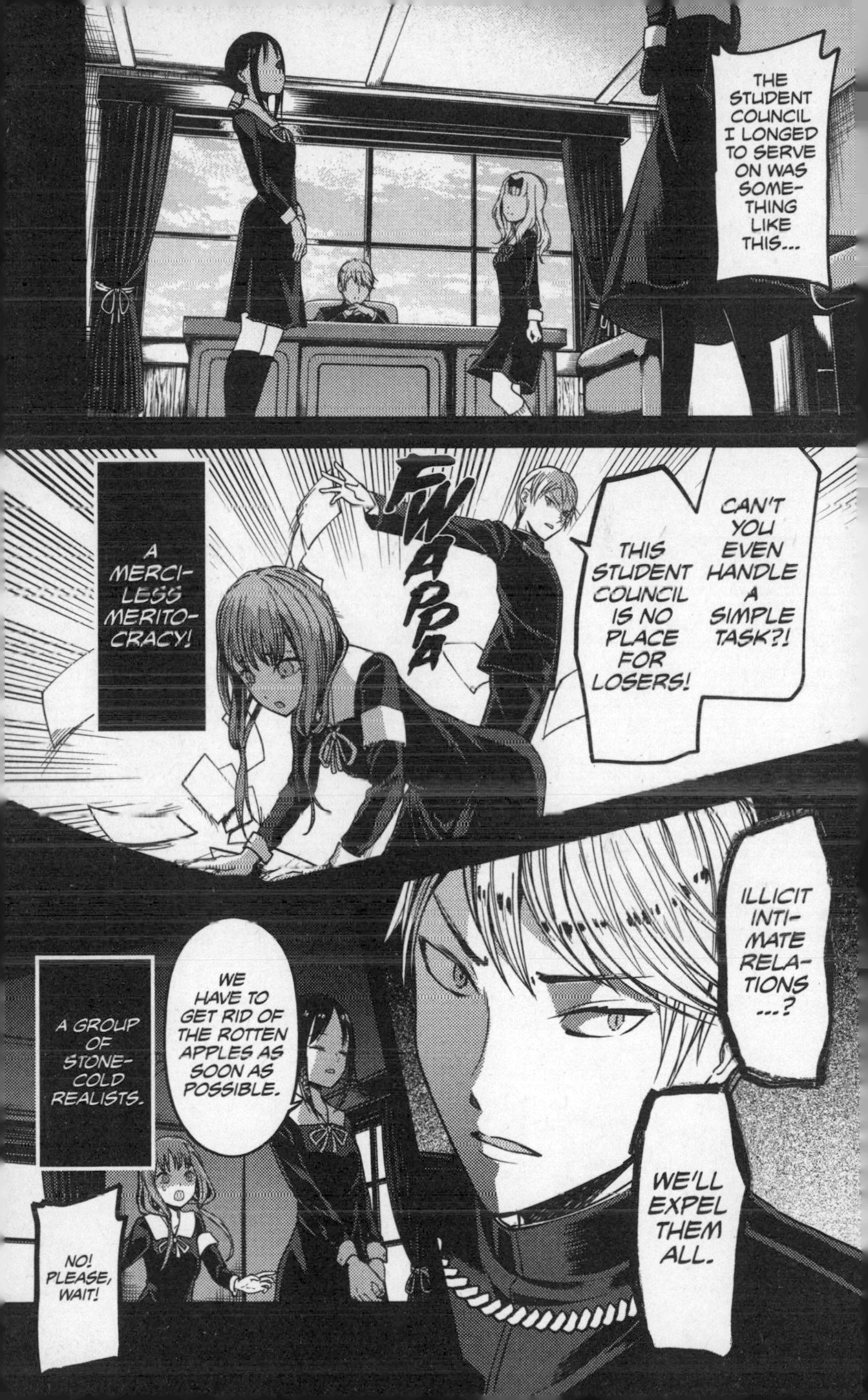
THE STUDENT COUNCIL I LONGED TO SERVE ON WAS SOMETHING LIKE THIS...
CAN'T YOU EVEN HANDLE A SIMPLE TASK?!
THIS STUDENT COUNCIL IS NO PLACE FOR LOSERS!
FWAPPA
A MERCILESS MERITOCRACY!
ILLICIT INTIMATE RELATIONS...?
WE'LL EXPEL THEM ALL.
WE HAVE TO GET RID OF THE ROTTEN APPLES AS SOON AS POSSIBLE.
A GROUP OF STONE-COLD REALISTS.
NO! PLEASE, WAIT!

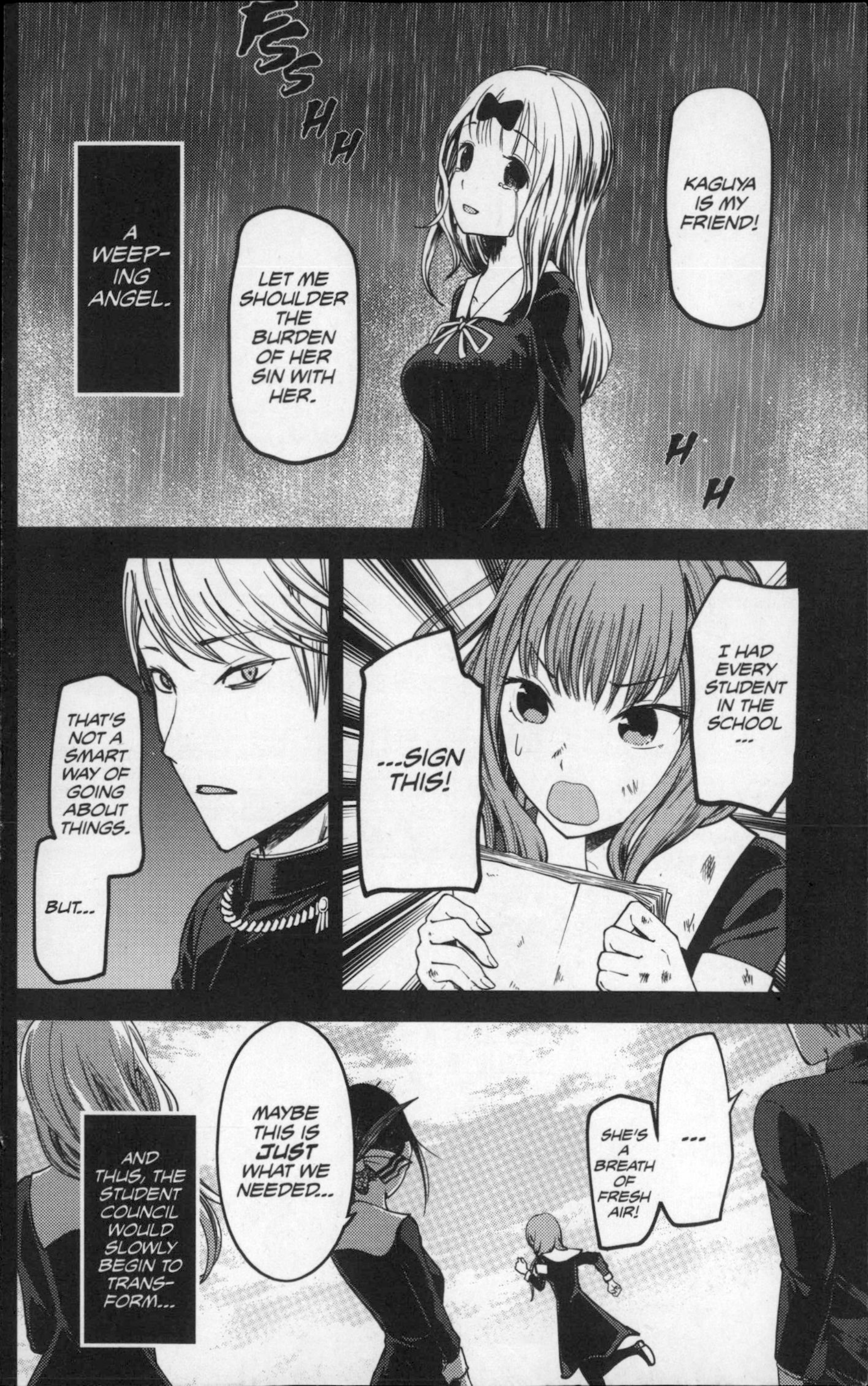
FSSHH
KAGUYA IS MY FRIEND!
LET ME SHOULDER THE BURDEN OF HER SIN WITH HER.
A WEEPING ANGEL.
HH
I HAD EVERY STUDENT IN THE SCHOOL...
...SIGN THIS!
THAT'S NOT A SMART WAY OF GOING ABOUT THINGS.
BUT...
...
SHE'S A BREATH OF FRESH AIR!
MAYBE THIS IS JUST WHAT WE NEEDED...
AND THUS, THE STUDENT COUNCIL WOULD SLOWLY BEGIN TO TRANSFORM...

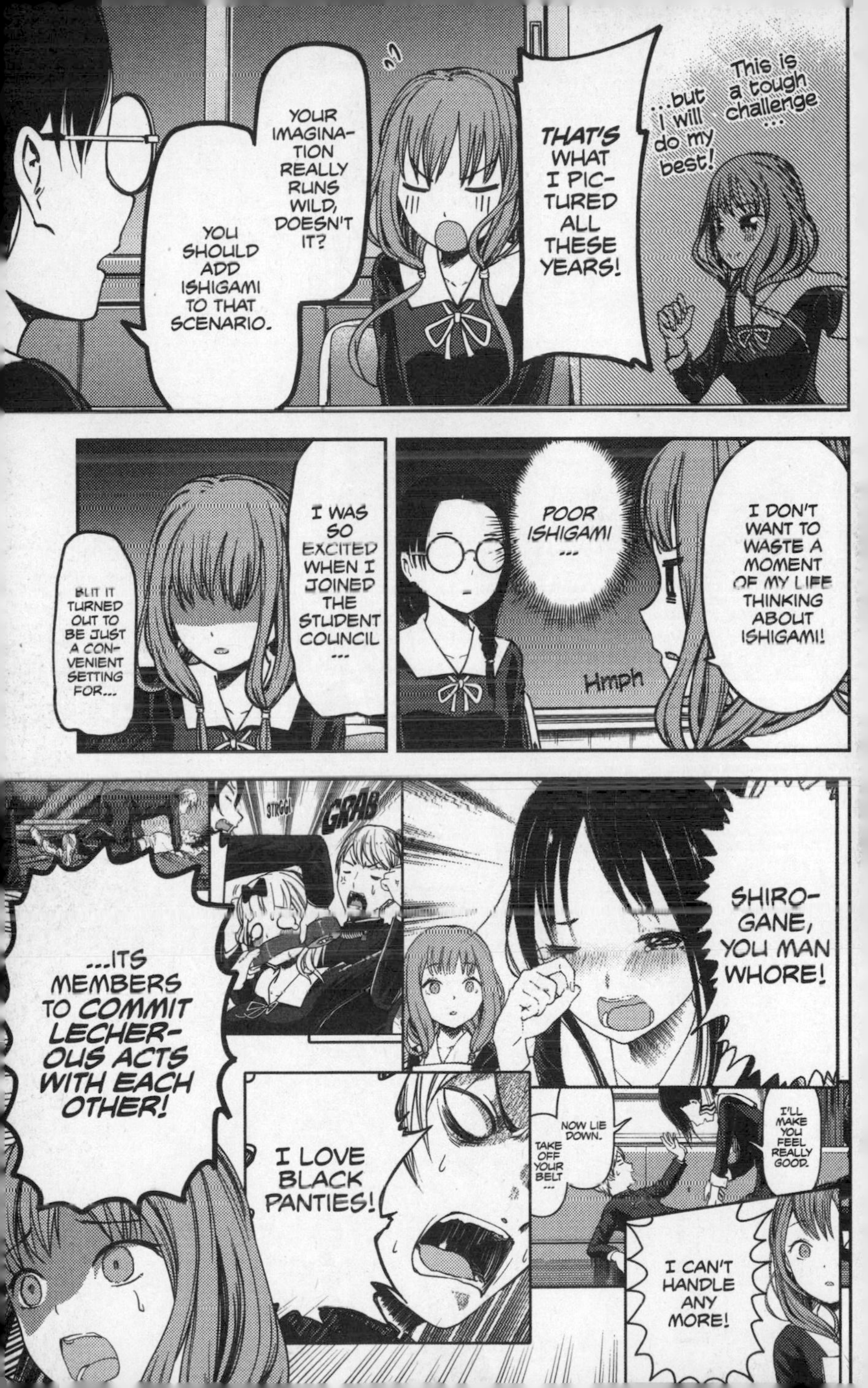
This is a tough challenge...
...but I will do my best!
THAT'S WHAT I PICTURED ALL THESE YEARS!
YOUR IMAGINATION REALLY RUNS WILD, DOESN'T IT?
YOU SHOULD ADD ISHIGAMI TO THAT SCENARIO.
I DON'T WANT TO WASTE A MOMENT OF MY LIFE THINKING ABOUT ISHIGAMI!
POOR ISHIGAMI...
Hmph
I WAS SO EXCITED WHEN I JOINED THE STUDENT COUNCIL...
BUT IT TURNED OUT TO BE JUST A CONVENIENT SETTING FOR...
SHIROGANE, YOU MAN WHORE!
GRAB
STRGGL
...ITS MEMBERS TO COMMIT LECHEROUS ACTS WITH EACH OTHER!
I'LL MAKE YOU FEEL REALLY GOOD.
NOW LIE DOWN.
TAKE OFF YOUR BELT...
I CAN'T HANDLE ANY MORE!
I LOVE BLACK PANTIES!

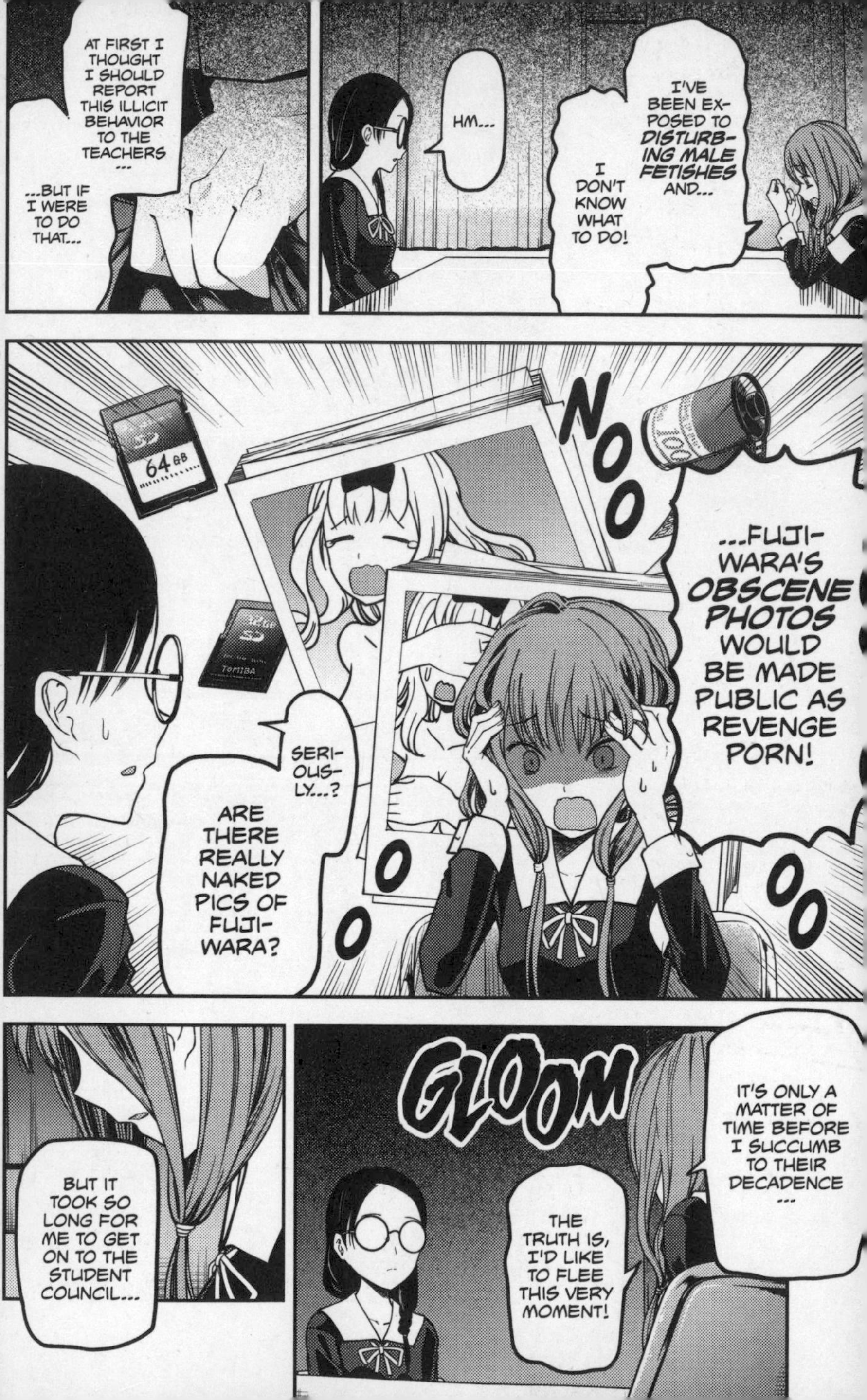
I'VE BEEN EXPOSED TO DISTURBING MALE FETISHES AND...
I DON'T KNOW WHAT TO DO!
HM...
AT FIRST I THOUGHT I SHOULD REPORT THIS ILLICIT BEHAVIOR TO THE TEACHERS...
...BUT IF I WERE TO DO THAT...
64GB
SD
TOMIBA
NOOOOOO
...FUJIWARA'S OBSCENE PHOTOS WOULD BE MADE PUBLIC AS REVENGE PORN!
SERIOUSLY...?
ARE THERE REALLY NAKED PICS OF FUJIWARA?
IT'S ONLY A MATTER OF TIME BEFORE I SUCCUMB TO THEIR DECADENCE...
GLOOM
THE TRUTH IS, I'D LIKE TO FLEE THIS VERY MOMENT!
BUT IT TOOK SO LONG FOR ME TO GET ON TO THE STUDENT COUNCIL...

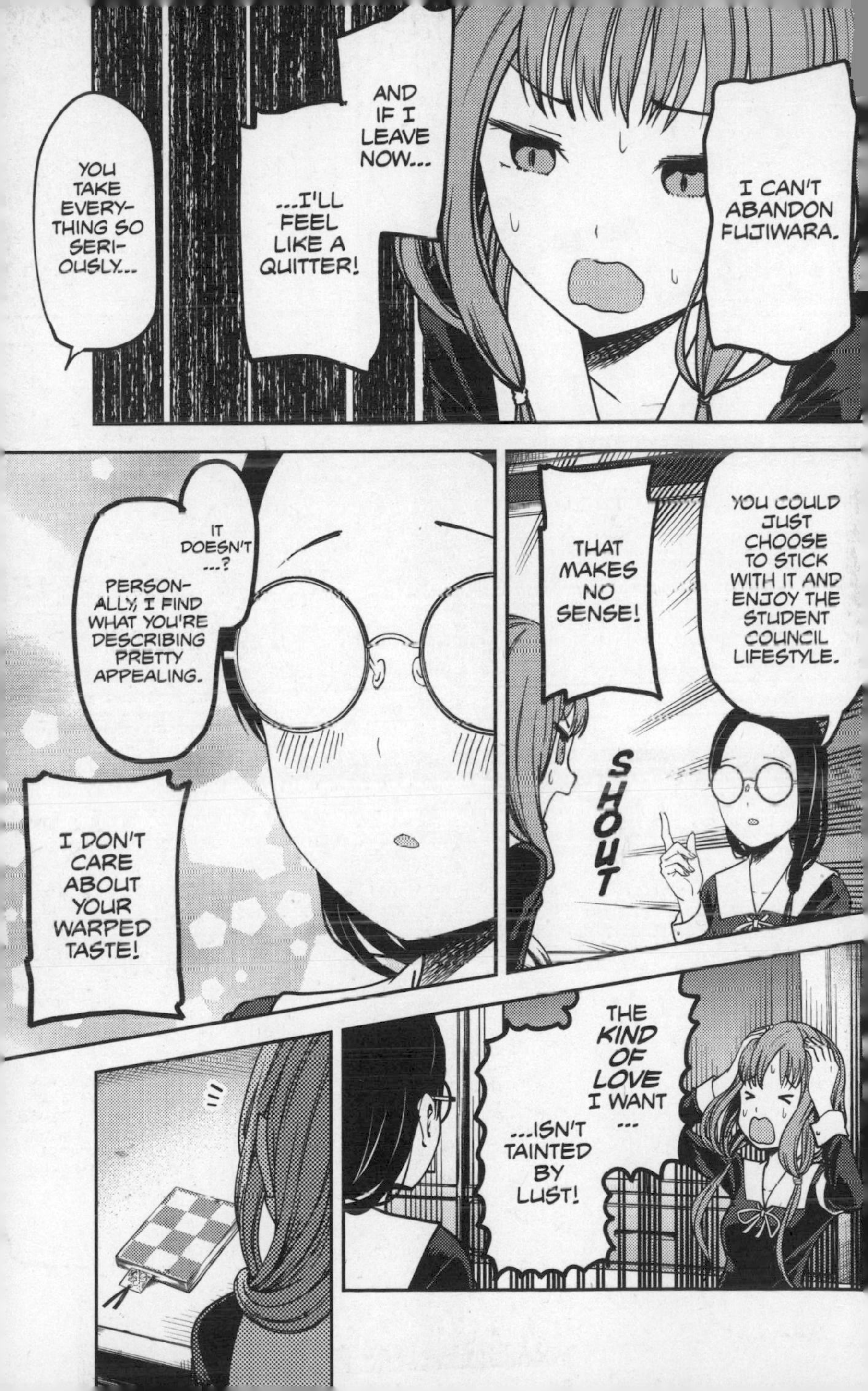
I CAN'T ABANDON FUJIWARA.
AND IF I LEAVE NOW...
...I'LL FEEL LIKE A QUITTER!
YOU TAKE EVERYTHING SO SERIOUSLY...
YOU COULD JUST CHOOSE TO STICK WITH IT AND ENJOY THE STUDENT COUNCIL LIFESTYLE.
SHOUT
THAT MAKES NO SENSE!
IT DOESN'T...?
PERSONALLY, I FIND WHAT YOU'RE DESCRIBING PRETTY APPEALING.
I DON'T CARE ABOUT YOUR WARPED TASTE!
THE *KIND OF LOVE* I WANT...
...ISN'T TAINTED BY LUST!

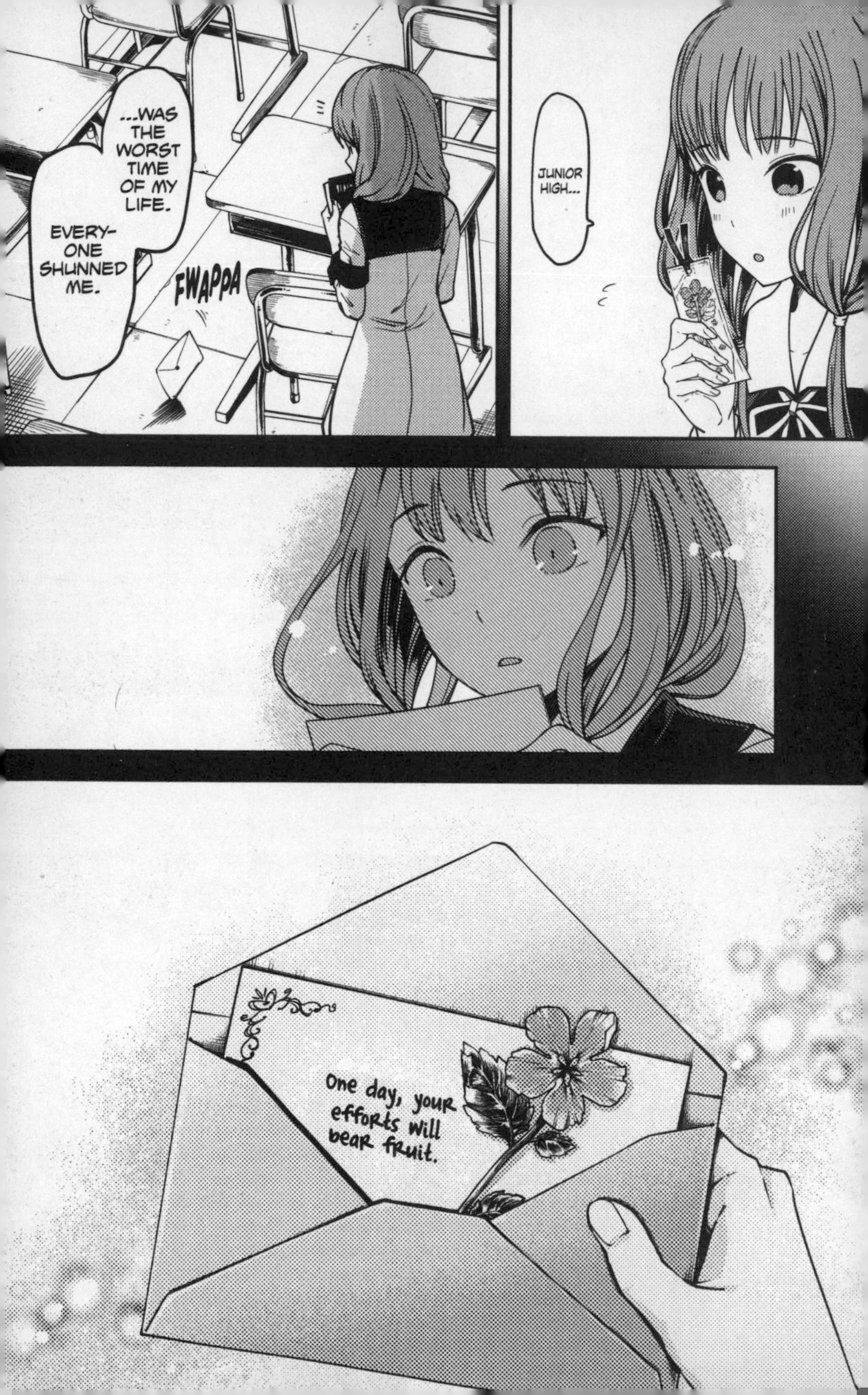
JUNIOR HIGH...
...WAS THE WORST TIME OF MY LIFE.
EVERY-ONE SHUNNED ME.
FWAPPA
One day, your efforts will bear fruit.

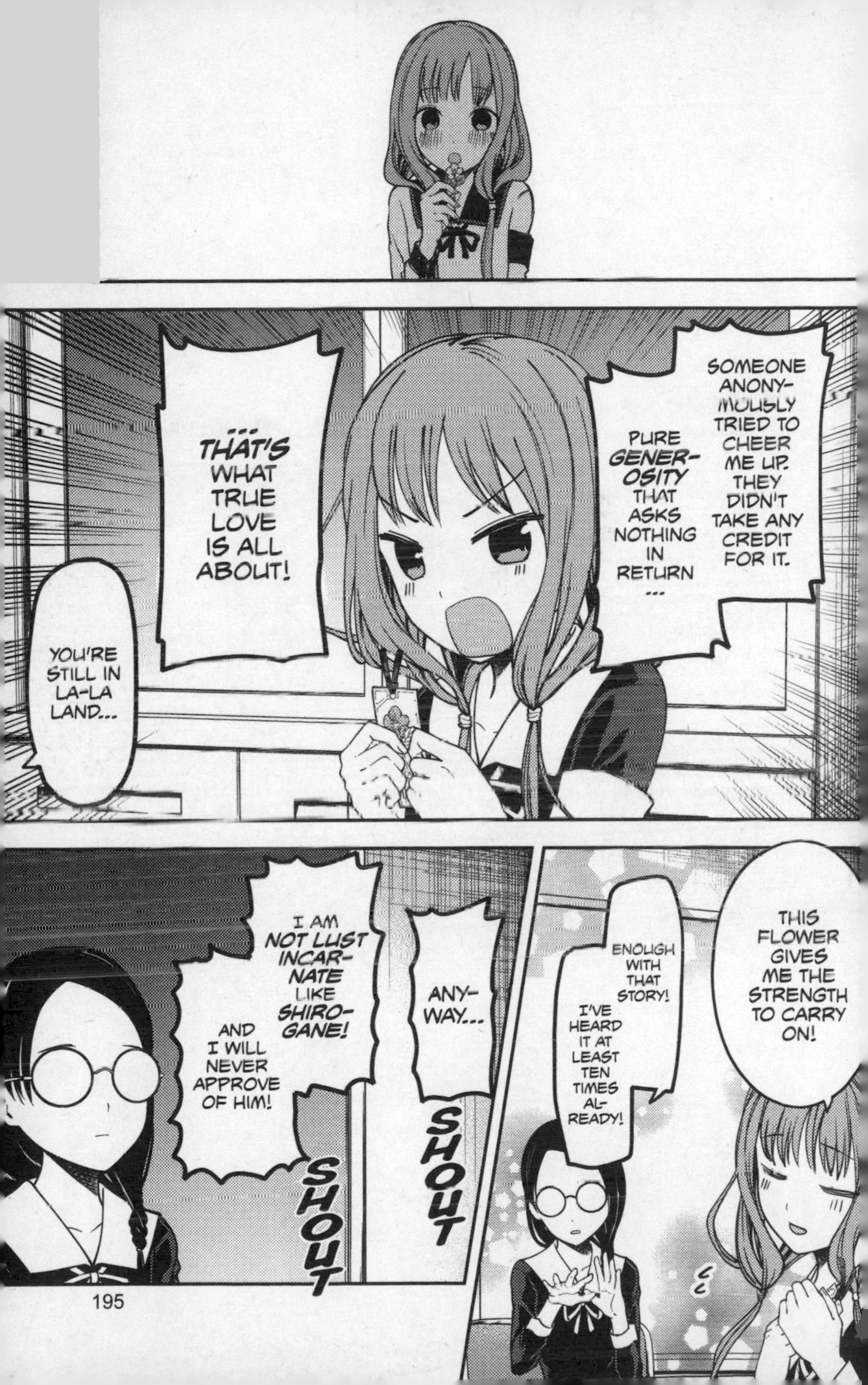
SOMEONE ANONYMOUSLY TRIED TO CHEER ME UP. THEY DIDN'T TAKE ANY CREDIT FOR IT.
PURE GENEROSITY THAT ASKS NOTHING IN RETURN...
...THAT'S WHAT TRUE LOVE IS ALL ABOUT!
YOU'RE STILL IN LA-LA LAND...
THIS FLOWER GIVES ME THE STRENGTH TO CARRY ON!
ENOUGH WITH THAT STORY!
I'VE HEARD IT AT LEAST TEN TIMES ALREADY!
ANYWAY...
SHOUT
I AM NOT LUST INCARNATE LIKE SHIROGANE!
AND I WILL NEVER APPROVE OF HIM!
SHOUT

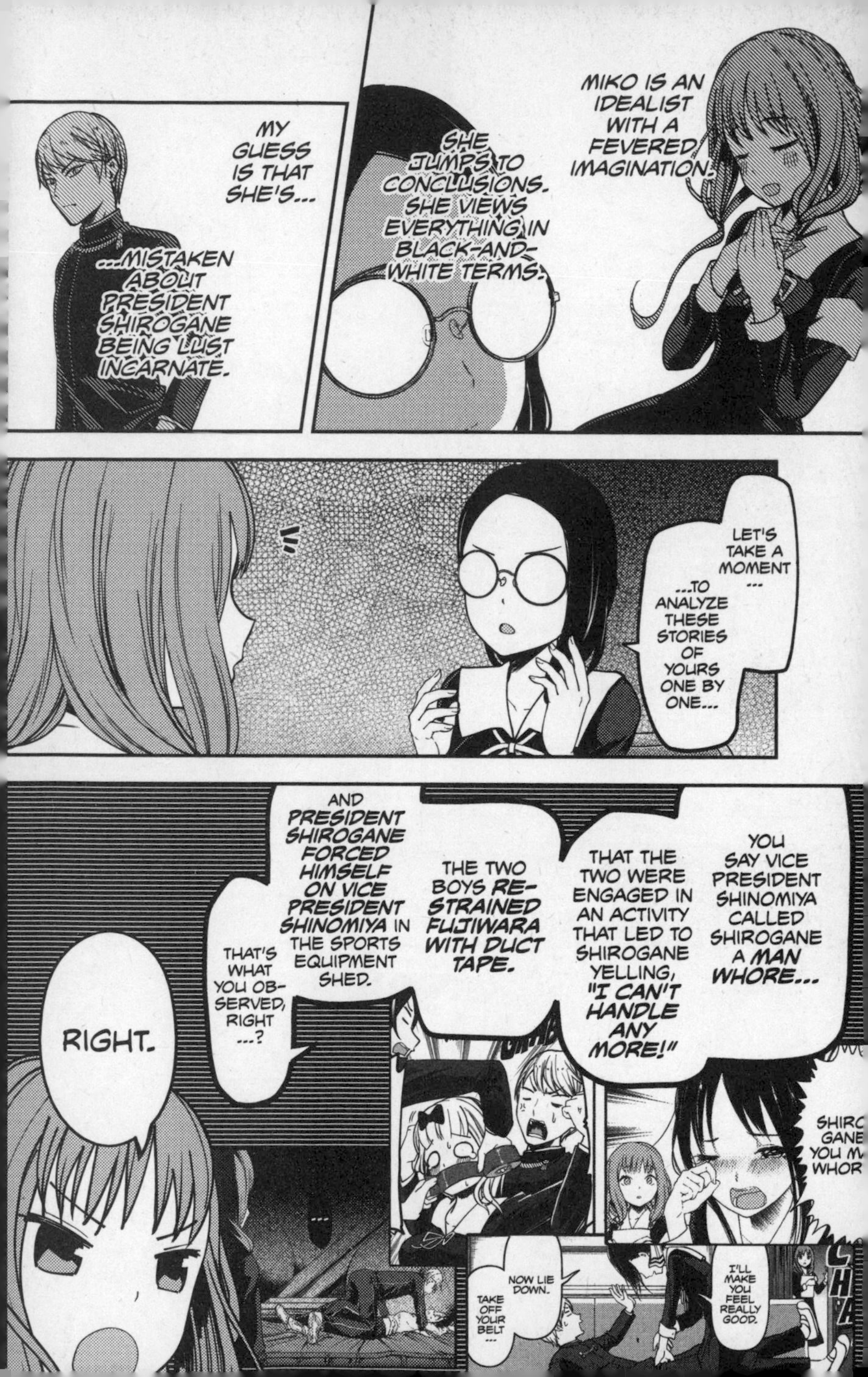
MIKO IS AN IDEALIST WITH A FEVERED IMAGINATION.
SHE JUMPS TO CONCLUSIONS. SHE VIEWS EVERYTHING IN BLACK-AND-WHITE TERMS.
MY GUESS IS THAT SHE'S...
...MISTAKEN ABOUT PRESIDENT SHIROGANE BEING LUST INCARNATE.
LET'S TAKE A MOMENT ---
...TO ANALYZE THESE STORIES OF YOURS ONE BY ONE...
YOU SAY VICE PRESIDENT SHINOMIYA CALLED SHIROGANE A MAN WHORE...
THAT THE TWO WERE ENGAGED IN AN ACTIVITY THAT LED TO SHIROGANE YELLING, "I CAN'T HANDLE ANY MORE!"
THE TWO BOYS RE-STRAINED FUJIWARA WITH DUCT TAPE.
AND PRESIDENT SHIROGANE FORCED HIMSELF ON VICE PRESIDENT SHINOMIYA IN THE SPORTS EQUIPMENT SHED.
THAT'S WHAT YOU OB-SERVED, RIGHT ---?
RIGHT.
I'LL MAKE YOU FEEL REALLY GOOD.
NOW LIE DOWN.
TAKE OFF YOUR BELT ---

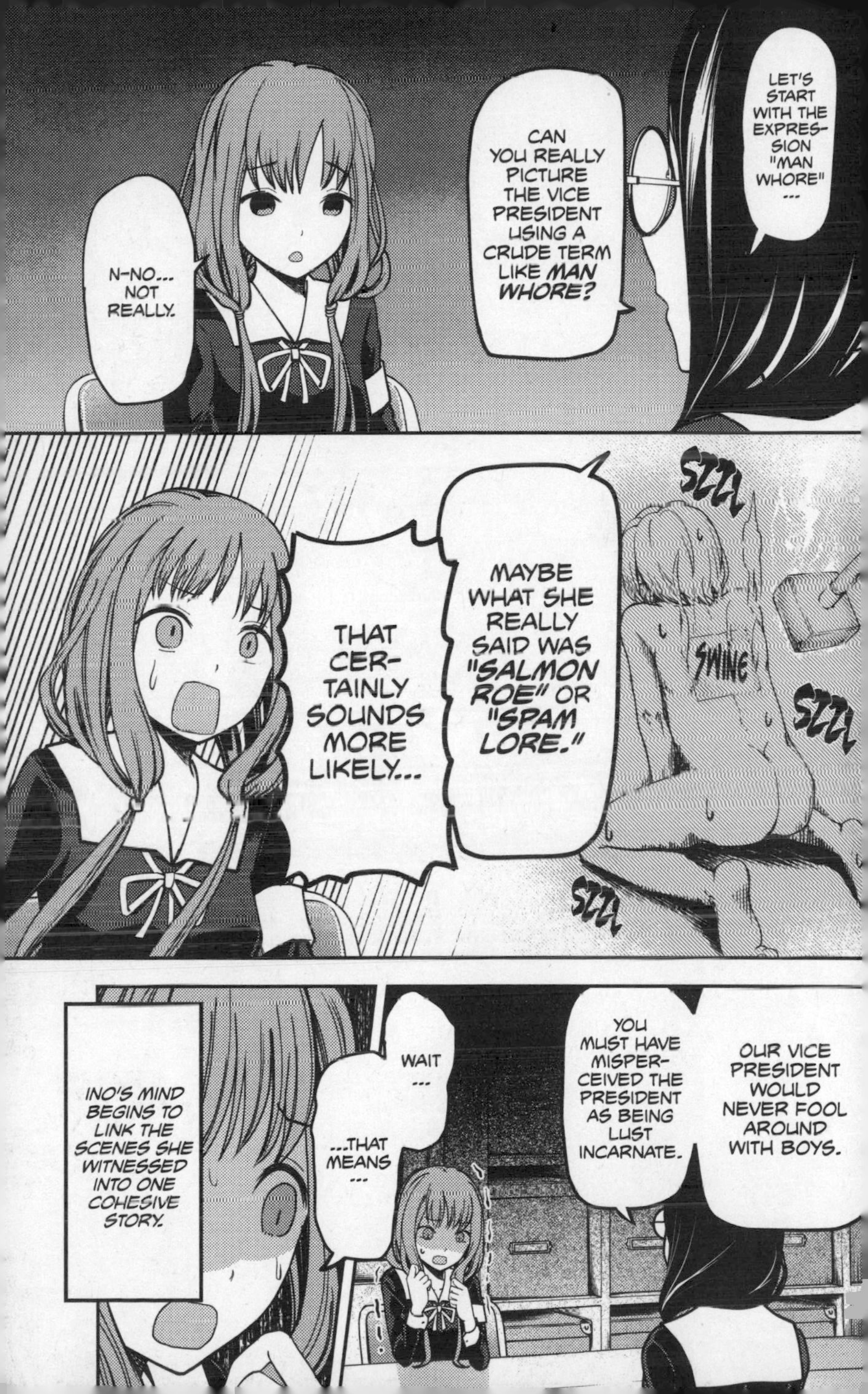

LET'S START WITH THE EXPRESSION "MAN WHORE"...
CAN YOU REALLY PICTURE THE VICE PRESIDENT USING A CRUDE TERM LIKE *MAN WHORE?*
N-NO... NOT REALLY.
SZZL
SWINE
SZZL
SZZL
MAYBE WHAT SHE REALLY SAID WAS "*SALMON ROE*" OR "*SPAM LORE.*"
THAT CERTAINLY SOUNDS MORE LIKELY...
OUR VICE PRESIDENT WOULD NEVER FOOL AROUND WITH BOYS.
YOU MUST HAVE MISPERCEIVED THE PRESIDENT AS BEING LUST INCARNATE.
WAIT...
...THAT MEANS...
INO'S MIND BEGINS TO LINK THE SCENES SHE WITNESSED INTO ONE COHESIVE STORY.

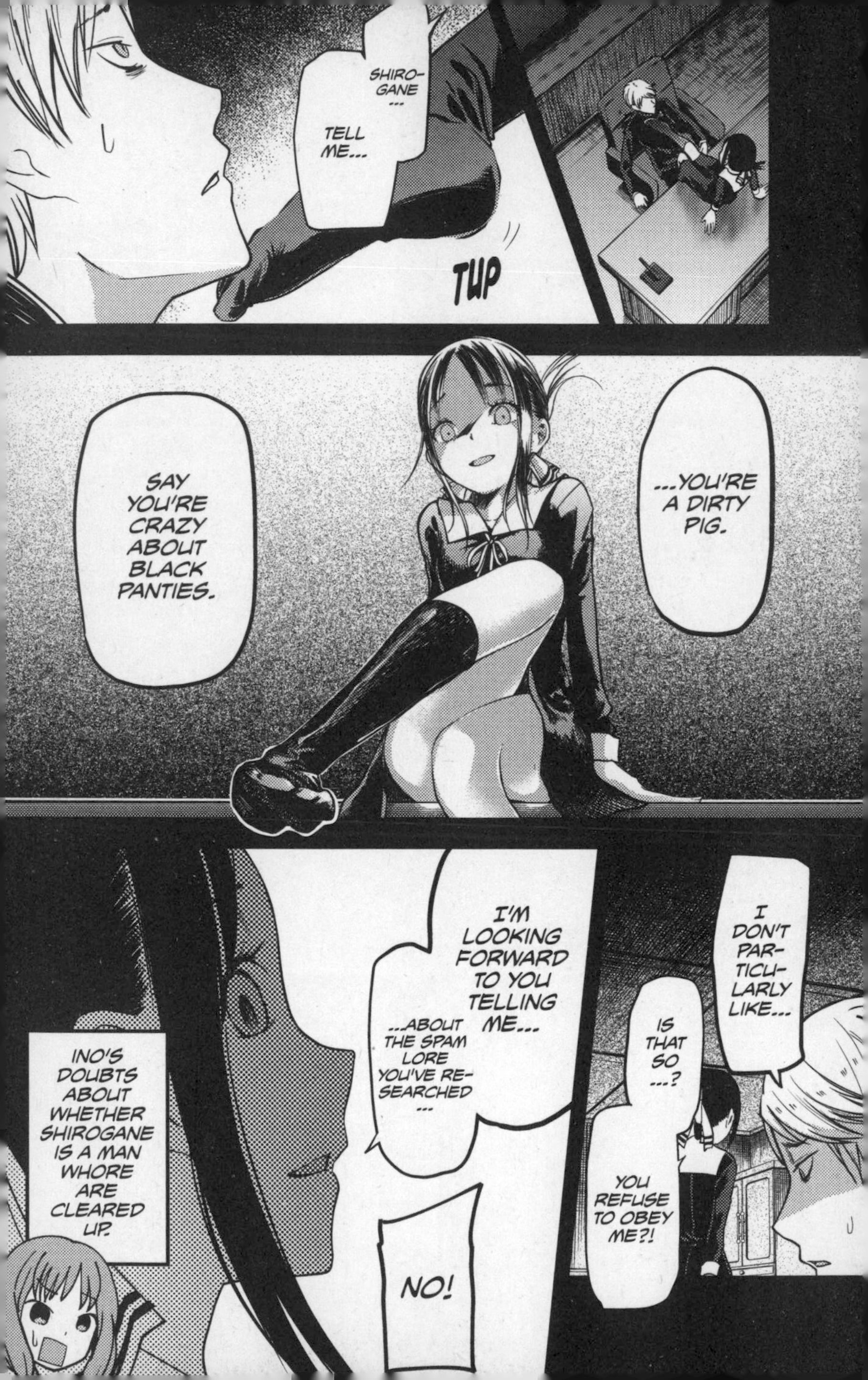
SHIRO-GANE ... TELL ME...
TUP
...YOU'RE A DIRTY PIG.
SAY YOU'RE CRAZY ABOUT BLACK PANTIES.
I DON'T PAR-TICU-LARLY LIKE...
IS THAT SO ...?
YOU REFUSE TO OBEY ME?!
I'M LOOKING FORWARD TO YOU TELLING ME...
...ABOUT THE SPAM LORE YOU'VE RE-SEARCHED ...
INO'S DOUBTS ABOUT WHETHER SHIROGANE IS A MAN WHORE ARE CLEARED UP.
NO!

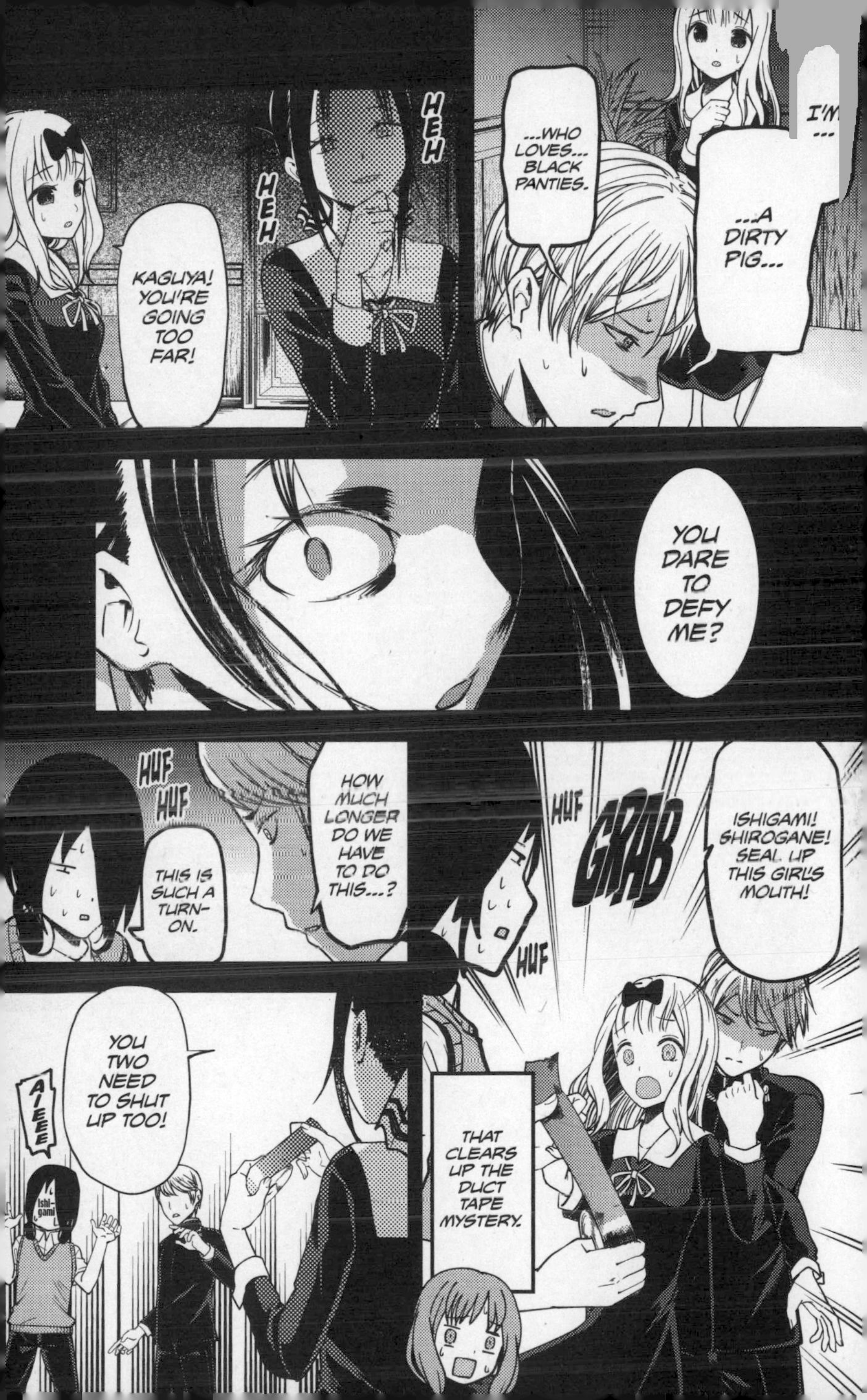
I'M ---
...A DIRTY PIG...
...WHO LOVES... BLACK PANTIES.
HEH HEH
KAGUYA! YOU'RE GOING TOO FAR!
YOU DARE TO DEFY ME?
ISHIGAMI! SHIROGANE! SEAL UP THIS GIRL'S MOUTH!
GRAB
HUF
HUF
HOW MUCH LONGER DO WE HAVE TO DO THIS...?
HUF HUF
THIS IS SUCH A TURN-ON.
THAT CLEARS UP THE DUCT TAPE MYSTERY.
YOU TWO NEED TO SHUT UP TOO!
AIEEE
Ishi-gami

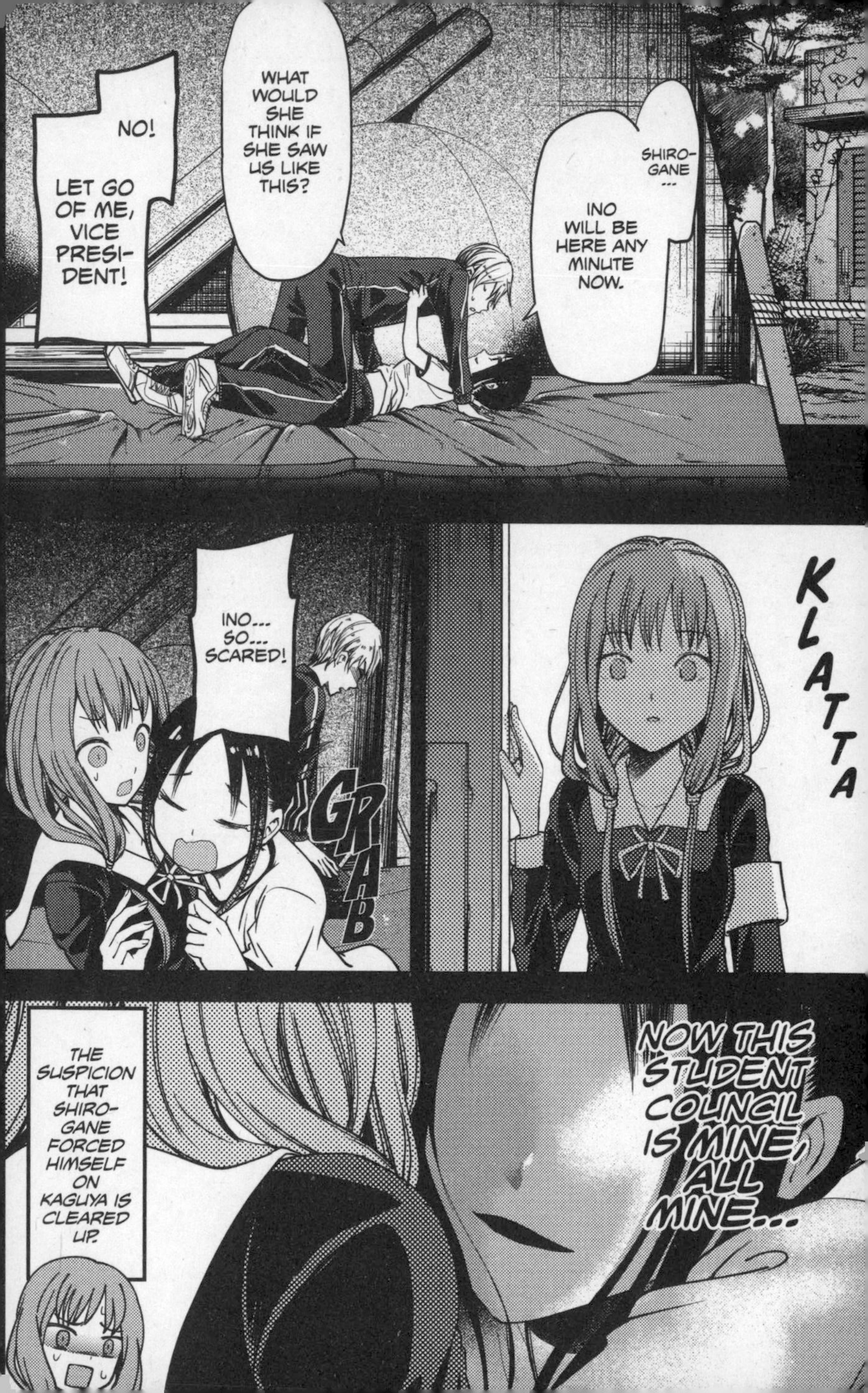
SHIRO-GANE...
INO WILL BE HERE ANY MINUTE NOW.
WHAT WOULD SHE THINK IF SHE SAW US LIKE THIS?
NO!
LET GO OF ME, VICE PRESIDENT!
KLATTA
INO... SO... SCARED!
GRAB
NOW THIS STUDENT COUNCIL IS MINE, ALL MINE...
THE SUSPICION THAT SHIROGANE FORCED HIMSELF ON KAGUYA IS CLEARED UP.

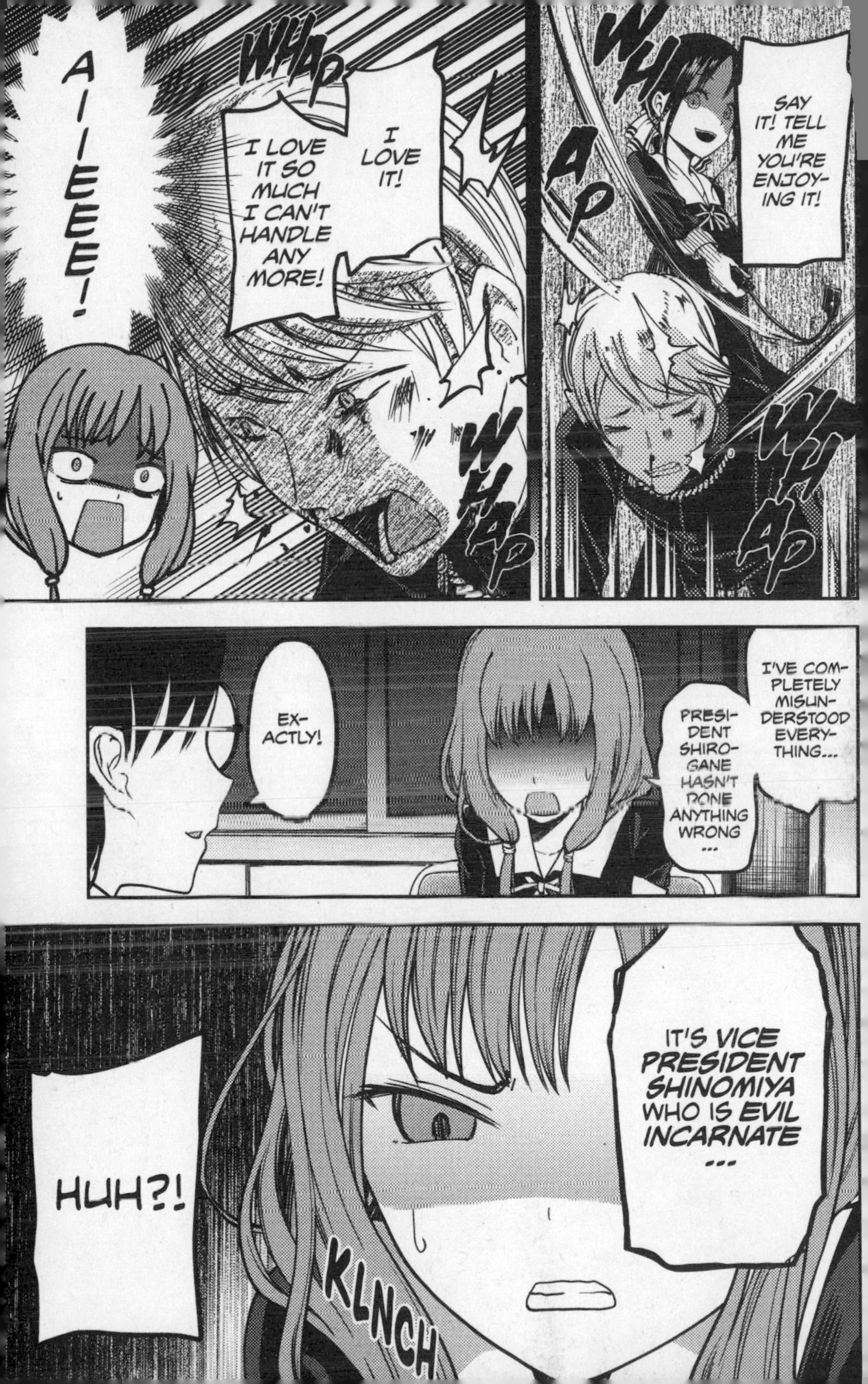
WHAP
SAY IT! TELL ME YOU'RE ENJOYING IT!
WHAP
WHAP
I LOVE IT!
I LOVE IT SO MUCH I CAN'T HANDLE ANY MORE!
AIIEEEE!
WHAP
I'VE COMPLETELY MISUNDERSTOOD EVERYTHING...
PRESIDENT SHIROGANE HASN'T DONE ANYTHING WRONG...
EXACTLY!
IT'S VICE PRESIDENT SHINOMIYA WHO IS EVIL INCARNATE...
KLNCH
HUH?!

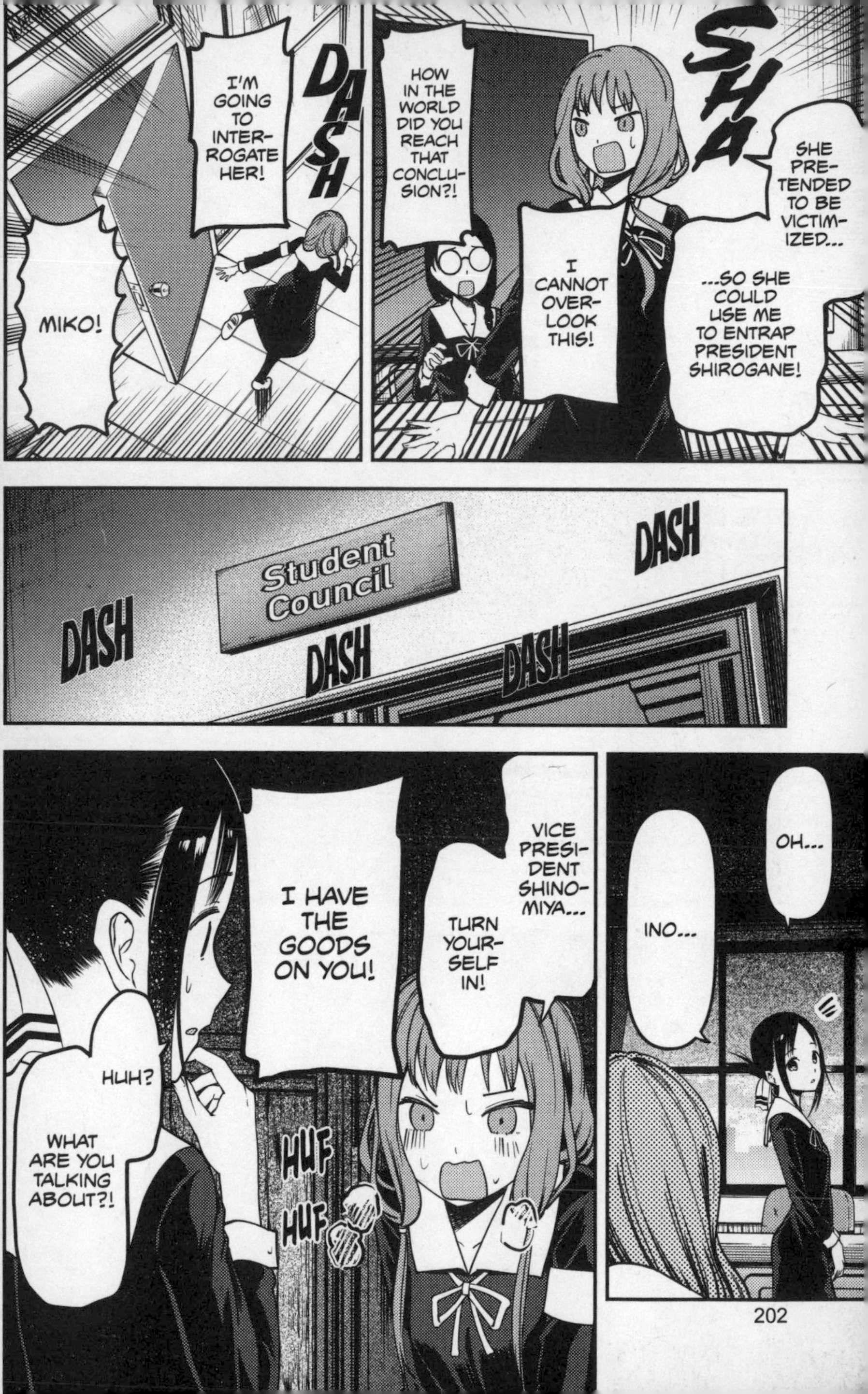
SHA
SHE PRETENDED TO BE VICTIMIZED...
...SO SHE COULD USE ME TO ENTRAP PRESIDENT SHIROGANE!
I CANNOT OVERLOOK THIS!
HOW IN THE WORLD DID YOU REACH THAT CONCLUSION?!
DASH
I'M GOING TO INTERROGATE HER!
MIKO!
DASH
Student Council
DASH
DASH
DASH
OH...
INO...
VICE PRESIDENT SHINOMIYA...
TURN YOURSELF IN!
I HAVE THE GOODS ON YOU!
HUF HUF
HUH?
WHAT ARE YOU TALKING ABOUT?!

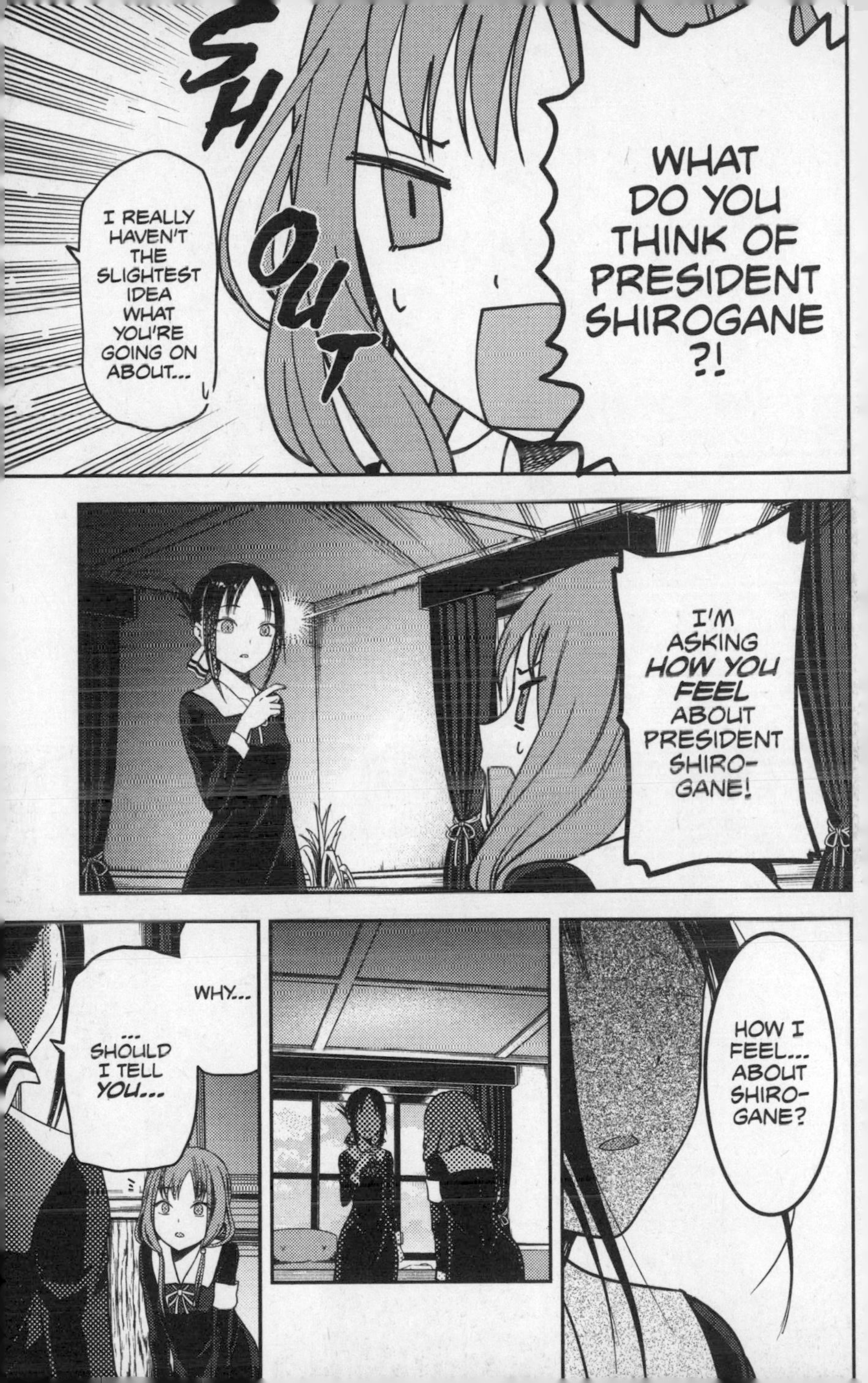
WHAT DO YOU THINK OF PRESIDENT SHIROGANE?!
SHOUT
I REALLY HAVEN'T THE SLIGHTEST IDEA WHAT YOU'RE GOING ON ABOUT...
I'M ASKING HOW YOU FEEL ABOUT PRESIDENT SHIROGANE!
HOW I FEEL... ABOUT SHIROGANE?
WHY...
...SHOULD I TELL YOU...

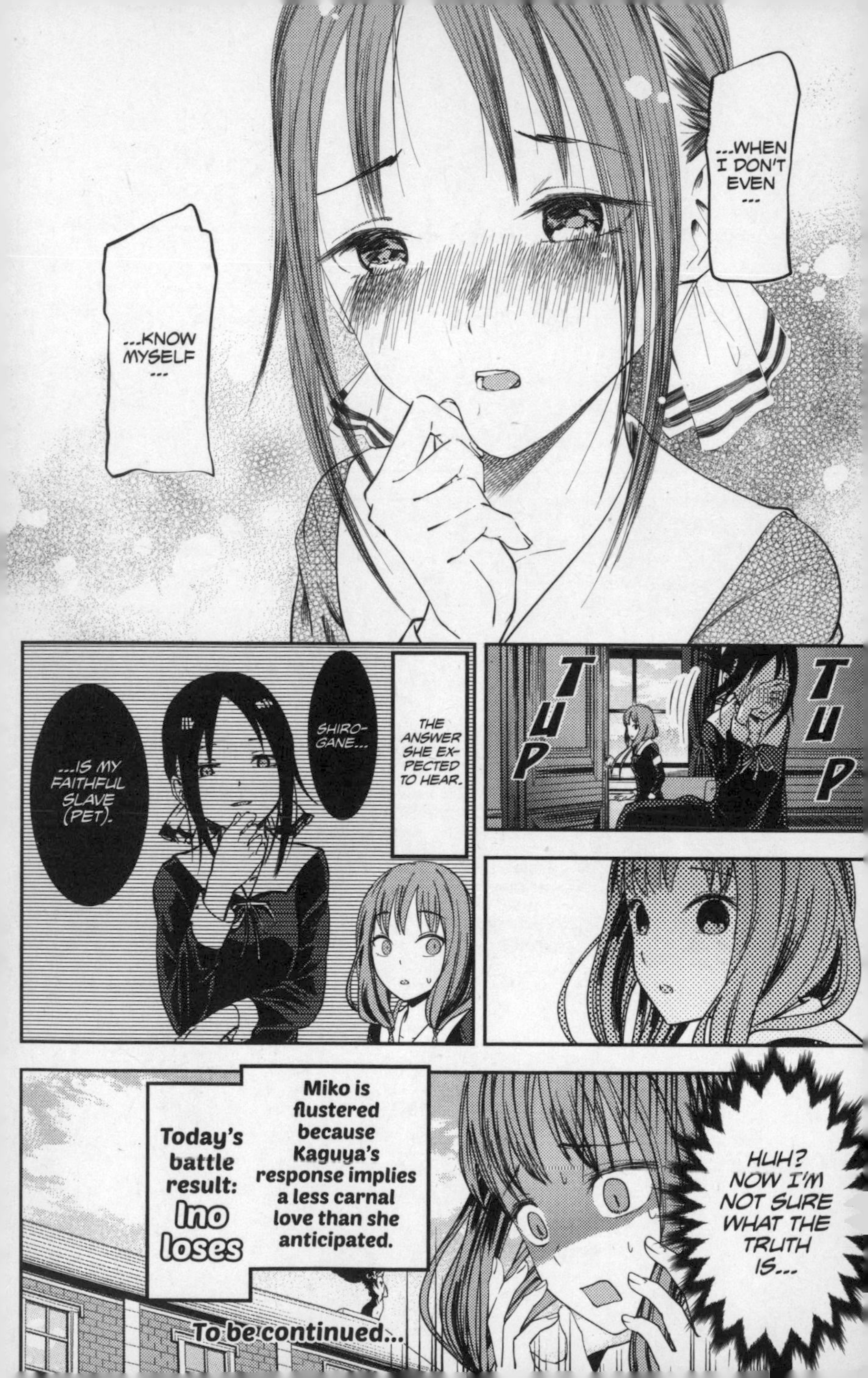
...WHEN I DON'T EVEN ...
...KNOW MYSELF ...
TUP
TUP
THE ANSWER SHE EXPECTED TO HEAR.
SHIRO-GANE...
...IS MY FAITHFUL SLAVE (PET).
HUH? NOW I'M NOT SURE WHAT THE TRUTH IS...
Miko is flustered because Kaguya's response implies a less carnal love than she anticipated.
Today's battle result: Ino loses
To be continued...

MIKO INO

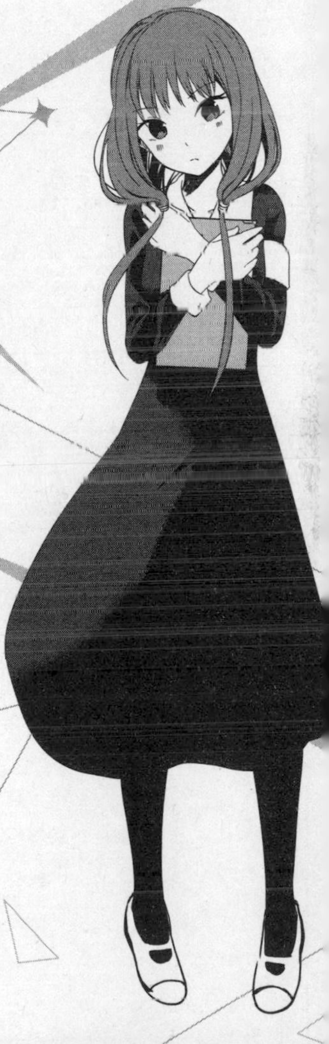

Miko Ino

- Shuchiin Academy High School First-Year
- Student Council Financial Auditor
- Notable characteristics: short
- Background character

Her father is a high court judge.

Her mother works for an international humanitarian aid organization.

Her parents are so busy that she spends more time with the family housekeeper than with them.

She is so lonely that she pursues justice as a way to connect with her parents. She is self-righteous and seeks justice for the sake of justice, betraying an immature understanding of true morality.

REACHING OUT TO SOMEONE CAN BE SCARY, BUT SOMEBODY NEEDS TO MAKE THE FIRST MOVE.

AKA AKASAKA

Aka Akasaka got his start as an assistant to Jinsei Kataoka and Kazuma Kondou, the creators of *Deadman Wonderland*. His first serialized manga was an adaptation of the light novel series *Sayonara Piano Sonata*, published by Kadokawa in 2011. *Kaguya-sama: Love Is War* began serialization in *Miracle Jump* in 2015 but was later moved to *Weekly Young Jump* in 2016 due to its popularity.

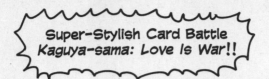

Super-Stylish Card Battle *Kaguya-sama: Love Is War!!*

What You Need

★ All the volumes of *Kaguya* x 2

★ A friend

x2
&
Friend

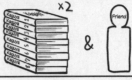

The Rules!!

This game is a card battle wherein players choose a volume from their hand (i.e., all current volumes of *Kaguya*), then play that volume on the count of "One, two, three!!" The character on the cover determines who wins or loses.

One, two, three!!
4
Kaguya
1
Kaguya

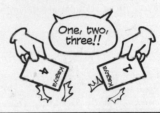

Each character has certain compatibilities. Cards that win or lose or end in a draw are placed in the discard pile.

Hand
Discard pile
Win
Lose
Hand
Discard pile

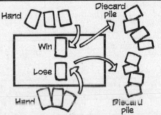

Continue battling until you've finished playing your hand (all the *Kaguya* volumes that have already been published). The player who has won the most rounds or the player who fulfills the "special condition victory" requirement wins the game.

Game example
Total
Player A
win win win win
Ai Chika Kei Miko Kaguya Yu Miyuki Nagisa
4 wins
Player B
draw
win win win
Chika Kaguya Nagisa Yu Miko Ai Kei Miyuki
3 wins
Player A wins today's game!!

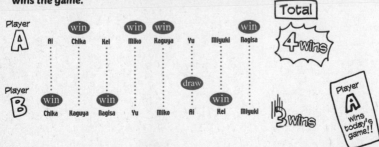

Card Rules and Values

Volume 1
Kaguya Shinomiya

May win against Ai, Miyuki, Yu.

★ **Skill <Strategy>**
May nullify one of your opponent's currently active special effects.

Volume 2
Chika Fujiwara

May win against Kaguya, Ai, Miko.

★ **Skill <Intensive Training>**
If this card has already been used, the student council president can win the "special condition victory" against Kaguya.

Volume 3
Ai Hayasaka

May win against Kei and Miko.

★ **Skill <Advice>**
The player who first used this card wins if the game results in a draw.

Volume 4
Kei Shirogane

★ **Skill <Rebellious Phase>**
May win against all other male characters.

Volume 5
Miyuki Shirogane

May win against Chika and Miko.

★ **Skill <Hard Worker>**
If Chika's <Intensive Training> is currently active and your opponent plays Kaguya's card, the game ends, and you win by default.

Volume 6
Nagisa Kashiwagi

★ **Skill <Spiritual Couple>**
May win against male or female virgins.

Volume 7
Miko Iino

May win against Yu.

★ **Skill <Childish Justice>**
If this card is retrieved from the discard pile using Yu's <Observation Skill>, her skill changes to the one below.

★ **Skill <True Justice>**
May win against characters other than Yu regardless of compatibilities or skills.

Volume 8
Manual

★ **Skill <Complicated Rules>**
You may use this to verify the explanations of the rules. You don't actually use this card in the game, but it's convenient to keep it nearby.

Volume 9
Yu Ishigami

May win against Chika.

★ **Skill <Observation Skill>**
You may exchange a card from your hand with a card from the discard pile.

*Regarding expansion packs: You'll get new cards as new volumes are published. Use your intuition to figure out how to use those cards.
**No game-play tests have been conducted.

KAGUYA-SAMA
LOVE IS WAR

SHONEN JUMP MANGA EDITION

8

STORY AND ART BY
AKA AKASAKA

Translation/Tomoko Kimura
English Adaptation/Annette Roman
Touch-Up Art & Lettering/Stephen Dutro
Cover & Interior Design/Alice Lewis
Editor/Annette Roman

KAGUYA-SAMA WA KOKURASETAI~TENSAITACHI NO REN'AI ZUNO SEN~
© 2015 by Aka Akasaka
All rights reserved.
First published in Japan in 2015 by SHUEISHA Inc., Tokyo
English translation rights arranged by SHUEISHA Inc.

The stories, characters and incidents mentioned in this publication
are entirely fictional.

Printed in the U.S.A.

Published by VIZ Media, LLC
P.O. Box 77010
San Francisco, CA 94107

10 9 8 7 6 5 4 3 2 1
First printing, May 2019

PARENTAL ADVISORY
KAGUYA-SAMA: LOVE IS WAR is rated T for Teen
and is recommended for ages 13 and up. It contains
mild language and first-love shenanigans.

viz.com

shonenjump.com

COMING NEXT VOLUME

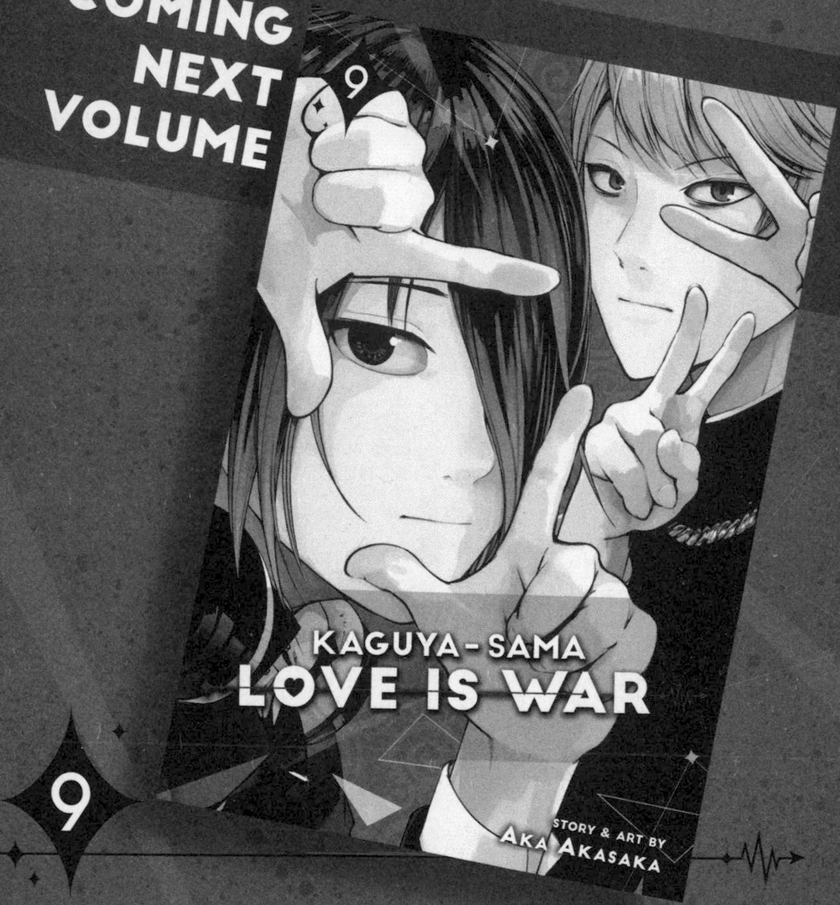
9
KAGUYA-SAMA
LOVE IS WAR
9
STORY & ART BY
AKA AKASAKA

Will Chika agree to train Miyuki one more time to make up for yet another of his surprising deficiencies? Then, Miyuki's sister and father meddle in his (mostly hypothetical) love life. Are they too early or too late? Rumors that plague Yu have serious personal and academic consequences. The much-anticipated, much-dreaded Sports Day finally arrives! And Chika dreams up a new game for the student council to play together—with literally explosive results.

Who cares what other people think?

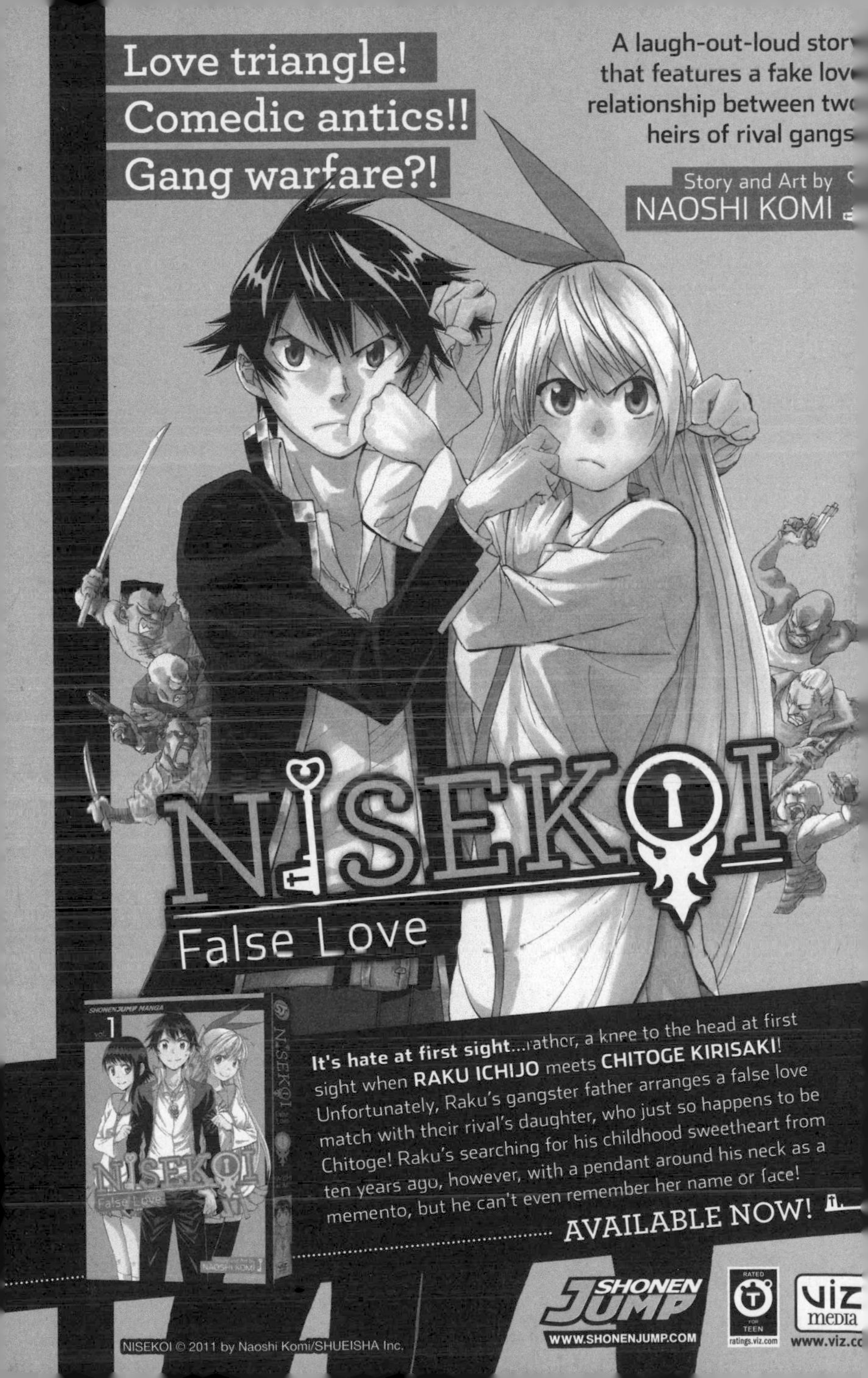

Love triangle!
Comedic antics!!
Gang warfare?!
A laugh-out-loud stor
that features a fake lov
relationship between tw
heirs of rival gangs
Story and Art by
NAOSHI KOMI
NISEKOI
False Love
SHONEN JUMP MANGA
vol. 1
It's hate at first sight...rather, a knee to the head at first sight when RAKU ICHIJO meets CHITOGE KIRISAKI! Unfortunately, Raku's gangster father arranges a false love match with their rival's daughter, who just so happens to be Chitoge! Raku's searching for his childhood sweetheart from ten years ago, however, with a pendant around his neck as a memento, but he can't even remember her name or face!
AVAILABLE NOW!
SHONEN JUMP
WWW.SHONENJUMP.COM
RATED T FOR TEEN
ratings.viz.com
viz media
www.viz.c
NISEKOI © 2011 by Naoshi Komi/SHUEISHA Inc.

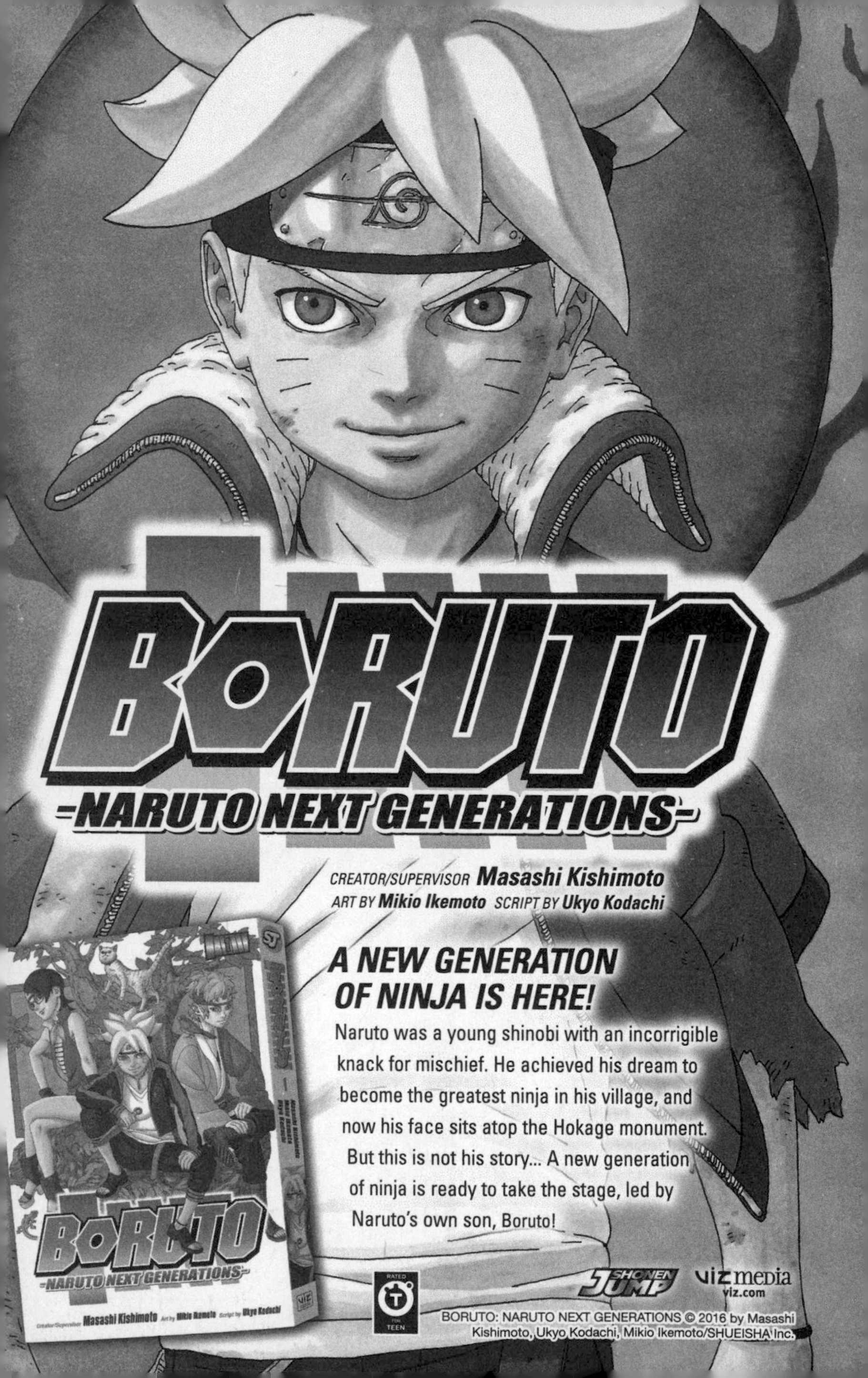
BORUTO
-NARUTO NEXT GENERATIONS-
CREATOR/SUPERVISOR Masashi Kishimoto
ART BY Mikio Ikemoto SCRIPT BY Ukyo Kodachi
A NEW GENERATION OF NINJA IS HERE!
Naruto was a young shinobi with an incorrigible knack for mischief. He achieved his dream to become the greatest ninja in his village, and now his face sits atop the Hokage monument. But this is not his story... A new generation of ninja is ready to take the stage, led by Naruto's own son, Boruto!
RATED T FOR TEEN
SHONEN JUMP
VIZ media
viz.com
BORUTO: NARUTO NEXT GENERATIONS © 2016 by Masashi Kishimoto, Ukyo Kodachi, Mikio Ikemoto/SHUEISHA Inc.

Dr.STONE

STORY BY
RIICHIRO INAGAKI

ART BY
BOICHI

One fateful day, all of humanity turned to stone. Many millenni
later, Taiju frees himself from petrification and finds himse
surrounded by statues. The situation looks grim—until he rur
into his science-loving friend Senku! Together they plan to resta
civilization with the power of science!

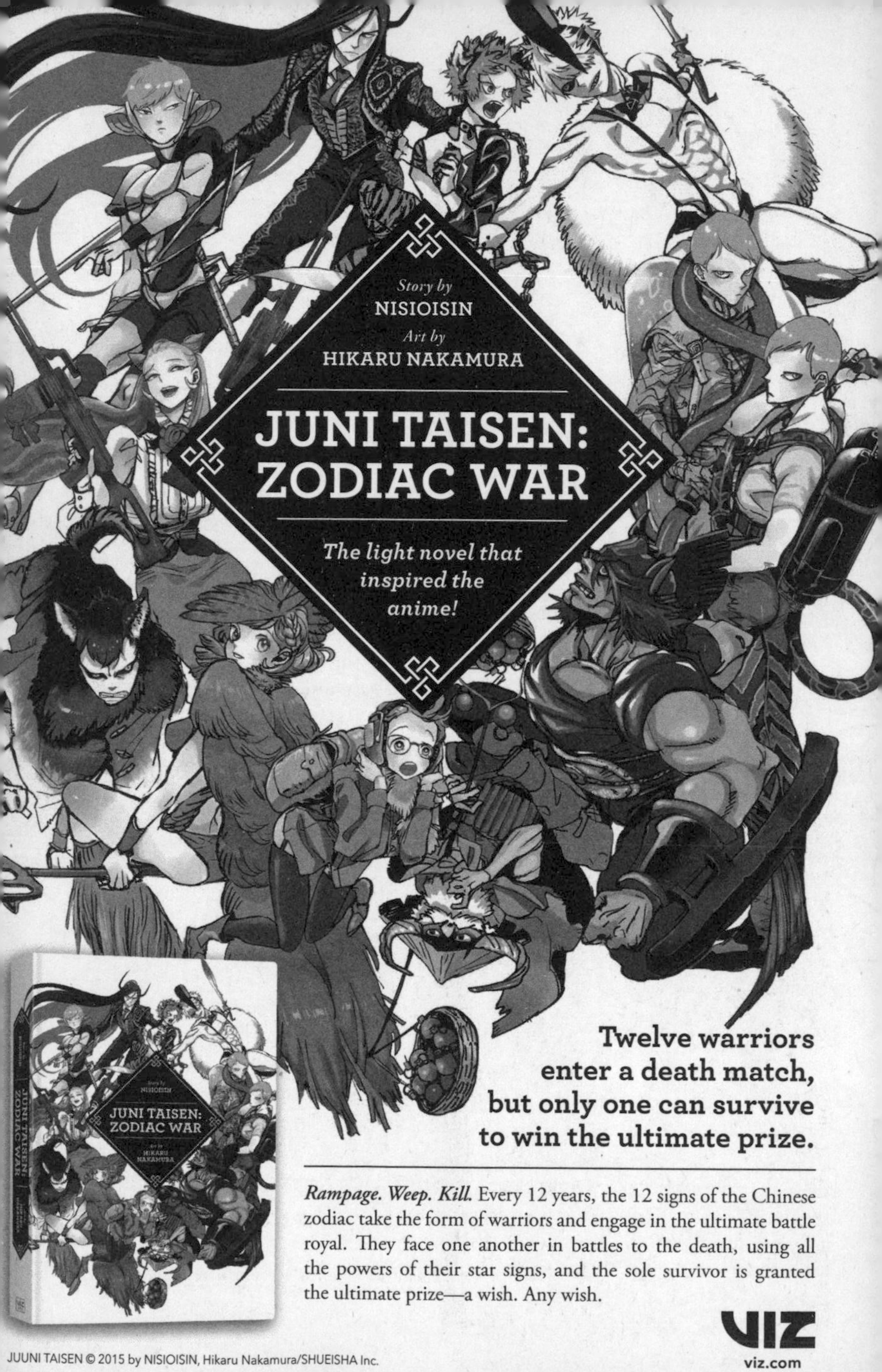
Story by
NISIOISIN
Art by
HIKARU NAKAMURA
JUNI TAISEN:
ZODIAC WAR
The light novel that inspired the anime!
Twelve warriors enter a death match, but only one can survive to win the ultimate prize.
Rampage. Weep. Kill. Every 12 years, the 12 signs of the Chinese zodiac take the form of warriors and engage in the ultimate battle royal. They face one another in battles to the death, using all the powers of their star signs, and the sole survivor is granted the ultimate prize—a wish. Any wish.
VIZ
viz.com
JUUNI TAISEN © 2015 by NISIOISIN, Hikaru Nakamura/SHUEISHA Inc.

DEMON SLAYER
KIMETSU NO YAIBA

Story and Art by
KOYOHARU GOTOUGE

In Taisho-era Japan, kindhearted Tanjiro Kamado makes a living selling charcoal. But his peaceful life is shattered when a demon slaughters his entire family. His little sister Nezuko is the only survivor, but she has been transformed into a demon herself! Tanjiro sets out on a dangerous journey to find a way to return his sister to normal and destroy the demon who ruined his life.

YOU'RE READING THE WRONG WAY!

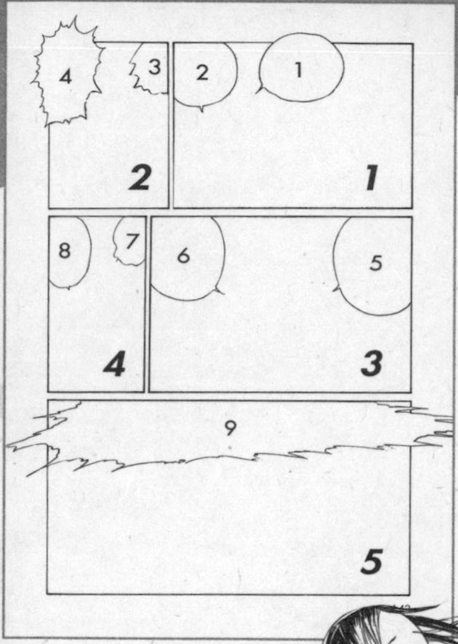
1
2
3
4
5
6
7
8
9
1
2
3
4
5

KAGUYA-SAMA: LOVE IS WAR reads from right to left, starting in the upper-right corner. Japanese is read from right to left, meaning that action, sound effects and word-balloon order are completely reversed from English order.

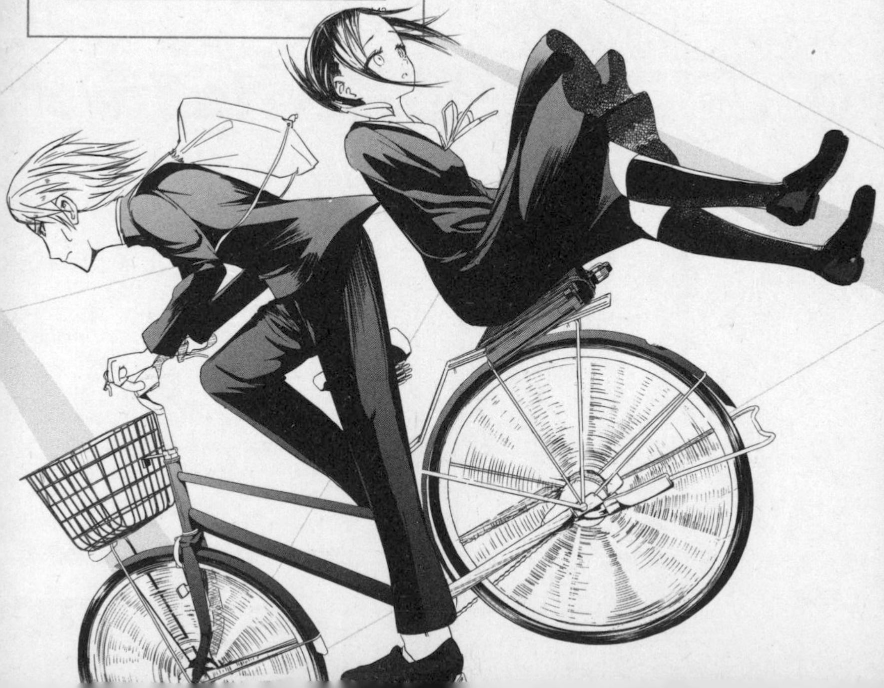